The Explorer's Guide to the
ABBEYS, MONASTERIES
and CHURCHES
of Great Britain

The Explorer's Guide to the
ABBEYS, MONASTERIES
and CHURCHES
of Great Britain

FRANK BOTTOMLEY

Illustrated by Paul Bottemley

St. Cuthbert's Cross,
Durham

AVENEL BOOKS
NEW YORK

To Pam, supporter and chauffeuse

Copyright © 1981 by Kaye & Ward Ltd.
All rights reserved.

This 1984 edition is published by Avenel Books,
distributed by Crown Publishers, Inc., by arrangement with Kaye & Ward Ltd.

Manufactured in the United States of America

Library of Congress Cataloging in Publication Data

Bottemley, Frank.
    The explorer's guide to abbeys, monasteries, and
churches of Great Britian.

    Reprint. Originally published: The abbey explorer's
guide. London : Kaye & Ward, c1981.
    Bibliography: p.
    1. Monasticism and religious orders—Great Britain—
Dictionaries.   2. Monasteries—Great Britain—Guide-books.
I. Title.
BX2592.B67   1984   271'.00941   84-6300
ISBN: 0-517-44853X

h g f e d c b a

HOW TO USE THIS BOOK

Its purpose is to help the explorer to understand the remains, fill in the missing parts and imagine the life which once existed in mediaeval religious houses.

It is divided into two sections: a Glossary (pages 1 to 193) which covers all major aspects of abbeys, etc. — buildings and their use, officials and customs, work and prayer, terminology. The entries are in alphabetical order for easy reference and the explorer is further guided by a large plan over pages vi and vii and other plans and illustrations distributed throughout this section.

The second section is a Gazetteer (pages 196 to 248), listing under each country all the notable religious houses in England, Scotland and Wales, identified by name and with brief details of their location, foundation, type, access and extent of remains.

Numbers in parentheses at end of entry indicate page references in Glossary. There may be more than one reference on a page.

Byland Trinity (preserved at
Ampleforth)

v

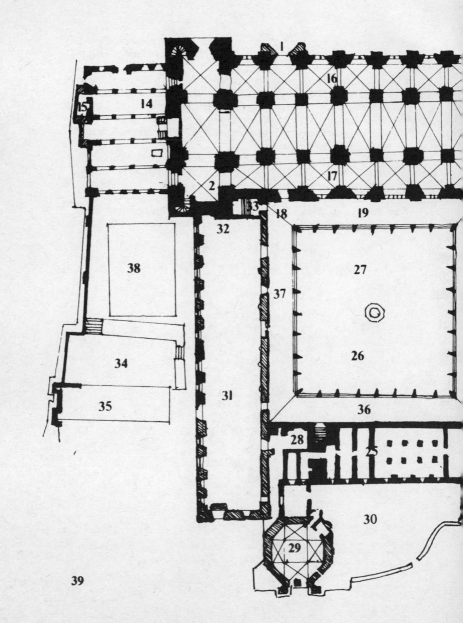

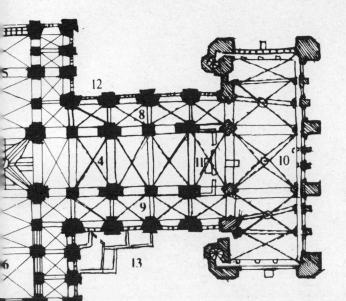

Key to Plan

1. Sanctuary knocker on north (people's) door
2. Site of night stairs entrance
3. Sacrist's oven for eucharistic bread
4. Quire
5. North transept and chapels
6. South transept and chapels
7. Central lantern house
8. North quire aisle
9. South quire aisle
10. Chapel of nine altars
11. St Cuthbert's shrine
12. Site of sacristan's checker
13. Vestry and sacristy
14. Galilee with St Bede's tomb
15. Well
16. North nave aisle
17. South nave aisle
18. Door to cloister
19. North cloister alley (site of carrels)
20. Slype and parlour
21. Chapter-house (restored)
22. Prison with two solitary cells
23. Day stair
24. Prior's lodging (a) hall with undercroft
                     (b) chambers
                     (c) chapel with crypt
25. Frater with undercroft and cellar
26. Site of hexagonal laver
27. Cloister-garth with basin of laver
28. The 'covey'
29. Great kitchen formerly surrounded by ancillary buildings
30. Coal-garth
31. Dorter over cellarium, common house etc
32. Treasury
33. Night stair
34. Rere-dorter
35. Prison ('lying house')
36. South cloister alley
37. West cloister alley (and novices' school)
38. Garden and bowling green
39. Site of farmery
40. Cemetery-garth
41. Access to outer court

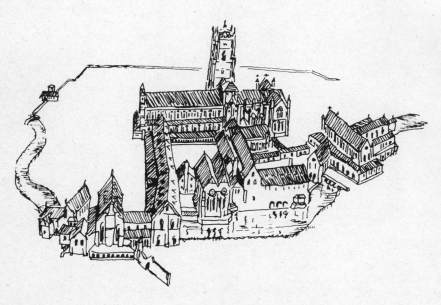

Fountains

ABBACY

The position of abbot or abbess. Initially, the appointment was for life but resignation was tolerated. The office was absolute and therefore a convent was at the mercy of a bad appointment who could be cruel to individuals and prodigal of communal resources.

Deposition could be effected by visiting bishop (see Visitation), head of order or pope (according to status of house) but procedures to bring this about were only the beginning of costly litigation. Should a deposed abbot win his fight for restoration, life in the convent became unbearable and, even when they were unsuccessful, some abbots were not above reprisals, e.g. at Lilleshall in 1331, and Bindon (slightly earlier).

ABBESS

Head of abbey of nuns. Like the abbot, she had jurisdiction over the lives of her subjects and like him bore a crozier as a symbol of her rank and office. She took tithes of appropriated churches (q.v.), presented secular vicars to serve parochial churches and had all the privileges of a feudal landlord over the temporal estates attached to the abbey e.g. the abbess of Shaftsbury found seven knights for the king's service and held her own manorial courts. The abbesses of Barking, Nunnaminster (Winchester) and Wilton were also feudal barons and, by right of this tenure, had for a time the privilege of being summoned to parliament. There were famous abbesses, such as Euphemia of Wherwell (1226-57) of whom her convent chartulary speaks:

'It is most fitting that we should always perpetuate the memory, in our special prayers and suffrages, of one who ever worked to the glory of God and for the weal of both our souls and bodies. For she increased the number of the Lord's handmaids in this monastery from 40 to 80 to the exaltation of the worship of God . . . She also, with maternal piety and careful forethought, built for the use both of the sick and of the sound a new and large farmery away from the main buildings and in conjunction with a dorter and other necessary offices. Beneath the farmery she constructed a watercourse, through which a stream flowed with sufficient force to carry off all refuse that might corrupt the air. Moreover, she built there a place set apart for the refreshment of the soul, namely a chapel of the Blessed Virgin. With the chapel she enclosed a large place

Benedictine Abbess

which was adorned on the north side with pleasant vines and trees. On the other side, by the river bank, she built offices for various uses, a space being left in the centre, where the nuns are able from time to time to enjoy the pure air . .'.

ABBEYS

The largest monasteries were usually known as abbeys because their head was an abbot or abbess (q.v.). The title is an indication of status and independence but some priories (q.v.) were as independent, large and well-endowed as the abbeys, particularly the cathedral priories (q.v.).

The chief abbeys, apart from cathedral priories in England include the following:

Beaulieu, Bury, Byland, Cockersand, Cleeve, Egglestone, Fountains, Furness, Glastonbury, Kirkstall, Malmesbury, Meaux, Netley, Rievaulx, Roche, Sawley, Selby, Tewkesbury, Thornton, Westminster, Whalley, Whitby.

Abbey Town

Wales: Aberconwy, Bardsey, Basingwerk, Cwmhir, Cymmer, Llantwit Major, Margam, Neath, St Dogmael's, Strata Florida, Tintern, Talley, Valle Crucis.
Scotland: Arbroath, Balmerino, Cambuskenneth, Crosraguel, Culross, Deer, Drybergh, Dunfermline, Dundrennan, Glenluce, Holyrood, Inchcolm, Iona, Jedburgh, Kelso, Kinloss, Kilwinning, Lindores, Melrose, Paisley, Sweetheart.

ABBEY TOWN   see also *Town*

Besides the place with this name in Cumbria, many towns were the creation of abbeys, growing up on its lands and under its protection e.g. Abingdon, Battle, Bury, Canterbury, Durham, Norwich, Peterborough, Reading, St Albans. The abbots exercised almost complete jurisdiction over such places and maintained roads and bridges, appointed civic officers, controlled trade, markets and fairs, and set up courts of justice. The towns eventually desired autonomy and usually this developed peaceably but occasionally there were notorious conflicts between citizens and abbey officials, especially in Bury.

ABBOT

Investiture of Abbot

'Abbas' or 'abba' means 'father' (cf. Rom.viii, 15) and expresses the paternal and authoritative qualities that should characterise a superior 'In the monastery he is considered to represent the person of Christ, seeing that he is called by His name'. (Benedict: Rule chap.ii). The supremacy of the abbot is central to Benedictine and derived orders. Obedience is one of the basic monastic vows and the superior is to be obeyed 'as if the command had come from God.' Since the abbot takes Christ's place, interior and external honour is to be shown him at all times and in all places.

St Dunstan

The abbot's absolute authority is limited only to conscience and the rule, though Benedict reminds him that he is to be a father not a tryant: 'An abbot who is worthy to have charge of a monastery ought always to remember by what title he is called'. Yet, though the rule gives direction about abbatial government, lays down principles and requires that he should consult the brethren in some matters, the monk is instructed always to give unquestioning and unhesitating obedience. On the other hand, the rule (especially ii and lxiv) has much to say about the use of this God-given power: 'Let him always put mercy before judgment, that he might find mercy himself; let him not be jealous or suspicious for so he will never find peace; let him strive rather to be loved than to be feared; let him be prudent in his correction, lest while he strive to scour off the rust, he break the vessel; let him realise what a difficult task he has undertaken — that of directing souls and adapting himself to many varied characters'.

Normally and ideally the appointment of the abbot was by free election of all full members of the house but the secular ruler had to give his consent and sometimes he interfered, as did the pope, especially in the case of Christchurch, Canterbury which was associated with the Primacy of All England. Election was for life but an abbot could resign without disgrace e.g. Maurice, second abbot of Rievaulx.

The social position of an abbot was often equal to that of a nobleman and one Cistercian abbot had the title of earl. Their rank involved them in feudal duties and secular affairs (they far outnumbered the bishops in the House of Lords, where, at one time, there were 52 abbots to 18 bishops) and consequently their monastic duties were largely delegated to the prior (q.v.).

ABBOT'S SERVANTS

Besides his obedientiaries (q.v.) an abbot employed bailiffs on his granges, expert laymen (sometimes knights) as his legal advisers, and a staff of clerks for accounting, letter-writing, etc. His household also included a chaplain and (at least in later Middle Ages) a staff of upper and lower servants: waiters at table, grooms etc. as well as escorts when he travelled abroad. There was an unseemly tendency for abbots (as feudal lords) to ape the display of their secular peers.

ABBOT'S TABLE

Originally this was the 'high table' in the frater but later he had his own table in his private hall (see Superior's Lodgings) where he could offer appropriate hospitality to distinguished guests. As there was no pressure to make them eat as monks, the food there was more generous and varied (including meat) and supplied from the abbot's kitchen. Sometimes monks of the community were invited to this misericord (q.v.) and it was usual, on great feasts, for the abbot to invite the ministers of the High Mass, together with the precentor and organist.

ABLUTIONS

1. The ritual washing of the liturgical vessels in the piscina. (q.v.)
2. The toilet of the monks.

This generally took place after Prime in the cloister or wherever the laver (q.v.) was placed. Monks took up their position in order of seniority, the juniors waiting in their places, reading or praying, until it was their turn. When the professed had finished, a sign was given that the lavatorium was free and the novice-master ceased his instruction, the novices laid down their psalters, the juniors returned their books to the book-cupboard and they washed in turn, smoothing their hair and tidying up in the corner of the cloister near the frater door. On Sundays and Feast Days the start of the early mass (q.v.) was delayed until the washing was finished.

Provision for spiritual cleansing was made at the same time by arranging for a priest to be in attendance in the chapter-house during the washing period to administer the sacrament of Penance.

Monk Travelling

ABSENCE

Even the Benedictine principle of 'stability' (q.v.) allowed for monks to be absent from the convent on necessary business. If the absence was protracted i.e. involving two nights or more outside the monastery, he was to receive a solemn blessing on departure and at his return. While away the monk was expected to say the canonical hours, by dismounting from his horse on the way, making use of a convenient church or saying them in his lodgings. Where practicable, he was also expected to attend mass. It was also assumed that he would keep the rule of silence as far as possible as well as the other regulations of his monastic state.

Monk in Travelling Dress

ABSTINENCE

The penitential or disciplinary practice of abstaining from certain kinds of food (e.g. flesh meat), as distinct from fasting which means not eating or reducing any kind of food to a strictly limited quantity.

A Friday abstinence (in memory of Christ's Passion) was practised by all Christians from very early times and more or less severe abstinence is still practised by contemplative orders (Carthusians, Carmelite nuns).

'**Accusations**'

In the Middle Ages, abstinence was practised, not only on Fridays but on Wednesdays in Lent, Ember Days, Rogation Days and on the vigils of certain major Feasts.

'ACCUSATIONS'

The first 'reserved business' of the chapter meeting was concerned with the revelation of faults against discipline. It included self-accusation as well as drawing attention to the faults of others. All could speak (except novices) though certain disciplinary officers had a special responsibility. Matters referred to generally fell into one of three classes:

i Negligences of all kinds, breaches of rule or observances, offences against the custom of the house, mistakes in the Divine Service.

ii Breaches of the rule of silence — a subject usually opened by the superior or guardian of the cloister.

iii Neglect of hospitality or almsgiving, on which the almoner or his assistant would have most to say.

The superior or his deputy presided and he was responsible for deciding the punishment (q.v.) of erring brethren and for deciding the treatment of other complaints.

ADMINISTRATOR   see also *Commendator*

A non-member of the community, sometimes a layman who was deputised to take care of the temporal affairs of a religious house by acting as a kind of estate-agent or manager. Such an officer was commonly attached to nunneries and was almost essential in the case of enclosed communities. In other cases this duty was carried out by a religious superior or by a delegated religious.

Administrators were sometimes appointed to correct the business affairs of a house which had acquired unmanageable debts (the king's steward was so delegated to Flaxley abbey in 1277). Such temporary custodians and managers of the revenues of a house were usually laymen of good social position, often friends and neighbours of the convent who could give personal attention to the crisis. Often they seem to have been carefully selected so that their qualifications corresponded to the specific nature of a particular difficulty — lawyers, knights or military men.

Their main duties were twofold: negative to reduce expenses (by diminishing number of servants, economising in food and 'state' maintained by house), sometimes this involved temporarily retiring the superior to a dependency and using his account and any other surplus funds to pay off immediate debts; positively, to see that the foundation number of religious was maintained (if possible) and that alms and donations were properly administered 'else the souls of the donors be imperilled'.

ADVOWSON

The right of nomination or presentation to an ecclesiastical benefice e.g. rectory or vicarage. This right was a property and could be bought, sold or given away.

AISLE

Literally 'wing' — a passage alongside the nave, choir or transept of a church, usually separated by columns or piers. Its purpose was to provide a processional path and its development was associated with the elaboration of the liturgy. (Examples at Bridlington, Christchurch, Colchester, Guisborough, Worksop, etc.). Early non-Benedictine churches were not provided with this facility (e.g. Haughmond, Kirkham, Lilleshall, Shap). Later rebuildings sometimes produced a single nave aisle on the north as the south could not be extended because of pre-existing cloister (e.g. Abergavenny, Bolton, Bromfield, Brinkburn, Canons Ashby,

Coverham, Dorchester, Haughmond, Lanercost, Newstead, Shap, Thurgarton, Torre, Ulverscroft.)

Unaisled naves are found in churches of all the orders, e.g. Bromholm, Hulme, Kelso, Sawley and there is an entirely aisle-less plan at Cymmer and in the churches of other small communities (e.g. Nun Monkton). This plan was preferred by the Carthusians (e.g. Mount Grace) and by the friars (e.g. Brecon, Hulne, Lynn, Richmond). Some of the later churches in towns were provided with aisles in order to increase accommodation (e.g. Norwich). The double houses of the Gilbertines (e.g. Watton) possessed unaisled churches.

Gatehouse Worksop Priory

ALIEN PRIORIES

Direct dependencies of continental houses, generally arising from benefactions made by William I's followers from English lands to monasteries in their home country. Some may have been used as 'holiday' homes, others for disciplinary banishment.

Bolton Priory

Basically, there were two types: conventual and manorial. The former had a full complement of religious pursuing the complete claustral life under a prior (e.g. Blyth, St Neots). The latter, which were more common, consisted of a manor (sometimes with an appropriated church) where two or three religious resided, leading no regular life but simply acting as agents for the collection of revenues which they conveyed to the mother house.

Chester South Aisle

At one time there were more than 100 'alien priories' in England including Boxgrove from Lessay, Blyth from Rouen, St Neots from Bec. At Ecclesfield, Yorkshire (probably from St Wandrille, Belgium) the 'custos' served the cure of the parish church. Small alien priories need leave no trace either of their domestic buildings or of conventual arrangements in the parish church.

They came under royal displeasure during the Hundred Years War with France both as channels for the transmission of revenue to foreign countries and as possible security risks. In the war of 1295 the crown confiscated their temporalities and imposed restrictions on the convents, including forbidding their members to dwell within 13 miles of the coast. There were also religious problems inasmuch as a handful of monks could hardly live the full religious life far separated from the discipline and inspiration of the mother house, much occupied by administration and with both communication and revenues frequently interrupted by political disturbance. Some were suppressed and their personnel and resources allocated to other religious uses — colleges, chantries or supplementing larger monastic establishments. Larger houses solved their problems by gaining charters of denization and became independent monasteries under English priors (e.g. Blyth, St Neots). Others became dependencies of great English houses so that, shortly after 1414, 'alien priories' no longer existed.

ALIEN HOSPITALS

There were about half a dozen hospitals in England which were subordinate to foreign convents. In general, their history parallels that of 'alien priories'.

ALMONER   (Elemosinarius)

The official responsible for the house's external works of mercy. Every religious house was under an obligation to distribute 'alms' which usually consisted of

Almonry

food and clothing, sometimes money and medicine but could include board, lodging and education. Apart from the house's own products in kind, definite income was allocated to this work and its administration required a man of parts. The Barnwell Observances are very specific.

Almoner

'Every almoner must have his heart aglow with charity. His pity should know no bounds and he should possess the love of others in a most marked degree. He must show himself as the helper of orphans, the father of the needy, and as one who is ever ready to cheer the lot of the poor and help them to bear their hard life.' While ministering to the wants of the body, he was not to forget the needs of the soul and should take opportunity to speak of spiritual matters, reception of the sacraments etc.

The work was demanding and besides servants the almoner often had a sub-almoner to assist him and he had permission to be absent from the morning offices in order to be free to distribute alms. He received the old clothes of religious and was ordered to lay in a special stock of clothing for distribution at Christmas. The monastery kitchens and buttery always prepared more food and drink than was needed so that the surplus could go to the almoner's stock. It was also the custom to give the rations of a dead monk for 30 days to the poor. Almsgiving was intended to be mutual and self-respect was preserved by the recipient offering his prayers for the community.

Besides the above, the almoner's duties included the supervision of the daily maundy and the great maundy (q.v.). He was also responsible for any extern school conducted by the monastery and for any (child) boarders in the almonry. He also had to find rods for discipline: in the school if there was one and also for the community (see Chapter, Discipline). Apart from these general duties, individual houses attached their own particular ones which could include renewing mats in the choir, providing rushes for the cloisters, dorter-floor and elsewhere, and even providing walking sticks for aged monks at the Rogationtide processions.

Nunneries also had their almoners and they operated on the same principles as did the monks, with converse regulations to avoid scandal, i.e. nuns were not allowed to visit bed-ridden males.

ALMONRY   (Domus elemosinaria)

Almonry, Evesham

At first, alms were distributed at the monastic gateway but later a special building was provided nearby and the services were extended. The almonry at Durham had an infirmary which maintained four old women and such monastic almshouses were not uncommon (paralleled by the bede-houses attached to some secular colleges in the later Middle Ages) and sometimes their offerings extended to education (so at Evesham where the almshouse substantially survives. The Augustinian abbey at Leicester had a school attached to its almonry.). The chamber over the great gate at Fountains was a bede-house and in the upper rooms of the almonry at Durham were lodged 'the children of the almonry' who were fed, clothed and educated at the expense of the monastery (They were taught in the outer farmery). Elsewhere (e.g. Barnwell, Thornton) these children were known as 'the clerks of the almonry' and their position was similar to those of 'clerici secundae formae' who in secular colleges were taught under the direction of the cathedral chancellor (e.g. Lincoln). The almonry at St Albans in earlier C14 contained 'hall, chapel, chamber, kitchens, cellar and all other buildings necessary for the scholars and their masters'. At Dorchester the almonry was combined with the guest-house and the dole window can still be seen together with the seat on which the almoner sat. There is a similar window at St Cross, Winchester. Traces of the destroyed almonry can sometimes be discerned on the walls of the gatehouse (e.g Kirkham, Thetford). The North Hall at Canterbury, of which a fine C12 staircase survives, adjoined the almonry and provided a casual ward for destitute wayfarers.

ALMS   see also *Almoner, Hospitality*

Pilgrims were specially due Alms

Every religious house was under exemplary obligations in regard to the corporal works of mercy as far as they could be applied. No needy person was ever to be sent empty away but there were also fixed times for the wholesale distribution of alms at the gatehouse or almonry (q.v.). At Canterbury, it was at noon on two specified days in the week. Spiritual alms were also obligatory — the raison d'etre of a religious house included intercessory prayer not only for named founders and benefactors but also for all Christ's people, living and dead.

The provided food was sometimes consumed on the premises: Worcester had a 'guesten house', Canterbury its North Hall, while the Benedictine priory of St Nicholas, Exeter had its 'poor man's parlour'.

Hospital Alms Box

The distribution of alms represented a very considerable expenditure. In C16, Gloucester abbey was spending £140.16.8 a year, the Carmelites of Norwich £77.6.9 and the nuns of Romsey in 1412 the sum of £8.19.4. This represented about a tenth of their total income and multiplication of the sums by something like 250 would give a rough approximation of their present equivalent.

Almsgiving could include education (see Almonry), board and lodging for orphans and sometimes the expenses of their apprenticing. In C16 at Westminster e.g. the sub-almoner took the children of the almonry (who had a school uniform of russet-coloured fustian, lined with white cotton, bound with black velvet and tied with silken points) to London to be apprenticed to masters of various trades and crafts. The abbey continued to keep some kind of supervision over them and cases are known of its representatives visiting them with gifts when they were sick.

ALMSHOUSE   see also *Bede-house*

Building for quasi-religious community, living under modified rule usually with the obligation of praying for the repose of the founder in return for free lodging and partial or complete board. The accommodation usually included small independent lodgings (sometimes for married couples) together with some common provisions — always a chapel and sometimes a hall. They were usually governed by a master or warden who lived on the premises. The institution is another form of the pervasive application of the corporal works of mercy and is one of the many forms of the mediaeval 'hospital' (q.v.). The contract for Tattershall survives, by which a carpenter agrees to construct, out of re-used and new timber provided by the warden, an almshouse 172ft long, 19ft deep and 16ft high to the top of the wall-plate. He is to provide a gallery on the south side, supported on pillars with a porch towards the churchyard and a door at the other end. Within, there are to be 12 separate chambers, each with two windows; a common hall and buttery; two staircases to the upper floor; and a chapel. The upper floor is to be two feet higher over hall and chapel. He is also to provide fittings. For all this he is to be paid £16 in weekly instalments and mutual bonds of 40 marks each are to be deposited for performance of contract.

ALTAR

The monastic church, like the Christian church-building in general, originated as a location for the altar on which Christ's atoning sacrifice was recalled in the mass. Originally, there was but one altar (retained in the later High Altar in the presbytery) and great effort and ingenuity were expended to provide a fitting erection. About 700 A.D. St Aldhelm returned from Rome, bringing with him 'an altar of shining white marble six feet long, four feet deep and three palms (c.12ins) thick, with a lip projecting from the stone and beautifully carved round the edge. . . He gave the altar to Ine who placed it for the service of the Mother of God in a royal villa called Briwetune (Bruton, Somerset) where it stands to this day (c.1125), a living proof, so to speak, of the sanctity of Adlhelm'. (William of Malmesbury).

The High Altar is usually raised on one or more steps which are often all that remain to indicate its site as mediaeval altars were particularly objectionable to the Reformers. The High Altar of Byland is reverently preserved at Ampleforth.

As more monks entered the priesthood and with the growth of the notion of the 'private mass' (a mass with celebrant and acolyte only), there was pressing need for the provision of more altars. This resulted in developments at the east end of the church. At Dore an eastern aisle gave access to a row of five chapels, at Byland the eastern aisle itself was divided into chapels, Jervaulx had five chapels against the eastern wall. The eastern arm of the church was generally developed e.g.
Thornton, Rievaulx, Whitby, Carlisle, Kirkham, York.
Fountains is perhaps the ultimate with its eastern transept to accommodate nine altars, a plan copied at Durham.

ALTAR

Altars were also provided at either side of the entrance to the pulpitum, before the rood screen, against the eastern walls of the transepts and against the western faces of nave piers. Apart from these, there were altars before shrines in chantries, in the farmery, chapter-house and elsewhere, almost invariably in guest-house, often in gatehouse, always in capella ante portas and rarely in dorter.

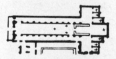
Westminster Abbey. Tomb of Edward The Confessor

e.g. in front of piers : St Albans, Byland, Fountains, Rievaulx.
before shrines : Durham, St Albans.
chapter-house : Mount Grace.
presbytery aisles : St Albans, St Mary's, York.
eastern extension : Guisborough, Jervaulx, Selby.
At Jervaulx some of the minor altars survive almost intact.

Fountains Abbey (twelfth century). Church Plan (C12) showing Altars

AMBULATORY   see also Processions

The enclosed 'walking-space' for liturgical procession provided within a church. The term is particularly used of the semi-circular or polygonal aisle enclosing an apse and characteristic of the Norman period. The apse did not retain its popularity long in England and Wales and was replaced by the square-ended eastern termination generally by mid C12. On the continent it was replaced by the chevet, adopted at Battle, Canterbury, Coventry, Tewkesbury and Westminster but the latter is the only survivor. The chapter-house at Rievaulx seems unique in having an ambulatory (to provide convenient access to shrine.).

ANARCHY

The period of the civil wars between Stephen and Matilda (1135-53) when 'it was openly said that Christ and His saints slept'. But it was also a time remarkable for new religious foundations (no less than 119) and is particularly the period of Cistercian consolidation and expansion.

ANCHORITE, ANCHORESS

A person who withdraws from the world to live a solitary life of silence, prayer and mortification. As distinct from a hermit (q.v.), he or she lived in strictly enclosed quarters (anchorage or cell) which might be attached to a church, provided within a monastery or be located on an otherwise uninhabited island. This life required formal approval of superior and permission of bishop who had to be assured not only of spiritual resources but also of provision of material ones. The 'Ancren Riwle' (c.1200) was written for the guidance of such solitaries (perhaps at Tarrant). St Ailred, abbot of Rievaulx, also wrote a treatise on the eremitical life for his sister who was an anchoress.

Some monasteries provided for their members who had received this special vocation and there was a succssion of anchorities at Westminster. Two monks from the Augustinian abbey of St Mary de Pré 'sought the life of anchorets' at Chester and Leicester St Michael during the abbacy of William of Clown (d. 1378). Durham had an anchorite's cell between the two piers at the end of the north alley of the quire which seems to have consisted of a kind of chapel in a loft overlooking St Cuthbert's shrine. There was apparently a similar arrangement in the parish church of Compton, Surrey on the Canterbury Pilgrim's Way.

ANGLICAN RELIGIOUS ORDERS

From 1626 to 1646 at Little Gidding, some 30 relatives of Nicholas Ferrar lived an ordered life in an impressivè but idiosyncratic community. Another attempt within the Anglican communion was made by Newman at Littlemore in 1842 and the Oxford Movement produced a steady, if not large, stream of foundations mostly of women (including enclosed comtemplatives) so that about 50 years ago Coulton could write that the present number of Anglican nuns exceeded that of Catholic nuns in the Middle Ages. Of the 34 'orders and societies' of men that appeared between 1842 and 1961, five joined the Catholic church and 19 became extinct. Of the ten survivors, the most important are those of Cowley, Kelham, Mirfield and Nashdom (though Kelham has recently abandoned its mother house). The Church of England Year Book gives a list of all religious communities with their addresses, dates of foundation and a brief summary of their nature.

St Augustinc's Chair

ANGLO-SAXON CHURCH

In C6-7, England was being evangelised by two currents: a Celtic mission (influenced by Eastern monasticism via Lerins through Ireland and Scotland) and a Benedictine mission from Rome instigated by St Gregory the Great under the leadership of St Augustine. The latter reached Kent in 597 bringing grammar schools and plainsong and establishing episcopal centres at Canterbury, London, Rochester and York. Meanwhile the Celtic St Aidan had established a missionary centre at Lindisfarne which was working in southern Scotland and northern England. The total effort of the two enterprises was somewhat hindered by different observances, including the date of Easter and the form of the monastic tonsure (q.v.) but these were decided in favour of the Roman custom at the Synod of Whitby in 664. The organisation of the missionary territory was established by the reform and

Bede's Chair,
Monkwearmouth

9

effective administration of archbishop Theodore,
appointed to Canterbury by pope Vitalian in 668.
Important synods of the English clergy were held and new
dioceses founded. The Danish invasions of C9 brought
destruction and havoc but the tide was turned and
reconstruction begun under Alfred the Great. Further
advances were made by the Benedictine St Dunstan and his
coadjutors in C10 and close connections with the rest of
Western Christendom were re-established. There was a
decline in the following century and most of the Anglo-
Saxon hierarchy were moved after the Conquest with the
notable exception of St Wulstan, the Benedictine bishop of
Worcester.

Wilfred's Stool, Hexham

Monasticism had been a powerful force in the Anglo-
Saxon church, most of the evangelisation had been effected
by monks and this may be the source of the English custom
of cathedral priories (q.v.). Double monasteries of men and
women, often ruled by an abbess (e.g. St Hilda at Whitby)
were not uncommon during the period but most of them
had disappeared by 1066. The period, particularly its first
part, is illuminated by the life of numerous saints (Bede,
Wilfrid, Benedict Biscop, Chad, Cedd and Cuthbert) as
well as by magnificent art and intensive learning under the
inspiration, and often the direction, of the church.

St Augustine

ANTIPHON
Originally a piece of music sung by two choirs. The
opposing seating in the quire is related to this practice.
Later, the term was applied to the setting of sentences,
usually from Scripture, which were sung before and after
the Canticles in the Divine Office. Antiphonal singing may
be divided between two equal choirs (cantoris and decani)
or between choir and a small group of soloists (cantors) and
may consist either of verses sung alternately or of a psalm
broken at intervals by a refrain or response.
The musical development of the antiphon (anthem) led
to the production of an elaborate free-standing piece of
music, especially the anthems of Our Lady sung after
Compline and on other occasions.

Tower Arch: St Benet's,
Cambridgeshire

ANTIPHONARIUM
The collection of chants used in quire and the book
containing them which normally rested on a lectern in the
middle of the quire. St Gregory collected the Roman chants
into an antiphonarium which was said to be chained to the
altar in St Peter's. The papal song school developed
plainsong or plainchant which the Benedictines spread
across Europe (St Augustine brought it to England).

Stone Lectern

APOSTACY
Leaving the religious life after solemn profession was called apostacy and
considered a serious crime in the eyes of both state and church. It was not only a
breach of faith with God but with the founders and benefactors of a religious house
which had been established to pray for them. A warrant for the arrest of a deserter-

monk could be issued and executed by the secular authorities who would return him to his house and to his superior for condign punishment. There are a number of recorded instances of the king ordering his serjeant-at-arms to arrest runagates. In C14, the abbot of Winchcombe reported the unauthorised departure of a troublesome monk to the king who appointed officers to arrest him and return him to the abbey 'to be chastened according to the rule of the order'.

APPROPRIATION

Before a parish church could be consecrated, it had to be endowed with an assured and adequate income for the maintenance of its incumbent. Advowson (q.v.) thus involved the disposition of an endowment. This right was sometimes awarded to a religious house by a benefactor (whose ancestors had often provided the original endowment) who allowed for the appropriation of the revenue provided that a curate was provided. This led to the development of vicars (representatives), with the rectory resting with the religious house (or other institution). There were opportunities here for abuse; the appropriator increasing the difference between the salary of the vicar and the income of the rectory, leaving the parish without an incumbent while enjoying its revenue, economising on expenditure needed for repairs, etc.

Monasteries sought appropriation as a means of 'saving' money (often to dispense it in hospitality and alms) or with a sincere intention of improving the quality of pastoral care but the practice of appropriation was often, though by no means always, detrimental to the fabric of the church concerned.

In an appropriated church, the monks almost invariably appointed a resident secular priest as they were not allowed, save in very exceptional circumstances, to serve parochial cures since this would interfere with their prime duty and vocation in quire and cloister. An example of the exception lies in the institution of a monk of Winchcombe to the rectory of Rowell in 1361.

ARCHITECTURE, MONASTIC

This was deliberately symbolic. From the time of abbot Suger of St Denys there was a whole spirituality springing from and expressed through light.

Malmesbury Tympanum

Contemporaries saw a consonance between the virtues of the inner life and a zeal for edifying the material dwelling-place of God — both were matters of harmony and proportion. Certainly many of the most saintly abbots were great builders.

Monastic buildings exemplified a devotion to light and to cleanliness. Much fresh air and light were admitted and water was plentifully supplied. Churches were not only adorned with costly materials, further enriched with the highest skill, but their very structure was in accordance with accepted and well-understood symbolic principles. The number seven as a module has been fully revealed at Cluny and it probably signified the Gifts of the Spirit. Other identified modules include three, five and nine and lay-outs based on a quadrille of 15 squares, dimensions based on 100 (for plenitude or perfection), 'perfect numbers', mean and extreme ratio and special Vitruvian constructions were also used.

Monastic architecture was so fitted for its purpose and so often a stylistic leader that it became the pattern for imitation in other large non-monastic churches: collegiate and cathedral. Cathedrals not only developed (unneccessary) cloisters e.g. Chichester, Lincoln, Salisbury, Wells but often a 'close' in imitation of the monastic curia (e.g. Lichfield, Salisbury, Wells) which was surrounded by an enclosing wall.

ARCHIVIST

This office was usually performed by the librarian (armarius) q.v. The archivist kept the deeds and charters of the house, licences and records including the necrology (q.v.). He also preserved the documents recording the solemn vows of each professed monk. Either he or the almoner drew up the brief or mortuary roll which informed other houses of the death of a member of the house and asked for their prayers. He might also be responsible for other legal documents deposited by lay-folks for safe-keeping in the monastery.

ARMARIUS (Librarian)

This post was usually conflated with the office of precentor (q.v.). He had charge of all books in the book-cupboard or, later, in the library or book-room. He had also to provide all materials required in the scriptorium (q.v.) which included the manufacture of ink, the provision of colours for illumination, the tools for ruling, writing and erasure and the materials on which to write (vellum or parchment). He was not only responsible for the storage of books, but also for their disposition, condition, binding and repair. He had to know the titles and location of all books possessed by the monastery and, by constant inspection and attention, to protect them from misuse, from the ravages of dust or damp (particularly difficult) and from the inroads of insects and other livestock.

For some of this work he employed skilled professionals, particularly in later Middle Ages, and accounts show his allowances 'for cleaning bindings of choir books' etc. Special revenues were sometimes placed at the disposal of the librarian for the making or buying of new books and monks travelling abroad on other business were sometimes asked to search for particular volumes. He kept a list of donors or makers of the house's books and arranged that such benefactors should be commemorated at mass and offices (usually at the beginning of Lent when books were distributed for spiritual reading). He brought books into the chapter-house for the abbot to distribute appropriately and entered, as always, the names of the borrowers in his register. If a book was lent outside the monastery he was responsible for its safe return and usually ensured this by extracting a sufficient pledge from the borrower.

He was also responsible for all official internal lists for the weekly rosters to tabulae of duties. These temporary documents were often inscribed on wax tablets and he had to supply the wax. He was in charge of all service books and lectionaries (including those read in chapter and frater) and for giving necessary instructions to appointed reader or singers. He was usually archivist (q.v.) and, in his capacity of precentor, one of the three custodians of the convent seal.

The Abingdon regulations about the precentor lay down that 'when he is away, the succentor (q.v.), if he is fit for office, shall keep the library keys: but should he be giddy and light-minded, (the precentor) shall give them to the prior or sub-prior'.

ART

Though the personal contribution of monks has been sometimes overstated, there was an undoubted monastic contribution to art. More is known about the art of Celtic monks than about their rudimentary architecture. They produced books (mainly Scriptural and Patristic works) that are world-renowned for their illumination. A distinctive style emanating from Irish monasteries was spread far and wide by monk missionaries e.g. Book of Kells (C7), Lindisfarne Gospels (C8). This style was also transferred to stone and appears on some 'Celtic' crosses.

According to the rule, individual artistic talent was always to be subordinate to the spiritual life as is clearly stated in chapter lvii:

Monk engaged in Artwork

'Artificers, if there are any in the monastery, shall practise with all humility their special arts, if the abbot permit it. But if any one of them becomes inflated with pride on account of his art, to the extent that he appears to be conferring something on the monastery — such a one shall be plucked away from that art and shall not again return to it unless the abbot again perchance orders him to, he having become humble'.

Figure from Chapter-House, York

The work of later scriptoria is of undoubted beauty but towards the end of Middle Ages, this work was being taken over by professional scribes. Throughout the period, the embroidery work of nuns was prized everywhere in Europe as 'opus Anglicanum.' Bury was celebrated for book-binding in C14 and C15. There were individual monk-architects, and monk craftsmen of great skill but the later contribution of monasteries was through patronage rather than through executants. e.g. Gandulph (designer of Ely octagon), and a Franciscan from Dundee was so proficient that he was appointed 'king's limner' in C14 and another friar from the same convent had distinguished himself as military engineer at Dumbarton. Dunstan was a highly skilled metal-worker in both iron and gold and there was a legendary Benedictine maker of clocks in the later Middle Ages. But these are all merely individuals extracted from a very long period of time. The later practice at least was to hire professionals but if one of their number had the appropriate skill, and its use would not beget pride, his talents were employed e.g. Master Walter of Colchester, sacrist of St Albans (1214 +), 'an incomparable painter and carver', designed and executed the rood screen for his abbey.

ASCETICISM

The word means 'training' or 'discipline'. St Benedict called his ascetics 'the athletes of God'. 'Ascetae' existed from the earliest days of Christianity, men and women trying to follow 'the more perfect way' but living in the world. In some early documents ascetics are considered as a special class of believers between laity and clergy. The ascetic movement intensified after the conversion of Constantine removed the danger of persecution, reduced standards and attracted more lukewarm or uncommitted Christians. Ascetics aimed at mortifying the flesh, of achieving a kind of self martyrdom when external martyrdom was no longer likely. They tended to withdraw from the world into a desert, actual or figurative. Some ascetics were solitaries, others formed groups of greater or less cohesion. Later some joined formal religious orders such as the Cistercians or Austin Canons. Asceticism was more characteristic (at least in its more extreme forms) of the Eastern church and the eastern-influenced Celtic church than it was of the West.

ASPERGES   see also *Procession*

Solemn sanctification by sprinkling with holy water. This ceremony usually took place before High Mass when water was blessed and the community moved in formal procession throughout the whole house asking for God's blessing on all its departments and the activities of all its parts, especially the church and its individual altars. The ceremony dates from at least C9 and takes its name from the antiphon with which it opens: 'Asperges me hyssopo, Domine' (Thou shalt purge me with hyssop, O Lord — Ps.li.).

AUDITORIUM

Occasional alternative name for parlour (q.v.) or locutorium but it seems sometimes to have been used to mean a school-house or lecture theatre.

AUGUSTINIAN CANONS, etc.   see *Austin Canons* etc.

AUMBRY

A cupboard or locker, usually set in thickness of wall, to provide safe-keeping for requirements of sacraments. Frequently found in association with site of altar to provide securely for vessels used at mass. There are usually a number in the presbytery where some were used to keep relics. Occasionally they were made beneath the mensa of the altar (e.g. St John the Baptist, York). The recesses survive in many monastic churches (e.g. Durham, Kirkstall, Tynemouth) and in other buildings, e.g. frater and cloister. In the latter location they were probably used for book storage (Examples at Dryburgh, Lacock).

Similar cupboards occur as 'ready use' storage e.g. table furnishings in frater, towels for laver. Sometimes, they are called 'civerys' (serveries?) as at Norwich where there are eight or more around the cloister.

Armaries is a word cognate with aumbry and is used of the library provisions for book storage, hence 'armarius' (q.v.)

Besides being recessed, cupboards could be free-standing and elaborate examples of the joiner's craft, but survivals are very rare.

AUSTIN CANONS   see also *Twelfth Century*

An order of Canons Regular (q.v.) which arrived in England, probably encouraged by Lanfranc, at beginning of C12 (St Botolph's Priory, Colchester c.1106 which had primacy over all other English foundations). They spread rapidly with 140 foundations in English and Wales in C12 and achieving over 200 houses at their height, declining to 170 at Dissolution. Each house was governed by a 'prelate', usually a prior but an abbot in about two dozen cases. Most of the abbeys were in the Midlands but Carlisle became a cathedral priory (q.v.) in 1133. The abbots of Waltham and Cirencester had seats in the House of Lords and their houses were exempt from episcopal visitation.

Augustinian Canon

Austin Canons first reached Scotland c.1120 with important houses at Holyrood St Andrews and Scone, derived from the English foundations at Merton and Nostell. Eventually, there were about a score of houses of which there are remains at Cambuskenneth, Holyrood, Inchcolm, Jedburgh, Moneymusk, Restenneth, St Andrews.

The Black Canons often seem to have settled on an ancient monastic site and when there were survivors of that (Celtic) community they seem to have joined the new foundation (e.g. Bardsey Island, Wales and St Andrews, Scotland).

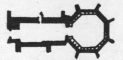

Bolton Priory / Chapter-House (Augustinian Canons)

The average revenues were quite modest approximating to about a third that of a Benedictine house and this poverty may explain the disappearance in Middle Ages of about a fifth of their foundations. They often had parochial responsibilities hence the survival, in whole or part of many of their churches e.g. Bristol, Carlisle, Oxford, Portsmouth, Southwark (now Anglican Cathedrals); Brinkburn, Cartmel, Bolton, Bourne, Breedon, Bridlington, Chetwode, Christchurch, Dorchester, Dunstable, Goring, Hexham, Lanercost, Letheringham, Little Dunmow, Portchester, London St Bartholomew's, St German's, Thurgarton, Waltham, Worksop.

Cloister walks survive at Oxford and at Lacock (with many intact apartments above). Ruins only at Haughmond and Ulverscroft and very little of the transmogrified Nostell which was notable for the number of its daughters (six, of which Bamburgh was the most important). There were other important houses at Barnwell, Leeds (Kent), Llanthony, London Holy Trinity Aldgate, Merton, St Osyth, Walsingham.

Guisborough Priory
(Augustinian Canons)

They made a notable contribution to the provision of hospitals, originating in London St Thomas' and St Bartholomew's which have survived and St Mary's Spital which has not, not to mention numerous smaller examples.

Their rule was based on St Augustine's 109th letter and they, like monks, were obliged to the Opus Dei, communal life and had a similar domestic organisation of obedientiaries, etc. But there were differences: all canons were priests, they were not bound to the house, their discipline was less austere. Their habit consisted of a black cassock with a white surplice and a hooded black cloak overall, hence their name of Black Canons. One of their most illustrious members was Walter Hilton (d.1396), mystic, author and sometime prior of Thurgarton.

AUSTIN CANONESSES

Nuns following the rule of St Augustine and whose chaplains were Austin Canons. They had about two dozen houses in mediaeval England and Wales of which half have left some material trace. They ranked as priories except for Burnham Canonsleigh (no remains) and Lacock which were abbeys. The houses were usually small and poor and when the endowment was inadequate the canonesses seem to have supported themselves by begging. The order returned in C19 and have about a dozen houses serving schools, hospices, etc. (Aconbury, Brewood, Campsey Ash, Cornworthy, Easebourne, Flixton, Goring, Grace Dieu, Holystone, Lacock, Limebrook, Minster).

AUSTIN FRIARS

Also known as the Hermit Friars of St Augustine. They were constituted from three small bodies of hermits who had been living according to the Augustinian rule (1256) and seem to have established some 40 priories in England and Wales. They were mendicants organised in areas called 'limites' and wore a long black gown and hood over a white cassock. In late Middle Ages one is recorded as confessor at St Bartholomew's hospital, Bristol, where he was paid 10 marks p.a. for this service to lepers. He was more highly rewarded (50 marks) for dressing their sores, saying 'lette us cure both spryte and bodye'.

There are remains of their establishments at Atherstone, Canterbury, Clare, Blackmore, Rye and Stamford. The Austin Friars had only a single house in Scotland, at Berwick, of which there are no remains.

In 1558 a strict reform, emanating from Spain produced the Augustinian Recollects who returned to England in C19 with three houses and responsibility for a number of parishes in Devon. The Austin Friars are now known as the Order of St Augustine. They too returned in C19 and have eight priories including one with a school in their old home at Carlisle.

BAKEHOUSE

A large community required vast quantities of bread, not only for its own use (the least of its needs) but for hospitality and alms. The great bakehouse (pistrinum) was situated in the outer court, usually near the granary and mill. Abbot Thomas of St Albans (1349-96), a great builder, paid his attention to this amenity: 'His bakehouse, also, weak from its great age, he restored most usefully, spending a great sum of money thereon; and he added, for the use of the same, a vessel of bronze holding 1,000 gallons (!)'. In spite of this record, bakehouses were usually less substantial and there are few remains (e.g. Canterbury, Fountains).

Besides the great general bakehouse, there was a special place (sometimes within the church itself) for baking the 'singing bread' i.e. the unleavenend bread used at mass and communion. This operation, under the direction of the sacrist, was conducted with scrupulous care and much ceremonial.

Monastic Barn, Bradford

BARN   see also *Granary*

The monastic barn or 'granarium' was a necessary storehouse for produce of, often distant, farmlands.

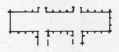

A fine barn survives at Bolton and an even finer one at Glastonbury (85ft × 25ft with porches extending a further 20ft). The barn was often the most imposing building on the monastic grange (q.v.) and sometimes incorporated accommodation for the granger and his assistant. There are particularly good examples belonging to Shaftsbury at Bradford-on-Avon and Tisbury. The barn at Enstone has an inscription recording that it was built by the abbot of Winchcombe at the instance of his bailiff. Barns belonging to Beaulieu survive in Coxwell, Berkshire and St Leonard's, Hampshire, and there is one which belonged to Kingswood at Calcot, Gloucestershire. Other examples at Temple Cressing, Llantarnam, Taunton.

Bradford-on-Avon,
Monastic Barn (plan)

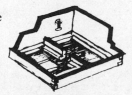

Barn at Littleton, Nr
Evesham

BATH

The rule of St Benedict (chap.xxxvi) prescribed that 'the use of baths shall be offered to the sick as often as is necessary; to the healthy, especially the young, it shall not so readily be conceded.' Thus, on the one hand, baths were seen as therapeutic, on the other, as smacking of self-indulgence. However, too much indentification should not be made between bathing and more or less thorough washing. Attitudes and customs fluctuated to some extent during the Middle Ages e.g. at St Augustine's, Canterbury

Laundry and Bath House

in C14 it was stated that there had been an allowance of four baths a year but at that time it was halved. Baths were normally prescribed before the festal seasons of Christmas, Easter and Pentecost.

Ascetics frequently immersed in cold water as a discipline (St Cuthbert is a notable example and St Ailred seems to have provided for this within his own cell). Many diseases were treated by bathing in hot water and one might expect to find signs of this provision in farmeries but their ruins are never sufficiently complete to provide this information though there is much evidence of complex water supply and draining. The documentation of hospitals shows that baths were frequent and regular and the Barnwell Observances declare:
'A bath should by no means be refused to a body when compelled thereto by needs of ill-health. Let it be taken without grumbling when ordered by a physician so that, even though a brother be unwilling, what ought to be done for health may be done at the order of him who is set over you. Should he wish for one, however, when it is not advantageous then his desire is not to be gratified. Sometimes, what gives pleasure is thought to do good even though it may do harm'. (One should not forget the long association between baths and lasciviousness, extending from imperial Rome to mediaeval England where 'stews' could mean equally 'public baths' or 'house of ill-fame').

There seems to have been a 'balnearium' (bath house) at Canterbury, located some distance east of the cloister, and there are dubious structures at Kirkstall and Shap which some have identified with permanent baths. There were considerable technical problems involved in the heating of large quantities of water and, like the arrangements for shaving, its provision was the responsibility of the chamberlain. He also had to provide the tubs, the soap, the linen for towels and see that naked and hot feet were protected by rushes or herbs on the floor of the bathing area.

BED TIME

Bed followed Compline (q.v.) usually sung about seven p.m. in winter and an hour later in summer. It was followed by an anthem to Our Lady and the recitation of the Pater, Ave and Credo before the crucifix or Majestas. When this short office was over the monks left the church, being sprinkled with holy water at the doorway, and they processed in order and solemn silence to the dorter where they slept until the bell called them back for Mattins, between midnight and three a.m. according to the season.

BEE KEEPING

Bee Keeping

Most monasteries kept bees both for their honey (which was the only mediaeval sweetener) and for their wax (required for the production of liturgical candles and also for writing-tablets). Honey was also used in the manufacture of mead. Bee keeping was also appropriate because of the symbolism of bees which represented order and industry in a common purpose. One of the contemporary authorities on bee keeping is a member of the community at Buckfast. In the Middle Ages the hives were usually kept in the curia or outer court and came under the ultimate responsibility of the cellarer.

BEER

Since beer was a staple drink of all classes in the Middle Ages, it was brewed in the monastery both for internal consumption and for hospitality and alms. A brewhouse (and its associated kiln) can be assumed among the ancillary buildings as surely as a bakehouse. Beer supply and its maintenance in good condition was one of the duties of the sub-cellarer in a large house. Some observances specify that the religious shall be served 'neuer withe newe ale, nor palled or ouer sowre.'

Beer normally accompanied monastic meals, it was usually part of the Mixtum (q.v.) and often followed Collation (q.v.) in later period. Its replacement by water was usually penitential or disciplinary. On the other hand, we know of a sick monk (at Westminster) who claimed to be unable to drink beer and was allowed wine instead. Servants and employees were often granted a bread and beer allowance as part of their remuneration.

Because it was the staple drink, beer is as common in female religious establishments as in male. In later mediaeval nunneries the weekly allowance of beer to each member was supposed to be seven gallons, four of the better sort and three of the weaker, but the amount varied in different houses. The Syon nuns had water on certain days as a mortification of the flesh and generally water could be substituted in times of financial stringency.

BELL

The order and discipline of a monastery was supported by constant signals on bells — so relentless that the monks of Byland had to move out of earshot of Rievaulx. There were a variety of bells — not only the great bells which could be heard all over the house and into the fields beyond but smaller bells signalling the end of meals, etc. (Sometimes both liturgical bells and other signalling bells were replaced by a clapper). Bells called them to rise, to move from church to laver, to gather for procession to frater and to assemble for chapter but above all they announced the time of the Hours. There were also passing-bells, angelus bells, occasional alarm bells and rejoicing bells at the great festivals, to welcome distinguished visitors, etc.

'The sound of bells was rarely absent from the air, either the small bells of the dorter, frater, chapter and church or the greater bells of the tower. They seem to have punctuated every occasion throughout the day and they must have given an air of animation both within and without the monastery.' (Crossley).

Great Bell

The large bells were housed in towers specially built for the purpose. Sometimes such belfries are detached (e.g. Cambuskenneth, Evesham) or, as an afterthought, 'butted on' to an existing building (e.g. Bolton, Fountains). The great bell from Osney went into the tower of Christ Church gateway at Oxford (recast 1679). These great bells fixed the central points of the monastic diurnal and consequently their accurate operation was a responsible and onerous task for which the abbot selected 'a careful brother'. Some of the responsibility was reduced by mechanisation in the later Middle Ages which saw the introduction of bells attached to clocks which had neither face nor hands but indicated time by striking a bell. This did not abolish the need for celebratory ringers and these were often rewarded with special rations from frater. Such celebratory ringing in a great abbey might extend to 40 days per annum and the job was transferred to paid servants. The central tower at Durham had 'three goodly bells' rung by four men to indicate the Hours. Their duties also seem to have included preparation for services: laying out vestments for mass, arranging books, light and other necessities. They slept in a chamber over the vestry, attached to the sacristan's chamber and besides preparing for the morrow's services they filled the holy water stoups, kept the church clean, lit the cressets and locked up the church every night.

BENEDICT, RULE OF

'In living our life . . . the path of God's commandments is run with unspeakable loving sweetness; so that never leaving His school, but persevering in the monastery until death in His teaching, we share by our patience the sufferings of Christ and so merit to be partakers of His kingdom.' (Prologue).

The rule is so adequate an expression of the devout sobriety of Roman Christianity that it became the norm of Western monasticism and the most powerful influence on all subsequent forms of the religious life. Against the excesses and individual pursuit of excellence which tended to characterise Eastern monasticism it opposed sanity and a statesmanlike adjustment to capacity and environment. It required habitual self-control but aimed to avoid ruining the body by pious excess or the mind by fanatic enthusiasm. Above all it was a corporate endeavour with the family as its model.

St Benedict

This demanding, yet merciful rule supplanted all other forms of monasticism in Western Europe by the end of C7. It was introduced into England by St Augustine, former prior of St Gregory's monastery on the Coelian

Hill in Rome, who was sent by the latter to fulfil his desire to evangelise the Angles. It gradually gained ground even in the northern strongholds of Celtic Christianity as is evidenced by St Wilfrid's taking over the monastery at Ripon and the departure of the Scottish monks who had previously occupied the site. This success should be linked to the outcome of the Synod of Whitby (A.D.664) after which English church life, including monasticism, increasingly approximated to the Roman model. This change can be discerned even in the Dark Age nunnery at Hackness (an offshoot of Whitby) and in the monasteries of Jarrow and Monkwearmouth (the home of the great St Bede). The fact that Canterbury, which was to become the primatial see, was from its foundation served by a Benedictine community and for most of its mediaeval history produced monk-archbishops, no doubt influenced the establishment of other cathedral priories, though earlier sees were also centred on (Celtic) monasteries.

BENEDICTINES

For some five centuries they were the very type and model of the monastic life: the schoolmasters of Europe, restorers, preservers and initiators in human culture, agriculture and the realms of spirituality. They provided stability in chaotic and restless times, regulation in anarchy and continuity in a time of dissolution. The moving spirits of the revival of English spiritual life Dunstan, Oswald and Etholwold and their tenth century reforms were centred on the refounding of old abbeys, the foundation of new ones and the replacement of groups of secular priests by monastic communities. They drew from Benedictine houses on the continent and their construction of a single code of observance for all the monasteries in their charge gave the monastic life of the country a unity and stability which, apart from its spiritual effects, encouraged a remarkable development of learning and the arts.

Mitred Abbot (Benedictine)

In 1066 there were some three dozen autonomous houses of Black Monks: Abbotsbury, Abingdon, Athelney, Bath, Buckfast, Burton, Bury, Canterbury, (two — St Augustine's and Christ Church), Cerne, Chertsey, Coventry, Cranborne, Crowland, Ely, Evesham, Glastonbury, Gloucester, Hulme, Horton, Malmesbury, Milton, Muchelney, Pershore, Peterborough,

St Albans (Benedictine)

Ramsey, St Albans, Sherborne, Tavistock, Thorney, Westminster, Winchcombe, Winchester (Old and New Minsters) with traces of houses at Swavesey, and St Neots. The following earlier foundations had ceased to exist by this date: Bedford, Deerhurst, Exeter, Eynsham, Hereford, Peakirk, Ripon, Westbury. Western monasticism came comparatively late to Scotland (there were no foundations before the late C11) for the Benedictine tradition to have the weight and influence which it had built up over centuries of establishment south of the border. In spite of Queen Margaret's foundation of Dunfermline and the lavish support of her son, David, which made it the northern equivalent of Westminster it remained the only sizeable Benedictine house in Scotland which, in the Middle Ages, had only seven at the most (May was possibly Cluniac and Rindalgros is dubious).

Because of its moderation, Benedictinism was open to laxity but found sources of strength and reform within itself. Those who were dissatisfied with the state of English church life in the mid C11, whether Normans comparing it with Bec or such Englishmen as Aethelwig of Evesham, were ardent supporters of Benedictinism as reformed, enthused and energised by the Cluniac (q.v.) revival of C10.

Benedictine Nuns

The Benedictine habit was a black cowl over a cassock of black, white or russet warmed with black or white fur. From the enveloping cape and hood they were and are known as Black Monks, they were only referred to as Benedictines in the later Middle Ages.

In 1569 it was calculated that there had been 37,000 Benedictine monasteries and that their inmates had included 11 emperors, 20 kings, 15 sovereign dukes and electors, 13 sovereign earls, 9 empresses and 10 queens.

Their thousand years of continuous history in these islands was brought to a savage and abrupt end in the middle of C16. Just before the Dissolution in England and Wales, there were 50 abbeys of monks, over 40 conventual priories, and about the same number of lesser houses and cells — a total of c.136 establishments with nearly 2,000 inmates, not counting servants, dependents, employees, etc. The nuns were always much smaller in numbers in the Middle Ages and at the same period they are estimated to have had rather more than 60 houses containing some 900 sisters.

The Benedictines were never strictly speaking an order but a confederation of self-governing houses following the same rule. In the Middle Ages some general association was developed, that of congregations, mainly on a national basis. The English congregation was set up by the Holy See in 1215 and re-established in 1633, having been exiled and diminished but never completely dying out. They returned in C19 and today the English congregation has eight abbeys and there are four abbeys of Benedictine nuns.

BENEDICTINE NUNS   see also *above*

Their most important houses were in the dioceses of Salisbury and Winchester. Though numerous elsewhere the houses were small, comparatively poor and have left few traces. Modified churches survive at Amesbury, Barrow Gurney, Bungay, Cambridge, Davington, Elstow, Farewell, Higham, London (St Helens, Bishopgate), Lyminster, Minster, Nuneaton, Nunmonkton, Polesworth, Redlington, Romsey, Shaftesbury, Usk, Wix, Wroxall.

Their chaplains may have been Benedictine priests but some of the older nunneries were provided with secular chaplains with prebends in the monastic estates. Such benefices generally became the perquisites of royal clerks who provided vicars for the nunneries (e.g. Romsey, Shaftesbury, Wilton, Wherwell, Winchester).

BENEDICTINE REMAINS

Besides the nuns' churches mentioned above, the remains of great Benedictine churches are numerous. They include the cathedral priories of Canterbury, Durham, Ely, Norwich, Rochester, Winchester and Worcester, which were retained as Anglican cathedrals together with the Henrician 'new foundations' of Chester, Gloucester, Peterborough and Westminster. St Albans became an Anglican cathedral in 1877. In parochial use are Bath, Great Malvern, Selby, Sherborne and Tewkesbury.

Smaller parish churches in which some part of the Benedictine structure survives include: Binham, Blyth, Boxgrove, Bristol St James, Bromfield, Chepstow, Cranborne, Crowland, Deeping St James, Deerhurst, Dunster, Freiston, Hatfield Broadoak, Hatfield Peveril, Hurley, Kings Lynn St Margaret, Lapley, Leominster, Little Malvern, Malmesbury, Milton, Pershore, St Bees, Shrewsbury, Thorney, Tutbury, Upholland, Wymondham, York Holy Trinity.

Of conventual buildings there are substantial remains at Chester, Canterbury Christchurch, Gloucester, Westminster, Worcester. Cloisters survive at Canterbury Christchurch, Gloucester, Norwich, Westminster, Worcester. Those at Durham were drastically altered in C18.

There are illuminating ruins at Finchdale, Glastonbury, Lindisfarne, Whitby and York St Mary. Practically nothing remains of the famous Bury and practically the only site marker at Evesham is the beautiful detached belfry.

There were never many houses in Scotland and remains survive only at Coldingham, Dunfermline, Iona and Pluscarden.

BENEFACTORS

There was a tradition nearly as old as English Christianity by which laymen contributed to building or extension of a monastery in return for the prayers of the beneficiaries for their welfare in both this world and the next. Such benefactors were often made confrater (see Confraternity) or 'familiares' of the house and their names entered, on a bede-roll or inscribed in such a splendid book as Durham's *Liber Vitae* or St Albans *Catalogus Benefactorum* so that future generations of religious could remember them before God and the community.

King founding Hospital for Lame

A relatively poor man could qualify as a benefactor but to be a 'founder' required the disposal of considerable wealth. Besides commemoration in a book, remembrance at mass and on the other occasions, benefactors (if they were armigerous) often had their shields carved on work to which they had contributed. There are 825 heraldic bosses on the roof of Canterbury cloisters (rebuilt c.1400).

The Normans were notable contributors to religious houses. Motivation extended from a simple practical faith which accepted that sinful men could ease their way to Paradise by strengthening the Church Militant with money, lands, goods or privileges to a mere social fashion; e.g. Henry of Blois made magnificent additions to Glastonbury, Gundulph reformed and largely rebuilt the monastery at Rochester and began a nunnery at nearby Malling. William I built Battle as a thank-offering and subscribed substantially to new building at Bury. Priories founded by continental houses included Lancaster and Northampton. Other noteworthy new building took place at Colchester, Durham, Selby, Tewkesbury, and old abbeys rescued from decay and neglect included Ely, Gloucester and the twin foundation of Jarrow-Monkwearmouth.

BERNARD ST

An individual who not only was responsible for the establishment and great success of the Cistercian order of which he was luminary but influential in politics, war (Crusades), the history of human thought (courtly love), and Catholic theology and devotion. He was a great devotee of Our Lady (from whom much of his other work stemmed), extended her cult and promulgated the doctrine of her Immaculate Conception.

BIBLE   see *Formation, Legend, Psalter, Reader*

St Bernard of Clairvaux

BLACK FRIARS   see *Dominicans*

BLACK MONKS

Except in Celtic parts of Britain there were no other monks before C11 and the word Benedictine (q.v.) does not occur before that time when it comes into use to distinguish the traditionalists from the reformed orders of Cluny, Citeaux, Savigny, Thiron, etc. These all appealed to the Benedictine rule and only differed in its interpretation and in their ideas about how the relations between individual houses should be constituted.

Black Monk

BLEEDING

It is uncertain when the popular mediaeval therapy of blood-letting was introduced into monasteries; there is no hint of this practice in the rule of St Benedict. Those undergoing this treatment, sometimes described as 'seynies', were called 'minuti' (from Latin 'minutio' — diminishment).

Later regulations provide detailed instructions in regard to this practice. (Those coming to be bled were instructed to change their 'working shoes' for their 'night shoes' (slippers)).

There was no fixed number of these occasions and practice varied greatly: sometimes the individual was allowed to choose, elsewhere 'seynies' occurred at intervals which could vary from five times a year to every six weeks and everywhere there seems to have been provision for individual exceptions. The Cistercians were normally bled four times a year; February, April, September and June (St John's Day). The Black Canons seem to have been bled

Blood Letting
(Phlebotomy)

every seven weeks as a rule but with shorter intervals allowed for individual needs while the White Canons had the operation six times a year and the Carthusians five. The larger houses of monks seem to have provided facilities for a barber to perform this operation once a week.

After 'seynies', religious were not only excused from night office and other demands of the rule but they were allowed to convalesce in the farmery, given special food and allowed other indulgences. Some houses granted the indulgence of meals at the abbot's table during the period of convalescence after bleeding e.g. C14 St Mary de Pré.

Monastic constitutions attempted to prevent the occasion becoming purely recreative, but this inevitably occurred and the periodical blood-letting became a kind of holiday. The rule of silence was relaxed: the Chronicler of Bury tells us that the monks there were 'wont to open to one another the secrets of the heart and take counsel together' but there was always some danger that this spiritual conversation might degenerate into gossip and idle talk. The recreation allowed walks within a limited area outside the enclosure and this too could be abused. Similarly, the fortifying food could become a kind of banquet: at Ely, on 1 August, 1388, seven 'minuti' and 11 other patients in the farmery consumed inter alia, beef, mutton, pork, veal, pullets, capons, salt and fresh fish, eggs, milk, cream, mustard, cheese and spices. About 300 years earlier, the abbot of St Albans had orderd that the 'minuti' there, instead of feeding on meat pasties should have a diet of salt-fish and slices of cake called 'karpie'.

Orginally the Cistercian 'minuti' had to be content with the normal sparse fare of the frater but this hardness was gradually relaxed and they were allowed into the farmery. Elsewhere the indulgence of the farmery was restricted to the general 'seynies': at Barnwell e.g. the patient demanding more frequent blood-letting than once in seven weeks was not allowed to convalesce in the farmery.

In the later Middle Ages, Benedictines seem to have sent their 'minuti' to small houses or granges at a little distance from the mother house which became a kind of convalescent home. The monks of Spalding usually took their 'seynies' at Wickham, those of Bardney at Southrey and those of Peterborough at Oxney.

There was sometimes a special room for bleeding — at Evesham it was a vaulted room beneath the rere-dorter. In Cluniac houses the parlour seems to have been the usual location.

BOARDERS   see also *Corrodians' Sanctuary*

Besides the hordes of guests using or abusing its hospitality (q.v.), abbeys sometimes had less common boarders.

In later Middle Ages, royal and other benefactors, claiming the privilege of founders, tended to foist off old retainers or others to whom they owed benefits as non-paying guests of the monasteries where they were housed and fed for the rest of their lives. A servant of Edward I survived for 34 years at Bath and Edward II sent his retired cook to Great Malvern and another retainer to Reading. They were also used as places of confinement with greater or less honour: the king of France, captured by the Black Prince in 1536 was honourably detained at St Albans and Elizabeth Woodville was confined until her death at Bermondsey by Henry VII. Ecclesiastical offenders could also be placed in custody of an abbey e.g. in 1457 the heretical bishop of Chichester was committed to Thorney (with a generous allowance of £40 p.a. for his maintenance), and, on a lesser scale, a scandalous canon of St Oysth's was sent to St Bartholomew's Smithfield for a period of penance during which his superior paid 12d a week for his support.

BONSHOMMES

An obscure order of friars, apparently of English origin, who may be derived from the Friars of the Sack. Their first foundation in England was by Henry III (who may have met them in Germany) at Ashridge. Their only other house in this country was at Edington, Wiltshire with possibly one at Ruthin.

They wore a blue habit similar in form to that of the Austin hermits and they followed an Augustinian rule, resembling the regular canons in their way of life. The name of Bonshommes was adopted by other orders, notably the Grandmontines (q.v.).

BOOKS

The copying, composition, binding and illumination of books formed the basic employment of the major part of the monastic community at least until end of C13. This work was particularly fitting to the monastic vocation — it was domestic, scholarly, quiet and useful. With the invention of printing the need for solitary, concentrated scholars engaged in this slow and laborious task disappeared and it may he said that monks since have not discovered a universal replacement for this ancillary work

Monastic Reading Desk

to which almost all could contribute and from which all would derive benefit. (Post-reformation monasteries have taken to schooling, bee keeping, pottery, perfumery and even tourism but none of these seem entirely satisfactory or capable of generalisation).

Some of their choicest products survive in museums (e.g. Lindisfarne Gospels, Winchester Bible), great libraries and private collections but the majority of their work vanished at the Dissolution.

Boots

The care and repair of the essential service books in particular and other books in general was the responsibility of the precentor who usually doubled as librarian (see Armarius). Initially, the number of books was very small and could be contained in a cupboard or small room attached to the sacristy but special provision was made as the volume increased (see Library).

Apart from the Bridgettines, no religious was allowed to possess books of his own. Books for spiritual reading were distributed in the chapter-house and those required for study or copying in the cloister (see Carrell) were kept in 'ready use' lockers (almeries, armaria) ranged against the church wall or in a kind of shelved recess or book-press.

Valle Crucis, Library Cupboard

BOOTS see also *Shoes*.

Boots were part of the monastic habit and were provided by the chamberlain at the rate of two pairs a year. Sometimes they were made on the premises but later they were bought or were provided from a monastic dependency in lieu of rent. Besides the heavy 'work boots', religious were issued with 'night boots', akin to felt Besides being quiet, they were also more comfortable and monks were allowed to wear them as an indulgence when they were bled or when they were in the farmery.

BREAD see also *Bakehouse*

Bread was a staple and produced in vast quantities for the community's own use, for almsgiving and for sustenance of guests. Doles frequently consisted of bread and beer.

Bread was symbolical of all food and exemplified God's providence as well as having sacramental associations.

Baking

Benedict had ordered, 'Let a good pound weight of bread suffice for the day' as the individual ration irrespective of whether there were two meals or one. But, characteristically, he allowed modification; 'If their work chance to be heavier, the abbot shall have the choice and power, should it be expedient, to increase the allowance.' (Rule chap.xxxix).

It does not seem to have increased in nunneries where the weekly individual allowance was seven (pound) loaves. New bread was served as a kind of compensation on 'water days'. In C15 Shaftesbury where there were about 50 nuns and a large household the weekly baking and brewing used at least 36 quarters of wheat and malt and could extend to 42.

In early Benedictine houses a good deal of ceremony attended the distribution of bread. The whole amount was placed in a basket suspended above the abbot's table by a rope and pulley. When all were assembled the basket, 'shall descend on to the abbot's table, in order that the rations of God's labourers may appear to descend to them from heaven.' The abbot distributes to those at his table who kiss his hand as they receive their portion. He then distributes the allowance for every other table through its head (provost) with similar ceremony. Even the crumbs were collected reverently and at the end of each week made into a sort of bread pudding which was distributed as a kind of sacramental on Saturday evening when it was blessed by the abbot.

Besides ordinary bread, monasteries produced their own bread for use in the eucharist which, because of its signal destiny, was prepared with the utmost care and solemnity. The sacrist and his assistants who made it were vested in albs and were required to take every precaution to ensure immaculate cleanliness. Psalms and prayers were recited during the process and there was sometimes a special oven for baking this bread situated within the church itself.

BREAKFAST   see also *Mixtum*
Monks (unless they were priests with later celebrations) broke their fast after the early mass which followed Prime, usually between seven and eight a.m. With the superior's permission, it could be anticipated by young monks who were not priests. This very slight refection was signalled by three strokes of a bell and accompanied by some ceremony. The weekly reader asked a blessing, the small portion was served and consumed in silence while standing and at its completion each said a silent prayer for the repose of benefactors (q.v.).

BREVIATOR
A name given to the monastic scribe (usually the precentor) responsible for drawing up the 'brief' or mortuary roll — the formal document which announced the death of any brother to other religious houses and asked their prayers on his behalf.
The title was more frequently given to the messenger who actually carried the brief around. He was usually one of the almoner's staff but was appointed by the abbot (for life). He was usually a salaried servant who was fed from the monastic kitchen and in later Middle Ages, could claim a sort of mortuary for his services.

BREVIARY
A single book which contained the text (and often the music) of all the quire offices, together with certain additions such as prayers for the dead.
In a religious house, the complexity of the music (and the size of the music books) often involved the use of many books (Antiphoner, Graduale, etc.) during a single service.

BREWHOUSE   (Bracinum)
Inside the monastery, as in the world outside, beer was the staple drink. It was made in the monastic brewhouse which usually stood in the outer court. The later brewhouses at Thicket and Yedingham gave on to the cloister. In the much-divided responsibilities of the greater religious houses, the brewer was one of the chief assistants to the sub-cellarer. In the later Middle Ages he was often a paid servant and not a member of the community. A kiln for malting was provided near the brewhouse.
Brewhouses survive, in part, at Canterbury, Fountains and Nuneaton but generally they were comparatively insubstantial buildings which have left no remains.

BRIDGETTINES
A religious order following a modification of the Augustinian rule as reformed and adapted c.1346 by St Bridget, former queen of Sweden. The vow of poverty was modified to allow the personal possession of a number of books for private study. They are a learned and zealous community much concerned with mystical prayer and originally resembled the Gilbertines (q.v.) in being organised as a 'double community' of nuns and canons with a shared chapel but this arrangement was given up in the later C16.
There was only one house in England, the famous foundation at Syon, richly endowed by Henry V as a penance in 1414. It survived the Reformation after much travel and vicissitudes and, much impoverished, maintains its enclosed and contemplative life in Devon.

BRIEF   see also *Breviator*
The formal document, often elaborately executed and illuminated, recording the death of a religious, which was sent by special messenger to other religious houses

for information and to request prayers. On reception it was endorsed with the assurance of the requested prayers to which was added sometimes Latin verses in praise of the dead or an expression of sympathy with the bereaved before being returned via the almoner to the breviator.

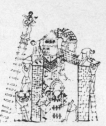

Bringing Building Materials

BUILDING MATERIALS

It is sometimes worth asking oneself on a site such questions as: What materials have been robbed or completely destroyed? Were the building materials from a local source or were they conveyed from a distance? What kind of stone was used, is there more than one variety, is there re-used material?

St Albans makes use of flint and Roman brick, Colchester also uses much brick from the Roman site. Winchester's limestone comes from the Isle of Wight while Peterborough used Barnack stone from its own quarries. The limestone of Fountains was quarried from the side of the dale in which it is set but, for details, it also makes use of a local 'marble'. Purbeck marble is used to embellish a number of (former) monastic churches. Chester makes use of red sandstone, while Durham utilised carboniferous sandstone.

Building

Major roofs could be carried on stone vaults or complex timber structures. Some ceilings were panelled (survivals at St Albans). Their coverings could be of tile, stone flags, slate or lead while minor buildings were roofed with thatch or shingles. Lead was particularly valued by the looting agents of the suppression and was usually melted into ingots on site by fires fuelled with the carved stalls, canopies and screens.

BURIAL   see also *Cemetery*

As a privilege, distinguished monks were sometimes buried in the chapter-house, east walk of the cloister, or within the church and stone-coffins from these inhumations are sometimes found in the vicinity of their burial.

Most monks were buried (without coffins) in the monastic cemetery which is nearly always positioned east of the chapter-house and south of the church. The cloister-garth was not used for burial except in the case of the Carthusians.

Priors, abbots and bishops seem to have been buried in their vestments, together with a pastoral staff and mass

Abbot's Grave Stone from Peterborough

vessels (usually of less valuable materials than those used for community masses). St Cuthbert was buried with his episcopal ring and pectoral cross.

The importance of burial of a monk in his own house was sufficiently great for it to be carried out at great inconvenience e.g. in C11 the body of Turgot was brought from St Andrews to Durham and that of Edmund from Gloucester, while in C13 Robert, also of Durham who died in France had his heart brought home for burial in the cathedral priory.

In accordance with the usual mediaeval practice the bones from the cemetery were exhumed after a time and gathered into a charnel-house or bone-hole near the burial ground. This sometimes took the form of a crypt with a chapel above. That at

Worcester, placed on the north side of the church was 58ft long, 22ft wide and 14ft high and was served by a small college of chantry priests who lived in a house west of the chapel.

Founders (q.v.) sometimes received distinguished burial in their foundation and royalty were often buried in or near monastic churches e.g. Abbey Cwmhir, Cambuskenneth, Dunfermline, Hailes, Iona, Peterborough, Worcester.

BURSAR

The keeper of the purse (burse). A late introduction among the monastic officers and seems to originate at the instigation of visitors brought in when finances were in disorder. Originally, he was the chief financial officer through whose hands the entire revenues passed in the first instance but because of the long tradition of obedientiaries he tended to become merely an additional financial officer who looked after such revenues as were not already appropriated to specified objects or officials.

He had his own office close to the church to which his food was brought from the communal kitchen. At their greatest extent his duties seem to have been to receive all the rents appertaining to the house, to receive and check the accounts of all other monastic officers and to pay all expenses which were not specific to other obedientiaries e.g. servants' wages, the bills for outside wages and those due on contracts for maintenance and repair.

BUTTERY

Strictly speaking, the wine-store (bottlery) and usually placed near the cellarer's office. In its more general application it is associated with the pantry and is an annexe to the kitchen from which food and drink were served to the frater. Service hatches remain at e.g. Mattersey, Monk Bretton and a pair giving on to a service lobby or large screens passage survive at Muchelney.

The president's lodging in a large house (e.g. Gloucester) might possess as many as four butteries and the same number of pantries.

BYLAND CAPITAL

An architectural feature, typical of this abbey, which can be seen clearly e.g. in the chapter-house. It consisted of the application to capitals of a water-leaf motif: a broad leaf-shape with a tied ribbon effect at the top. It probably originated at Byland and spread to become a common decorative device in C12.

Byland, Capital

CALDARIUM

The great cauldron for boiling water which was essential furniture in the monastic kitchen. The Custumals usually require three: one for cooking the beans, a second for the vegetables and a third, with an iron tripod to stand it upon, to provide hot water for washing plates, dishes, cloths, etc.

CALEFACTORY   see *Warming-house*

CAMERARIUS   see *Chamberlain*

Caldarium

CANDLES   see also *Lights*

The provision of church candles came within the sacrist's area of responsibility. They had to be made of wax and were an expensive commodity which were sometimes left as bequests or the money to purchase them. Few are used on altars (one was normal in the mediaeval period) but they were offered as votive lights before images, shrines, tombs, etc. A monastery committed to maintain votive lights in connection with a royal tomb was involved in considerable expense: the tombs of Queen Eleanor, King Richard II, Henry III, Henry V and Henry VI in Westminster consumed over 1434 lbs of wax p.a. In the funeral of Henry V 60 attendants carried beeswax torches weighing 14½ lbs each. The provision of a candle of a given weight before a particular image was often made in fulfilment of a vow or as a final bequest.

Ordinary candles to provide light were made from tallow and were the responsibility of the fraterer. The allocation was generally one between two places at e.g. meals but if a brother sat by himself he was allowed an individual candle. There were also candles to be provided for the lanthorns used at night by disciplinary and other officials.

Candles and candlesticks in the guest-house were provided by the hostellar or guest-master. Provision of board and lodging, as in a corrody (q.v.) often included specifically fuel and light e.g. a clerk at Worcester was granted, inter alia, six pounds of candles of Paris tallow p.a. Candles were not allowed in the dorter, except within a lantern. The supply of lamps there, their lighting and extinction, was the responsibility of the sub-chamberlain.

Apart from the candles in church, candles accompanied all liturgical processions (q.v.) and they too had to be of the best beeswax. Liturgical candles were usually supported on candlesticks or prickets made of wood, iron, pewter, latten or precious metals. One of a magnificent pair made for Gloucester survives in the Victoria and Albert Museum.

CANONS REGULAR   see *Austin, Gilbertine, Premonstratensian*

CANONESSES OF ST AUGUSTINE   see *Austin Canonesses*

CANTOR   see also *Precentor, Succentor*
The 'lead singer' who announced the tone, set the pitch and either led the choral singing or sang solo or antiphonal parts. They stood at the great lectern which bore the antiphonarium in the midst of the quire. They were chosen by the precentor and officiated for a week after their names had been posted on the duty-roster or tabula (q.v.). When officiating on major occasions they were vested in surplice and cope and their number varied from one to two or four according to the solemnity of the festival.

CAPELLA ANTE PORTAS
The chapel at the gate of a religious house. As the convent chapel was private, religious communities almost invariably (if there was no other facility nearby) provided a chapel for the use of visitors and their own servants and employees at or near the main gate. This provision sometimes developed into a parish church when a permanent community grew up outside the monastery and they were provided with their own cemeteries e.g. Abingdon, Bury, Evesham, Westminster.

Porch of All Saints', Evesham

The Cistercian rule specifically required this provision, probably because of the remoteness of their sites. There are ruins of this chapel at Fountains and Furness and it is documented at Byland and Meaux. At Kirkstead it is complete and it survives in modified use at Coggeshall, Rievaulx and Tilty. It survived at Croxden until 1884. The one at Merevale, now used as an Anglican parish church, was built for the benefit of thronging crowds of pilgrims and the monastery provided it with a penitentiary possessed of special powers to serve their spiritual difficulties.

CAPITULUM
'The little chapter' or short reading from the rule which gave the chapter-house (q.v.) its name.

CARMELITE
The friars of the order of Our Lady of Mount Carmel were founded in Palestine c.1154 by St Berthold but they claimed continuity with much earlier settlements of hermits in this sacred place. The primitive rule of extreme asceticism required absolute poverty, total abstinence from

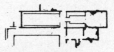

Hulne Friary (Carmelite), Plan of Church

flesh and solitude. After the failure of the Crusades many of the order came to Europe. They came to England c.1240 and St Simon Stock was one of the first Englishmen to join them. He re-organised them as mendicant friars living in priories and became General of the order in 1247. They increased rapidly under his leadership, especially in this country, where they had about 50 houses organised, for administrative purposes, into areas called 'Distinctions'. Because of their predominantly white habit they were generally known as White Friars. Very little survives of their houses: the scant remains of Denbigh are in the guardianship of DE and there are others sometimes absorbed in private houses, at Aylesford (now restored to its original purpose), Blakeney, Burnham Norton, Coventry, Hulne, Kings Lynn and Stamford. There were 11 Carmelite friaries in mediaeval Scotland and they have left minor material remains at Luffness and Queensferry.

Carmelite sisters were founded in 1452 and though they projected houses in England they were delayed and eventually prevented by the impact of the Reformation. They were reformed in C16 under the inspiration of St John of the Cross and St Theresa.

The Carmelites returned to England in 1926, re-establishing the English Province in 1952. There are about eight houses of friars and many more of nuns, including houses of the reformed (Discalced) Carmelites who are enclosed and contemplative.

CARRELLS
A set of study-cubicles set against the windows of the cloister alley next to the church. At Durham there were three to each window making 30 in all, divided from each other and the access passage by wainscotting. The more elaborate, and largely stone, carrells which substantially remain at Gloucester are 20 in number — two to each of the ten four light windows. They were roofed at the level of the window transom so that the walk behind them was lit by the upper part of the window. There are traces of six carrells in north cloister alley at Beaulieu. A reconstructed set of stone carrells can be seen at Chester but as the divisions were normally wainscotted there are no remains elsewhere. At Durham they were entered by individual doors with pierced

Carrels in Gloucester Cloister

tops so that their interior could be seen from the walkway behind. Each contained a desk for reading, writing and storing materials. In the church at Bishops Canning, Wiltshire is preserved a strange piece of furniture which might have belonged to a carrell. Some monasteries had an additional scriptorium (q.v.) apart from the carrells in the cloister walk and the Dominican friary at Gloucester had the 'studies' in the south range. It consisted of a long room with wall recesses to serve as carrells and provision for a library. It is probable that there was similar provision at other friaries (e.g. Clare).

Mount Grace (Carthusian)

CARTHUSIAN

Order formed by St Bruno at the Grande Chartreuse, near Grenoble in 1086. To the ordinary vows were added continual fasting and a life of solitude. Their houses consisted of one or more courts around which were arranged the separate cells (with private gardens) of each monk. The members only met in church to sing Vespers, the night office, and mass. The lesser offices were said privately and the two meagre meals, except on certain festivals, were served through a hatch or turntable to the cell in which he ate, slept, worked and prayed.

The order was thus a return to an earlier anchorite ideal and consisted of a group of hermits. Its austerity kept down the number of recruits and therefore the number of houses: only two foundations were made in England before mid C14, Witham and Hinton. There was only one foundation in Scotland : at Perth (1429-1569) (of which there are no remains). The order retained its high ideals and strict observance and has never needed reform. In C14 it expanded substantially and seven new charterhouses were established after 1340, including the royal foundation at Sheen. Their austere contemplative life steeled them to accept almost universal martyrdom rather than yield to Henry VIII's ecclesiastical usurpations. The order returned to England in C19 (St Hugh's, near Horsham, Sussex) — its dedication commemorates St Hugh of Lincoln (1135-1200), a Carthusian from Witham, the last of a long line of sainted monk-bishops.

Hinton Priory (Carthusian)

Carthusian Cell, Mount Grace

Ironically, the rich liqueur which takes its name from the Grande Chartreuse originated as a tonic from their herb gardens but a small part of its profits still goes to the upkeep of the mother house. There are scant remains of mediaeval charterhouses at Beauvale, Hinton and London but the most complete picture is to be gathered from the emotive remains of Mount Grace. The beautiful and tranquil sites of the latter and Hinton, together with the austere material remains of their homes, still speak of 'the lonely blessedness and the blessed loneliness' which was the Carthusian ideal.

CATERER

Possibly the most important of the cellarer's staff, attached to the kitchener. He supervised the cook and his assistants in preparing meals and often seems to have been responsible for bulk purchases of food. He oversaw the service at meals, usually standing by the dresser window (q.v.) and checked for promptitude, efficiency and fittingness. He had two servants to help him in marketing and to carry his purchases. One custumal says, 'he ought to be a broadminded and strongminded man. One who acts with decision, wise, just, upright in all things belonging to his office; one who is prudent, knowing, discreet and careful when purchasing meat and fish in the markets.'

CATHEDRAL PRIORIES

The seats of bishoprics were established in some of the more important monasteries and the monastic church became the cathedral with the bishop as titular abbot but not necessarily a member of the community which was governed by the prior. The form seems to have been established by the Benedictine St Dunstan (909-988) bishop in turn of Worcester, London and Canterbury and had affected four cathedrals (Canterbury, Sherborne, Winchester, Worcester,) before 1066. The institution was strongly supported by reforming Norman bishops (especially Lanfranc), largely because of the slack and unedifying lives of the secular canons. By the end of the Middle Ages, the following sees had monastic chapters: Bath, Carlisle, Canterbury, Coventry, Durham, Ely, Norwich, Rochester, Winchester, Worcester; all of them Benedictine except Carlisle which was a house of Austin Canons. The cathedral priory became so much the norm that even non-monastic cathedrals adopted a quasi-conventual plan with cloisters, chapter-house, etc. e.g. Salisbury, Wells.

In a cathedral priory the bishop was given the style and honour of abbot but he had no voice in chapter and sometimes he could be at variance with the prior and his community (so for a long time at Durham). He sometimes claimed the right to appoint some obedientiaries (q.v.) such as the sacrist and precentor and even the prior. Such claims were stoutly resisted.

CELL

i.   The individual accommodation for a monk in a semi-eremetical institution like a Celtic monastery or charterhouse.

ii.   A small house of less than four religious, dependent on a mother house. Such cells had many purposes: to keep an eye on distant property, to serve as a penitentiary, Tynemouth, a cell of St Albans, seem sometimes to have been regarded as a disciplinary posting but this was not its main purpose, or to provide a 'desert' for monks desiring a more solitary existence (e.g. Farne Island), as a 'rest' or convalescent home (e.g. Finchale for Durham, Hackness for Whitby, King's Lynn for Norwich).

Celtic Cell

CELLAR

The cellarium or great storehouse of the monastery often occupied the entire ground floor of the west range. It was usually vaulted from a central row of columns (c.g. Chester, Norton). Its position was related to the great court through which provisions reached the monastery. The

Undercroft, Fountains

entrance was often large to admit such bulky stores as beer barrels or large sacks and at e.g. Bradsole it was big enough to take a horse and cart. Sometimes there were additional cellars (e.g. under frater), and cellarage was always supplemented by a variety of external store-houses. Part of the undercroft in the west range or the ground floor was divided off for other uses such as providing outer parlour or, in Cistercian houses, as a frater for conversi. There are a number of impressive remains of cellars, e.g. Byland, Furness, Rufford but Fountains has the most impressive west range in Europe, 300ft long and vaulted in 22 double bays from a central row of columns. It was originally divided by partitions into a number of rooms: store, offices and frater.

CELLARER

Perhaps the most responsible and demanding office after that of the superior: 'the second father of the house.' The cellarer had charge of everything concerning food, drink, fuel and other constant requirements. He had not only to organise, check and store farm produce but he leased and sold land and appointed overseers for the monastic estates. His care embraced the mills, malt-house, brewhouse and bakehouse, tolls and carriage of goods, the staffing of granges and the oversight of the convent's immediate servants. For this extensive work he had the assistance of a number of subordinate or associated officials: sub-cellarer, fraterer, chamberlain, kitchener and guest-master but nevertheless the appointment of a bad cellarer could be disastrous for the whole community.

Cellarer's Checker,
Fountains

His duties not only frequently took him away from the convent but would require his presence at all hours. He was therefore excused from many of the quire offices and allowed to sleep in the farmery so as to be both more accessible and prevent disturbance to the rest of the community. He was the chief means of communication between the convent and the outside world, attending fairs and markets, interviewing salesmen and keeping accounts.

He was responsible for all storage vessels for the equipment of the cellar, kitchen and frater in all their details. He had particular responsibility for provisions of the sick and those seeking the house's hospitality. This could be vastly increased if the house became a pilgrimage centre e.g. in 1347 the Durham cellarer, during the week-long festival of St Cuthbert provided 600 salt herrings, 400 white herrings, 30 salted salmon, 12 fresh salmon, 14 ling, 4 turbot, 2 horse-loads of white fish, 9 oxen, 7½ pigs, 14 calves, 3 kids, 26 suckling pigs, 71 geese, 14 capons, 59 chickens, 60 pigeons, 5 stones of hog's lard, 4 stones of cheese and butter, 2 quarts of vinegar, 2 quarts of honey, 14 lbs of figs and raisins and 1300 eggs. (These provisions may have been for men only as women were not admitted to the shrine).

The demanding nature of this office was recognised from the beginning in Chap.31 of St Benedict's rule. When that part of the rule was about to be read in chapter, the cellarer was given advance notice by the precentor so that 'he may on that day make a seemly feast in the frater' preceded by an act of reparation for his short-comings. He was provided with a special form of confession for his official faults which was recited in chapter and in return the community recited particular psalms and prayers to support him in his onerous duties.

He had his own checker or accounts office, usually near the cellar and kitchen (as at Durham and Fountains) where he could maintain close contact with the fraterer and kitchener. Here he did the costing and forward planning, checked the weekly accounts in all the kitchens (including conventual, farmery guest-house and superior's when they existed). He had to ensure that supplies never ran out, whether large of grain or small of spices.

CELTIC MONASTICISM

Derived from the east, via Lerins, it was characterised by the eremetical tradition and extreme asceticism. It was brought into Northern Britain from Iona by St Columba and the sites mainly consisted of individual cells grouped within an enclosure (wall, bank, ditch, water). Occasionally there was a community building: a possible writing room at Tintagel, a suggested frater at Whitby, a dorter at Hackness, and a church at Abingdon (though each cell seems to have its own small altar). The habitations were simple and austere, the art rich and complex and the lives of the monks often of great beauty and sanctity.

Their foundations were particularly frequent in C6 ('the age of the saints' who include Columba and David) and cluster in Cornwall, Wales and Strathclyde though St Cuthbert on Farne and Guthlac amid the marshes of Crowland belong to this tradition.

The buildings were primitive and generally insubstantial but the site retained its hallowed memory and often became the burial ground, and distinguished by its near circular shape, of a later church. Sometimes a memorial stone survives with inscription in Latin (Ogham). Another marker is in place-names (Cloŋ in Ireland, Llan in Wales, followed by the name of the monk-founder e.g. Llandudno 'the monastery of Tudno'). 'Clas' indicated a mother church (e.g. Glasbury, Glascwm) and probably consisted of a group of priests ruled by an abbot. Knowles and Hadcock list more than 50 early monasteries but there are remains, usually extremely scanty, only at Bardsey, Llantwit Major, Penmon, Puffin Island, St Piran and Towyn).

CEMETERY

St Dunstan was credited with the enclosure and design of the first monastic cemetery at Glastonbury (c.950). He surrounded it with a wall of cut stone so that 'it seems like a charming meadow, removed from all noise of passers-by, so that it may be justly said of the holy men who lie there, "Their bodies are buried in peace".'

C8 Tombstone
(Lindisfarne)

It was usually situated around the east end of the church and approached from the cloister via a slype (q.v.) e.g. Gloucester, Worcester or, in Cistercian houses, from the church through a door in the transept away from the cloister, e.g. Byland, Jervaulx, Rievaulx, Strata Florida, Valle Crucis. There was similar access in Premonstratensian houses, e.g. Easby. In Carthusian houses part of the cloister was used as a cemetery.

Part of 'Monks' Stone',
Peterborough

The right of burial in a monastic cemetery was usually confined to members of the house and confraters but monasteries in towns sometimes provided a separate lay cemetery within the precinct but with its own entrance gate, e.g. Bury.

CHAMBERLAIN   (Camerarius)

An official unmentioned in Benedict's original rule but of considerable importance later. His duties could include the general oversight of the stables, provision of pasturage, winter feeding, harness and furniture for horses and wagons (i.e. similar to a marshal in a large lay establishment) as well as the maintenance of lamps in dorter and elsewhere. He was also responsible for providing hot water and soap for shaving and baths. He was charged to keep an eye on the laver and its furnishings and if it froze in winter he had to provide hot water and warm dry towels. He bought the wood to heat the bath water and supplied the sweet hay spread on the stone floor round the bath tubs. He provided hot water for the feet-washing on Saturdays between November and Easter and was told to keep a good fire in the warming room on Christmas Eve to welcome the monks when they came back from midnight mass and office in the cold church. In some houses the offices of chamberlain and cellarer were combined or one person performed both functions. In such cases the chamberlain/cellarer seems to have been assisted by a sub-camerarius who was often a lay-brother.

The chamberlain had his own office or checker. At Bury it was at the end of the undercroft in the dorter range, elsewhere it occurs in the curia — at Durham over the tailor's shop.

CHAMBERS   see also *Superior's lodging*

Private or semi-private accommodation, usually for the president of the house and his guests, sometimes associated with the dorter, sometimes in the vicinity of the farmery (e.g. Kirkstall, Furness, Waverley). Such accommodation was sometimes provided for ex-superiors, e.g. Daventry, Easby (which at one time had three ex-abbots), St Albans. The prior's lodging at Ely gave opportunity to accommodate guests varying in number and rank while the palatial house of the abbot at Gloucester had no less than 13 chambers, in addition to a variety of 'specialist' rooms and apartments.

The disposition of apartments was often modified in the course of the history of a religious house (e.g. Forde, Hailes, Rievaulx, Sawley, Wykeham) but it was C14 which saw a general development of private chambers. This was partly due to changing social fashions and also for efficiency. It had become customary to allocate their own rooms to obedientiaries and scholars and increasing provision was made for maintaining some kind of state for retired superiors. The introduction of corrodians also implied increased private accommodation. Larger buildings were sub-divided, e.g. Byland, Wilberfoss. The movement towards privacy also resulted in the subdivision of the dorter by wooden partitions and the development of 'private wards' in the farmery (e.g. Fountains, Tintern).

CHANT

All services and prayers (except private ones) were intoned and the monastic life made considerable contributions to the development of western music but it is perhaps most associated with the development and perfection of plainsong or plainchant associated with the name of St Gregory. Modern continental abbeys have done much to recover and popularise the music that was universal in the western church for nearly 1,000 years.

CHANTRIES

Name derived from the 'singing' of a Requiem mass. The late mediaeval custom of endowing an altar or chapel for continuing masses for the donor, his relatives and friends extended to monastic churches and there are a number of notable architectural survivals, e.g. Canterbury, Christchurch, Durham, St Albans, Tewkesbury, Thetford, Tynemouth, Winchester, Westminster, Worcester.

CHANTRY COLLEGE

An institution intermediary between a religious community and a chantry. It involved clergy living in a regulated community and secured 'in perpetuity' a constant round of masses for the founder and others. Its function was extended in two ways: in many the master had a cure of souls and others had an academic function. There was little legal or constitutional (or even practical) difference between a chantry college and an academic college e.g. All Souls.

Chantry

The foundation of such an institution was a long and costly process not dissimilar to the problems of founding a monastic house and legally it was perhaps even more costly but it became an alternative in C14.

CHAPELS   see also *Altar*

A small subsidiary church or a sub-division of a larger one with its own altar. They originate in the need to provide altar space for large numbers of priests to say mass and with the intention to do honour to particular saints, devotions or aspects of the Christian faith. There was a particular development of Lady chapels in monastic churches in C12 and after (except in Cistercian houses where the entire abbey had this dedication.) Minor chapels within the great church were usually dedicated to monastic saints (but cf.Chantries, above) and there are remains at e.g. Byland, Fountains, Rievaulx.

Chapels were also provided outside the minster e.g. in the president's lodging, over the gatehouse, in the cemetery, farmery and elsewhere. Besides the gate-chapel (see Capella ante Portas) monasteries provided extern chapels for dependents and pilgrims e.g. Red Chapel, King's Lynn; St Michael's on Glastonbury Tor and the little chapel with the same dedication on a knoll a few miles south-east of Fountains. Chapels were also built on granges e.g. Brimham, Bewerley, Yorkshire WR (Fountains), St. Leonards, Hampshire (Beaulieu); Tetbury, Gloucestershire (Kingswood); Thrintoft, Yorkshire ER (Jervaulx);

CHAPLAIN

Prioress and Chaplain

Besides the resident priest required by nuns for mass and sacraments, there were also private chaplains attached to abbots and major priors. He acted as a sort of personal assistant and secretary as well as performing spiritual duties. He collected his superior's allowance from the bursar and saw to its spending in the former's maintenance, the expenses of his household and in his duty of alms-giving. In the later Middle Ages he supervised the abbot or prior's household and saw to its service and good order. He was also responsible for his superior's private plate and the payment of his servants. He had a private chamber within the superior's house and his own office which, at Durham, was conveniently near the bursar's. Female superiors often had a nun 'chaplain' who acted as a personal assistant.

CHAPTER   see also *Accusations*

The daily conference of the entire community which gave its name to the building in which it was held. Though the larger houses had possessed chapter-houses from at least C11, in 1334 Benedict XII ordered that there was to be a daily chapter whenever there were at least six in the community.

It usually followed the office of Prime (q.v.) and, at the ringing of a small bell, the monks processed in order to the chapter-house. When they were assembled they remembered the dead and their benefactors and then a chapter (which gave its name to the whole proceedings) of their rule was read by a chosen lector. In Benedictine houses the entire rule was read through three times a year and once a year in Cistercian establishments. This was often accompanied by a commentary or followed by a sermon on it by the abbot or his delegate. There was also a business section with notices, correspondence, allocation of weekly duties, perhaps reports from officials etc. and there may have been a choir practice or the rehearsal of some important ritual. The most solemn part was opened by the superior announcing 'Let us now speak of matters of discipline' and this was followed by self-accusation and the accusations of others in regard to breaches of the rule of the order and the constitutions or customs of the house. Punishment was decreed by the superior and was often corporal, scourging 'with a single stout rod while he lies in his shift on the ground or with a bundle of finer rods while he sits with his back bare.' During these unpleasant proceedings 'all the brethren should bow down with a kind and brotherly compassion.'

There were detailed rules of procedure in chapter e.g. 'No one shall speak privately with another or with several. Whatever is said shall be audible to the superior and the entire community. Only matters of utility and pertaining to the religious life shall be discussed. While one is speaking the rest shall keep silence. No one shall interrupt a speaker save the president who may bid a speaker to have done if it seems to him that his words are too many or to no purpose. When the president begins to speak, even if one is already speaking, he shall cease and absolute silence shall be preserved by all present.' (Lanfranc: Constitutions). There was also a rule forbidding the discussion of chapter business or proceedings outside the actual meetings.

It is said that business proceedings of the monastic chapter, affected those of parliament which sometimes met in the Westminster chapter-house. It appears that the chapter was not so important among Regular Canons and possibly only took place weekly.

CHAPTER, GENERAL   see *General-Chapter*

CHAPTER-HOUSE

Second only to the church in importance, it was the location of business meetings, considerations of the rule of the house and the place where the visitor (q.v.) held his periodical enquiries. It was the place where confraters and distinguished visitors were sometimes received and, rarely, if the monastery was in a town, it could be used for important secular purposes such as a session of parliament or a public meeting.

Chapter-House

In C12-13 it was the customary burial place for superiors and the bodies of other monks rested here while Matins of the Dead was sung about them before they were carried out through the parlour into the cemetery. It is always positioned in the dorter range near the church and actually adjoined the church at Chester, Castle Acre and other houses where this position was not occupied by slype or sacristy.

Fountains Abbey, Chapter-House

The building was usually oblong and vaulted and in Benedictine houses often ended in an apse (e.g. Castle Acre, Durham, Gloucester, Reading, Shrewsbury). Even when they were square ended they usually projected eastwards from the range (e.g. Chester, York) and only in small houses such as Finchale and Monk Bretton were retained within the main walls.

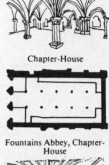

Chapter-House, Rievaulx (reconstruction)

It contained a raised seat for the superior in the centre of its east end with his obedientaries ranged on either side. Seating was strictly hierarchical, the 'upper rooms' being

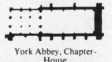

York Abbey, Chapter-House

nearest the president and farthest from the door and in the upper rows of seats when there was more than one tier. The seats were usually stone benches of which there are often remains round the walls. Other furniture included a lectern from which the readings were given, and often a book cupboard or small library. The socket for the desk or lectern (analogium) survives in front of the president's seat at Byland and Waverley. The Cistercians often had a library in the chapter-house: the bays flanking the entrance were partitioned in stone for this purpose (Fountains, Furness) and there is a single book closet at the west end in the chapter-houses at Calder and Valle Crucis.

The importance of this room led to considerable architectural elaboration and it must have had a church-like atmosphere (indeed occasionally there was an altar in it). Though the chapter-house at St Mary's, York was of the usual early rectangular form with a vestibule (known as the Galilee), it seems to have been unique in its monumental decoration. This is believed to have consisted of large coloured and guilded statues of the precursors of Christ in the vestibule, of apostles along the side-walls of the chapter-house proper and culminated in a magnificent effigy of Christ in Majesty which occupied an elevated position on the east wall above the abbot's chair. Some of these statues, more or less mutilated, survive in the nearby museum and they have been described as comprising 'a series unique in England'. Chapter-houses were built end-on to the cloister, their breadth usually occupying three bays with a central door flanked by windows, e.g. Furness, Kirkstall. Most chapter-houses were aisle-less halls but the Cistercians had a room divided by rows of columns, varying in length from three bays at Byland to six at Fountains. This beautiful design was copied elsewhere (e.g. Beeleigh, Lacock) and there is additional internal arcading at Bristol and Much Wenlock.

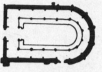

Rievaulx Abbey, Chapter-House

Usually the chapter-house was a single storey high (Haugmond, Lacock, Valle Crucis), to allow for the dorter or its continuation above, but the desire to dignify the building led to raising its height to two storeys (Bristol, Canterbury, Chester, Gloucester, Reading, Westminster) producing problems of direct communication between the dorter and church. At Rochester and Bindon the problem was solved by vaulting the westermost bay at a lower level to leave room for a passage above to the night stairs. In other places (Bristol, Chester, Westminster) the solution lay in treating the space between the main walls of the range as a vestibule and building the chapter-house proper entirely to the east. This was particularly necessary when the peculiarly English form of a polygonal chapter-house was adopted (e.g. Bolton, Carlisle, Cockersand, Pontefract, Thornton, Westminster). There are unusual plans at Alnwick (a combination of circle and rectangle), Gloucester (three sided apse), Margam (internal circle, external polygon), Rievaulx (five aisles and a unique ambulatory, probably connected with shrine). Grandmontine chapter-houses had their long axes north and south and did not project beyond the main walls of the dorter range (Alberbury, Craswall, Grosmont).

There are substantial and interesting remains of chapter-houses not only in formerly monastic cathedrals or the large secular churches which imitated them in this provision e.g. Lincoln, Salisbury, Southwell, Wells, York but also at Birkenhead where it is used as a church and in the ruined houses of Cleeve, Furness and Kirkstall.

CHARTERHOUSE
A house of Carthusian monks.

CHECKER   (Cheker, Chequer)
Generally an office but particularly an accounts office, especially the monastic counting house (usually controlled by the cellarer) where accounts were tallied and recorded, payments made, etc. In the Middle Ages a checked cloth or check board marked in squares were used to assist calculation.

Usually this office was located near the great cellar but at Canterbury in early C14 a new one was built over the east alley of the farmery cloister. The monastic treasurer sometimes had his own checker. At Durham this contained a quadripartite money-box containing the separate funds for the obedientiaries who had to make cash transactions, e.g. almoner, bursar, hostellar and sacrist.

CHILDREN
Children were sometimes found in monasteries, more frequently in the early ages when parents offered their children to God in the religious life. A notable example of child oblation is St Bede. Sometimes orphans were also accepted to whom monks acted as foster-parents and saw to child's education and general formation. These children wore a variant of the habit, acted as choristers and acolytes and usually made their monastic profession when they reached canonical age. This practice was rejected by the Cistercians and by C12 was generally on the wane.

Later, children were brought up in a separate part of the monastery such as the almonry and if they did not join the community the monastery might pay their apprenticeship fees.

CHOIR   see *Quire*

West Door, Bolton

CHURCH

The monastic church was orginally called the oratory, later the 'minster' (monasterium). Benedict instructs his followers that those who would pray there should 'simply go straight in and pray' and remembering the manifold uses to which churches could be put (general assembly place, town hall even market), he writes, 'Let the oratory be what its name implies (i.e. place of prayer) and let nothing else be done there or anything alien to this purpose be placed there.' (Rule, chap. lii).

Abbey Dore (Carthusian)

As the main purpose of the monk's life was the communal service of God, the most important building in the monastery was the church in which more than half his waking hours might be spent. Except in the smallest monasteries, it was built in the symbolic cruciform shape and consisted of a presbytery, quire, transepts and nave. It was entered from the cloister by two doors, one at either end of the southern alley and by a staircase from the dorter into south transept. Because the Cistercian procession (q.v.) followed a slightly different route from that of the Black Monks they sometimes dispensed with the doorway opposite the west alley of the cloister (e.g. Croxden, Jervaulx) and used the west doorway which elsewhere was used only on special occasions (even if it existed).

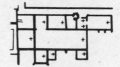

London Charterhouse, Plan of Church

The design of monastic churches was not only affected by changing architectural fashions which increased or accumulated income might allow to be followed but also by other factors such as changing devotions, liturgical developments, cult of saints, provision of shrines, access for large number of pilgrims, declining numbers or new purposes (such as the friars' churches which were basically preaching halls). Some churches were deliberately plain on religious principles, others were highly decorated because only the best was good enough for God or because of the pride of man. The Cistercian church was originally austere on principle and had to provide for large numbers of lay-brethren.

All monastic churches shared some of the same requirements:
a. A quire for the common singing of the canonical Hours
b. A presbytery to provide a suitable setting for the High Altar and its ministers
c. Adequate altar provision to allow all priest-monks the opportunity to say their daily mass (except on Good Friday)
d. Space for the formation and movement of processions.

CIRCAS, CIRCATOR

Responsible for 'rounds' of monastery to see that all was as it should be both day and night. The chief officer had to tour the church and the claustral buildings at night with his lantern. He was to see that no-one had fallen asleep in the church, he inspected the dorter and the rere-dorter to see that all were asleep in the former and none in the latter. He inspected the farmery and if the brethren were in bed he stood in the centre of the hall and shone his lantern all round. When he had completed his tour of inspection, which included checking security (especially for unlocked doors and danger of fire) he extinguished his lantern and retired himself.

CISTERCIAN   see also *C12*
   An austere reform of Benedictinism emanating from Citeaux at the end of C11. Its real founders were the Englishman, St Stephen Harding, abbot of Citeaux (1109-) and his greater disciple St Bernard, abbot of Clairvaux (1115-). The order spread with extraordinary rapidity. By 1128, when the first house was established in England, Citeaux had more than 30 daughters. In 1152 new foundations were forbidden when there were 339 foundations with 50 in England and Wales. In spite of this prohibition there were more than 600 abbeys in C13 of which there were 75 in England and Wales, some with dependent cells. In Scotland there was a family of 11 abbeys, 'the most compact and in some ways the most remarkable group of religious houses in the country'. The first, Melrose, was founded by King David's stepson, St Aldef (a monk of Rievaulx who became first abbot of Melrose). It had at least five daughters who included Kinloss and Newbattle. Dundrennan was established by another 'hive' of Rievaulx supported by David and filiated two later abbeys in Galloway. There are some remains of all the Scottish houses: Balmerino, Coupar Angus, Culross, Deer, Dundrennan, Glenluce, Kinloss, Melrose, Newbattle, Saddell, Sweetheart.
   Citeaux, like Cluny (q.v.) was the head of a religious federation with papal exemption from episcopal authority. But, unlike, Cluny, the abbeys enjoyed some independence under their own abbots. Apart from other advantages, this freedom saved them from the difficulties of 'alien priories' (q.v.). The principles of the order, its manner of growth and the inter-relations between its member houses were set out in the Charter of Charity (1119). When the numbers in a house grew too large it might, with the assent of the General-Chapter (q.v.) at Citeaux send out a minimum of 12 monks under an abbot to make a new foundation.
   The excellent principle of visitation by the mother of the filiated house ran into practical difficulties due to the number of foundations and their widespread character.
   All Cistercian churches were dedicated in honour of Our Lady for whom St Bernard had a deep and mystical devotion. Like hers so Cistercian life was to be hidden and so its favoured sites were secluded valleys — Valle Crucis, Vale Royal, Vaudrey, Vallis Dei, Merivale. Even insalubrious sites were not to be despised since sickness or death could be a salutary warning of the ultimate realities. Buildings were to be simple and severe; a church tower smacked of ostentation as did stained glass and excessive decoration. Paintings apart from representations of the Passion were prohibited and even the vestments and altar furniture were to be of the plainest and cheapest fashion compatible with dignity.
   The seclusion had to be maintained, remote not only from wordly conversation but even from the bells of another abbey. All workshops and other offices were to be within the precinct and lay settlement under its walls was to be discouraged. Temporary guests were admitted under special conditions but women were not allowed within the precinct.

   'With astounding consistency, perhaps even more remarkable to contemporaries than to ourselves, the Cistercians rejected the proffered gifts of proprietorial churches and of manors, the working units of an economy they affected — a little self-righteously — to despise. Unencumbered lands on the margins of existing settlements were to become the basis of the Cistercian's agricultural economy, and it was upon these primarily that their zeal and their genius would be lavished in the creation of that characteristically Cistercian institution, the independent

Strata Florida (Carthusian)

monastic farm or grange.' (Platt, pp.11f). These granges were at fixed distances from each other according to a system which unified everything from the plan of the abbey to the details of the meagre food and the simple habit of undied wool which gave them the name of White Monks. St Bernard saw his monks as 'soldiers of Christ', disciplined, drilled, well trained and travelling light.

A particular feature of the Cistercian economy was its attraction and use of lay brothers, 'conversi' whose large numbers and dedication obviated the need for tenants, hired help or other lay dependents. The rule emphasised manual labour and their horarium provided additional time for this purpose. From centres such as Fountains and Rievaulx in Yorkshire, Furness and Whalley in Lancashire, Vale Royal in Cheshire, Tintern in the Wye Valley, Valle Crucis in North Wales and Holmcultram in Cumberland, dedicated monks and conversi cleared scrub and forest, drained marshes, altered water-courses, ploughed valleys, turned fell and wold into rich sheep pasture and, where possible, mined iron ore and smelted it with charcoal. From all this came great wealth and with it decline from the original high ideals.

They returned to Mount Melleray in Ireland in 1833 from which new foundations sprang: Mount St Bernard in Leicestershire (1835), Caldey, Pembrokeshire (1913) and Nunraw, East Lothian (1946). All these are 'Trappists' (q.v.).

CISTERCIAN NUNS

There were nearly 40 houses in mediaeval England and Wales, mostly small and ranking as priories except for Marham and Tarrant which were abbeys. They usually had associated conversi until the Black Death and chaplains from the regular canons. They were not exempt but subject to diocesan visitation. The majority have left no visible remains including Hampole, Yorkshire, where Richard Rolle was an anchorite. Some of these churches in whole or part, survive in Anglican use: Heynings, Llanllugan and Swine.

They returned in 1802 and have an abbey near Wimborne, Dorset, (Stapehill).

Cistercian Nun

CISTERCIAN REMAINS

No church survives in its entirety as their site and constitution inhibited parochial function, thus at the Dissolution there was little competition with the looters and cannibalisers. Besides the nuns' churches mentioned above, parts of the following survive in use : Abbey Dore, Holmcultram, Margam.

There are substantial ruins of an entire monastery at Fountains, Furness, Kirkstall, Rievaulx, Tintern. The church has gone at Cleeve but the buildings round the cloister are well preserved.

A list of interesting and accessible remains would include: Balmerino, Basingwerk, Bindon, Buildwas, Byland, Calder, Cleeve, Croxden, Coupar Angus, Culross, Cymmer, Deer, Dore, Dundrennan, Glenluce, Hailes, Jervaulx, Kinloss, Kingswood, Margam, Melrose, Neath, Newbattle, Netley, Roche, Rufford, Sawley, Strata Florida, Valle Crucis, Waverley, Whalley.

CITEAUX

In later C11 a group of hermits gathered in Burgundian forest of Colan founded a strict monastery on Benedictine principles at Molesme but in a short time benefactions and numerous recruits overlaid the intentions of the reformers so that a group of 20, under abbot and including many of original hermits of Colan, resolved to make yet another fresh start, seeking solitude, poverty and severity of life. In 1098, according to the traditional account, 'There were 21 monks who joyfully proceeded from Molesme to the desert called Citeaux a spot situated in the diocese of Chalon which was at that time almost inaccessible by reason of thickets and thorns, and was inhabited only by wild beasts.'

CLAUSTRAL PRIOR

To be distinguished from the 'great prior' who was the superior, if not second-in-command. The claustral prior's responsibilities were entirely interior and involved maintenance of the rule. He was a disciplinary officer, watching for incorrect dress and minor breaches of good conduct as he made his rounds in the early morning and after Vespers checking on security, etc. (cf. Circator). Later in the period, in large houses, his duties were taken over by the second prior in an abbey and the third prior in a priory.

CLOCK

The demands of the horarium (q.v.) led the monks to concern themselves with the more exact computation of time. They developed not only time-measuring devices (there was a clepsydra at Bury in C12) but also mechanical clocks which would ring bells to waken the brethren in time for the night office (thus inventing the alarm-clock). The time for the day office had been more or less satisfactorily indicated by sun dials (mass dials). The first clocks were merely striking clocks, a dial was later added (with a single hand at first), and later complex astronomical clocks with a variety of functions were developed. A legendary Benedictine monk has had clocks at Exeter, Ottery St Mary, Wells and Wimborne attributed to him. Another Benedictine, Richard of Wallingford, c.1320 constructed a mechanical clock which not only indicated the time in hours

Prior Castell's Clock, Durham (Benedictine)

and minutes but also showed tides, phases of the moon and the positions of the sun and planets. He set up this complex apparatus at St Albans where it became one of the first public clocks in the country

The clock was under the care of the sacrist and was usually placed in the south transept of the church.

CLOISTER (Claustrum) see also *East, North, South, West Ranges*

The heart of a religious house, often used as its synonym, consisting of a rectangular walk, covered with a pentise roof, between the external walls of the main buildings and an arcaded wall (sometimes closed with shutters) which looked on to a grassy court or garden (see Garth). The open arcades (e.g. Bridlington, Jervaulx, Newminster, Rievaulx) were sometimes glazed later (e.g.

Cloister

Gloucester). The capitals of Romanesque arcade columns were often elaborately carved (Bermondsey, Bridlington, Norwich, Reading) but the Cistercians, under the influence of St Bernard, preferred a simple leaf form (e.g. Byland). Carvers also found scope in the roof bosses (especially Norwich). The favoured position of the cloister was on the south side of the nave but it is at the north side at Buildwas, Lacock, Tintern. In town sites it is placed away from the hubbub (Canterbury, Chester). It is rarely placed south of the chancel (Penmon, Rochester). At Waltham it is north of chancel.

Most surviving cloisters are single-storeyed but some in later Middle Ages had an upper floor (e.g. Muchelney, traces at Fountains). This floor contained carrels at Evesham and a library at St Albans. In some small houses the cloisters were mere passages (see Lane) and this form was adopted by friaries (e.g. Coventry) by Gilbertines at Watton and by small nunneries (Handale, Kirklees, Thicket, Wilberfoss). An additional cloister was always provided in double houses and sometimes for farmery or conversi.

Besides acting as passages, processional ways or place for perambulating meditation the cloister alleys had fixed uses. Except in Carthusian houses, that nearest the church was the study area with stone benches or individual carrels (q.v.). The western alley often served as novices' school-room (traces of children's games at Canterbury, Gloucester, Norwich, Westminster) while the 'Maundy' (q.v.) took place in another alley. The 'tabula' (q.v.) hung in the cloister and books were stored in wall-recesses or free-standing cupboards. In Cistercian houses, the collation (q.v.) took place here.

The 'working areas' were carpeted with straw, hay or mats for warmth and quiet, and draughts were reduced by wooden screens and/or leather curtains. At night the cloister was lit by lamps (bracket at Lilleshall). The entrance from outer court was variously placed: through western range (e.g. Finchdale, Lanercost, Torre), through vaulted passage in east walk (Durham, Worcester). Near this entrance was a seat for porter or 'guardian of cloister'.

CLOTHING   see also *Habit*

Its provision was the responsibility of the chamberlain (q.v.) who was in charge of the tailory: 'He should provide tailors, trustworthy, sober, unassuming, secret, not talkative, nor drunken or lying, as they were summoned into the interior privacy of the monastery where they could hear and see the secrets of the brethren. Such men should not be lightly engaged or lightly discharged. The tailor should know exactly the shape and cut of the brethren's woollen and linen garments. They should be neither sumptuous nor sordid.' He bought the materials for clothing: cloth, wool, skins, etc. and was responsible for the laundry of the completed garments. Sometimes the material was produced and processed on the premises or in the house's dependencies. Durham had a fulling mill on the banks of the Wear below the monastery and tanneries are recorded in connection with some houses. The chamberlain provided the boots and saw to their preservation by greasing (pig's fat was supplied from the kitchen three times a year for this purpose).

The general nature of monastic clothing was laid down in the rule (chap.55): it was to be simple and inexpensive but not too much mended as old clothes were to be given to the poor. This mending also came into the chamberlain's domain: some houses had the custom that a member should leave clothing needing repair in a specified place whence it was collected and to which it was returned after mending. There was variation between orders, not only in relation to their specific habit but in their austerity, e.g. the Cistercians wore unbleached and undyed wool, the Benedictines at Durham never descended to the sybaritism of linen which was allowed e.g. at Barnwell. There were also variations in regard to the system of replacement: at Westminster, the brethren were re-equipped in rotation, at Barnwell they were all given their allowance at a specified time: the summer allowance was issued at Easter and consisted of a surplice, shirt, three pairs of leather shoes, one pair of gaiters (serge or canvas), a cloak of frieze without fur. The winter issue took place shortly before St Michael's Day (Sept. 29th): one new woollen tunic or cassock of lambskin, one pair of felt boots, one pair of woollen gaiters, two pairs of woollen (night?) shoes, a black lambskin to mend the fur hood of the cloak.

In 1301 the Benedictines of Gloucester were issued with a new frock and cowl at least once a year, day shoes once in 18 months, boots once in five years, a pair of woollen shirts every four years. Other garments were issued irregularly but apparently more frequently and included: thick and thin tunics, a pilch or fur cloak, undershirts and drawers.

Normally all religious seem to have slept fully dressed apart from their footwear and outdoor clothes. The austere Cistercians wore no underclothes on principle of mortification so that their rough habit was in general contact with the flesh.

CLUNIAC

A reform of the Benedictine order, stemming from Cluny (q.v.), characterised by an emphasis on elaborate liturgy and ceremonial and a centralised organisation by which daughter foundations remained dependent priories under the abbot of Cluny. The observant principles of Cluny influenced the C10 reform of English religious life as well as the later Norman reorganisation before the development of a distinct group of Cluniac priories of which Lewes was the chief followed by Bermondsey (made the only Cluniac abbey in England in 1399), Castle Acre and Wenlock. Eventually, the English province had 32 Cluniac houses all founded before end of C12. Apart from those mentioned earlier, the largest and wealthiest were at Lenton, Montacute, Northampton and Pontefract. The major foundations established many cells, e.g. Lewes: Castle Acre, Farley, Monk's Horton, Prittlewell, Stanegate, Thetford; Castle Acre: Bromholm, Mendham, Normansburgh, Slevesholm (last foundation in England

Cluniac

1222.) They came into danger as 'alien priories' (q.v.) but most achieved 'denizen' status under an English superior.

The most complete remains are at Wenlock and Castle Acre but there are substantial remains at Bromholm. In Scotland, there were three or four foundations (May being doubtful) and the only material remains are at Crossraguel and Paisley.

CLUNIAC NUNS

There were only three or four Cluniac nunneries in England and Wales: Arthington, Fotheringay, Northampton and possibly Sewardesley. The only material remains are at Northampton (De la Pré) which had the status of an abbey.

CLUNY

'A monastery to which European civilisation owes a great debt.' (Zarnecki). It was founded in Burgundy in 910 by William the Pious, Duke of Aquitaine and placed under direct papal control to free it from episcopal or lay interference. It was essentially aristocratic, recruiting from the aristocracy and replacing manual work by elaborate and lengthy liturgical worship. This was considered the highest human activity and nothing was too good or costly for its use or environment. The movement spread with phenomenal speed, became an order under Cluny with some 1500 monasteries in Europe, championed by popes some of whom were themselves Cluniacs. Its ideals much influenced English Church under the leadership of Dunstan and later Lanfranc. Its impetus died after two centuries (apparently due to its over-elaboration which produced the reaction, among others, of St Bernard).

Cluny

COFFIN

Though monks were normally buried without a coffin, distinguished members or confraters of the house sometimes had the privilege of a stone coffin which was sunk

shallowly in church, chapter-house or cloister so that its
stone lid was level with the floor. Such coffins often survive
on a monastic site (e.g. St Andrew's which also possesses a
rare finely-carved stone table-tomb or sarcophagus).

Coffin

COLLEGES   see also *Chantry College*

Groups, of greater or less cohesion, and bound by rules
of varying strictness and detail, which were formed to
further common purposes of a religious or charitable
nature. They could be concerned with the provision of
parochial worship, with alms-giving or with education.
'Colleges of one sort or another (were) the last and most
diluted embodiment of the monastic ideal of the Middle
Ages and . . . the colleges of the two universities were the
only religious communities of the mediaeval world to
escape the Tudor bonfire and to remain, almost within
living memory, the only bodies of celibate clergy in England
with a status recognised by authority.' (Knowles).

Two Cambridge colleges occupy parts of former
conventual buildings, two more are on the site of a religious
house while a fifth has inherited some of the buildings of
what was a monastic house of studies. In the hall, raised on
an undercroft and in the cloister of Neville's Court at
Trinity College can be traced the relationship to, if not
descent from, the frater and garth of an abbey.

Mediaeval College
Almhouse?

COLLATION

After supper, the monks said grace in church and
returned to the cloister for the last time in the day to hear
the evening 'collation', a short reading on the monastic life
usually taken from Cassian's 'Collationes Patrum'. This
reading could take place in the chapter-house but it seems
to have been Cistercian practice for it to take place in the
south walk of the cloister where a seat and lectern were

Collation

placed for this purpose. There are signs of this provision at Cleeve, Strata Florida
and Tintern. When there was no supper, the monks were allowed a 'snack' in the
frater consisting of a drink and a small portion of bread ('potum caritatis'). By
association, this 'snack' later acquired the name 'collation'.

COMMANDERY

An estate or manor in the charge of a member of the Hospitallers. The
corresponding institution among the Templars was the 'preceptory'. Much of the
latters' property was transferred to the Hospitallers in early C14 and retained the
name of preceptory.

COMMENDATORS

A system which began in C8 in face of Saracen invasions whereby a layman
might be appointed to title and income of superior in return for his physical
protection of a religious house. When this prime purpose was lost the system became
much abused as a means of rewarding favourites of king or pope without expense to
themselves. It was particularly obnoxious in Scotland in C15 and C16 when
commendators not only gave nothing to the abbey but took more than the abbot's
portion, encouraged indiscipline, prevented reform and effected both spiritual and
material decline of abbey.

COMMON HOUSE
Common room or combination room. A late development of the warming-house (q.v.) whereby it developed into a recreation room, the scene for small celebrations, a place of entertainment for visitors where there might be a mitigation of the rule especially in regard to silence.

COMMON LIFE, COMMUNITY
From St Benedict's time the monastic rule was eminently social or communal. In both theory and practice the regular observance was based on the principle of the common life — 'all things in common' — not only no private possessions but no privacy as they lived, worked and prayed together in the closest possible association. The community or corporation was the sole entity : particular interests were merged in the general and the life of the individual was merely an item in the total life of the corporate body. This is emphasized in all rules and customaries, requiring from each the greatest respect for the whole, especially when it was formally assembled in its corporate capacity — in church, cloister, chapter, frater or in procession.

COMPLINE   ('Completorium')

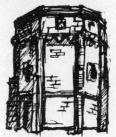

The last of the canonical Hours said before the community retired for the night. It received its liturgical form from St Benedict, who included it in his rule. It was a short office, including the singing of psalms xxiv, xxxi, 1-6, xci, cxxxiv, a hymn 'Te lucis ante terminum' and a short lesson. It was preceded by a formal confession and followed by an anthem of Our Lady.

It was not always said in quire (e.g. at York it was said in the Galilee, q.v.) and when it was finished the brethren were sprinkled with holy water as they passed through the cloisters to the dorter at about seven thirty in winter and eight thirty in summer.

Conduit House, Durham

CONDUIT   see also *Water Supply, Well*
Conduits were the water mains, often distributed from a central point contained in a conduit house where the tank was raised up to give some pressure (examples at Beaulieu, Canterbury, Durham, Monkton, Farleigh.) The water was conducted to the distribution point, usually from a spring or separate source from that used for drains, etc. and thence was fed, often by a very complex system of pipes, to various points in the domestic quarters. Friaries were celebrated for their conduits of running water which they sometimes shared with the town where they were established (as did abbeys in some places).

CONFEDERATION   see also *Confraternity*
Confederated abbeys formed a kind of spiritual union by which they agreed to offer prayers for the departed of other houses in the group. Usually once a year, a special messenger (rotularius) was despatched from each house to

Water Tower, Canterbury

the others in the confederation bearing a roll inscribed with the names of those for whom prayers were desired.

An obit roll of c.1230 records the death of the founder and first prioress of Hedingham. It was sent to 120 houses, all of which acknowledged its receipt as follows: 'May the soul of Lady Lucy, prioress of Hedingham and the souls of all the faithful departed, by the mercy of God, rest in peace. We concede to her the benefits of our church. We pray for you; pray for us'.

For a later example of this confederation: the abbeys of Abingdon, Chertsey, Romsey, Tewkesbury, Wherwell are named, among others, as being in spiritual confraternity with Winchester. There were also treaties of pious fraternity and mutual support between the abbeys of Peterborough and Ramsey.

CONFESSION

Usually public, as offences were against the community (q.v.) as well as against God. Both the mass and the offices began with a general confession of faults and unworthiness. More particular offences, especially breaches of rule, observances or courtesy, were admitted before the community in chapter (q.v.).

In addition, there were opportunities for private (or auricular) confession with provision of spiritual counsel and direction. This facility was normally provided after chapter but it could be provided at all times and was used by members of the public who desired it. The monasteries seem to have provided a public penitentiary (hearer of confessions and giver of penances) for pilgrims and the romances of the later Middle Ages frequently show knights consulting ghostly fathers, hermits or monks.

CONFRATERNITY

Individual as opposed to confederation (q.v.). This was a rare privilege and honour by which a benefactor was given honorary membership of a religious community. He thus shared in the 'good works' of the community, benefitting from their prayers and self-sacrifice. It often carried the right of being buried in the monastic cemetery, clothed in the habit of the order, together with certain other privileges. This honour was solemnly conferred in the chapter-house. The person seeking confraternity, either for himself or his house (see Confederation), was brought before the assembled community to whom he made his request with appropriate humility. If the petition was favourably received, it was ceremoniously granted by the act of giving a copy of the rule (to a religious) or the gospels (to a layman). The new confrater was then given the kiss of peace by each member of the community and allocated a seat in the chapter-house. This kiss of peace was not given to a woman confrater in a male community and vice versa (the hand was kissed instead).

An illustrious confrater of Cluny was William de Warenne (together with his lady) and his influence brought the first settlement of Cluniacs to England. It appears that King John made a late entry into the confraternity of Worcester where he was buried in a Benedictine habit. William I was a confrater of Battle, Henry VI of Bury and Crowland, Wolsey of Evesham and Sir Thomas More of Christchurch, Canterbury. Nuns were sometimes received as 'consores' of an abbey e.g. two nuns of Sopwell received this privilege at St Albans in 1428 at the same time as the Earl of Warwick and the Duke of Gloucester were made confraters.

The privilege was not confined to the upper classes and in some form it was often granted to long-serving employees. Servants were also granted similar privileges in a diminished form as when in 1466 the enclosed Minoresses of Denney allowed two domestic servants to be married in their private chapel.

The words 'con-socius' and 'familiar' — 'fellow-member', 'one of the family' have similar associations and all such were entered in a special book and for the names of all so recorded, the abbey regularly and religiously offered prayers for their good estate in life or death.

CONVENT   see also *Building*

From Latin, 'convenire' — to assemble. A community of either sex and not necessarily a nunnery.

CONVERSUS   (pl. Conversi)

An important element in the Cistercian (q.v.) order. A layman who had been 'turned' from the service of the world to that of God and more or less equivalent to later lay brothers. They were monks in that they lived according to the rule in community, wore a modified form of the habit and occupied their day in a combination of work and prayer. But their work was manual, though not necessarily unskilled, and their prayers were simplified and shortened, being excused from quire and saying a diminished office in their own church. They said special prayers which they had learnt by heart at the time of the offices as they paused from their labour in workshop, field or grange. In terms of abstinence, silence and other essentials, their life was that of the other Cistercians but they had a separate common room, frater, farmery and church and the equivalent of their own cloister (see Lane). They rose at a later hour than the other monks because of the nature of their work and they had a supplemented diet for the same reason and only had chapters on Sundays and major festivals.

Conversus sowing

In C12 and 13 there seem to have been about twice as many 'conversi' as quire 'monks' in the Cistercian communities e.g. Waverley (1187) and 70 monks, 120 conversi; Rievaulx (1167) c.140 monks, c.240 conversi and c.260 lay servants or employees; Louth Park (end C12) had 66 monks and 150 conversi. The number at Fountains is unknown but the large frater, even larger dorter and separate farmery indicates numbers in excess of those at Rievaulx.

Though all orders had lay brethren up to the Black Death (1348-9) when they largely disappeared, the conversi occupied a special place among the Cistercians and were provided with special regulations in the Carta Caritatis.

Conversus ploughing

They seem to have included skilled masons who often prepared the buildings in advance for the arrival of the quire monks. They formed small priories to manage the outlying granges which were characteristic of the order. They were attached to houses of Cistercian nuns to do the heavy and manual work. They could equal the monk in social position but to be a conversus was enough, it was not a stage to being in quire. Consequently they were not allowed to become quire monks and it was forbidden to give them a literary education. Ambition was to be rooted out at all costs. They not only took the monastic vows of poverty, chastity and obedience but their obedience was more extensive ('de bono' as distinct from the monk's 'secundum regulam Sancti Benedicti').

They were dressed in a white cloak, tunic, stockings, boots and a cowl which was shorter than that of the monk and covered only the shoulders and breasts (more practical for their work).

CORRODIANS

Persons who paid the convent a capital sum in cash or kind (corrody) for lodging, fuel and food from a specific time until their death. From the corrodians' point of view it was a kind of life insurance or old age pension, to the religious house it was a means, in time of financial stress, of raising ready money but it was something of a gamble from either side. The outgoings to support the long old age of a couple could far exceed the initial capital payment. Conversely, in early C15 an abbey sold an annual corrody of £5-6-8 to one Thomas Stone for £150 and he died after only five years of receiving it.

Corruption

Corrodies could take the form of a pension paid in return to a benefactor for a gift or loan and it was not infrequently used as a means of paying wages. In the early C14 this happened at Bath in the case of a plumber and at Worcester of a master mason. In C16 and earlier the crown sometimes bought corrodies for its retired servants (ushers, clerks, secretaries, soldiers). It also abused its privileges and claims as a founder by forcing such corrodians on an abbey without reimbursement. Corrodies could differ in the details of the contract: the nature of the accommodation, the quality of food (ie. which kitchen supplied it), the amount of fuel allowance and other perks (some included stabling for a number of horses). There can be little doubt that corrodies were a burden (Kirkham sold 16 at end of C13; Great Malvern was paying about 30 at the Dissolution) — not only financial but in their effect on religious observance.

Corrodian?

CORRUPTION   see also *Decline, Laxity*

A Latin inscription on the former quire-stalls of Easby abbey (now in Richmond church) can be translated: 'There are ten abuses of those in a cloister; costly living, choice food, noise in cloister, strife in chapter, disorder in quire, a neglectful discipline, a disobedient youth, a lazy old man, a headstrong youth, a wordly religious'.

There is no doubt about the existence of these faults, especially in C14-16. The cloistered life produced all the strains of human beings in close and unchanging proximity and they would be aggravated in houses which had inadequate superiors and where a comfortable existence replaced a zealous austerity.

On the other hand, these weaknesses have received undue prominence because they are so inconsistent with the professed and extremely difficult ideal. Its very challenge almost produces a demand for scandal. Even good historians with their proper dependence on written evidence sometimes forget that, by the nature of things, the inner life leaves little documentation and visitation reports, though they disclose a good deal of scandal, rarely indicate general corruption in any house or that back-sliding went unpunished. The evidence of Henry's commissioners is hardly worth considering: their function was to provide evidence for an already decided verdict.

Nevertheless, it is true that in C14 and 15 there was a decline in both quantity and quality of the regular religious life. There is evidence of a slow revival in the C16 and perhaps one should remember the words of one of the greatest of the monastic saints (Ailred of Rievaulx) : 'The house which witholds its toleration from the weak is not to be regarded as a house of religion.'

COSTS

It is very difficult to compute the costs involved in building a religious house and even when figures exist it is a complex operation to transpose them into contemporary money equivalents. It may help to remember that for a long time in the Middle Ages 1d. a day was a reasonable wage i.e. £1.25 a month as against say £250 today. To multiply mediaeval figures by 200 is both naive and simplistic but it may give a very rough idea.

Three years of building at Vale Royal (1278-80) cost £15,000. Rebuilding work at Westminster in 1253 was costing about £53 a week. Syon (f.1431) cost £4,833 for the church, dorter and cloister alone. These were all royal foundations, probably using state contractors and with little expense spared. Money could be saved by using local materials, their own labour, etc., but initial building or extension in stone would always require either princely benefactors or the building up of a considerable building fund. This latter could be based on self-sacrificial labour and continued good management (as in the Cistercian houses), generous benefactions or the funds accruing from pilgrims attracted to the shrine. (New buildings at Canterbury, Gloucester and Westminster were financed from pilgrims' offerings).

Iron Worker

Apart from the main buildings there were repairs and additions: most of the replacement of Durham cloister (c. 1400) cost £600, but they received from Bishop Skirlaugh a contribution towards the new dorter of 330 marks (i.e. £220). A little earlier (1372) they had provided a new base for St Cuthbert's shrine at over £200. About the same time the Austin Canons at Guisborough (1381) spent 5500 marks on their bell-tower (a mark is 13s.4d.). There was a good deal of building at Guisborough at this time as their confrater, Lord Latimer, after his burial there, required his executors to complete the vaulting which he had begun in the north aisle (as well as paying for the belfry).

Sometimes benefactors would present a single article of furniture of which the much depleted screen at Durham is a conspicuous example.

Another element in the on-going costs of a monastery which is often forgotten is the sum required for the maintenance of the community itself. It has been estimated that it cost £10 p.a. for a Benedictine and £3 p.a. for an Austin Canon in endowment. The friars claimed to exist on what they could beg and therefore had no endowments at all. There is of course no relation between the income of an abbey and the amount put aside for subsistence for each individual monk. Some of former went into the prior's account for travel, hospitality and maintenance; similar but smaller amounts were ear-marked for particular departments e.g. farmery, almonry, sacristy. A considerable sum was also disbursed to servants and employees.

COURTS

As feudal lords, abbots (particularly those of town abbeys) had their own courts and prisons to deal with errant dependents. There was a prison in the great gate at Bury, court-rooms over the gate at Ely and a separate court-room (Tribunal) in the main street at Glastonbury. The abbot of Gloucester had a court-room in his extensive house.

COWL

The distinctive outward vesture of a religious (remembering the monastic proverb: cucullus non facit monachum — the cowl does not make the monk). By St Benedict's time it consisted of a long cloak or mantle with an attached hood. The cowl of the Austin Canons was an unattached hood. The colour of this vesture gave the popular name to the various religious orders: Black, White Monks; Black, White Canons: Black, White and Grey Friars; White Ladies, etc.

Monastic Craftsmen

CRAFTSMANSHIP   see also *Art, Book*

'It was due to the fostering care of the monasteries and the bishops, and the commissions of royalty that craftsmen were able to develop and continue their work'. (Crossley). (Some detailed evidence of this patronage is available in W.R. Lethaby; *Westminster and the King's Craftsmen* (1906).)

Apart from the finer arts and crafts which were not always distinguished in the Middle Ages, religious houses provided constant employment for masons, glaziers, plumbers, smiths and carpenters as well as less frequent (but common) contracts for bell-founders, goldsmiths, silversmiths and workers in bronze and latten.

There is evidence that large religious houses sometimes hired out a skilled member of the community e.g. Thomas the Plumber, a C14 monk of Combermere, spent no less than 166 days in a single year working for the king on the lead roofs of Beeston and Chester castles and in an earlier period we know that Gandulph, the 'weeping monk' of Bec designed both ecclesiastical and secular buildings.

CRUTCHED FRIARS

The Fratres Cruciferi, Friars of the Holy Cross. One of the lesser orders of friars, recognised in 1169. They had, at the most, only a dozen houses in England of which a number disappeared during the Middle Ages. There are no remains apart from a street name in London where there was a house from 1298 to 1538.

Sculpture from York Chapter-House

CRYPT

Crypts were built to house the bodies of saints beneath the High Altar (cf. Rev.vi,19) and there are monastic examples at e.g. Lastingham, Ripon, St Dogmaels. These are part of the church and should be distinguished from cellars and undercrofts.

CULDEE

Celtic monks, apparently originating in C8, whose name appears to mean 'companions of God'. They seem to have

Goldsmith making Pyx

been anchorites who banded together in groups (often of 13) and apparently survived as late as C14 in some places though they began to be absorbed into the more regular Latin orders from C11. The community of hermits at Kirkstall were largely absorbed into the Cistercian foundation and from C12 priories of Austin Canons were often founded on Culdee sites, presumably taking in their predecessors.

CURIA

The outer court of a religious house, within the enclosure but outside the main claustral buildings. It contained the guest-house, outer parlour, bakehouse, brewhouse and granary. It was a somewhat busy place, providing a meeting-point between the convent and the outside world and therefore cut off from the cloister from which it could be entered by a passage. The Cistercians often had a further court outside the main gatehouse in which they located noisy or offensive workshops or processes e.g. the carpenters' shop, the masons' lodge, smithy, tannery, iron-works, mill etc. (e.g. Beaulieu, Furness). Other orders were usually content with a single

Gate of Curia, Norwich

outer court though many of them had several offices outside the precinct (e.g the mill and guest-stable at Tewkesbury).

The curia could contain malthouse, kiln, beehives, dairy, scullery, sundry workshops (e.g. for glazier, plumber), stables, and a variety of store-places, including stew-ponds. Later, the abbot's lodging was located here, sometimes with its own courtyard. Often little survives of its buildings as they might be made of comparatively impermanent materials such as wood and thatch.

CUSTODIAN

Large houses had officials called 'custodes ordinis', responsible for the order of the house: they might include the claustral prior, the custodian of the cloister, the circators, etc. They sometimes had a short private meeting in the inner parlour before chapter to consult on any matter which might need correction or to which the attention of the community should be called. The custodians of the cloister were responsible for security, to see that no strangers penetrated the domestic buildings, and their duties included locking the monastery precincts at night and during the chapter meeting.

CUSTOS   see *Administrator, Custodian, Guardian*

CUSTOMARIES, CUSTUMALS

The rule of an order was concerned primarily with principles and touched on practice only in the most general way. It was therefore supplemented by customaries or observances which applied these generalities in some detail to a particular house which had its own use, conventions and customs. The rule (e.g. of Benedict or Augustine) could be very brief indeed and therefore needed to be filled out. The 'observances' of Barnwell have, among others, survived and give a vivid and detailed picture of the daily life of a house of Austin Canons. Customaries lay down, for instance, the kind of behaviour expected at meals or they may instance the necessary signs to be used during silence.

DAILY ROUND   see also *Horarium*

The monastic life was regular by definition and unvarying in its general terms, though there were modifications due to feasts and fasts, celebrations and penitential times. It could also be affected by such occasional events as visitations, the installation of a new superior, and (increasingly in the later Middle Ages) by involvement in secular affairs and the abuse of hospitality by the aristocracy. Very occasionally a great abbey might have to suffer the great upheaval consequent on its being the seat of a parliament.

There were minor variations in the daily service as saints' days were celebrated and the community progressed through the seasons of the liturgical year and perhaps also in the allocation of work which was generally organised on a weekly basis. St Benedict's working day was basically divided into three or more or less equal parts: the Opus Dei which was to have pre-eminence, meditation and study, manual work. There were slight differences between orders but in all cases the year was divided into two seasons : winter (from mid-September to Easter) and summer. The day was the natural day from sunrise to sunset and it was divided into 12 equal hours (whose length varied from season to season). It began at midnight when the first and longest service (Matins) took place. This was followed, after a brief pause, by Lauds ending between one and two a.m. when the monks returned to their dorter. They were re-awakened at daybreak and assembled in church for Prime which was immediately followed by the early mass

Summoned by Bells

51

for servants and manual workers. Only the necessary participants attended this function, the rest went to the cloisters where they attended to their toilet. This done, the senior priests said their private masses, other monks took their books for study and the novices began their lessons. If it was not a fast day, a light breakfast, (mixtum) was taken as the bell rang for morning mass (Lady Mass or Chapter Mass) which was said in a low audible voice with no particular ceremonial. This was followed by Chapter, Terce and the solemn High Mass which on Sundays and festivals was preceded by the great procession. Sext followed and the community then returned to the cloister for further attention to their toilet (and sometimes to sharpen their knives ready for dinner). This main meal, taken shortly after noon was accompanied by considerable formality. The next quire service was None which in summer was followed by a brief siesta. A short period of recreation was sometimes fitted into the afternoon and any other time was occupied by work until Vespers about six p.m. This was longer than any other quire office (apart from Matins) and was followed, except during fasts, by supper. After supper there were private devotions in church and perhaps some time in cloister or chapter until Compline. After Compline the monks processed to the dormitory for a few hours' sleep until the bells for Matins called them back to worship and the beginning of another round.

Silence lay over all (unless the monks were reading or singing) except for brief periods in the parlour. All spare moments between the unceasing round of services was occupied by personal tasks or the common duties which were issued at chapter or prescribed on the weekly roster.

All this however is only the scaffolding within which the monk 'made his soul'. The horarium of Rievaulx in 1160 or of St Joseph's, Avila in 1565 is little compared with the writings or life of St Ailred or the autobiography of St Theresa and the sketches of her nuns in 'Foundations'. The life of a true religious is veritably 'hid with God'.

DANE, DAN, DOM
The English form of the title 'Dominus' (Sir, Master) which was initially given to members of religious orders and then applied, like 'Father', to other clerics.

DAUGHTER HOUSE
A foundation made by 'hiving' from another abbey, either as a result of missionary zeal or because the mother had outgrown her resources. The form was to send out a community of 12 under a superior (in imitation of Christ and his apostles). Usually the endowments of the new house were secured and the buildings were more or less ready before the move but in early days such colonisations were made at what seems a great risk to us and a firm trust in providence to them. Originally the mother house had control over the daughters which usually began as priories but many developed independence.

St Albans had eight 'daughters' including Binham, Hatfield Peveril, Tynemouth, and two dependent houses of nuns (St Mary de Pré, Sopwell). Durham had seven cells, including Finchale priory. St Mary's York had seven dependencies and Fountains was a daughter who outgrew her mother in prestige and influence making many great foundations of her own.

DAVID I
King of Scotland (1124-1153), a prodigal founder and benefactor of religious houses: Augustinians at Holyrood, St Andrews; Premonstratensians at Dryburgh; Cistercians at Dundrennan, etc. ; Arrousians at Cambuskenneth and other canons at Jedburgh; Tironians at Selkirk (moving to Kelso).

'Whether judged by their number, their size, their wide distribution or the variety of their rule, the foundations of David I must rank as the most remarkable of any Scottish monarch, or indeed of any monarch of the age.' (Knowles)

DAY ROOM

Seems to have been equivalent to the common room or parlour (q.v.), though sometimes it may have developed from the warming room. It was generally used for 'recreation' periods, lay brothers having their own provision, but it appears to have been used for other purposes outside these times e.g. novices sometimes were taught in their day room.

DAY STAIR   see also *Night Stair*

The access from the cloister to the dorter. Its usual position was next to the chapter-house on the side furthest from the church (e.g. Thetford, Westminster). Other sites were used in smaller houses which often had difficulty in finding a space for it (e.g. Lacock, St Radegund) and it has an unusual position in the larger houses of Chester (within a thickened wall at north end of west range) and Bolton (east end of frater range — a position generally adopted by Cistercians e.g. Fountains, Jervaulx, Neath, Rievaulx). The day stairs of St Mary's York were contrived in the thickness of the parlour wall. The narrowness of the stair is indicated by a regulation in the eustomary which requires monks descending to give way to those ascending.

Day Stair

Lay brothers had their own dorter and consequent day stairs — on cloister side at Byland and on west side at Fountains where they rise above the cellarer's office. The Grandmontines tended to follow the Cistercian custom of placing their day stairs in the south east angle of the cloister.

Survivals at e.g. Chester, Cleeve, Valle Crucis.

DEATH   see also *Burial, Cemetery, Illness*

Death was treated as a solemn and critical occasion in the Middle Ages and that of a monk was treated with much ceremony. As death approached he was fortified by the prayers of his brethren and the rites of the church: Unction, Confession and Absolution, Viaticum (Glastonbury had a portable altar of saphire for use by the bedside). The customaries give in great detail the rites, ceremonies and pious practices that accompanied the death of a religious. These varied a little in different places but they were alike in their solemnity and in the significance given to death.

Laying a Brother to rest

In early times, ashes were strewn on the floor and covered with a hair-cloth onto which the dying man was gently lifted from his bed. Later the custom was adopted of putting the sackcloth and ashes onto the bed. (St Martin, much honoured by monks, had told his disciples that a Christian should die on sackcloth and ashes).

After death the corpse was washed and reclothed in the monastic habit, set on a hearse and covered with a pall, then it was treated with various rites before being carried in solemn procession from the infirmary or its mortuary-annexe to the church. For some 24 hours the community kept watch over the body with continual prayer and silence was maintained throughout the house. Masses and formal prayers were said on his behalf for 30 days, after which he was remembered annually by name. Doles were made to the poor on behalf of the deceased and notice of his passing was transmitted to other religious houses (see Brief).

If monks died away from home the body was, if possible, solemnly returned to the community who had been informed of the death in a special chapter as soon as the news was received. The place of a dead monk was reserved in frater for 30 days and a portion of food was placed there before being given to the poor.

The burial (q.v.) was naturally a solemn affair attended by the whole company and accompanied by continuous tolling of the great bell.

DEBT

There was no reason to suppose that a religious superior would be a good business man and monasteries, from time to time, found themselves in severe financial difficulties from which they extricated themselves in a variety of ways: resource to the king, money-lenders, benefactors, disposal of land or amenities (see Corrodian).

Debts could arise from many causes: commercial miscalculation such as forward selling of produce, especially wool; bad harvests or disease among stock; fire, flood or other accidents; devastation due to war or invasions; careless supervision, improvidence or corruption on part of obedientiaries; dissension between abbot and convent; extravagance of a personal kind, usually due to the superior maintaining himself in the manner of a lay magnate; legal expenses, required for confirmation of charter, election etc.

Perhaps the most frequent source of financial embarassment was the abuse of hospitality: self-invited guests who found free lodgings for long periods, not only for themselves but for very considerable retinues (kings were far from guiltless in this respect). In 1331, the Black Prince informed his justices in Cheshire that 'the abbeys of Chester, Combermere and Vale Royal all in the county, are so excessively burdened by frequent visits of people of the county with their grooms, horses and greyhounds, that their possessions hardly suffice for the maintenance of the monks'

Even reasonable hospitality for the needy could be a great burden if the house was on a pilgrimage route or main line of communication (especially when located near a ferry or port).

At Bristol Priory in 1371 'it was found that owing to lack of good governance and neglect, the abbot has brought it low by sale of corrodies, by hurtful demises to farm or the possessions bringing little or no profit, by waste, sale and destruction of the said possessions, excessive and fruitless expenses on manors, lands, rents, that alms and piety are withdrawn, and it is to be feared that the canons will be dispersed through lack of sustenance.'

In the reign of Edward III, no less than 36 monasteries applied for royal relief and in 23 cases the need was due to large debts.

DECLINE   see also *Corruption, Laxity*

There were many periods of decline, followed by periods of reform, development and recovery. The Benedictine rule, because of its very moderation, was particularly susceptible to developing slackness. There was a notable period of decline in C9 and C10 which had two main causes: repeated invasions, the breakdown of general law and order, the sacking and burning of monasteries (particularly by Danes) leaving monks denuded and dispersed fugitives when they survived at all; secondly,

"Naughties"

weaknesses due to the transposition of Benedict's rule from Italy, autonomy and consequent isolation of individual monastery. Furthermore, the absolutism of the abbot made his appointment critical and sometimes he was the creature of a powerful lay lord.

'That monastic life, and with it European civilisation, was saved from complete disintegration was due to a few men of great faith and courage, who set, themselves the task of restoring moral values by first reforming the monasteries.' (Zarnecki). This task was performed by the great abbots of Cluny such as Hugh and when the Cluniacs themselves declined, new vigour was instilled into the monastic life by the Cistercian reform and leaders such as St Stephen and St Bernard.

The Cistercians were the victims of their own success, particularly their vast wealth created by continuous good husbandry and the benefactions attracted by the sacrificial quality of their life. All houses were affected by institutionalisation and increasing administration together with involvement in feudal society as landlords, royal officials.

The arrival of the friars brought new vigour and a new form of religious commitment but their very dependence on begging made them despised in some quarters and their success produced envy of older orders.

Everywhere necessity forced some relaxation of the original austerity, good excuses were found for increasing number of exceptions and indulgences, whether of fasting, private property, or leaving the house. There was the awesome catastrophe of the Black Death with its economic and psychological repercussions. To some extent there was a 'crisis of identity' and real questioning about the place of monasticism in the contemporary world which was certainly over endowed with religious houses. More than once, leaders in church and state had suppressed small

Savings Box

houses and put their endowments to more fruitful use and this false precedent was abused by Henry VIII for personal, political and economic ends.

There is a tendency for critics to concentrate on the decline in the late Middle Ages and especially C16 to justify increasing nationalisation of charity or to justify the Henrician suppression. The facts seem to be that in the long history of monasticism, apart from an occasional brief period following its foundation, some religious institution, somewhere or another, was in decline and not only a particular house but even a whole order was in need of revitalisation. The history of western monasticism is, to no small degree, a history of alternating decline and revival — realistically foreseen by St Benedict himself. More often than not real reform (as distinct from destruction) did take place. The C15 was to some extent a period of decline in religious fervour, the age as a whole was acquisitive, concerned with worldly success and 'fame' but towards its end there were also signs of reform and of new devotion. What the outcome might have been in England, Scotland and Wales is a matter of complete hypothesis as the entire monastic structure went down in a welter of greed, and destruction rationalised as religious reform.

> '*For sum bene devowte, holy and towarde,*
> *And holden the right way to blysse;*
> *And sum bene feble, lewde and frowarde,*
> *Now God amend that ys amys.* (C16 poem)*

Modern House,
Mt St Bernard

DECORUM

Rules and customaries give both general and particular instruction about decorum: forbidding levity, demanding obedience to superiors and the formal acknowledgement of hierarchy, requiring courteous deference to age and office and paying considerable attention to behaviour at meals. Religious were to wash their hands before and after eating, there was to be no noise as they assembled outside the frater — 'if the monks persisted in holding their parliament at the door of the frater or near it, they were to be put on bread and water until they promised better obedience' (injunction at Ely). There were many directions about behaviour in frater (q.v.). Similarly the servers or waiters are neither to rush about nor stand aimlessly in one place, nor are they to gossip with the kitchen staff about the dishes.

These outward observances were seen as a crutch to and symbol of desirable interior attitudes: humility, self-control, consideration for others etc. on the principle of William of Wykeham's motto: 'Manners makyth man'.

DEDICATION

The explorer may find it interesting to discover and collect the dedications of monastic houses and churches. The universal (secondary) dedication of Cistercian abbeys was to Our Lady with some differentia e.g. Our Lady of the Fountains, Our Lady of the Cliffs, Our Lady of the Rock, etc.

The Hospitallers were under the patronage of John the Eleemosynary, a sainted patriarch of Alexandria, remarkable for his exceeding charity. It might be found that particular religious orders have their favourite dedications or no pattern may be discernible because of the preferences of individual founders. In Scotland for example, an examination of the dedications of Dominican houses reveals a number of Marian mysteries: the Annunciation, Nativity, Assumption, Coronation; saints from the New Testament: Andrew, Bartholomew, James, John the Baptist, John the Evangelist; popular saints; Catherine, Lawrence; local saints, St Moran; obscure saints: St Peter of Milan.

St Augustine

DENIZATION

The process by which 'alien priories' (q.v.) were 'naturalised', its most significant element being the grant of a royal charter by which they gave up sending contributions to foreign mother house and replaced superior, if not entire community, by Englishmen e.g. Barnstaple in 1403 paid the large sum of £106-13-4 to the king in order to gain its charter of denization and consequently to free itself from restrictions, confiscations and penal taxation.

DEPOSITION

Except in the case of a small dependent house where it could be affected by the mother house, the removal of a superior was a difficult, and often costly, process. When he had rights of visitation, the diocesan bishop could begin the canonical process of deposition. In exempt houses it was more difficult and required action either from the papacy or from the superior of the whole order. This process could be prevented by the sovereign refusing admission to country of foreign visitors.

Fountains, Tower Niche

DETAILS

Some of the treasures of ruins (and even non-ruins) only reveal themselves by scrupulous search for details and questions about their meaning. The following items are worthy of special attention: bosses, key-stones, corbels, mouldings round arches, capitals, canopies of niches, remains of sculptures (e.g. Chichester, Ely, Malmesbury, York). Some of these may be stacked apart from the ruins or collected in a nearby museum. Often there are interesting inscriptions (Easby stalls, Fountains tower). Piscinas indicate sites of altars, holes in pillars and walls indicate vanished screens, a recess may be the remains of a cupboard, the standing for a lamp or the recess for the 'tabula'.

Close examination reveals modifications of roof, changed function of rooms, points of repair or rebuilding, etc.

C15 detail; Quire Roof
St Albans (Benedictine)

Arms of Whalley

DINING HALL   see *Frater, Misericord*

DINNER

The main and sometimes the only meal of the day, following High Mass and Sext shortly after midday. There were usually two courses with some provision for choice. Originally it seems to have been based on vegetables but the meagre and repetitive food of the earlier days was gradually modified in most houses by increasing both quantity and nature so that a wide variety of dishes involving fish, cheese, pastry, vegetables, fruit, wine, water, milk could be offered. Bread and beer were always available and vast

Fishing

quantities of eggs seem to have been consumed. The reduced food of Lent became more palatable with the addition of spices, figs, cakes and ale. Eventually, meat appeared at festivals: pork-pies, capons and more exotic poultry, such sweets as blancmange with rice and almonds, fig and other fruit tarts.

In a relaxed monastery of the late Middle Ages the dinner of a feast day could approximate to a secular banquet.

DISCARIUS

The waiter or server of dishes in the frater. He received them from the caterer at the serving hatch and placed them on the tables, beginning with the high table. Customaries give instruction about his behaviour mentioning care and efficiency in his work. After meals he seems to have helped with the washing-up and seen to the proper storage of utensils so that they would be ready for their next use. Outside meal times he served in the kitchen, helping to bring in fuel, seeing that the wheelbarrow for kitchen refuse was in position and that it was properly emptied when necessary.

DISCIPLINE   see also *Order, Punishment*

Fundamentally, the religious life was one of self-discipline in which, helped by his brethren, each was 'to discipline his body in respect of food, drink, sleep, chatter, and mirth'. Decisions affecting all were to be discussed by all in chapter (q.v.). Discipline was necessary not only for the good of the individual but to allow the whole community to work and pray without distraction and to live together without unnecessary friction. If a brother was disobedient or insubordinate, proud or a grumbler, he was to be privately admonished. If he did not amend or seemed incorrigible, he was to undergo punishment with reform as its prime purpose. This could vary from spiritual tasks (extra prayers, etc.), reduced or solitary meals, through corporal punishment (which was quite frequent) to solitary imprisonment of greater or less severity. In the last, and rarely taken, resort he was expelled from the community.

The punishments at St Augustine's, Canterbury, were, for lighter faults: separation from the common table with meals served three hours later, lower place in quire and chapter, loss of ritual rights i.e. function in services; for graver faults the punishments included: imposition of total silence (including quire), fasting on bread and water for a specified number of days, taking the last place in the community, prostration at church door so that brethren had to step over his body.

There are examples of a monk being put on bread and water every Friday until Christmas for not rising to Matins and of another being ordered a severe beating with a 'ferula' for illicit absence from the house.

The internal discipline of a house was administered by the superior and responsible officers such as the claustral prior and circators. Discipline from external sources depended on effective visitation (q.v.).

The word discipline is also used in monastic circles of the short whip or strap with which a religious castigated himself in the pursuit of mortification.

57

DISSOLUTION   see also *Suppression*

On some real, and more fraudulent, evidence the smaller religious houses were suppressed by an act of parliament in 1536 whose 'preamble' speaks in distinction of 'divers and great solemn monasteries of this realm wherein, thanks be to God, religion is right well kept and observed.' The implication was that an annual income of less than £200 was productive of vice and lax observance. Those with a less arithmetical yardstick objected to this attack and the northern counties rose in organised and orderly protest (see Pilgrimage of Grace).

This 'treason' was used to implicate some of the greater houses and by a combination of bribes, cajolery and outright terror they were all by a legal fiction brought to surrender themselves into the king's hands for the disposal of their property and personnel. Those who had given in most easily (about half) were given pensions for their former members. Abbots (sometimes intruded) who had co-operated with the king in his 'take-over' were given very substantial pensions of £100 p.a. and more, often with preferment to high office in Henry's new national church. Others were barbarously executed notably Becke of Colchester, Cooke of Reading, Whiting of Glastonbury. Almost every single Carthusian (whose austere observant religion no one questioned), was cruelly done to death.

Articles of value, plate, votive offerings, altar furniture, etc. were transported under guard to the king's Wardrobe. Bells, brasses and other re-usable metal went to his armouries, lead from the roofs was melted down on the spot and cast into ingots bearing Henry's mark. Libraries were burnt at the worst and dispersed at the best. Lands were sold to landlords to increase their vested interest in maintaining the suppression. The profits which did not go to Henry's personal expenditure went largely on armaments. In spire of promises nothing accrued to new charities including education (on the contrary much was diminished) and even the limited deployment of a small part of the revenue on new bishoprics was fulfilled only in five out of the promised twelve cases.

DIURNAL   see also *Horarium*

The daily round (q.v.) of services interspersed with work and sleep.

DIVINE OFFICE

The duty owed by religious to God, called by Benedict the 'opus Dei' (God's work), consisting of the seven day offices (Lauds, Prime, Terce, Sext, Nones, Vespers, Compline) inspired by the Ps.cxix,164: 'Seven times a day do I praise Thee, because of Thy righteous judgements' to which was added the long night office of Nocturns or Mattins (q.v.).

DOGS

Seem to have been very popular in religious houses, particularly of the later Middle Ages. Nuns kept them as pets but they were only allowed in the stricter orders if they were 'ready barkers used to drive away thieves' from the house. Some laxer houses kept hunting-dogs, sometimes allegedly for the entertainment of distinguished visitors. The Dominicans ('Domini canes') were nicknamed the 'hounds of the Lord'.

DOMINIC, St.

A Castilian aristocrat who became an Austin Canon in 1199. In 1203 he was sent to preach against the Albigensians and he continued in this dangerous work until 1214 when, in view of his lack of success, he decided to found an order aimed at combating heresy by learned preaching and devoutness of life. This, the Order of Preachers, received papal approbation in 1216 and spread rapidly. Dominic died in 1221 and was canonised in 1234. Though less popular than his contemporary and fellow-founder of friars, Francis, he was a man of heroic sanctity whose humility equalled his courage. His followers popularised the rosary as a lay devotion, more or less equivalent to the Divine Office of the clergy.

DOMINICANS

The Order of Friars Preacher, O.P., mendicants and evangelists with a mission to towns, like the Franciscans, but learning was a Dominican ideal, necessary for preaching and controversy — particularly for the rational (as distinct from the forced) conversion of heretics. This order produced the great intellectual systematisers of the Middle Ages: Albert the Great. St Thomas Aquinas, and was much involved in the development of the nascent universities.

They arrived in England about middle of C13 and for administrative purposes they were divided into four 'visitations' centred on London, York, Oxford and Cambridge. There is a dearth of information about their foundations, the dates given in the Gazetteer are those of first mention (the actual foundation is usually a fair time earlier).

Dominican Friar

They had about 60 houses in England and Wales but there are very few material remains. In mediaeval Scotland there were 16 priories and there are material traces of their houses at St Andrews and St Monans. All differed considerably from those of the older orders because of their purpose: base of operations and missionary HQ rather than permanent home. As late-comers they tucked themselves into cramped and often inconvenient sites in the corners of towns and cities. When space permitted they arranged their buildings round a cloister but not necessarily in the traditional order. The church was often separated by a space like a lane and its chapel was adapted to its prime purpose of providing a preaching hall as nave and the friar's section divided by a tower over a passage (e.g. Norwich).

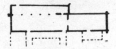

Brecon Friary (Dominican)

They returned in C19 and have about a dozen priories, including a house of studies at Oxford.

DOMINICAN NUNS

Possessed only one house in mediaeval England, though that was a very large one, at Dartford. The Dominican nuns developed into two forms (a) enclosed contemplatives and (b) which was not enclosed and undertakes active work. There are two houses of the former and 30 of the latter in England, Wales and Scotland.

Dominican Nun

DOMUS CONVERSORUM

The 'home of conversi' (q.v.) normally the west range (q.v.) of a Cistercian abbey. Even before their virtual disappearance in C14 the 'conversi' seem to have been troublesome, in some places at least (e.g. Meaux in C13), and therefore their decline may have been viewed with some relief. Their former accommodation was put to new use in C14 e.g. at Hailes it became the abbot's lodging.

DOOR-KEEPER   see *Porter*

DOORWAY

The great western door of the church was rarely used: arrival of new abbot, visit of bishop, royal personage and during procession of Palm Sunday and it does not always exist in an abbey (e.g. Brinkburn, Buildwas, Cartmel, Furness, Romsey).

The general entrance was by two doors from the cloister whose purpose was to facilitate the route of processions but they sometimes had other uses. Sometimes the conversi entered their church from the westernmost one. Sometimes a particular door is ascribed to the superior but this does not imply a monopoly (e.g prior's door at Ely).

Sometimes there was a special entrance to the church for the use of the public, normally in churches which had parochial use. This is sometimes on the north side but more often on west beyond cloister (and equipped with porch for certain lay ceremonies e.g. marriage, churching). Examples at Canterbury, Chester, Gloucester, Malmesbury, Malvern. The north door at Durham was connected with rights of sanctuary and still possesses its sanctuary knocker.

There are fine surviving doorways, apart from those still in use, e.g at Fountains, Holmcultram, Kirkstall, Norton, Strata Florida.

There were of course a large number of interior doorways in the church, giving access to towers, triforium, etc. as well as many piercing the screens which once divided the church into a variety of chapels. As most of these latter were of wood, they rarely survive.

DORTER (Dormitorium)

Dorter

The sleeping-place of the monks. Originally it was a long open hall with bed-heads placed against the longer walls, leaving an aisle down the middle. The beds of the younger monks were interspersed with the older. This communal provision among other things, was intended to give mutual support when they had to rise for Mattins: 'and when they rise for the service of God, they shall exhort each other mutually with moderation, on account of the excuses that those who are sleepy are inclined to make.' (Rule of St Benedict). Regulations required that a light should constantly burn there through the hours of darkness. There were also strict instructions about behaviour in dorter: manner of taking to bed, tidiness, bed-making, consideration for others, modesty, etc. There was strong insistence that it 'ought to be a place of quiet and privacy' and access was strictly limited except for the farmerer and his assistants.

Lamp Niche and Window, Conversi' Dorter, Fountains

The demands of the abbot's office and the relaxation of the original rule led to the abbot withdrawing first to one end of the dorter, then to a separate chamber connected with it by a passage and finally into his own lodging. The developing habit of privacy through the Middle Ages also led to the subdivision of the dorter into wainscotted cubicles each lit by a separate window, approached by a central passage. In the later arrangements at Durham each

Dorter Undercroft Torre

cubicle was equipped with a writing desk at which the monk could work, if he wished, during the afternoon resting period in summer. None of these internal partitions have survived but there are substantial dorter remains at Beeleigh, Cleeve, Durham, Forde, Valle Crucis, Westminster.

In the late Middle Ages, not only the abbot had his own sleeping quarters but the cellarer (for convenience) was allowed to sleep in the farmery. It was the duty of the prior (or the sub-prior in greater priories) to check the dorter, calling each monk by name at his cubicle 'to see good order kept and to check that no-one was missing'.

The dorter was usually carpeted with straw and the beds consisted of straw pallets but St Albans had oak bedsteads in the time of Matthew Paris. The usual 'bed linen' was a mat, a woollen covering, a woollen cloth under the pillow and the pillow itself. The monks slept in their habit apart from the outer garment. The latrines (rere-dorter, q.v.) communicated with the dorter and the dorter was usually provided with night stairs (q.v.) to the church and 'day stairs' (q.v.) to the cloister.

Its position is usually over the eastern cloister range where it gained a little heat from the warming-house (q.v.) beneath but it could be located elsewhere (e.g. Durham where the new dorter was built over the western range, so too at Easby and Worcester).

Cistercian houses had a separate dorter for the conversi which was larger than that of the monks (e.g. Fountains, Rievaulx). There was no dorter in Carthusian houses since the monks slept in their cells. Some Benedictine abbeys (e.g. Canterbury) had two dorters, presumably to accommodate expanded numbers.

DORTER UNDERCROFT

The basement or ground floor which carried the dorter above. Its utilisation was not standardised but generally it had to accommodate the day stairs, the warming-house, a parlour or slype or an inner parlour and a passage to the farmery. It usually contained the vestibule of the chapter-house (sometimes used as a library). At Durham there was a prison and crypt under the old dorter. When the dorter extended beyond the cloister this undercroft was put to various and sometimes unidentifiable use. At Bury it houses the chamberlain, occasionally it was used by the novices (e.g. Peterborough).

DOUBLE ORDERS

A name given to foundations which included both men and women. Sometimes these were basically nunneries served by a small community of chaplains but others consisted of two distinct communities of men and women, within one total enclosure and under a single superior (usually a woman). They generally worshipped under one roof, though the church was walled down the middle, and considerable pains were taken to separate the adjoining convents. This institution was common in early monasticism (see Celtic Monasticism) and Whitby under St Hilda is a famous example but it disappeared with the establishment of Benedictinism. The idea was later revived, first in the order of Fontrevault, then by the Gilbertines and Bridgettines (q.v.).

DOVECOT (Plumbarium)

A dovecot was often provided among the outbuildings of the curia or in the eaves of a major building. Doves and pigeons provided an important and cheap source of meat during the dearth of the mediaeval winter. There are substantial remains of a fine C13 dovecot at Penmon, Anglesey.

Dovecote at Penmon

DRAIN

The draining of the site and the effective flushing of the rere-dorter were important criteria in the choice of a site. The main drain is often notable for its fine masonry even in such a small house as Monk Bretton and its wide substantial construction is the origin of many a legend about secret passages. At Fountains its ramifications and design are a

Monastic Dovecote

constant source of wonder, while at Kirkham its necessary passage has affected the siting of not only the rere-dorter but also of the kitchens, farmery and prior's lodging which follow its course in a quadrant of buildings more than 100 yds long. The great drain usually traverses the site, flowing from the kitchen to the rere-dorter block, sometimes taking in the farmery. The original planners sought an appropriate slope, usually from north west to south east and the explorer might care to check the course of the drain, explain its planning and check the subsidiary water supplies which fed the kitchen, laver, etc.

There were problems of disposal of the water from roofs, used water from lavatorium and kitchen and particularly from farmery. Careful arrangements were made when water was re-used that the more polluting use was lower in the system than the less. The system was maintained by channels, sluices and drains, there are examples of balancing tanks and syphons and one must recognise the skill of the monks as hydraulic and even civil engineers.

DRESSER WINDOW   see also *Rota*

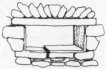

The serving hatch between kitchen and frater, provided with a dresser or serving table on either side for the convenient transfer of dishes and vessels. Sometimes there were two 'dresser windows' side by side. At meal times the caterer was stationed at one side of this hatch and the discarius at the other to see that dishes were served in proper condition, on suitable vessels and in a proper manner. (e.g. Mattersey, Monk Bretton, Muchelney).

Basingwerk Abbey, Kitchen Hatch to Frater

DRINK

Could vary between water, milk, beer and wine. Water seems to have been punitive or penitential, milk medicinal, beer normal and wine either festive or restorative (medicinal).

There was no puritanical element in the Benedictine rule:

'Every man has his proper gift to God; the one in this way, the other in that. We hesitate therefore when we have to decide how much others should eat or drink. Nevertheless, keeping in mind the weakness of the less robust, we think that half a pint of wine a day is sufficient for each. But those on whom God bestows the gift of abstinence must know that they will have a reward. But if local conditions or work, or summer heats demand more, let the abbot decide, taking care that neither surfeit nor drunkenness result. We read, indeed, that wine is no drink for monks: but since nowadays monks cannot be persuaded of this, let us at least agree on this: that we drink sparingly and do not take our fill, for "wine maketh even the wise to fall away".' (Rule, chap.x1).

DRYING ROOM

The Cistercians sometimes had a special drying room or drying house in the south east corner of the cloister. This is thought to have been for the benefit of the conversi who spent so much time in the fields and therefore were likely to be both wet and cold when they returned to their quarters.

DUES

The dues to a monastery included all the normal obligations to a feudal landlord. The dues from a monastery were similarly generally all those required from a feudal lordship but in some cases these were, as a special privilege, commuted, modified or abolished. The Templars were particularly favoured in this respect but the average religious house had little advantage over any other lord in its obligations to the king. Indeed kings had a habit of claiming to be 'founders' of religious houses and claiming considerable rights from this position (especially of board and lodging at all times and the imposition of 'free' corrodies for their servants in the later Middle Ages.) These rights, often claimed by other lay magnates were often indistinguishable from crippling dues.

DUTIES

In a monastic household some duties devolved from position or office (see Obedientiaries), others were allocated from day to day or from week to week. (See Tabula). Though I have come across no examples of demarcation disputes, the exact division of responsibilities could be very precise e.g. the provision of the dorter bell was the duty of the sacrist, but the rope or cord to ring it devolved upon the chamberlain. Similarly, in the tailor's shop, the sub-almoner provided the needles but the sub-chamberlain the thread.

EARLY MASS

Alternatively known as Morrow Mass, Missa Familiaris. It followed Prime and was chiefly intended for servants, work-people and lay brethren. It was taken in turn by priests of the community (except the infirmarian who said mass for the sick in the farmery. Some of the other obedientiaries were also excepted). The duty priest was named on the 'tabula' (q.v.) and it was his responsibility to see to the advance preparation of the altar and other necessities so that there would be no delay in its starting.

During the time of the early mass (usually between six and seven a.m.) the monks in priests' orders said their private masses at one of the many altars in the house, assisted by a junior monk who acted as acolyte or server. When two priests were allocated to the same altar, the senior said mass first. This duplication of masses (arising from over-emphasis of certain doctrinal aspects of the service) is the reason for the development of hagioscopes or squints and the increasing provision of altars.

EASTERN RANGE

Normally adjunct to or continuation of east transept of church. At the point of juncture is often a slype (q.v.) or a library in the Cistercian plan. The slype was often used as the inner parlour though there could be separate provision. Further south was the chapter-house (q.v.) with the warming-house (q.v.) beyond it. The Cistercians sometimes had a vaulted hall in this position whose purpose is not clear. Above these buildings the dorter extended with its day stairs to cloister and night stairs to transept. Adjoining it was the 'necessarium' or the rere-dorter (nicknamed 'tertium dormitorium' at Canterbury) with its position affected by the availability of the main drain (q.v.) On this first floor was often a treasury or muniment room (e.g. Fountains). There is no parlour at Rochester or Wenlock and its position at Westminster is occupied by the chapel of St Faith which can only be entered from the south transept of the church.

EATING   see also *Abstinence, Beer, Bread, Fasting, Food, Frater, Meals*

In the early days the main meal consisted of potage, bread, fish, eggs and sometimes cheese and/or fruit. The original Benedictine rule forebade meat or game except to the sick or infirm but this rule was relaxed at the General-Chapter at Oxford in 1300. Even this relaxation only allowed meat on certain days and never on such fast days as Advent, Lent, Rogation Days and the eves of some festivals.

The Cluniacs, Cistercians and Carthusians maintained the meatless diet longer. The Cistercians never allowing it in the frater and the Carthusians never allowing it at all.

Some information about amounts is available for later Middle Ages e.g. in mid C14 the large community with its dependents at Durham seem to have consumed in one week : 1,000 eggs at 6s.9d., a cartload of whiting at 4s.0d., seven salmon with plaice and smelts at 4s.2d., pork and veal at 9s.0½d., seven sucking pigs, 14 geese, 17 fowls at 7s.4½d.,

Economy

wild fowl at 3s.0d., butter and honey at 10d., 48 fowls at 8s.0d., and 700 eggs. The total cost was about 12s.3d. a day and at this time there were probably about 60 monks, the same number of servants and unnumbered dependents, guests and recipients of charity.

Eggs were generally a substitute for meat and vast quantities appear to have been consumed e.g. in the year 1333/4 the Durham cellarer bought 44,140 but this is only 121 a day i.e. one each for the community and its servants.

In late C15, Winchester provided for one day : two dishes of 'moile' (marrow and grated bread), tripe, beef, mutton, calves feet and 170 eggs. There were about 32 monks at this time and, allowing for dependents, the objection would rather be to unbalance than quantity. The cost was 8s.4d.

ECONOMY

The foundation of a religious house, except in the case of the Mendicants, depended on an endowment calculated to support a community (usually 13 in first instance). This was usually in land and the establishment depended on clearing, developing and exploiting this land by direct labour. Later, direct exploitation was increasingly replaced by a rent economy, supplemented from other sources which could be very varied and might include markets, tolls and appropriated benefices.

Tenant rendering Dues to Steward

The heart of the finances of many houses, not only the Cistercians, lay in its great flocks of sheep.

EDUCATION

In the Dark Ages, the monasteries were centres of education and culture but this was not their purpose which was to be 'schools of Christ', encouraging the spiritual growth of their members under direction and rule. Formal, classical education could be seen not only as pagan but as generally irrelevant as Walter Daniel, the Cistercian biographer of St Ailred and a man of considerable education himself, wrote: 'Our master, Christ, did not

Educating Quire Monks

teach grammar, rhetoric or dialect in the schools; he taught humility, pity and righteousness.'

Nevertheless, the duties of a quire monk required some academic education and this was given during the novitiate and included literary, musical and religious instruction. Later in the Middle Ages, after the rise of the universities, some monasteries maintained houses of study in the universities so their members might pursue higher academic work.

At a lower level, some houses (particularly those situated in towns) provided education for poor children through the almonry (q.v.) and its schools.

Nunneries were particularly prone to taking in school-girls as boarders (usually to supplement the income of poorer houses) in spite of the frequent prohibition of this practice as distracting from their prime function. There were boarders at about 50 houses including: Barking, Burnham, Cambridge, Catesby, Cornworthy, Dartford, Elstow, Esholt, Farewell, Godstow, Grace Dieu, Heynings, Marrick. Norwich, Nunmonkton, Polesworth, Redlington, Romsey, Rosedale, St Helen's Bishopgate, Swaffham Bulbeck, Swine, Thetford, Winchester.

Among the monasteries with almonry schools were Barnwell, Bermondsey, Burton, Bury, Canterbury, Durham, Evesham, St Albans, St Augustine's Westminster.

ELECTION

Superiors of religious houses were elected, other officers were nominated by the superior. When a superior died, some members of the community were delegated to inform the king and obtain his permission to elect a successor. The king usually appointed an interim administrator and issued licence for the community to choose a new head. These preliminaries could sometimes take a long time, particularly if the king was irresponsible or absent from the country. The new superior was often chosen from an experienced member of the community such as the cellarer, prior or sub-prior; sometimes the appointment was under particular pressure from the patron (especially king), sometimes an appointment was made from another community e.g. in 1360 the convent of Winchcombe left the choice of its new abbot to the bishop of Worcester who presented the cellarer from his own abbey.

Abbot's Chair from Evesham

The formal election procedure could theoretically take one of three forms:
(a) acclamation, expressing the unanimous wish of the convent.
(b) proposing 'a short list' (often drawn up by senior members of community) who were then voted on individually, 'per viam scrutinii'.
(c) delegation to an individual (as in case of Worcester above) or to a small number of community to elect on behalf of all. 'per compromissum'.

The founder, his descendant, or the patron was often consulted before any election procedure.

Henry of Blois, Bishop of Winchester, Abbot of Glastonbury, Brother of King

EMPLOYEES & DEPENDENTS   see *Servants*

EMPTOR

The marketing agent of the kitchener. He was a servant of the latter, trusted with the intelligent purchase of provisions and expected to be knowledgeable in regard to the means, substance and timing of the replenishment of kitchen stores.

ENCLOSURE   see also *Curia, Precinct*

The symbolic withdrawal from the world was indicated by actual boundaries and the precinct of a religious house

Gatehouse to Enclosure

was usually marked by an enclosing wall or dyke with a gatehouse to provide admission to the outer court (curia). In this outer enclosure stood various offices or storehouses which might disturb the monastery either by the processes taking place or the necessary communication with the outer world. Beyond the curia was a further enclosure, to which laity were not normally admitted, formed by the buildings round the cloister. Monks were not allowed to leave the claustral enclosure without permission (which was assumed in the case of certain officers).

There was even greater emphasis on the notion of enclosure in the case of nuns and those of Prémontré and Fontrevault were strictly enclosed from their foundation as were the Poor Clares from 1263. A general regulation about the enclosure of nuns was promulgated by Boniface VIII c.1229 and it became effective among the contemplative orders of both sexes.

Countervailing notions of a ministry of good works to the world produced the distinction between 'active' and 'contemplative' orders.

ENGLISH MONASTICISM

Early monastic life was extinguished in the greater part of the country by the Danish invasions which, inter alia, destroyed Jarrow, Monkwearmouth, Whitby and set the monks of Lindisfarne on a long trek with their most precious possession — the body of St Cuthbert. Revival began tentatively under Odo, Archbishop of Canterbury (942-59) and prevailed under his successor Dunstan with the powerful assistance of King Edgar, Oswald Archbishop of York and Ethelwold Bishop of Winchester. Monks were introduced to Worcester and abbeys established at Evesham, Pershore, Winchcombe and elsewhere in the diocese. Ramsey was founded in 971 and a few years later the abbot of the reformed and reforming Fleury was persuaded to visit England to give his advice and assistance. Destroyed monsteries were reconstituted (e.g. Ely, Peterborough) and failing abbeys (e.g. Glastonbury) were reinvigorated.

Monkwearmouth

This revival was ended by the disasters of early C11 but Cnut and Edward the Confessor were notable monastic benefactors (the latter founded Westminster). The lasting dominance of monasticism followed the Norman Conquest and was initiated by William's thank-offering of Battle, shortly followed by Selby and many other Benedictine foundations. The most notable agents of the Norman reform and revival were Lanfranc and Anselm, both Benedictines.

After the Benedictines followed the Cluniac and Cistercian reforms (the latter being particularly attractive to the inhabitants of the north of England), the development of the Mendicants and the foundations of chantries and colleges. In all these developments, England played its full part and contributed names of European significance; Alexander of Hayles, Roger Bacon, Stephen Harding and others. There was also a fine school of English mysticism and the country produced some notable spiritual writers: Ailred, Richard Rolle of Hampole, the authors of the Ancren Riwle, the Cloud of Unknowing, and Walter Hilton (to name but the most outstanding),

After a continuous history of nearly 1,000 years, English monasticism was substantially destroyed by Henry VIII but the life returned later and even affected the church which he founded.

ENGLISH ORDERS

Though England only produced one religious order in the Middle Ages (the Gilbertines who eventually died out in spite of an unsuccessful attempt at revival in modern times), it has been more successful since, significantly among women. It is an interesting fact that in mediaeval religious life men far exceeded women and the position is now reversed. Among the modern English orders might be listed those of the Cross and Passion (1852), Carmelites of Corpus Christi (1908), Sisters of Charity of St Paul (1847), Institute of B.V.M. (1609).

EREMITE   see also *Anchorite, Hermit*

An ambiguous term which, particularly in C11 and 12, was used indiscriminately of individuals in coenobitic monasteries in the country, of the inhabitants of grouped hermitages, of isolated hermits attached to a monastery and of hermits who had no connection with any other hermit or with any institution.

Nevertheless, words like 'eremus', 'eremita', 'solitudo', 'vita solitaria' seem always in C11 and 12 to refer to rural monasticism (as opposed to urban), characterised by withdrawal from civilisation and by emphasis on a simple, poor and austere manner of life.

ESTATES   see also *Granges*

Land was the normal form of endowment and the basis of the material existence of a religious house. As the land of a benefactor was scattered, so the estates of a monastery might be at a considerable distance (though good superiors, like other landlords, tried to consolidate their holdings.) Possession of land by a religious house normally involved all the obligations of any other feudal landlord.

Generally speaking, initial land grants were a waste and only made profitable by hard and long continued work on them. Some land remained waste and was used for rough pasture, turf-cutting, hay, wood-gathering. The other was gradually brought into cultivation by laborious clearing, draining, ploughing and marling. Arable land was sometimes held jointly by a religious house and its tenants and farmed according to normal mediaeval practice, including customary service. Later tenants fell into two classes: money-tenants and service-tenants. The former ('censarii') paid a money rent instead of giving their labour but they still had some service obligations such as finding oxen to help with ploughing and providing extra hands at harvest-time, etc. The latter ('villeins') usually held two bovates or ploughlands in return for two days service a week, providing cartage when necessary, ploughing twice a year and reaping thrice, together with many occasional charges in kind.

The religious seem to have been rather more humane in their treatment of poorer tenants than the average lay landlord but their innate conservatism produced some disadvantages to their tenants. They seem to have been particularly generous in their provision of free food at harvest etc. (It has been estimated that at e.g. Battle the liberal dispensation of food exceeded in value that of the labour returned). Until C13 or thereabouts there was a bottom class of serfs or slaves who could be bought, sold or given away and such existed on monastic land as elsewhere. Recent research seems to indicate that the accusation made of Cistercians that they depopulated their land to provide sheep runs or granges is ill-founded.

Estates were usually managed by a steward or bailiff, sometimes assisted by under-bailiffs, though religious houses sometimes established a cell on distant property to supervise it. The estates of Cistercian houses could be vast, the distance of Fountains fell from Fountains Abbey is some indication. The acreage of the Meaux granges varied in size from 85 at Sutton to nearly 1500 at Skerne, totalling 6,056 divided among 13 granges. An average lowland grange in Yorkshire possessed between 300 and 500 acres, an area probably similar to that of an average Benedictine one.

EVENSONG

The English name of the monastic office of Vespers.

EXEMPTION   see also *Jurisdiction, Visitation*

Normally the bishop of the diocese in which a religious house was situated was its visitor and ultimate authority. Appeals could be made to the pope, as in most matters, from his judgment or actions.

Monastic houses, particularly male, became increasingly exempt from this diocesan control: whole orders (Cistercians, Cluniacs, Premonstratensians, Gilbertines) were under the jurisdiction of their mother house which appointed regular visitors. Apart from these, great Benedictine houses (e.g. Bury, Evesham, St Albans, Westminster) on one ground or another claimed exemption and would only receive papal visitors. In C13, the mendicant orders, as international bodies, became independent from local control and were visited by representatives of their order. Other religious houses individually obtained the privilege of exemption at great expense from the pope, though the privilege saved other expenses.

EXENNIA

Small tokens of affectionate remembrance which, in later Middle Ages, monks were allowed to send four times a year to their relatives and friends. These were obtained from the cellarer.

EXPENDITURE

The outgoings of a great house could include board and lodgings for community upkeep and extension of buildings, alms and hospitality. In addition there were the wages and/or board of servants and employees and the necessary expenditure on appropriated churches and vicarages, maintenance, repairs and salary. There was also considerable demand from distant property of other kinds: granges, mills, farm buildings, etc. Then there was a group of feudal obligations including knights' fees, ordinary and extraordinary taxation, forced loans and compulsory corrodies for retired royal servants, together with benefices demanded by king, pope, or patron for their nominees. There could be sequestration of income during a vacant abbacy, sometimes artificially prolonged for the benefit of the king. There were the normal legal fees, involved in appointments and land transactions, which could be very heavy apart from abnormal fees resulting from disputes, appeals and the vindication of challenged rights. Apart from the legal costs there were the expenses of travelling to courts (which could be at Rome) and on monastic and royal business. There were the expenses of General-Chapters, of provincial chapters and visitations and the losses due to natural disasters such as flood, murrain and disease of men and stock. There were also the losses due to riot, civil disorder and outright war, endemic on the borders of Scotland and Wales and sometimes much further afield (Bolton was sacked by Scottish raiders in 1316).

As a result of such expenses (particularly hospitality) and losses, a house could become so impoverished that its resources scarcely sufficed for the minimum subsistence of its community. (Many houses were inadequately endowed from the beginning). By the end of C14, even Winchcombe e.g. had been brought to a dangerous degree of poverty by 'compulsory ceaseless hospitality, costly lawsuits, barren lands, services and rents reduced to almost half by deaths of tenants and servants in the pestilence, the ruin that had befallen the monastery and its manors in frightful gales and by dilapidation and the various corrodies anddebts.'
(G. Haigh).

EXTRA-CLAUSTRAL BUILDINGS

Usually applied to the immediate buildings of the abbey, particularly those in the curia, as distinct from the ranges round the cloister. These latter followed a more or less uniform pattern but the buildings outside these ranges are more haphazard and their siting is often related to convenience. They included the farmery from the beginning as well as the guest-house, to which were soon added the superior's lodging, bakehouse, brewhouse mill etc. These had usually been built or rebuilt in stone by the end of the Middle Ages but there were always additional structures, including a variety of sheds, offices, stores and workshops which remained in wood and often have left no trace above ground.

FAMILY

Popular name for religious community, which often consisted of a superior and twelve brethren in imitation of Christ and his apostles. The abbot was the father of the family and stood in the place of Christ; on these grounds he was to receive respect and complete obedience but, according to the rule, he was to be democratically elected.

In spite of its feudal background the monastery remained democratic in principle: there was to be no favouritism and no class distinction. The only distinction that Benedict was prepared to tolerate was excellence in good works and/or obedience. Otherwise slave and noble were equal in the community. In fact, the requirements of literacy tended to bring about a predominance of 'upper' or 'middle class' (on the grounds of education rather than birth) and the leaders in religious and in national life tended to come from the same families.

FARMERY   (Infirmary)   see also *Illness, Medicine, Pharmacy*
    'Before all else and above all else must come the care of the sick, so that the
service may be rendered to them which is in truth rendered to Christ, for He said : "I
was sick and ye visited Me" and, "What ye have done to one of these little ones, ye
have done to Me." ' (Benedict: Rule, chap.xxxvi). The old monks, on account of
their infirmity, were to be treated with particular indulgence and Benedict has a
short chapter on the special consideration to be given them. The farmery had its own
kitchen where 'more subtle and delicate meats' could be
prepared for the benefit of the aged, sick and convalescent.
In C14 this amenity became more generally used and the
farmery frater or 'misericord' (q.v.) became the normal
eating place of the community on the increased number of
permitted 'flesh days'. At Fountains this dining hall was
positioned between the farmery and the abbot's lodging.

    The developed monastic farmery was a religious house
in miniature with dorter, chapel, frater and sometimes its
own cloister where the religious life could be fully
maintained, howbeit with some relaxation of rigour in view
of the age or health of its inmates. They were provided with
a fire, given special diets including meat and permitted a
modified office. The occupants fell into three classes:

Infirmary Passage,
Canterbury

1. The 'sempectae' 'stagiarii' or 'stationarii' —monks
    who had been professed for 50 years and whose age
    both required and deserved the better food, warmth
    and personal attention provided by the farmery.
    Perhaps we should include in this class the rare
    examples of retired superiors. Normally only death
    brought retirement but there were cases of heads of
    households being relieved of their duties on grounds of
    the intolerable burden of office or age or sickness (e.g.
    Richard de Idbury, abbot of Winchcombe, retired in
    1340).

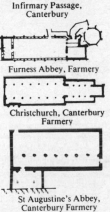

Furness Abbey, Farmery

Christchurch, Canterbury
Farmery

2. The sick, for whom careful provision was made in all
    rules and customaries.
3. Those who were recuperating from the regular bleeding
    (q.v.) At Ely there was a weekly 'minutio' which monks
    attended every seven weeks. The 'minuti' usually
    stayed in the farmery for three days.

St Augustine's Abbey,
Canterbury Farmery

    The farmery complex usually lay east of the cloister, away from the noise of the
curia. Its essential parts were the hall and its chapel, its own kitchen to provide more
delicate and nourishing food, the frater or misericord where meat eating was
allowed, and accommodation for the master of the farmery and his staff. The latter
might include a physician and nurses.
    Apart from the care of its own, religious houses seem to have extended the care
of sick and infirm beyond their walls, particularly remote Cistercian abbeys, e.g.
Fountains, Jervaulx, and Roche. Durham had a second infirmary 'without the south
gate' and the infirmary at Castle Acre (whose chapel altar still partly stands)
provided the last care for the sick and dying heading for Walsingham. The present
parish church at Ramsey may have originally been the hall of the abbey's extern
farmery, serving travellers and possibly also accommodating the 13 poor boys
maintained at the abbey.
    Charterhouses did not possess a farmery, caring for the sick in their private cells
until they rejoined the austere life or were buried coffinless in the cloister-garth.
    The farmeries originally took the same form as a mediaeval hospital (q.v.),
similar to a simple church plan where the nave formed the hall and the chancel

contained the chapel. Great houses (e.g. Canterbury, Christchurch, Ely, Peterborough) had grand farmeries of this type. There were less grandiose farmeries at Norwich and Canterbury St Augustine, and there was a tendency for later farmeries to have unaligned chapels which were not necessarily part of the hall. Sometimes the farmery buildings were grouped round a cloister (e.g Waverley, Winchester). Ely had a similar plan but also retained the old hall. The vast aisled hall of the main farmery at Fountains had a complex water supply and highly sophisticated draining arrangements. Beds were placed with their heads to the long walls, there was usually a central fireplace around which meals were sometimes taken. There was a tendency to break up this draughty communal space by separating it into single cubicles or 'private wards', sometimes provided with individual fireplaces. The baths were often placed near the farmery (e.g Canterbury). Obedientiaries tended to find accommodation near the farmery (e.g. Bardney, Durham, Ely). Similar provision was sometimes made for retired superiors (e.g. Meaux).

The later farmeries were uniform neither in plan nor location. The halls at Furness and Jervaulx are a reversion to the earliest plan, while Thetford had a series of small chambers ranged round three sides of a small cloister with the hall and chapel occupying the fourth. At Rievaulx and Tintern the farmery shared a small cloister with the dorter range and rere-dorter. At Wenlock an aisle-less hall was built beyond east range in C12 to which a large east wing, of two floors containing a chapel and prior's lodging was added in C15. Easby has a wide arch from the farmery hall to the chapel to enable the bed-ridden to join in the services.

The Cistercians had separate farmeries for their conversi, usually in the form of an aisled hall with a north south axis, placed near their rere-dorter (e.g Fountains, Jervaulx, Roche).

The position was always related to isolation and water-supply and it was usually connected to the main group of buildings by a covered passage or pentise. At Haughmond (substantial remains) it was south of the frater, at Easby north of the church, at Durham and Worcester it was on west side of cloister, at Canterbury and Gloucester (where there are ruins of the hall) it was attained from a lesser cloister; at Jervaulx and Netley it seems to have been under the dorter. Where the infirmary was west of cloister the access was by a passage in east range next to chapter-house or through an isolated bay of dorter undercroft.

There are substantial remains of the farmeries at e.g. Canterbury, Ely, Gloucester, Peterborough, (archdeacon's house encloses hall of late C12 farmery), St Dogmael's.

FARMING

Apart from the educational and cultural work of the early Benedictines, perhaps the most important secular contribution made by monasticism was in the development of agriculture (where the Cistercians were pioneers and innovators, see Grange). 'A new "scientific" agriculture began with the Cistercians and their imitators, and it is to their initiative that we owe, among other things, the first establishment of many of those great farms on the hills and in the flood-plains of our rivers that have survived intact as

Farming

units to this day. Here, indeed, is the lasting significance of the entire grange experiment. It led naturally in the next (thirteenth) century to an era of high farming that was itself a peak and turning-point in mediaeval society, the genesis, through its accompanying urban and commercial expansion, of the world we are familiar with today.' (C. Platt)

FASTING   see also *Abstinence*

The reduction of food and drink, as an act of penitence, mortification and self-control. Besides individual fasts undertaken out of private devotion, the mediaeval church imposed on all, except the very young and very old, a variety of fasts which alternated with the feasts of the liturgical year including the seasons of Advent and Lent.

FEASTS

Festival, fiesta originated in the joyful celebration of Christian mysteries and the devotion in particular places to patronal saints. In mediaeval monasteries, there were five great feasts: Christmas, Easter and Pentecost (Whit Sunday) together with the Assumption (kept as their patronal festival in Cistercian houses) and the feast of patron (e.g. St Cuthbert at Durham, St Alban at St Albans, St Edmund at Bury, St Edwin at Evesham, St Peter at Westminster, etc.). When the Assumption was kept as the patronal festival (as in Cistercian and other houses dedicated to St Mary), the feast of St Peter and St Paul seems to have been included among the five great rejoicings.

Mazer used at feasts

On such days there was great ceremony and the whole house strove to do honour to the occasion. The entire church was decorated, the finest furnishings were placed on the altars, the best vestments were brought out, the whole house was 'spring cleaned' on the vigil, seats were draped, and floor coverings renewed. There was more elaborate music, much ringing of bells, multiplication of lights and incense, longer services and shorter chapter. There were festal tablecloths and table decorations, soft towels to replace the rough usual ones and an improvement in food.

Feretory of St Alban
carried in Festal Procession

Other solemn festivals, less exalted than the above, celebrated in convents included Epiphany (Jan 6), Candlemass (Feb 2), St Gregory (March 12), Annunciation (March 25), Ascension, St Augustine (May 26), St John Baptist (June 24), Nativity BVM (Sep 8), Michaelmas (Sep 29), All Saints (Nov 1), St Andrew (Nov 30). St Benedict

Cook

was feasted on July 11 (the day of his Translation) since his commemoration on March 21 always fell in Lent. In this group came the celebration of local saints such as that of St Alphege at Canterbury, the commemoration of the church's dedication, the Octaves of Easter and Pentecost.

There were also feasts of the third rank, kept with three lessons or nocturns instead of six or nine of the greater festivals, which included the Conversion of St Paul, St Vincent, SS Philip and James, the Finding of the Cross, St James the Less, St Peter's Keys, St Lawerence, St Bartholomew, St Augustine of Hippo, Beheading of St John the Baptist, the Exaltation of the Cross, St Matthew, SS Simon and Jude, St Martin, St Thomas the Apostle, and many others.

A variety of other days brought distinct rites and ceremonies to the round of offices: the first Sunday of Advent, Septuagesima, the first Sunday of Lent, Midlent Sunday, Palm Sunday, Rogation Days, etc.

There were other celebrations such as those at the reception of a visitor, the installation of a new superior and minor occasions such as jubilees of profession, the keeping of 'O's, the cellarer's feast, etc.

FERETORY

A saint's tomb above ground level, hence a shrine or a chapel containing a shrine for relics. These were originally placed in a crypt built for the purpose, but convenience, and a growing cult of relics, led to their elevation into the church proper, and the erection of costly shrines for their reception, usually placed in a bay behind the altar (as at Winchester and Durham where some remains of the feretory survive). This chapel or shrine was usually separated from the presbytery by an elaborate screen behind the High Altar (e.g. St Albans, Durham) and was approached by doorways in the screen and/or processional paths (aisles, ambulatory).

FERETRAR

An assistant to the sacrist, occasionally found in religious houses possessing a shrine or major relic (e.g. Durham), who was responsible for the care and custodianship of the shrine and its associated treasures.

FEUDAL OBLIGATIONS

For three centuries after Norman Conquest, great abbeys, like other major tenants had to provide knight service to the king for their holdings. C11 Ely was responsible for 40 soldiers with their full equipment, Barking nunnery was held at 13 knights' fees and as late as C14 the abbess of Romsey had to provide military contingents in Edward II's causes at home and abroad. In the reign of Henry II, the abbot of Peterborough had to provide and equip 60 knights, while his brother at Bury was responsible for 40. This responsibility was at variance with the nature of a religious house and eventually it was replaced by 'scutage', a cash commutation. In C12, the abbot of Bury owed the service of 50 knights or the equivalent in scutage. He also contributed 7s every 20 weeks for 'castle-guard' at Norwich and 20s p.a. to its watchman as 'wayte-fee'. Even in the late Middle Ages the abbot of Selby was in personal combat against the Scots and the aged abbot Littlington of Westminster volunteered for service against the French in 1386. The titular abbot of Durham was a secular prince, ruling a county palatine, and much involved in warfare against the Scots when the holy banner of St Cuthbert was frequently carried in the van.

25 abbots in England ranked as barons which not only implied knight service but attendance at parliament with all the consequent absence from their houses and involvement in secular affairs. This function should be related to the development of separate accommodation for religious superiors.

FILIATION

The reproduction of monasteries by a 'cell' or 'hive' of a mother house (usually of 12 monks and superior). The daughter ('filia') was independent but visited by superior of founding community. Characteristic of Cistercians (q.v.).

FINANCE   see also *Cellarer, Expenditure, Income, Sacrist*

The administration of monastic finance, like monasticism itself, was traditional and of slow growth. Many attempts were made to improve it but without much success. The revenues of a particular obedientiary became looked upon as almost personal and quite independent of the general fund. At times of stress, money might be transferred from one account to another but any attempt at external interference or amalgamation was viewed with suspicion. In their attempt to 'modernise' the system, visitors introduced the bursar through whose hands they intended that all the revenues should pass but tradition won, the obedientiaries kept their own accounts and the bursar merely gained control of revenues which were not already appropriated to specific objects. The autocratic power of the abbot could be disastrous when he was financially obtuse, imprudent or dishonest. Although he was given his own account, he ultimately controlled those of every department.

Debts were met by borrowing, forward selling or granting of corrodies but such expedients tended to aggravate the situation. More effective procedures could

include petitions to the king, including request for
protection against the abuse of hospitality by the powerful.
Sometimes the king appointed his steward as financial
administrator (so at Flaxley in 1277) or another prudent
administrator (q.v.) was appointed to clear the debts and
sort out the finances.

Financial problems seem to have had four chief causes:

1. Inadequate initial endowment
2. Demands of 'hospitality'
3. 'Natural disaster' — fire, flood, murrain
4. Overcommitment in building.

Finance

The monasteries, of course, did what they could in the way of self-help, reducing
expenditure, making economies, modifying the buildings, etc.

Apart from the problems mentioned above and under Expenditure there were
also cases of robbery and brigandage (especially in C14) when bands of armed men
attacked monasteries and feudal lords used force to acquire land and privileges.
These civil disturbances resulted in the fortification (q.v.) of some monasteries.

FIRES, PROVISION

Originally there were only three fires in the monastery enclosure: the warming-
house (q.v.), the necessary fire in the kitchen and an indulgent fire in the farmery.
Some extern buildings had this provision such as the blacksmith's shop out of
necessity and the guest-house out of charity. Later the superior's hall might be
heated on analogy with the guest-house but with relaxation of the rule and greater
domestic comfort in the external world fireplaces proliferated in religious houses as
well, often as a result of modifying the usage of buildings when the numbers
declined.

Small rooms with fireplaces, often in a row or an apparent suite probably
indicate accommodation for corrodians who were not bound to the rigours of the
religious house.

FISH

A plentiful supply of fish was essential for the monastic
diet and wherever possible the monks secured fishing rights.
Chester maintained a boat on the Dee and had a ship and
ten nets off Anglesey and tithes of some of the best fisheries
in the county. Vale Royal let its weirs at Warford on the
river Weaver and received '48 strikes of eels and 12 large
eels' each year. Titchfield had rights on the Meon and
St Dogmaels on the Teifi while the fishing rights in the
great mere of Skipsea were hotly contested between York
and Meaux and decided in trial by battle. Some great
houses maintained a cell or quasi-grange as a fishing H.Q.
located on the coast or inland e.g. Glastonbury's C14 fish-
house at Meare which still stands was built to exploit the
fishing in the Somerset marshes. The nuns of St
Radegund's had rights in a part of the Cam which long
retained its name of 'nunneslake'.

Income in kind from
Fishermen

In addition to this use of natural waters, monasteries followed the normal
mediaeval practice in a great house of constructing and stocking artificial fish-ponds
or hatcheries close to their precincts. These often survive or, even when dry, their
earthworks are recognisable (e.g. Buckland, Fountains, Thornton).

Besides fresh fish, a great deal of dried or salted fish was eaten. Monastic stores
also kept supplies of the dried cod known as stockfish. For Lent the chief articles of
food were herrings and salt salmon but lists show an impressive variety of fish. In
C16 Syon was eating fish from Scarborough and Iceland and the cellarers records
mention ling, cod, salmon, white and red herring, eels and 'muddefissh'.

FONTREVAULT

Apart from the Celtic monasteries, this was earliest formal order embracing men and women in 'double monasteries'. It arose from the monastic renaissance of C12 (about 1100) in the French abbey from which the order took its name. It consisted of a 'double order' of monks and nuns under the rule of an abbess based on a rigorous and austere development of the Benedictine rule. There were five houses of this order in England which were classed as 'alien priories'. One of these foundations only survived a few years and the others became Benedictine nunneries about the turn of fourteenth to fifteenth century. The order influenced the later constitution of the Gilbertine order (q.v.) and there are survivals of the church at Amesbury and other remains incorporated in a secular building at Nuneaton.

FOOD

Monastic food varied according to the austerity of the order, the season and the date (with a general increase in quantity and quality as the Middle Ages progressed) though the Carthusians and Observant friars maintained their vigour to the end. Even when the brethren restricted themselves, they were generous to their guests, providing a different menu from a separate kitchen and in many places the food in the guest-house was both excellent and lavish.

Milking Sheep for Cheese (Wensleydale)

The communities had little luxuries on celebratory days (see 'Pittance',) which later developed, in some places, into veritable feasts. Conversely there was the unpleasant and boring Lenten fare (q.v.) which extended to all fast days. At other times of the year in the later period convents ate fresh fish (when they could get it) or dried or salt-fish (q.v.) and on meat days either beef or some form of pig's flesh: pork, bacon or 'sowce' (pickled pork). Mutton was seldom eaten as mediaeval sheep were scraggy creatures kept for wool rather than meat. This diet was supplemented by milk-products, eggs and poultry and, of course, bread and beer (qq.v.). There were also seasonal foods such as pancakes on Shrove Tuesday, dried peas ('carlings') on Care Sunday (Passion Sunday), etc.

The food supply was the responsibility of the cellarer's department but its supply could be affected by dearth, mismanagement, and 'accidents' varying from crop failure to destruction by raiders.

Various kitchen bills have been preserved from early C16 which give information about food in the last years of the houses' existence e.g. at Winchester on Good Friday 1515, there was harburden, red herrings, minnows, and mustard! On the feast of Easter the menu included spiced vegetables, meat-pudding, eggs, venison, fish ground with crumbs, broth, open tarts, beef and mutton. At Dover in 1530 the cellarer received in one week: mutton, lamb, geese and capons, oysters (which then were a cheap and proletarian dish), plaice, whelks, salt salmon, fresh fish, butter and eggs.

FOOT WASHING

Apart from the requirements of hygiene, foot washing was given ritual significance in convents in the ceremony of the Mandatum (see Maundy).

FOOTWEAR

Included boots, shoes, (q.v.), sandals and slippers, depending on the order and the work being done. Every order included some ascetics who went bare-foot (discalced).

Washing Beggar's Feet

FORMATION   see also *Office, Divine*
The purpose of the religious life was spiritual formation and edification. The main instrument in this process was the Bible as it was used and commented upon in many activities:

(a)   The liturgy, the formal prayer of the church consisting of
  1.   The office, or opus Dei, which essentially is a monthly recitation of the psalter with interspersed Bible readings.
  2.   The mass which contains a variety of psalms and lections (chiefly from the New Testament).
(b)   Chapter and collation included readings and the main meals in the frater were taken in silence to meditate better on the accompanying reading.
(c)   Private reading and spiritual conversation. Monastic books are sprinkled with Biblical quotation and allusion. Much labour was spent in their study and teasing out the historical, moral and mystical meaning. Opportunities were provided for discussion of problems, for confession and absolution and for spiritual direction.
(d)   Sermons and homilies which were not only preached at mass, but given in chapter, at visitations and conferences and introduced into the offices as commentary. Ailred wrote an exegesis of Lk.xi,33 for the benefit of the monks at Westminster, applying it to St Edward, to be read on his feast day there. (St Ailred's biographer reckons that his subject preached about 200 sermons in monastic chapters, clerical synods and assemblies of the laity).

FORTIFICATION
Originally religious houses relied on their spiritual status as protection. Holmcultram, near the Scottish border, pointed out that 'the precincts of the monks' houses and granges . . . like cemeteries and churches are all by apostolic authority to be free and undisturbed by any invasion, terror or violence.' But papal declaration was not much defence against the Scots and in 1235 the house received royal permission to arm their servants with bows and arrows in defence of their home and property. Later, they raised a small castle close to their grange at Raby. In troublous times and districts other houses sought the help of lay lords and their forces (see Commendator).
Most monastic sites had a wall or ditch with a gatehouse but this was primarily for enclosure and protection against wild animals and sometimes secondarily to drain and improve site. But in unsettled times and regions monasteries acquired substantial fortifications: Newminster supplied peles on its estates at West Ritton, Greenleighton and Nunnikirk and castles at Carrycoats, Rytton and Filton. Tynemouth was a monastery within a castle and its dependencies were also fortified: Hebburn and Elswick. There are strong towers on the islands of Coquet and Farne and strong points at Carlisle, Cartmel and Lanercost. The tower at Dalton was an outpost of Furness, Titlington of Kirkham and Carrow of Hexham. Tweedmouth was a fortified annexe of Kepier hospital, Kirkoswald possessed a fortified 'college' as did Mettingham in Suffolk.
Many monastic gatehouses were free-standing strongpoints: Alnwick, Bury, Thornton, etc. but perhaps the best examples of a totally defended site are Tynemouth, Ewenny, Lanercost and Hulne.

FOUNDATION
The prescribed minimum number for an independent foundation was a community of 12 plus a superior, with an endowment to support them and a site on which to settle. Foundations were often planned to be much larger than this but the numbers varied considerably e.g. Battle was intended for 60, Canterbury, Christchurch for 150, Crowland had 58 in 1076, Beaulieu was founded for 30,

Founders

Peterborough had 110 in 1240, Fountains and Rievaulx numbered their inmates in hundreds within a score of years of their foundation, Westminster was planned for 50, St Albans was limited to 100 in C12, Ely was planned for 70 in C12 and Bath had over 40 in early C13.

Obviously numbers were related to size of endowment and successful management as well as number of vocations.

Thurstan of Fountains

FOUNDERS see also *Benefactors*

Ela, widow of William Longspee founded both Hinton charterhouse and the Austin house at Lacock. She retired to the latter and was abbess there until her death in 1261. It was not unusual for founders to join the community that they had established but not necessarily as superior e.g. Robert Fitzharding probably ended his life as an Austin Canon at Bristol and more than one Cistercian founder or benefactor ended his life as an obscure monk or lay brother. Walter L'Espec, founder of both Kirkham and Rievaulx ended his days as a humble monk at the latter in 1154. Much earlier, Ethelreda after founding Hexham in C7 became a nun at Coldingham before becoming abbess of her later foundation at Ely.

Great houses required wealthy and aristocratic founders but hospitals needed less resources. Nevertheless the highest in the land were among their instigators: Lanfranc founded hospitals at Canterbury and Harbledown; Gundulf a lazar-house near Rochester, Queen Maud, wife of Henry I, was a devoted friend and supporter of lepers and Henry himself founded a number of hospitals. Stephen and his wife Matilda founded or substantially benefited hospitals at London and York respectively. Richard founded a hospital at Stroud and a number of lazar-houses are attributed to John while Henry III founded or refounded a number of hospitals.

One of the greatest royal founders was David I of Scotland (q.v.) who settled Cistercians at Newbattle, Haddington, North Berwick, Dundrennan.

Founders were sometimes buried in the church e.g. Arbroath, St Dogmaels.

Canute presenting Cross to New Minsters Abbey

Matilda's Hospital, London

FOURTEENTH CENTURY

Often categorised as a period of religious decline. It was certainly a time of religious crisis, largely induced by the catastrophic experience of the Black Death (q.v.). There was a change of religious sentiment and the characteristic foundations were no longer monasteries or even friaries but chantries, chantry colleges, almshouses and the like. There were, however, rare foundations of the older type e.g. Haltemprice ('Haute Emprise') Yorkshire E.R. (no remains) and Kirkby Bellars, Leicestershire. Both these were Augustinian and A.H. Thompson remarks that 'between a house of Austin Canons and a college of chantry-priests there was no great difference'. The other notable exception to the contemporary trend is the foundation by Edward III in 1353 of St Mary Graces on the edge of London — the only new house of Cistercian order in C14.

FRANCIS

The apostle of poverty, taking Matt.x, 7-19 as a personal call. He attracted followers and sought papal approbation of a simple rule for them in 1209. In his humility he called them the 'little brothers', hence their formal designation as order of Friars Minor. His followers increased and included the noble Clare who founded a similar society for women (Poor Clares). By 1217 the Franciscan order was so large that it had to be organised into provinces and Francis, unhappy about some developments, resigned the leadership in 1220. Shortly afterwards he founded the Tertiaries for those adopting his ideals as far as possible within the context of an ordinary life. About this time the pope approved a more definite and settled rule which brought the friars closer to traditional orders. Francis received the stigmata in a vision in 1224, died in 1226 and was canonised in 1228.

His total devotion to absolute poverty was evaded among his followers by a nice distinction between owning and possessing, though they continued to exist on alms and never acquired great wealth. Francis declared, 'I desired and willed that, in accordance with the example of my Lord, my little brothers should pray more than they read' yet his followers became scholars and university teachers and produced such men as Bonaventura and Duns Scotus.

FRANCISCANS, Minorites, O.F.M.

The ideal of complete poverty proved impractical but it was maintained by 'Spirituals' until 1318 when corporate ownership was accepted by the whole order. The problem of poverty resurfaced particularly after the Black Death and Great Schism had led to decline and laxity. The Observants led a reform and they separated from the less strict Conventuals in the early C15. A further reform led to the Capuchins in 1529 but they did not reach pre-Reformation England.

The original Franciscans arrived in 1224 and made settlements in Canterbury, London and Oxford. (One of these, John Peckham, was archbishop of Canterbury from 1279-92). At first they captured the popular imagination but after about a century they suffered a partial eclipse in public favour and made few new foundations after mid C14.

They had about 50 houses, organised in 'custodies,' of which there are very few remains. Because of the nature of the friar's (q.v.) vocation they usually occupied cramped town sites. The superior of a house was usually called warden. Their churches were simple and designed for preaching, of which there are remains at Coventry, Lincoln, Reading and Yarmouth, rather less survives of their houses at Canterbury, Cardiff, Chichester, Gloucester, Kings Lynn, Lichfield, Richmond and Winchelsea. Some other fragments are absorbed in secular buildings at Shrewsbury, Walsingham and Ware. In Scotland there were eight friaries established in the Middle Ages of which material traces survive at Inverkeithing and Kirkcudbright.

The Observants were introduced by Henry VII and had houses at Canterbury, Greenwich, Newark, Newcastle, Richmond Surrey and Southampton. Nearly all were arrested under his son and imprisoned in appalling conditions from which about a third soon died. There are some remains of their house at Canterbury. The Observants reached Scotland half a century before England and eventually had nine houses of which there are remains only at Elgin.

The Friars Minor returned and the Capuchins arrived in C19 and currently have more than 50 houses. The Church of England has a community of men and another of women, inspired by the Franciscan ideal.

FRANCISCAN NUNS

In the Middle Ages there only seem to have been five houses in England, though all were fairly substantial with the rank of abbey. There are scant material remains in Denney and London. English Poor Clares were refounded in Brussels (1621) as cloistered contemplatives and returned to England (where they have two houses) in recent times. There are a number of modern orders of active Franciscan nuns with about 50 houses in Great Britain.

FRATER   (Refectorium)

The common dining-room where behaviour and food were governed by strict rules. The monks arrived in procession, washed at the nearby laver (q.v.), took their places in order, sang a grace and then ate in silence while a reader (appointed for a week) read aloud from the pulpit. A bell rang to indicate the end of the meal after which grace was sung, the departed remembered and the monks left in ordered procession. Whether it was a 'two meal' day or a fast day, the frater was to be a place of order, decorum and edification, dominated by the image of Christ and sounding only to the reader's voice from its pulpit (q.v.). Cleanliness is specially emphasized in all the customaries and the fraterer (q.v.) was directed to add to the atmosphere by strewing fresh rushes, supplying flowers and strong-smelling herbs to make an agreeable scent. In summer he was to supply fans or fly-flaps ('muscatorias'). Courteous hospitality allowed some relaxation of the strict rule of silence. 'if it be desirable to say anything by reason of the presence of guests, it must be done sparingly and in a low tone'. But the diners were also reminded, (e.g. in Barnwell Observances) 'Let not only your mouth take in food but let your ears too be hungry for the Word of God, wherefore, if anything be wanted, it should be asked for by a sign rather than by word of mouth'.

Nuns in Frater

There was generally a high table ('mensa major') on a dais where the abbot, prior or sub-prior presided at its 'upper end' and to which he invited guests. The other tables were placed at right angles in the body of the hall with the youngest members of the community placed nearest the door. Novices sat at a separate table presided over by the novice-master. Sometimes this was partitioned off or placed in a separate room. They had their own reader, provided from among themselves, who read aloud (usually from the Latin Bible) during their silent meal. Another novice was appointed to sing grace when the novice-master signalled. The dishes were served through a dresser hatch

Door to Frater, Chester

Frater Benedictine, (reconstruction)

(q.v.) beginning with the superior and ending with the juniors, by waiters (called 'servitors') who were appointed by roster and took their own meals later, together with the cooks and reader.

Very detailed instructions are given both about the service and behaviour at table e.g. 'The servitors are to serve the food quickly and actively, not running or jumping in an unbecoming fashion, and they are to hold the dishes neither too high nor too low, but so that the food might be seen by him who carries it. The dishes are not to be broken or dirty, or unsuitable, or smeared on the underside. The servitor should use both hands, and carry only a single dish, except when he is serving eggs. If he cannot bring the brethren all they ask for, he ought, nevertheless, to reply to them civilly . . . The brethren all ought to be careful not to wipe their noses or run their teeth on the napkins or tablecloths, nor staunch blood, with them, nor handle anything unclean with them nor cut them with their knives'. (Barnwell Observances).

The frater was the principal room in the cloister range opposite the church and generally occupied most of its length. It might be on the ground floor (e.g. Chester) or raised on an undercroft (e.g. Durham). In the latter case the undercroft might accommodate the great cellar (from c.1400, these cellars were sometimes equipped with a fireplace which both improved the storage facilities and gave some warmth to the frater above) and buttery with a stair to the west end of the hall, partitioned off by screens. These screens formed a passage to the kitchen and had a pantry on their west side (e.g Durham, Easby). The main entrance was near the west end opposite the high table. Early Cistercian plans seem to have followed the Benedictine pattern of locating the frater on an east-west axis parallel to cloister (traces of this original arrangement at Fountains, Kirkstall, Rievaulx and of its unaltered continuance at Merevale, Sibton). But with the standardisation of the late C12 the Cistercian frater was placed 'end-on' to the cloister to allow the insertion of a kitchen which could serve both it and the frater of the lay brethren to the west by means of 'rotas' (q.v.) in opposite walls. When the conversi disappeared in C14 this arrangement became unnecessary and in some places (e.g. C15 Cleeve) there was a reversion to the traditional Benedictine arrangement.

In all cases it was a handsome, church-like room (at Bury 171ft long, at Fountains 110ft × 46ft), aisle-less with a wooden roof (rare survival at Cleeve with its hammer-beams and carved angels). The church-like effect was increased by the pulpit (q.v.) and the devotional picture or image on the east wall (Durham seems to have had pictures on both east and west walls): at Cleeve it was a painted crucifix (still discernible), at Fountains a carved wooden crucifix, at York and Worcester (still discernible), a Majestas.

The resemblance of the frater to a church (so close that at Beaulieu the transition was not difficult) is not accidental. Meals were seen as sacramental in character, a symbol of community and friendship with strong familiar associations and an opportunity of thanksgiving, and past members of the community, living in God, were held in mind. At Durham after dinner, the monks went to the cemetery 'and there did stand a certain long space with their heads uncovered, praying among the tombs for their brethren buried there' until returning to study in the cloister.

FRATERER   (Refectorarias)

The official responsible for the frater, its equipment, service and meals. He ordered supplies from the cellarer (who e.g. at Durham supplied him daily with 72 loaves) and was in close touch with the kitchener.

He ordered the tablecloths and saw to their laundering, repair and replacement. He filled the jugs with beer and saw to their cleanliness. After dinner he provided two jugs of beer for the convent and its guests (one freshly drawn, the other from slops). He was responsible for the washing up and keeping tally of tableware (spoons, cups and dishes). He fetched bread from the cellar (and was instructed not to offer it if mice had been at it) and laid it, covered, on the tables. He provided mats and rushes for the frater and the neighbouring cloister alley. He was instructed to keep the frater well swept with besoms and in summer he sprinkled it with sweet-smelling herbs (and sometimes provided fans). In winter he supplied candles for the tables. He also had charge of the laver (q.v.).

FRATER PULPIT

Near the high table, in the wall opposite the cloister except in Cistercian houses when it was in south wall, was the pulpit or reading desk from which the weekly reader read during meals. Because of the importance of this office, its temporary holder was solemnly blessed on the Sunday when his duties began. 'The reader at table ought not to hurry with the view of reading much but he should read clearly and distinctly so as to be understood; and when he has found a good and noteworthy passage, he ought to repeat it again and again, that it may be thoroughly understood. He is to correct any mistake he may make at a nod from the President,' (Barnwell Observances).

Frater Pulpit, Bealieu

Fresco

The silence for this reading included the service of the meals and the manner in which they were consumed.

Fraters still occasionally contain the recesses for the aumbries in which books for this reading were kept at hand. (At Fountains it is by the pulpit stairs).

The pulpit was often located in a large window recess with its floor and parapet corbelled out towards the hall. It was approached by a staircase in the thickness of the wall, sometimes with an open arcade on its inner face (e.g. Beaulieu, Chester). The finest survival is at Beaulieu, preserved by its continuing use, but there are other good examples at Fountains, Rievaulx, Shrewsbury.

FRESCO

Painting on the plaster of a wall done while it was still wet or 'fresh'. These existed in monastic churches and buildings as elsewhere in the Middle Ages though they were frowned on by the Cistercians except behind the High Altar and on the east wall of the frater. There are survivals at Cleeve (frater), St Albans (piers), Westminster (chapter-house).

FRIARS

A vigorous religious movement of C13, to be distinguished from monks. Monks were stable (confined to their house at least in theory — 'a monk out of his cloistre is not worth an oyster') and local, concerned with prayer for themselves and others and having the least possible contact with the outside world which came to them rather than vice-versa. Friars were international, mobile and evangelical, rarely in their houses but more often in the streets and market places, using their friaries only for occasional rest, refreshment and the holding of services.

Friar travelling

Initially, they identified themselves with the meanest beggars and outcasts and rejected rents, tithes and feudal status, begging for their food and poor clothing, willing to work for it in field or workshop. Their enthusiasm and abnegation provoked a religious revival, a steady flow of recruits and considerable benefactions (leading ironically, to decline).

Friars preaching

They arrived in the 1220's and by end of C13 there were over 5,000 in England and Wales, perhaps one to every 1,000 inhabitants. The Dominicans (Blackfriars) arrived in 1221, the Franciscans (Greyfriars) in 1224, the Carmelites (Whitefriars) c.1240 and the Austin Friars in 1248. Besides these four main orders there were a number of lesser ones (q.v.). Since they required neither invitation nor endowment, the friars reached Scotland within a few years of their arrival in England. All four major orders were represented but the Austin Friars had only one house. On the other hand, the Trinitarians were more strongly

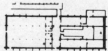

London Franciscan Friary,
Church Plan

represented than in England, as were the Red Friars. They emphasised preaching, studied to preach better and made a notable contribution to the growing universities. At Oxford, Robert Grosseteste tutored the first generation of friars at the university before becoming its chancellor. One of his pupils was Roger Bacon, O.F.M. Later the two leading Oxford astronomers were both friars: John Somer O.F.M. and William Lynn (O.Carm.). Notable Franciscan philosophers include John Duns Scotus and William Ockham. Initially at least, the friars were more popular with students than established masters, among other reasons because they lived on charity and taught for nothing. The friars' great general success roused the opposition of both traditional religious and parochial clergy, reflected both in satirical carving on misericords and in documentary evidence: the monks at Bristol objected to the arrival of friars in 1230 and there were complaints elsewhere in the last decades of the century. Established clergy saw the friars as criticising them by example, they envied their popularity and objected to the diversion of recruits and fees. The decline of the friars seems to have set in c.1350 when their success required the building of large churches to house the audiences for preaching, the requirements of study and learning led to the appointment of agents and proxies, even for begging (which had replaced work) which produced the notorious 'limitours' who were given 'farming' rights with permission to pocket any excess. These abuses should not obscure their continuing good work among rich and poor, in town and village, and especially in schools and universities.

FRIARS,   Lesser Orders
    Included the Trinitarians, the Crutched Friars and the Friars of the Sack. The General Council of Lyons (1274) forbade the lesser orders to admit new members so that they gradually became extinct. The small surviving communities were compelled to join one of the four major orders and their buildings were re-allocated to suitable use e.g. of the houses of the Friars of the Sack in Cambridge, one passed into the possession of Peterhouse, another became a chantry, while the third was taken over by Carmelites. Of their total of 17 houses there are no remains except for fragments at Rye. The Pied Friars (Friars of Blessed Mary) had four houses but there are no remains.

FRIARY
    The religious house of one of the orders of friars, together with its church. The latter had architectural peculiarities distinguishing it from monastic churches since its main purpose was not so much to provide a private oratory but to house large external congregations attracted by preaching. It tended to take the form of a hall, uninterrupted by screens or divisions, allowing uninterrupted sight and hearing of the preacher and altar. The 'private' church where the friars said their office was usually separated by a passage surmounted by a tower. Remains are rare as the churches were not parochial or required for the decreased functions of the established church. Sometimes remains of the tower survive e.g Dunbar, Richmond. Other survivals at Norwich (Dominican), Walsingham (Franciscan), Clare (Augustinian), Hulne (Carmelite) where at least the plan has been recovered. St David's cathedral uneasily holds Edmund Tudor's tomb from the dissolved friary in the city. Some glass in St Mary's Shrewsbury probably was rescued from the friary.

FUGITIVE
    For a professed religious to flee his house was a heinous crime in the eyes of both state and church. From the religious point of view it was turning back after 'putting the hand to the plough', not merely a lapse, but apostacy (q.v.). From the secular point of view it was a breach of contract, a failure to fulfil obligations underpinned by charter and charity — the return of prayer for benefaction.

FURNISHING
    The furnishing of the conventual buildings was sparse, at least until the end of the Middle Ages when privacy and a desire for comfort began to show, especially in the superior's accommodation. Generally the church had much work and treasure bestowed on it, particularly by the Cluniacs though the Cistercians reacted against this. All monastic churches had pulpitum, screens, stalls and many altars with appropriate furnishings. There was usually an altar of the Holy Rood before the rood-beam or rood-screen, two altars on either side of the pulpitum. Sometimes there was another beam above the High Altar — the one at Canterbury supported a Majestas, images of St Alphege and St Dunstan and seven reliquaries. The churches usually possessed an organ (q.v.) by end of the Middle Ages.

GALILEE

The westwards extension of a minster, taking the form of a chapel (e.g. Durham) or a porch (Neath, Tintern) or narthex (e.g. Byland, Ely, Fountains, Rievaulx). It usually seems to have consisted of a low pentise across the west end with an open colonnade facing outwards. Its use was possibly to have provided an assembly point or 'station' for monastic processions, this would explain its name as the celebrant, entering it in front of his community on Sunday, the weekly celebration of Christ's resurrection, symbolised the Master going before his disciples into Galilee (Matt.xxviii,10).

Galilee, Durham

Other uses have been suggested: an annexe to which women might be admitted, the place for lay brothers or monks under discipline who were not allowed to enter the church proper, etc. but such suggestions seems little more than unfounded hypotheses. It may, however, be relevant to point out that at York St Mary's the vestibule to the chapter-house was known as the Galilee.

GALLERY

There were sometimes galleries providing communication between different elements of the religious house above ground level e.g. there was one from the abbot's lodging at Fountains to a place above the Chapel of the Nine Altars. The Bridgettines at Syon occupied a gallery at first floor level around the church to ensure their segregation from the canons who served it.

GARDEN

The monastery precinct contained at least one garden but the use seems generally to have been purely practical: for fruit, herbs and vegetables. The cloister-garth at St Mary's York was occupied by a herb-garden whose products contributed to both kitchen and pharmacy (q.v.). There is some evidence of merely decorative provision (or a reminder that all beauty, whether natural, man-made or a combination of both, stems ultimately from God). St Francis, characteristically, required that every friary garden should set aside a corner for flowers alone so that brothers could contemplate in them the Author of all beauty. Carthusians had a private garden attached to each cell.

GARDENER

The appointee, at pleasure, of the cellarer. His chief duty seems to have been to keep the convent supplied with herbs four days a week in winter and spring and daily with vegetables in season. He was instructed to visit the kitchen frequently to see what was required of him there and always to return his produce cleaned and prepared for cooking.

GARDEROBE   see also *Rere-dorter*

Antiquaries' name for mediaeval privy or 'necessarium'. The chambers in the guest-house at Fountains had such conveniences as had the punishment cells in the basement of the abbot's house.

GARTH

A space enclosed by walls. The cloister-garth was usually kept under grass, it sometimes contained a fountain or laver. At York it was used as a herb-garden while Carthusians used it as a burial ground.

Besides the cloister-garths, there were other garths e.g. a coal-garth at Durham and wood-garths for the storage of fuel were quite often provided near kitchen (e.g. Fountains).

GATE

The formal entrance to the monastic precinct was generally by way of a gatehouse which, whether small and simple or large and ostentatious, was rarely less than two storeys high. The ground floor was pierced by one or more gated passages. Where there was only one opening (Bury, Kirkham, Peterborough and, Thetford), it was large and high, able to accept horsemen and wheeled traffic. Quite often this was flanked (usually on the right side) with a smaller access for pedestrians (e.g. Bridlington, Durham, St Osyths, Torre). The structure of these archways varies: sometimes they are in a cross-wall in the middle of the gate passage (e.g. Easby, Worksop) while at others (e.g. Battle) they are at one end of the passage.

A doorway in one of the side walls of the passage led to the accommodation of the porter. The gates were usually barred at Compline but could be opened for belated guests or travellers. Some houses did not allow laity, especially those of the opposite sex, beyond this point so the gatehouse might contain a chapel. (e.g. Beaulieu, Meaux, Peterborough, Whalley). If not, one was provided 'ante portas' immediately in front of the main gate.

Gatehouse, Kirkham

Gatehouses vary in size from the small gabled building at Kingswood to the magnificent structures of St Albans and Thornton and their upper floors had different uses. Sometimes a chapel was occupied by administrative offices. At St Albans and Ely it contained prisons and the latter had a courtroom as did York. Occasionally the gatehouse provided accommodation for the prior e.g. Thorney, Durham.

Gatehouse of Grange
(Benedictine, Shaftesbury)
near Tisbury, Wiltshire

An extensive precinct required more than one gatehouse. Bury had four of which two survive. Two also survive at Canterbury. Others remain at Gloucester, Norwich, Evesham, Cleeve. Some convents had watergates (e.g. York, Tintern) in addition to the great entrance for landborne traffic. Bury had a separate entrance to the vineyard and Furness, beside the two in the precinct wall, had a third giving access to the outer-courtyard usually found beyond the precinct in Cistercian abbeys (e.g. Fountains) and a fourth leading to the cemetery. Tisbury has two gatehouses, while at Waltham the entrance is only a facade, approached by a bridge.

Gateway, Canterbury

GENERAL-CHAPTER

In the great integrated orders: Cistercian, Cluniac, Premonstratensian, Carthusian, unity and uniformity was maintained through General-Chapters usually meeting at the mother house to which all the superiors of daughter houses came. The decisions there taken were binding on the other houses and it was the duty of their representatives to see that they were carried out. These chapters usually appointed visitors and elected new superiors. They were introduced by the Cistercians in 1119 and made compulsory for the others by the Fourth Council of the Lateran in 1215. Their frequency varied, usually taking place about every four years.

Attendance was difficult, sometimes dangerous and always expensive. Sometimes secular rulers forbade superiors to attend and this could seriously interfere with discipline and reform. The prohibitions increased with the increasing chauvinism of later Middle Ages.

Other orders took up the practice of general assemblies: the Benedictines moved towards a General-Chapter in C13 and also had provincial meetings. In C14, the

Benedictines seem to have held a chapter of all houses in the country about every three years. This normally took place in the first half of September and lasted between three and five days according to the pressure of business. In 1340 it was at Northampton and in 1343 at Oxford. In the same period the Augustinian Canons also developed General-Chapters.

GILBERT, ST

As rector of Sempringham he encouraged seven pious women of his parish to form a community based on Cistercian rule. A year later he received their profession as nuns and associated lay sisters and brethren with them to assist with their manual work. Their number grew, a second foundation was made in 1139 to be soon followed by others. In 1148 Gilbert went to Citeaux to seek their incorporation in the Cistercian order but the chapter declined to accept the government of nuns and Gilbert placed them under the direction of Austin Canons so that the communities took the form of a double order approved by the pope in the same year. When Gilbert died the sole English order had grown to nine double monasteries and four of canons only. It was generously treated by kings (especially Henry II and Henry VI).

GILBERTINES

An austere, exempt order with its mother house at Sempringham. It was double, with minutely composed statutes to ensure the complete segregation of the two communities. There were usually twice as many nuns as canons in a double house. Watton, their largest, was designed to accommodate 140 nuns and 70 canons. Besides the professed religious there were, on Cistercian analogy, lay brethren 'conversi and conversae', 'ready to labour in poor dress, content with the food of the poor.' The order was under the control of the Master of Sempringham and multiplied by the Cistercian principle of 'hiving'. The order never spread beyond England but had, at its suppression some 25 houses, concentrated in Yorkshire, Lincolnshire and East Anglia. Watton has been thoroughly excavated

Gilbertine

and there are scant remains elsewhere including the priory church at Malton and fragments at Bullington, Chicksands, Clattercote, Matterssy, Newstead, Ravenstonedale, and Sempringham. The Gilbertines attempted a foundation at Dalmilling, Ayrshire in 1220 but it did not establish itself and the endowments were transferred to Benedictine Paisley in 1238.

GLASS

The development of glass because light was a symbol of God seems to have been inspired by abbot Suger of St Denys. Its possibilities as a 'visual aid' were exploited in monasteries as in churches during the Middle Ages and it seems to have been so used in cloisters and other conventual buildings. Glass was too susceptible to iconoclasm and vandalism, quite apart from its natural fragility and the necessity to renew leading frequently, for much to survive but there are some ancient survivals in former monastic churches (e.g. Canterbury, Gloucester, Malvern, Selby.)

GRANARY   see also *Barn, Grange*

Monastic granaries occasionally survive (e.g. Abingdon, Bolton). They were usually placed in the curia but there were outliers in the granges. It was in charge of the granatorius who was responsible for supplying bakehouse. The Master of the Garners at Durham was an important official since in his barns 'all there whet and other corne did

Abbots Barn, Glastonbury

lye. His office was to recyve all the whet that came, and all the malte corne and to make accompte what malte was spente in the weeke, and what malte corne was delyvered to the kylne, and what what was receyved from the kylne and howe moche was spente in the house.'

GRANARY   Keeper of the
A necessary officer in every monastery but rarely mentioned as a separate office (which it was at Durham). He had his own office/store where he received all the wheat and malt corn, keeping account of income and expenditure (e.g.what went to the kiln for beer and what came back), as well as what was distributed to the kitchen and bakehouse.

GRANDMONT
A reformed Benedictine abbey f.1046 in diocese of Limoge that required plain and humble buildings as well as an austere and observant life, which also embraced lay brothers. It had affinities with both Benedictines and Augustinians and the habit of the Grandmontines, sometimes known as 'Bons Hommes', changed from brown to black. Like the similar movements of Savignac and

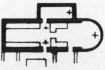

Grosmont Priory (Grandmontine), Plan of Church

Thiron it lacked the organising capacity to spread and endure and so tended to disappear. There are some remains at Alberbury and Craswall, both of which were dissolved as 'alien priories' (q.v.) and the third (of which there seem to be no remains) survived as a small denizen priory at Grosmont. The entire order disappeared in the French Revolution. Grandmontine houses, including their churches, were plain and humble. Their chapter-houses were orientated north-south within the limits of the main walls of dorter range, their day stairs located in south-east angle of cloister (like Cistercians), and, as an austere order modelled on groups of hermits, their dorters were from the beginning divided into separate cells.

GRANGE
An institution firmly associated with the Cistercians whereby they assembled the most important of their properties into easily manageable units at more or less fixed distances from each other (c.25 miles). They saw both its spiritual and economic advantages as it allowed them to be independent of more involving resources such as manors and rectories. Each grange was controlled by a team of lay brethren (often only two), under the general supervision of the cellarer. Considered as an administrative centre and store the institution was known as a grange, a word conventionally applied to a barn. (In many cases the accommodation of the 'conversi' was integral with the barn).

The Cistercians' successful organisation produced much imitation, in C12 and later, among both the regular canons and the established Cluniac and Benedictine communities, resulting in the achievement of a new standard of centralised agriculture. By mid C13, Furness had 18 granges; Kirkstead, Newminster and Stanlaw had eight each. Even minor houses such as Stoneleigh and Sibton had respectively eight and six in later C14. The great period of development was C12, it slowed down in C13 and had ceased or declined by C14. As early as 1220s the Cistercians had begun to lease granges to tenants because of the decreasing quality of the 'conversi' on which they so much depended. By 1300 this process had become common and was general by 1400, largely as a result of the Black Death, though the monks tended to retain in their own hands immediate home farms and granges used for resort and vacation.

The development of leasing was not always continuous or unreversed and, to the end, religious houses kept control of adequate demesne, produce rents and dairy for direct supply of the main needs of the house. The site of the 'home farm' of Whitby,

a little over a mile to the south of the abbey, is still marked
by its moats. Some granges were leased to friends or
granted to reward a benefactor and leases often reserved
useful rights varying from pasturage to lodgings.

In the later Middle Ages monastic granges developed
many uses. They could be a refuge from an infectious
epidemic, rest or convalescent homes for religious suffering
from mental or physical strain or infirmity, or for those

Abbot's Lodging, Grange,
Broadway

recuperating from the periodic bleeding. Particular establishments became favourite
retreats for superiors where they might escape the demands of office or find peace
for study or attention to pressing business. By C15 the attractions were becoming
too great and there was a royal decree that an abbot should not spend more than
three months on his manors and these were immediately to follow Easter (a
permitted summer holiday?).

Granges varied widely in size, situation and the quality
and extent of their buildings which could extend from the
merest necessities constructed from the humblest materials
to substantial stone buildings comprising a miniature
monastery (e.g. Minster, Thanet). Sometimes the grange
had a substantial chapel, usually built in C13 or C14. The
same period saw the development of defensive works in
vulnerable areas.

Piscina from Chapel at
Calcot Grange,
Gloucestershire

There are considerable remains of some monastic
granges, e.g. Broadway retains a good deal of the favoured
retreat of the abbot of Pershore. Other examples might
include the two granges of Abingdon at Sutton Courtney
and Charney Bassett, Salmstone of Canterbury, St
Augustine and Tisbury of Shaftesbury. Atherington,
Sussex belonged to Séez until 1414 when it was given to the
endowments of Syon; Lessingham, Norfolk was a grange of
Benedictine Ogbourne until it was transferred to King's
College, Cambridge in 1462; Melton Mowbray was possibly
a grange of Cluniac Lewes. Coxwell, Berkshire belonged to
Beaulieu; Leigh to Buckfast and St Leonards, Hampshire
also belonged to Beaulieu, East Hendred, Berkshire was a
grange of Carthusian Sheen. Bradford, with its magnificent
barn, belonged to Shaftesbury which was also patron of a
hospital in the village. Monks Hall at Appletreewick is the

Church Door, Calcot
Grange

remains of a grange of Fountains. St Mary's York had important granges at Kirkby
Lonsdale and Kirkby Stephen and there are some remains of former. Gloucester had
a grange at Llantwit Major, Glamorgan which may account for somewhat monastic
character of the surviving church. Minster in Thanet was an important grange of
Canterbury St Augustine as Saighton and Ince were of Chester. Salmstone, Kent
was an early grange which also belonged to Canterbury St Augustine.

GRANGE STAFFING

Could extend to a substantial monastic community. On the other hand it could
be reduced to a simple lodge occupied by a single lay brother with a shepherd or
cattleman to help him. These latters were not strictly granges but 'outliers' from a
grange e.g. Fountains had seven such lodges in Langstrothdale, centred on the
grange at Kilnsey, Guisborough and Rievaulx had similar lodges or huts in
Westerdale and Teesdale and Buckfast had one on Dartmoor.

The grange proper had a considerable permanent staff, probably originally of
lay brothers, but this kind of manning became impractical and was replaced by paid
servants with agricultural labourers, perhaps with the retention of a single lay

brother as manager. Staffing was obviously related to land utilisation: sheep would require much less than arable. In 1290, Hollingbourne (belonging to Canterbury Christchurch) had a labouring staff of eight ploughmen, a shepherd, a swineherd, oxherd, cowherd, goatherd and dairymaid. About the same time, Wellingborough (belonging to Crowland) had eight ploughmen, two carters, cowherd, swineherd, three shepherds, malster and maid. This kind of provision does not seem to have varied much throughout the Middle Ages. Such staff would be augmented when necessary e.g. at harvest-time. The permanent labour force would be at least 10 on average,

Shepherds

rising exceptionally to something over 20. Each unit was under the leadership of a grange-master or granger. When the religious staff were reduced the granger remained, acting as bailiff.

Besides the permanent staff there would be need of occasional specialist service in dairy, forge, bakery, brewery and sheep or cattle house. These were probably supplied from the mother house. Alleged depopulation involved in the foundation of some granges probably only meant a shift of housing and control, since peasant cultivators and their families were needed and their labour was often specifically included in the acquisition of land. There was thus reorganisation rather than dismissal and there is some evidence of a village settlement being shifted nearer the grange.

For examples of supervisory staff accommodation being built into the grange (or barn) see Hazeldon, Nr Cirencester; Leigh, Dorset.

GREYFRIARS   see also *Franciscans*

Place name is often all that survives since their churches were non-parochial and surplus to requirements of Anglican church.

GUARDIAN OF CLOISTER

The minor official responsible for the seclusion and order of the cloister. He was sometimes called porter and some of his duties may have been fulfilled by circator (q.v.). Apart from preventing disturbance by unlawful intruders, his chief duty was to see that silence was kept within the limits of cloister activities.

GUEST-HOUSE   see also *Inn, Pilgrim*

Hospitality was built into the monastic rule and the guest-house (hospitium) was an essential provision within the monastic precinct. In large houses it was a building of considerable size and elegance, placed away from the cloister 'so that guests may not disquiet the brethren by their untimely arrivals.' In smaller houses the provision might be confined to one or two chambers near the superior's chamber but large houses often had multiple provision: important guests in the abbot's lodging, middling ones in the cellarer's hospice and poor strangers in another one outside the precinct. Canterbury had multiple provision, there are ruins of a large 'Guesten Hall' in the close at Worcester and even remote Cistercian houses, deliberately sited away from the haunts of men, made provision for occasional visitors and passing wayfarers. Fountains had two hospices, situated some distance from the cloistral buildings. The guest-houses at Kirkstall and Bardney had aisled halls with cross-wings containing

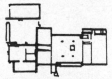

Kirkstall Abbey Guest-House (Developed)

Guesten Hall, Worcester

87

chambers. A later development at the former abbey had kitchen, service quarters and stables grouped round a small courtyard. A guest-house of the Hospitallers survives at Anstey, Wiltshire. The Guesten Hall of Sherborne survives in a modified form within the school buildings.

At York St Mary's there seems to have been a guest-hall or suite of chambers for guests above the cellarer's store in the west range of cloister. The south range also had a common hall where the abbot entertained strangers.

The guest-house of Worcester survived materially until 1859 when it was demolished and its roof, suitably truncated, was re-used in the building of St Mary Shrub Hill which is due for demolition if not demolished. The C14 roof, even in its modified form, was described by Pevsner as 'the most elegant mediaeval carpentry in the county'.

Besides the ordinary guest accommodation, some abbeys had special chambers for visiting monks (so St Albans in early C13). Distinguished guests were taken into the superior's lodging which allowed for this hospitality.

Entrance to Guest-House, Canterbury Christchurch (Benedictine)

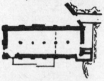

Fountains Abbey Guest-House (Plan)

GUEST-MASTER

Responsible for the welfare of all guests and usually subordinate to the cellarer. He was sometimes assisted by a hosteller or 'hostillar'. At Durham both these offices were combined in the function of the 'terrer'. He worked closely with cellarer and kitchener.

'His office was to see that all the guest chambers were cleanly kept and that all the tablecloths, table napkins and all the napery in the chambers (i.e. sheets and pillows) were sweet and clean. And he provided always two hogsheads of wine against the coming of any strangers and he provided provender for their horses that nothing should be lacking for any stranger whatsoever degree he was. He had (inter alia?) a staff of four yeomen to wait upon guests at whatever hour they arrived.' (Durham Rites)

Guest-master was a responsible office since he exemplified Christ's care for the homeless. For this reason and because of the temptations and distractions necessarily involved in the contact with 'the world', the role was usually given to a rare character. Cuthbert seems to have been the first guest-master of the Anglo-Saxon monastery at Ripon, St Benedict's rule declared: 'All guests who come shall be received as though they were Christ, for He himself said: "I was a stranger and ye took me in." '

Not only was he to show love and deference, he also had to make practical arrangements; 'The brother who is appointed to receive guests should have ready in the guest-house, beds, chairs, tables, towels, cloths, tankards, plates, spoons, basins and suchlike — firewood also. Bread and drink and other provisions he receives of the cellarer for his guests by means of the servants at his disposal.' (Lanfranc: Constitutions).

Because of his office, the guest-master was dispensed from the monastic rule of silence and he therefore became the natural go-between if any outsider wished to speak to the superior or any member of the community. Similarly, because of the 'extern' nature of his duties he was to keep an eye on monks in the curia as they returned from monastic business. If any visiting clerks or monks wished to dine in the frater, he transmitted their request to the superior and if granted, looked after them. He had a variety of such 'intermediatory' offices: guiding strange monks, transmitting mortuary rolls, introducing into chapter seculars seeking confraternity (q.v.), even acting as guide to sight-seers, 'taking care that the community is not in the cloister' and consequently likely to be disturbed. He was responsible for seeing that visitors to the cloister were properly dressed, silent and not likely to bring mud or dirt into the enclosure. He also introduced postulants and instructed them how to make their petition for entry into the order.

GUESTS

Monks (note crossed Sleeve) Welcoming distinguished Guest

Were to be treated as though they impersonated Christ — see above. The usual stay was for two days and two nights but an extension was allowed if the guest was sick. The powerful were likely to abuse this charity: in the reign of Henry VIII we hear of a man imposing himself as a guest for seven years, together with his wife and seven children. In the later mediaeval period the great houses seem to have provided for three classes of guests: the aristocracy of church or state entertained by the superior as his personal guests; the middling folk in the guest-house, the poor in the almonry. But in Durham, at least, right up to its Dissolution, there is evidence of unusual liberality and mixture of classes in most generous provision.

Apart from overnight guests, there was much provision of casual meals via the almonry (some of these were very 'regular') and this expenditure could be enormous at such occasions as the installation of a new abbot (e.g. the welcoming feast given in honour of Richard Sudbury when he was appointed abbot of Westminster in 1308).

HABIT

The distinct dress of a monk, intended to be an outward sign of an inward state: abandonment of the world, abnegation of natural ties, subjection of own will to that of superior, submergence of individuality within common life (cf. Luke xiv.26 etc.).

It had also some of the associations of a uniform, membership of a large and honourable body, to be respected by wearer and others. The religious was solemnly clothed with the habit after a ceremony which included the vows (q.v.). Each order had its own distinctive dress, which varied in colour, shape and nature though the cowl (q.v.) was common to all male orders and the whimple to female ones.

HALL

The central public building of a secular house, replaced by frater, chapter-house and parlour in a monastery. Nevertheless, there were a number of halls in the ancillary buildings: guest-house, superior's lodging almost always and the almonry sometimes had their own hall.

HEATING   see *Fires*

For most of their history there were generally only three fires, even in the northern hemisphere, in a religious house: kitchen, infirmary and warming-house. The latter was often so placed as to give a little heat to the dorter. The great church was utterly without heat and precautions had to be taken to prevent the priest's hands becoming so cold that he could not hold the sacred vessels. Among the many duties of the sacrist (q.v.) was the provision of warm coals in iron dishes to warm the hands of the altar ministers in winter. (Honnecourt has an ingenious drawing of such a device, mounted on gimbals to prevent the ashes spilling).

In winter, special precautions had to be taken in the cellars to prevent the contents freezing — beer barrels were insulated with straw and there was a later development of providing a fire in the cellar under the frater for this purpose (also incidentally taking a little of the chill from the frater above). Sometimes there was, in the later monasteries, a fire in the library or muniment room to protect the contents from damp. At the cold abbey of Lindisfarne, a brazier seems to have been provided in the frater during the winter months, at least in its later history.

When superiors developed separate lodgings, these had fires in the hall on the analogy of the guest-house and the accomodation for corrodians always seems to have its own heating.

HERBARIUM   see also *Garden*

The herb-garden which was probably a universal provision in a religious house. (At York St Mary's it occupied the cloister-garth). Herbs were the raw material of the pharmacy, were used as air-fresheners (particularly in frater), played a great part in mediaeval cookery and later provided tissanes, cordials and pick-me-ups (e.g. Chartreuse).

Hermit or Anchorite

HEBDOMARIAN

The 'duty officer' for the week, notified on the tabula (q.v.) and announced in chapter. He was the priest responsible for celebrating High Mass, leading certain offices, and fulfilling other 'chaplain' functions. His term of duty began at Evensong on Saturday and continued until he had sung High Mass and None on the following Saturday. He was the celebrant at all the quire offices, the daily High Mass, sang grace, etc. in frater and read the lessons at Mattins and Evensong.

If he was prevented by illness or other sufficient cause from fulfilling his duty he asked for a substitute and stood in for the latter when his turn came round. Everyone, except the superior, had to take his turn as hebdomarian and, at Barnwell at least, it seems to have been the custom for the hebdomarian of one week to sing the Morrow Mass during the next and the Lady Mass in the third week.

This spreading out of duties extended to all departments of the house from the kitchen to the quire where the Cantoris and Decani sides seem to have changed places in alternate weeks.

HERMIT   see also *Anchorite*

A solitary pursuing spiritual excellence e.g. John the Baptist, St Anthony, St Cuthbert. Even after the organisation of Benedictine monasticism the eremetical tradition persisted. St Benedict allowed for this choice after long probation in the communal life. There were hermits at the Benedictine houses of St Albans, Westminster and Durham (some of the latter removing themselves to St Cuthbert's own island of Farne). St Guthlac was a monk at Repton before moving to the wilderness of Crowland. Many others are known by name e.g. Robert of Knaresborough, St Godric of Finchale.

St Christopher (life size, Worton) Archetypical Hermit

Besides occupying themselves in prayer and contemplation, hermits also took on some work of public charity which could include spiritual counsel (so often in mediaeval romance), guiding travellers (cf. legend of St Christopher) and giving them other assistance such as maintaining bridges, keeping lighthouses, succouring injured. Otherwise he supported himself by manual work (especially gardening) or academic work (Richard Rolle,

St Guthlac of Crowland

Julian of Norwich, John Wittering). Some were supported by an annual pension from their sponsoring monastery. A north country hermit called Hugh was 'of great perfection, and by such charitable almes as he dyd gather in the countre he founded an hospital' at Cockersand which eventually became an abbey. Similarly Godric's hermitage at Finchale grew into a priory and many Celtic and early English groups of hermits were superceded by a religious house, specially of Cistercians (as at Kirkstall) and of Austin Canons. For insights into the spiritual life of hermits, see: *The Ancren Riwle, Cloud of Unknowing, Writings* of Richard Rolle and the Hermit of Lindisfarne.

Chapel, Warkworth Hermitage

HERMITAGES

Could be within church or precincts of a religious house as well as being 'cells' in remote places. These cells varied in amenity and complexity. Some were more or less modified caves (St Constantine's Cells, St Robert of Knaresborough's cell, Redstone Rock (Worcestershire) and other similar caves in same county at Airley Kings, Stanford-on-Teme, Wolveley). Others were simple houses of hall, bower and garden, while others were quite complex buildings, e.g. Pontefract, Warwick, Warkworth. The latter consists of a two-storeyed house cut in the rock with hall and kitchen, solar, chapel and sacristy. It had had a supporting garden and little farm.

HIERARCHY

The religious house had a strict hierarchy which was maintained particularly in choir, chapter, frater and processions. It was unconnected with worldly status but with religious merit which was often related to length of time since profession. The officers of the monastery were graded: abbot, prior, sub-prior, cellarer, etc. followed by their assistants in the same order: sub-cellarer, sub-sacristan, succentor, etc. Beyond this, clergy took precedence over laity, quire monks over lay brethren, old over young. Internal promotion could be affected by the superior literally bidding a monk 'to go up higher' (Luke xiv, 10) i.e. to take a seat of greater precedence in chapter or quire in order 'to do honour to one of the brethren on account of his deserts and to advance his place in the community on account of his excellent character' (Lanfranc: Constitutions). The principle was clearly declared in St Benedict's rule (chap. 1xiii).

HIGH MASS

The principal mass of the day, sung with a complement of three ministers, numerous acolytes, and accompanied by elaborate music and ritual which was increased in complexity on major feast days, when it was preceded by the great procession (q.v.). It was attended by the whole community and took place at High Altar in the presbytery. It took place daily at about 10 a.m., lasted about an hour and was followed by the office of Sext (q.v.). Some of the ritual furnishings of this function survive: piscina, aumbry, sedilia, altar-step, etc.

HOLY DAY   (Holiday)

The major festivals or Holy Days were, from the beginning of Christianity, given a spiritual significance by as far as possible abstaining from 'servile work'. With the conversion of states and the introduction of Christian laws this practice was given support both by canon and civil law and it was an offence to work on specified major festivals which were to be kept by attendance at mass, followed by feasting and other appropriate rejoicing. Thus Holy Days became holidays and their numbers constantly increased during the Middle Ages until with the triumph of the Protestant ethic they were largely abolished and replaced by bank holidays and later by national holidays. The current much reduced Holy Days of obligation where attendance at mass and abstinence from servile work are still commanded by the church are all Sundays in the year, January 1, 6., March 19, Ascension Day, Corpus Christi, June 29, August 15, November 1, December 8, 25. Though some of these are not kept in Great Britain viz. March 19 — St Joseph and December 8 — Immaculate Conception.

When the psychological pressures of the religious life became too much, or when a monk was recuperating from a serious illness or even from 'seynies', he could go (if he were the superior) or otherwise be sent to a small priory or grange which was retained by the greater religious houses for this purpose. Here the demands of the rule were somewhat mollified though the general religious life and main observance were still kept. There was some opportunity for relaxation and/or recreation and there was increased privacy, tranquillity and seclusion. This practice is still maintained in some modern religious houses under the name of 'villagiutura'. (q.v.). Even the great abbot Hugh of Cluny was wont to retire to a favourite grange at Berże to relax from an extremely active public life (a fine Romanesque chapel still survives at the farmhouse).

In England in 1421 the king decreed that no superior was to spend more than three months annually on his manors which testifies to a well-established practice whose consequences often included improved accommodation at granges and the building of a larger chapel attached to it.

HOLY WATER

Was considered as an important 'sacramental' i.e. a material thing which could remind and to some extent effect the assimilation of religious truths. Water always had been a potent symbol of life, cleanliness etc. and water blessed and with added ingredients (usually salt) was much sprinkled on places and persons as a reminder of pure life in God. Asperges (q.v.) preceding High Mass, was an important element in processions and people blessed themselves by signing their body with holy water on entering church. Occasionally holy water stoups survive (e.g. Fountains).

HOME

It is often salutary to remember that the religious house was the permanent home of the monk. It had to possess the necessary amenities of any home and monastic initiative and invention often led to these being more advanced than in comparative secular accommodation. As homes they were affected by cultural changes in the Middle Ages of which perhaps the most significant in this regard was the increased desire for and provision of privacy in domestic accommodation. This led to partitioning of rooms, more intimate accommodation and to some relaxation of original observances.

HORARIUM   see also *Daily Round, Hours, Time-Table*

The monastic daily time-table, created by its division into the canonical hours of Mattins etc. This varied in different orders and at different times though the general pattern remains constant. It is difficult to transpose into modern chronology because of the vagueness of the information and the late development of clocks (q.v.). The horarium also differed in summer and winter. The day, apart from meals, is divided into office (four hours), reading (four hours) and work (five to six hours).

At Lanfranc's abbey at Canterbury (c. 1075) the winter scheme was as follows:

2.30	Rise, prayers with seven psalms, psalms 119-150, Nocturns, several more psalms for the royal house, Mattins and Lauds of the dead, Mattins of All Saints
5.00- 6.00	Reading
6.00- 6.45	Lauds, psalm 51, psalms and prayers for royal house, anthems
6.45	Prime, seven penitential psalms, litany of the saints
7.30- 8.00	Reading
8.00	Seven psalms, Terce, psalms for royal house. Chapter or Morrow Mass, chapter-meeting, followed by psalms for the dead
9.45-12.00	Work
12.00	Sext, psalms and prayers for relatives, etc. High Mass
1.30	None, psalms and prayers for relatives, etc.
2.00	Dinner
2.45- 4.30	Reading or work
4.30	Vespers, psalms for relatives, etc., anthems, Vespers of All Saints, Vespers of dead
5.30	Reading
6.15	Compline, psalm 51, five psalms
6.30	Retire

There were some liturgical functions (e.g. processions) and some extra prayers which have been omitted from above. Liturgical time has expanded to eight hours, reading contracted to three and work to three at most.

HORTICULTURE   see *Garden*

HOSPICE, HOSPITIUM   see also *Guest-house, Hospital, Hospitality*

Mediaeval Hospice

Hostel for pilgrims and travellers, provided in outer court of religious house and sometimes as a separate and more or less independent entity where it is also referred to as hospital (q.v.) or college (q.v.). A hospice usually provided three amenities: a chapel to pray in, a frater to eat in and a dorter to sleep in. It usually had a staff and was under the control of a superior often called warden or master. Some of the university colleges developed from 'hospices' or 'halls'.

HOSPITAL.

There was an extremely large number of hospitals in the Middle Ages. They had a variety of names: Almshouse, Bede-house, Bedlam, Godshouse, Hospice, Hospitium, Lazar-house, Mallardy, Masendew (and other variants of 'Maison Dieu), Preceptory, Priory, Spital.

There were many different sizes and types: Leper hospitals, some for men, some for women, some for both: hospitals for aged and/or sick poor, some for men, some for women, some for both; refuges for aged or sick priests; hospitals for the sick in general, and single-sex institutions of the same kind; hospices for poor travellers and pilgrims, sometimes combined with another kind of hospital; hostels which were similar to an almshouse for resident brothers, sisters and/or poor people (including widows); hospices for orphans. In these latter cases they usually lived under a rule and could be either single sex or mixed institutions. Besides their being admitted to a general hospital there was special provision for the mentally sick. The most famous hospital of this kind was St Mary of Bethlehem, outside Bishopsgate, London — its dedication is the origin of the word 'bedlam'. There were hospitals for the care of women in childbirth (and for the child if the mother died) and for foundlings. In the early Middle Ages the most common special provision was for lepers who were _

St Mary's Hospital, Chichester

Hospital

given a distinctive habit of a grey coat and scarlet hat.
Harbledown is a conspicuous example of this provision
which later became less necessary and many original lazar-
houses became general hospitals or hospices.

In some cases the master, prior or warden, together with
the brethren and sisters who formed the staff, followed a
definite religious rule and wore a special habit. They were
assisted by lay brothers, lay sisters and servants. The
commonest rule followed was that of St Augustine, though
hospitals dependent on a religious house often followed its
rule. The dependency was not necessarily in the precinct or
even in the near neighbourhood.

Some orders were particular and only concerned with
hospital work : St Lazarus of Jerusalem (lepers), St Mary of
Bethlehem (particularly mental sick), St Thomas of Acon,
St Anthony of Vienne. Hospitals existed all over the
country; not only clustered in the mediaeval towns but
occuring in remote villages (e.g. the hamlet of
Killingwoldgraves, Yorkshire ER had a hospital from
before 1169 to the Reformation.) In C14 and C15, like
chantries and schools, they were a popular alternative to the
traditional endowment of religious houses (cf. Sir Richard
Whittington's foundations.)

The Scottish situation paralleled that of England and
Wales. The following hospitals were dependent on religious
houses: Arbroath (almshouse); Fife (poor, travellers) on
North Berwick nunnery; St Edwards, Berwick (poor, sick)
was staffed by Trinitarians; Cree, Kircudbrightshire (type
unkown) depended on Dundrennan; Dunbar (Maison Dieu)
seems to have belonged to Trinitarians; St Katherine's,
Dunfermline (almshouse); Edinburgh St Leonards
(almshouse) on Holyrood; Fail, Ayrshire (poor) was
another Trinitarian house; Helmsdale, Sutherland was
supported by Kinloss; Horndean, Berwickshire (almshouse)
by Kelso; Houston, East Lothian was another Trinitarian
establishment; Inverkeithing, Fife depended on Dryburgh;
Jedburgh provided an almshouse in the town as did Kelso;
the Trinitarians had another house at Loch Leven; the
nunnery at North Berwick supported a hospice in the town
for poor travellers; Dunfermline provided similarly at
Queensferry North; Rutherford, Roxburghshire had a
hospital (type unknown) dependent on Jedburgh; the
Dominicans at St Andrews provided a leper/poor-house;
the almshouse at Segden, Berwickshire was Augustinian;
the hospital at Smailholm, Roxburghshire depended on
Dryburgh; the provision for poor and travellers at Soutra,
Midlothian was Augustinian and a hospital at Stirling
depended on Cambuskenneth. Remains are rare but a
ruinous building in Lauderdale, east of Thirlestane, was
probably a hospital with the customary attached chapel (it
may have been given to Dryburgh c.1260). Apart from this, of the 150 mediaeval
hospitals which are recorded there are remains only of Edinburgh's St Mary
Magdalene and Soutra.

Hospital buildings were similar to monastic infirmaries, consisting of a large
heated hall with the bedheads arranged against the long outer walls with an alley

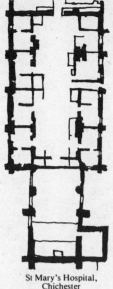

St Mary's Hospital,
Chichester

Infirm

Hospital

down the middle, they inevitably had a chapel (whose altar could normally be seen from the hall), a kitchen and sometimes a separate dining hall where meals were not served in the hall. There is a good survival at St Mary's Chichester.

The ideal was that no one in need was to be refused admission, that the patient was to be treated as Christ and the rules of the Hotel Dieu in Paris e.g. required each person to be treated 'as if he were the master of the place'. On admission the patient was washed and his clothes removed and disinfected. (Early in C16, the annual payment for bed linen at St Thomas' Hospital, Canterbury, was £2.6.8.) He was bathed every morning and the sheets were frequently changed. At Sherburn lazar-house there were two bath tubs for bathing and provision was made for washing heads weekly and personal clothing twice a week. At Higham Ferrers bede-house, the inmates were provided with hot water for daily washing and weekly attention from the barber. However, it appears that under pressure a hospital might require the sharing of beds (not uncommon in general mediaeval life). On discharge, the patient's clothes were returned, having been laundered and repaired. If he died in hospital he was guaranteed careful Christian burial with masses for the repose of his soul.

Some nunneries e.g. Romsey, had an attached hospital, and even more acted as 'old peoples' homes'. Nuns seem personally to have nursed their boarders and corrodians who must eventually have become old if not seriously sick and we occasionally find wills dated from convents.

HOSPITAL AS RELIGIOUS HOUSE

Though these institutions are often not numbered among the abbeys etc. they all resembled formal religious communities. They had a rule and their staff nearly always, and the inmates sometimes, were tonsured. Both staff and inmates wore a distinctive dress. There was one for all lepers and other hospitals and their inmates usually had their particular uniform. Generally, it was modelled on that of Austin Canons and Canonesses with a cross or other badge above the right breast. The staff and inmates took the three main monastic vows, recited the divine office and were subject to a superior. They were also subject to visitation but, as in the case of monasteries, there were

Holy Water

some 'exempt' (q.v.) hospitals. Their chapels, like those of monasteries, were usually 'private' or 'free' but some few had full parochial rights and duties e.g. Durham St Mary Magdalene, Armiston, Norwich St Paul's. Curiously, some chapels attached to lazar-houses seem to have been in this position: Northampton St Leonards, Lincoln, York St Nicholas. Hospitals lacking their own chapels used the local church, often with prescriptive rights in a particular chapel

Holy Water Stoup, Fountains

or aisle (e.g. Croydon) and even if they had a private chapel, they constantly resorted, when convenient, to the parish church (e.g. Ewelme). The essentially religious character of the mediaeval hospital is shown by the fact that some had anchorages attached to them (e.g. in 1320, the archbishop of York gave permission to a nun of Arden to be enclosed as an anchoress in the cell attached to the hospital of St Nicholas in Beverley where she joined another recluse already established there).

A considerable number of hospitals were fully conventual and of far greater importance than many lesser priories. Among the larger hospitals might be included: Bridgwater, St John Baptist; Bristol, St Mark; Bristol, St John Baptist; Burton Lazars; Bury, St Saviour; Canterbury, St John Baptist; Carlisle, St Nicholas; Coventry, St John Baptist; Dover St Mary (Maison Dieu); Durham St Giles

Hospital Chapels

(Kepier); Exeter, St John Baptist; Gloucester, St Bartholomew; Greatham Co. Durham; Harbledown, Kent; Leicester, Newark; London had eight large hospitals; Ludlow, St John Evangelist; Norwich, St Giles; Sherburn Co. Durham; Southampton, St Julian; Southwark, St Thomas the Martyr; Strood St Mary; Westminster, St James; Winchester, St Cross; Worcester, St Wulstan; York St. Leonard.

Hospice, Hospital

In the later Middle Ages, the generosity of hospitals was abused and they also had their 'corrodians' often imposed from outside. They also came to suffer from the vices of pluralism and non-residence on the part of their masters. It is worthwhile noticing that their reformation in 1424 sometimes took the form of replacing 'secular masters' by a religious prior (so at Pontefract). In their last years they also suffered from devaluation of coinage and inflation. Their inmates were sometimes known as 'eremites' which, at York was corrupted to 'cremettes'.

HOSPITAL CHAPELS

Centre and focus of community life, these were as richly furnished as any other mediaeval church. Gold altar vessels are recorded, rich vestments and valuable service-books (the manual and missal at Beverley Holy Trinity were valued at £4 each by Edward VI's assessors before they were pillaged with other spoil from chantries.)

Their altars survive at Glastonbury, Grantham, Ripon, Salisbury and Stamford while there are sedilia and stalls at Chichester, Stamford and wall-paintings at Wimborne. There are some rare fragments of glass at Bath St Mary Magdalene, Bristol St Mark, Salisbury Trinity, Sherborne, Stamford, Winchester.

The primary dedication was always to God but the normally used title is the distinguishing secondary dedication to saint or mystery. Sometimes they commemorate a monastic saint, possibly a member of the founding order, e.g. St Augustine, St Benedict, St Bernard, St Julian the Hospitaller is obviously appropriate as is St Lazarus; St Alexis was a patron of beggars; the popularity of St George and St Christopher extended to hospitals; St Mary Magdalene was also very popular (perhaps because of her care for Christ), dedications to Our Lady extend to hospitals, and other female saints include Anne, Catherine, Helen, Margaret, Ursula. There are many French saints: Eloi, Denys, Giles (patron of cripples) Laud, Leger, Louis, Leonard, Martin, Roche, Theobald. Others include the Holy Innocents, the Three Kings, and there were naturally dedications to local saints including: Brinstan, Chad, Cuthbert, David, Edmund the king, Edmund the confessor-bishop, Ethelbert, Godwald, Oswald, Wulstan and, above all, St Thomas of Canterbury (the pre-eminent healing saint). All Saints is rare, B.V.M. often appears under a 'mystery' especially the Salutation, or Annunciation. The angels, as ministering spirits, were obviously suitable patrons as were the particular archangels, Gabriel, Michael. Christ appears in many forms: St Saviour, Name of Jesus, Corpus Christi. Dedications to the Holy Spirit are rare in England as are those to the Trinity (the festival was only introduced by St Thomas of Canterbury,) there are a few C13 dedications but in C15 it became more common for almshouses.

HOSPITALS, DISSOLUTION OF

Those that were not dissolved as a result of the suppression of the religious houses which supported them, largely perished as a result of the Edwardian suppression of chantries (1548). Some staggered on into the reign of Elizabeth when Grindal (fruitlessly) asked for 'reformation rather than destruction'. It is said that the living conditions in hospitals were far superior to the common lot of the generality of patients, therefore many who were not ill sought admission. Most of them fell under the attack on 'superstition', the token 'Wayfarer's Dole' still issued at St Cross (a favourite dedication of Hospitallers as St Sepulchre was of Templars) is a pathetic and rare tourist attraction replacing a generous provision to the needy. Of over a thousand which once existed, there are material traces of c.100 e.g. Beverley had at least 10 hospitals of which not one survives.

HOSPITAL : MATERIAL PROVISION

It is necessary to distinguish between the provision for more or less permanent guests and the passers-by who normally only stayed one night.

(a) Lepers, bedesmen and sick who were given food, care and shelter until they recovered or died.

(b) Travellers, who either received doles to help them on their way or were provided with supper, bed and breakfast.

The allowance to cover an overnight stay at Canterbury St Thomas was 4d., a not inconsiderable sum in the currency of the period. The bodily necessities which were generally provided included food and drink, baths, bedding and clothes. At Sherburn, Co. Durham, each inmate received daily a large loaf and a gallon of beer; he was provided with meat three times a week and, on other days, eggs, herrings or cheese, together with butter, vegetables and salt. Hospital statutes required the provision of fresh food and forebade the consumption of rotten or blighted food which was quite common outside their walls. Some hospitals presented a pig at Christmas to each inmate, while others made special provision for vegetarians. In some later mediaeval hospitals, those 'on the foundation' were given a cash allowance with which to buy their own food which was cooked by the staff. Everywhere, festivals were celebrated by special food. Since St Cuthbert's Day fell in Lent, his almsfolk at Sherburn had to be content with fresh salmon. It was a common practice to keep Michaelmas with a goose-feast, with one goose to every four inmates.

St Mary Magdalene's Hospital, Glastonbury

For transients, there are also examples. The norm seems to have been bread and ale, loaves and fishes (or other meat), so at York St Leonards. This dole was modified on special days e.g. Norwich St Giles provided, on Lady Day, 180 portions each consisting of bread, cheese and three eggs.

Pilgrims, Travellers

Travellers reaching Lynn on Maunday Thursday received a herring and a farthing; lepers in York, on the Feast of SS Peter and Paul, received bread and ale, mullet with butter, cheese and salmon when it was in season.

HOSPITAL STAFF

Usually included warden, chaplain(s), professed brothers and/or sisters, devout and committed laity and visiting staff: expert nurses, physicians, (barber) surgeons. Apparently, when the latter came to operate in St Bartholomew's, Bristol 'whanne some doughtie worke ys to bee donne on a lazar', Austin friars also were present 'leste hurte and scathe bee done to the lepers.' Here it appears that friars were accepted as more knowledgeable than the surgeons since the latter were willing to attend 'wythoute paye to gayne knowleche of ayliments and theyr trew curis'.

HOSPITALITY

From its centrality in the rule, Benedictine hospitality was almost a matter of pride, there was dishonour in failing to provide the hospitality expected of the house. Hospitality could vary from the occasional great celebration to 'doles' for the passer-by and bed and board for the simple wayfarer (free accommodation was normally limited to two nights and a longer stay required the permission of the superior), to the accommodation of nobility, together with their retinues, at will. The expected provision for an ostentatious retinue could be an intolerable burden on resources, quite apart from the affect of this sort of hospitality on the life of the convent.

Even 'ordinary' entertainment could be an intolerable burden to a house sited on lines of communication. Yet so strong was the tradition that religious authorities passed enactments that the hospitable principles of the rule should be maintained in spite of costs and inconvenience. In C14 prior Chillenden of Canterbury extended the accommodation both within and without the precincts, including a great inn called the Cheker of the Hope (which cost him £876.14.4) in the city. Glastonbury and St Albans also provided great inns in the nearby town for the benefit of pilgrims.

Distinguished guests were accommodated by the superior in his own accommodation which was designed for this purpose with its hall, chambers, kitchen, etc. Others were put up in the 'hostry' or guest-house in the outer court. Cistercian abbeys seem to have had two guest-houses (e.g. Fountains, Kirkstall) and their charity seems to have extended to hospitals for sick lay-folk. Evesham built additional guest accommodation c.1300 and that at Gloucester could apparently cope with parliament. Guests were usually the responsiblity of the cellarer (q.v.) but normally there was an additional official, guest-master, hosteller, etc.

HOSPITALLERS   see also *Knights Hospitaller*

The Knights of St John of Jerusalem who, besides acting as dedicated Christian soldiers, maintained a number of hospitals. The order seems to have had two off-shoots: the Knights of St Lazarus, concerned with lepers, who maintained and served the great hospital at Burton Lazars with its dependencies and the order of St Anthony which had hospitals in London and Hereford. A number of other nursing orders were formed after the Reformation including the order of St Camillus, the Alexian Brothers, the Brothers of John of God, the Sisters of Bon Secours, Sisters of John of God, the Hospitaller Sisters of the Mercy of Jesus, many of whom maintain hospitals and nursing homes in this country.

Badge of Knights Hospitaller

For a short time the Knights Hospitaller administered St Cross Winchester and they were patrons of the hospitals at Stidd by Ribchester and St Leonard's Skirbeck. It is interesting that the title 'Commandery' was given to St Wulstan's Worcester and that the masters of both the hospitals in Worcester were called 'preceptor' though there is no known connection of either institution with the military orders.

Frater Furniture

HOSTELLER   (Hostillar)

The word is sometimes used as synonymous with guest-master, otherwise to describe one of his assistants responsible for the interior service of the hospice, guest-house or almonry. At Barnwell, the hosteller was required to 'have elegant manners and a respectable upbringing. By the help of these endowments, in walking, standing and in all his movements, he ought neither to do nor say anything but what sets monastic life in a creditable light . . . It is part of the hosteller's duty to be careful that perfect cleanliness and propriety should be found in his department namely: to keep clean cloths and clean towels, cups without flaws, spoons of silver, mattresses, blankets and sheets, not merely clean but untorn, proper pillows, quilts to cover the beds of full width and length and pleasing to the eye of those who enter the room; a proper laver of metal, a basin clean both inside and out, in winter a candle and candlesticks, a fire that does not smoke, writing materials, clean salt in salt-cellars that have been well scrubbed; food served in porringers that have been well washed and are unbroken; the whole guest-house kept free of spiders' webs and dirt and strewn with rushes underfoot . . . a sufficient quantity of straw in the beds, keys and locks to the doors and good bolts on the inside, so as to keep the doors securely closed while the guests are asleep. Further, in these as in all other matters relating to his office, he ought to love propriety and cleanliness, so ought he to avoid waste, theft and extravagance.' (Barnwell Observances).

Sometimes a specific income was allocated to this official e.g. Greenberry Grange, Yorkshire North Riding, was reserved for the purposes of the hosteller at Fountains.

HOURS   see also *Horarium, Time*

The canonical offices said (or usually sung) at specified times consecrating day and night to God and remembering the suffering by which Christ the Saviour effected our redemption. The day hours were Prime, Terce, Sext, None, Vespers, Compline while the night hours were Nocturns (Mattins) followed by Lauds at break of day. The establishment of the correct time for these 'hours' led to the development, by monastic inventors of clocks which indicated time to both sight and ear.

The Canonical Hours (later called the Great Hours) were not only developed and elaborated, particularly by the Cluniacs, but they steadily gathered accretions which included:

i. A short service 'Pro pace ecclesiae', usually appended to Mattins which also had the gradual psalms said before its commencement.

ii. The prayers in the Hours for the Dead were prescribed to be fitted in during the greater part of the year.

iii. The 'Trina Oratio', a kind of prescribed form of morning and evening (private) prayer was said by all before Mattins and after Compline.

iv. Two or three times a week there was likely to be a commemoration (special service in honour of Virgin, patron saint, etc.)

v. A daily service in chapter-house after Prime called 'Pretiosa' which was 'a prayerful remembrance of departed brethren, benefactors,' etc.

HOUSE

A house of religious was variously called: of men, a monastery; of women, a nunnery; of either, a convent. Apart from the house of monks, houses of other orders had different names: of friars, a friary; of Templars, a commandery; of Hospitallers a preceptory (though these get confused owing to the Hospitallers 'inheriting' Templar property). Other titles such as abbey or priory are usually related to status and generally a priory is smaller and dependent on an abbey though there were exceptions.

Church of Benedictine House, Durham

Cluniac houses, whatever their size, are usually called priories because they are dependencies of Cluny, though large Cistercian establishments have the rank of abbey. Houses of regular canons are usually priories (whatever their size) as are Carthusian houses. Very large Benedictine abbeys with attached cathedrals are usually called cathedral priories because they are governed by a prior, the titular abbot is the bishop. Abbeys are governed by an abbot or abbess. Other superiors, apart from prior, may be called master, warden, prelate, superior, etc.

HOUSEHOLD

The inhabitants of a large religious house at various times could include children (oblates), young monks (or nuns) who were between 15 and 21, full (professed) members of the community, old and sick (in farmery), lay brothers (or sisters) or 'conversi', associates (confraters or consorores), permanent employers who were counted as part of the establishment (especially chaplain(s), steward and lay brethren in nunneries), other permanent help (craftsmen, labourers, servants), permanent guests (corrodians), transitory guests using or abusing hospitality, official visitors (bishops, abbots), private guests of community, temporary help who might be lodged on premises (builders, masons, plumbers, carpenters) and who were usually given board as part of payment.

The numbers in a religious house were always far greater than the number of professed — sometimes they might be in the ratio of four to one or more.

ILLUMINATION see also *Farmery, Infirmarian*

ILLNESS   see also *Farmery, Infirmarian*

Monks who were infirm through age or other cause had special indulgences and the rule of St Benedict has a short chapter (xxxvi) on the special consideration which should be given to old monks.

Bench for Infirm Monks

If sickness or infirmity was such as to interfere with a monk's duties, he confessed his incapacity in chapter and, at Canterbury at least, the superior replied: 'May the Almighty God grant you such good health as He knows to be expedient for you. Meanwhile, treat yourself as your sickness demands and stay away from conventual duties at your discretion.'

Illness

If the sickness grew worse the superior commanded that the ailing monk should be removed to the farmery for care. 'where he might have both fyre and more convenient keepinge for that they were allowed no fyre in ye dorter' and improved diet. If he recovered, his return to full religious life in the community was celebrated with some ceremony. If the illness became mortal, then there were detailed regulations about the practical and ritual preparations for death. Henceforth, he is prayed for formally every day in quire and at mass. If his condition deteriorated even further, two brothers were delegated for a perpetual watch by his bedside where they read to him from the gospels, especially the Passion narratives.

When the point of death (articulo mortis) arrived, the whole house was informed of his death-agony by beating on a board. They hastened to his bed and recited prayers on his behalf. At death the bells are tolled, more prayers are said and the corpse is prepared for burial. It is shaved by the barber, washed by appropriate ministers and reclothed in new monastic garments which are sewn together to prevent indignity or disarray as they act as a winding sheet. The body is placed in the mortuary until evening when it is removed to the farmery chapel and watched over in vigil (q.v.) by two monks 'either in kindred or kyndness ye nearest unto him'. This vigil was sometimes shared by the 'children of the almonry' (so at Durham) who sang psalms over the body. At eight a.m. or thereabouts, according to the season, the corpse was transferred to the chapter-house for a final service attended by the entire convent. After this the body was conveyed, in solemn procession, to the monastic cemetery where it was normally interred without a coffin.

ILLUMINATION

The art of decorating and illustrating books to the glory of God and His saints was a monastic invention and tradition which contributed much to human art and culture. Their magnificent productions, made under conditions of the utmost physical and technical difficulty include the Book of Kells and the Lindisfarne Gospels. Some pages must have taken months to complete and the cost in materials would not be incomparable with the costs in labour and effort. We need to remember that the skins had to be prepared and scraped, pens frequently cut, paints mixed, lines ruled and there were no such aids as magnifying glasses, electric light or warmed studies.

Initial letters were a marked feature of mediaeval manuscripts and were often greatly elaborated and finely decorated. In 1489 a monk of Westminster applied for a transfer to Wenlock where he was welcomed as a celebrated maker of capital letters.

INCOME   see also *Costs, Expenditure*
The formal foundation of a religious house normally implied its endowment with an adequate income (usually for a community of 13). It has been estimated that this was about £10 per head for a Benedictine and about £3 for an Austin Canon (friars were unendowed). This initial endowment could be derived from a variety of sources: land (usually the prime element), impropriated churches, manors or other benefices such as tolls, salt-pans, etc. With time they might have become supplemented in many ways: 'one-off' gifts of money or chattels, gifts in kind (such as wood for fuel and building), grants of property, rents and tithes, profits of fairs, endowments in money, collections (sometimes associated with indulgences), tolls of markets, bridges, etc., 'entrance fee' on joining order ('dowry' etc.), thank-offerings or marks of gratitude from beneficiaries, alms of pilgrims, appropriations of rectories, ritual fees — sometimes customary, sometimes obligatory, e.g. sepulture. This income could be assisted by 'negative income' in the form of exemption from customary fees or dues involved in feudal system.

Technically, all religious as individuals were vowed to poverty and the acquisition of private possessions, including money, was always liable to punishment though there were tacit allowances in later period. In spite of this, in their corporate entity, the greater monasteries often became great land-owning corporations, endowed with manors and churches, in return for their duty of prayer for the donors. These alienations of property to religious corporations became so extensive that the state limited them by the Statute of Mortmain (1279) though considerable benefactions were continued within the terms of the act.

Land-owning led to slackening of the rule and involvement in the world of feudal society. In spite of their wealth, many monasteries at some point in their history were beset by money difficulties and it must not be forgotten that many (particularly nunneries) never were wealthy and found difficulty in subsisting. Hadcock and Knowles give the incomes of religious houses at the Dissolution. The average income of a Cistercian abbey seems to have been c.£200 p.a. with considerable variations from the average e.g. Fountains c.£1,115; Grace Dieu, Monmouth £19. A very rough contemporary and possibly over generous equivalent might be obtained by multiplying these figures by 200 which not only had to provide for the professed community but their servants and dependents, the expenses of the superior, building repair and maintenance, almsgiving, hospitality and support of some dependencies.

INDUSTRY   see also *Agriculture, Grange*
The artistic and agricultural activity of religious houses is perhaps well recognised but they made an increasing contribution to national trade from second half of C12. Apart from export of wool (q.v.) local markets and fairs saw larger monastic contributions, not only of wool but of metals, agricultural surplus and a variety of manufactured goods. They were also involved in industrial activities in the modern sense. Tynemouth had a cell at Monk Seaton where coal was mined. The Benedictines at Jarrow were involved in iron-working as were the Cistercians at Kirkstall (the forge is historically continuous with their activity). Durham had coal mines at Ferryhill and Gateshead (with rights of timber for pits and water-gate). Finchale had a coal mine with its pumping station operated by horse-power in 1486. In C12 there was iron mining from both St Bees and Byland. Kirkstead had four forges, two for smelting and two for working iron, with mineral and wood rights. Bolton owned lead mines and many houses owned pits: Birkenhead, Combermere, Chester, Stanlaw, Vale Royal, Lilleshall, Shrewsbury, Wenlock, Burton,

Dieulacres, Ranton, Basingwerk. Some derived a
considerable income from the production of salt: Vale
Royal held Northwich in farm for £76 p.a. in 1306 and
about 20 years earlier it had a 'farm' in Mottram Forest for
glass-making. St Albans had a monopolistic fulling-mill, so

Iron Workers

probably had Durham, Meaux had a tannery, Repton and Malvern had tile-works
and in C13 many houses (including Evesham and Tewkesbury) had vineyards.
Jervaulx was engaged in horse-breeding, a tradition which has persisted in the
district. Wensleydale cheese seems to have been invented in the same place. The
Tironensians of Arbroath and Kelso seem to have been involved in crafts such as
weaving and woodwork. Many nunneries were engaged in fine embroidery (opus
Anglicanum) which was much in demand throughout Europe. This commercial
activity and success was largely the result of good management and unbroken
exploitation of initial and subsequent endowments of land given by generations of
benefactors. The generally responsible management and continuity of inheritance
produced the agregation and consolidation of estates which were 'ploughed back'
into further holdings so that by C15 it has been estimated that the church (including
the religious houses) possessed nearly a third of the total wealth of England, with the
consequent problems of great wealth and the envy of land-hungry seculars.

INFIRMARY   see *Farmery*

INFIRMARER   (Infirmarius, Master of Farmery)

'The master of the farmery . . . ought to be gentle, good-humoured, kind,
compassionate to the sick and willing to gratify their needs with affectionate
sympathy. It should rarely or never happen that he has not ginger, cinammon,
peony and the like ready in his cupboard, so that he is able to render prompt
assistance to the sick if stricken by a sudden malady . . . If they cannot sing the
Canonical Hours for themselves, he ought to sing them for them and frequently, in
the spirit of gentleness, repeat to them words of consolation, of patience and of
hope in God . . . Further, he should in a spirit of fraternal sympathy provide a fire
on the hearth should it be required by the state of the weather, a candle, a cresset
and a lamp to burn all night, and everything else that is necessary, useful and
fitting'. (Barnwell Observances).

In a later age, at least, the infirmarian's duties also
included the feeding of monastic prisoners, and others, more
privileged, who were accommodated in the farmery or its
appurtenances (e.g. the cellarer). As is indicated above, he was
also responsible for the pharmacy and its stock of drugs, most
of which were processed from natural sources in the monastic
herb-garden. He usually had his office and accommodation in
close proximity to the farmery (e.g. Peterborough). At
Wenlock he had a suite of rooms on two floors connected by a
spiral staircase and each room had fitted cupboards in its
walls, probably to act as drug cupboards.

Infirmarer's Bronze Mortar
(York)

In C14 at Canterbury St Augustine's, a sick brother who needed his spirits
raising was taken into the farmery chapel where, behind closed doors, a monk or
servant played the harp 'for his delectation'.

IMPROPRIATION   see also *Appropriation*

A benefaction whereby a religious house took the income arising from the
endowment of a parish church to their own use and, in return, provided a vicar. This
system was not only open to abuse but involved parochial and pastoral responsibility
outside the monastic vocation and was therefore rejected by the Cistercians.

INNS

Often developed from the hospices of abbeys e.g. George and Pilgrim at Glastonbury built 1475 to house wealthy pilgrims to the abbey. Inn signs often show their ecclesiastical connections: Cross Keys, Lamb and Flag, Mitre, Seven Stars, Salutation, etc.

INSUBORDINATION

As monks sometimes suffered from a tyrranous superior so a superior could occasionally suffer from a contumacious community. A C13 prior of Dover, returning from Rome, found that the sub-prior had unsurped his position and was leading the convent in open mutiny: 'Neglecting all rule and decency, the brethren locked the prior in his room for seven weeks, during which time the monks used his horses for journeys to London and elsewhere, spending the revenues and scattering the property of the house.' Eventually the quiet and inoffensive prior escaped by night and trudged in the snow and mud to Canterbury which he eventually reached with his complaint in spite of danger from vagabonds on the way.

Besides trouble with the community itself, a superior could have problems with tenants. In 1481 the parishioners of Whaplode, which belonged to Crowland, threatened the life of the abbot's bailiff when he tried to prevent their cutting down the abbot's trees. General social disorder involved religious houses in their capacity of landlords: there was a rebellion at Dunstable in 1229 over tallage, in 1236 the villeins of Abotts Bromley made an unsuccessful claim of free tenancy as did those of Burton in 1280. In 1309 the abbot of Combermere was assaulted at Nantwich, one of his monks slain, his grange burnt and his goods stolen. In 1330 one of the abbot's servants was murdered at Vale Royal and the prior of Bury was beheaded by rebellious serfs in 1381.

INTELLECTUAL LIFE

Through the Dark Ages, art, literature and learning were kept alive in the monasteries. They not only preserved the learning of pagan antiquity but produced the wisdom of the Church Fathers, the religious experience of ascetics and mystics, scriptural exegesis and commentary, and developed new literary forms. Learning and the spiritual quest were associated from the Benedictine Gregory to the Cistercian Bernard. The monastic dominance and leadership in intellectual life moved from the monks in C12 to the friars who were much involved in the development of the

Abbot (St Albans) constructing Astrolobe

universities and new ways of thinking, not only in philosophy but in laying the foundations of western science.

ISLE OF MAN

In the Middle Ages, there were Cistercians at Mirescog (priory?) and Rushen (abbey). The latter was founded from Furness and the former possibly from Rievaulx. There were Franciscans at Bemaken from 1367 and Cistercian nuns at Douglas from before 1226. A hospital existed at Ballacgniba and possibly at Peel. The right to elect the bishop of the Isles was held by the monks of Furness from 1184 to C14. St German's cathedral at Peel was built in mid C13 and from third decade of C15 the diocese of Sodor and Man was resolved into two parts. There seems to have been a Celtic foundation at St Leoc which may have continued into C12.

JANITOR   (Doorkeeper)   see *Porter*

JESUS MASS

A votive mass in honour of Our Lord Jesus Christ, usually followed by the Jesus anthem. It was sung every Friday at the Jesus altar which stood in front of the great rood on the rood-screen or beam. The devotion was characteristic of later mediaeval piety which increasingly centred on the humanity, particularly in its suffering aspects, of Christ.

JOHN OF JERUSALEM, ORDER OF see *Hospitallers, Military Orders*

JUNIORS see also *Novices*
The young monks who were usually allowed some minor indulgences.

JURISDICTION
The area of legal authority and responsibility, see abbot, bishop, General-Chapter, government, mother house.

KEEPER OF THE GRANARY see *Granarius*

KITCHEN
The conventual kitchen possessed one of the few fires in the purely monastic buildings. This single kitchen was later supplemented by a variety of others: those of the infirmary, guest-house and superior's residence (e.g. Ely, Fountains, Gloucester, Kirkstall, Roche, Waverley). Some monasteries had a separate meat-kitchen since no meat was cooked in the frater-kitchen and later such kitchens developed under the name of misericord (q.v.) etc. (e.g Ely, Kirkstall).

The kitchen of a religious house was external to the cloister range (e.g. Castle Acre, Easby) but necessarily associated with the frater (q.v.). In some of the greater houses (e.g. Canterbury, St Augustine's, Durham, Glastonbury), it was a detached building of considerable architectural and ergonomic status.

In smaller houses economy sometimes led to kitchen being placed at the end of the west range nearest the frater e.g Exeter) and a similar modification took place in some of the larger houses in the later Middle Ages (e.g. Thetford with its hand-mill, well and impressive range of ovens). Cistercian kitchens were positioned so as to serve both monastic frater and dining hall of conversi (Fountains, Waverley) though some houses (e.g. Cymmer, Valle Crucis) retained the older plan of a frater parallel to cloister and kitchen beyond.

The kitchen was usually connected to the frater by a passage which issued behind the screens. At Durham there was a serving-hatch called the dresser-window in the wall of the frater. In most cases the kitchen was a simple rectangle and sometimes (e.g. Lacock) it stood west of frater in angle between it and west range.

Abbot's Kitchen
(Glastonbury)

In Cistercian houses the kitchen opened from the cloister in the west part of the south alley but elsewhere it was usually on the far side of the frater. Cistercian houses usually had a separate meat-kitchen for the benefit of guests and others (e.g. Jervaulx) since only vegetables were cooked in the ordinary kitchen. There was a small attached courtyard or garth serving the kitchen, provided with the usual offices and storage place for fuel. At Chester and Westminster this court had a tower and larder on its west side. The pantry, buttery and scullery were also near the kitchen and often separated from it by 'screens' as in a large secular house. Original monastic rules assumed that the cooking was done by all the brethren in turn and this

Reconstructed Kitchen

Kitchen Tripod

tradition long continued in Cluniac and Cistercian establishments but generally there was a tendency for the cook to become a professional and important official of the household. (see kitchener).

Kitchen furniture is minutely described in the Customals. There were to be three caldaria (cauldrons) for heating water: one for cooking beans, a second for other vegetables, the third (with an iron tripod to support it) to furnish hot water for washing plates, dishes, cloths, etc. Secondly, there were to be four great containers (sinks, cisterns, or tanks): one for half-cooked beans, another and much larger one (into which water was always to be kept running) to wash vegetables, a third for washing up and a fourth to contain the supply of hot water for the weekly maundy (q.v.), shaving and tonsuring. There were always to be four spoons, the first for beans, the second for other vegetables, the third (naturally a small one) for seasoning the soup and a fourth (an iron one of large size) for shovelling coals on the fire.

Other furnishings for the kitchen included: four pairs of sleeves for the servitors to protect their habits, two pairs of gloves for moving hot vessels, three kitchen cloths which had to be changed every Thursday. In addition there were knives and a sharpening stone, a small dish to get hot water quickly when required, a strainer, an urn to draw hot water from, two ladles, a fan to blow the fire, stands to set the pots upon, etc.

KITCHENER   (Coquinarius)   see also *Caterer*

Kitchener

The kitchen supervisor, responsible for the work of the cooks, the choice of meals, (including keeping the rules of fasting, abstinence and the ordinances of the particular order). He regulated and appointed the activities of the cooks and their assistants who could be extremely numerous in a large house with its heavy responsibilities of hospitality and almsgiving. His staff could include paid servants, including women. He naturally worked very closely with the fraterer and cellarer.

'The kitchener ought to know what food and how much should be set before the convent on each day according to traditional allowances . . . For gouty persons, and the sick who cannot eat their commons, he ought to provide an alternative meal . . . The kitchener ought to be careful that food is not served in vessels that are broken or dirty, and that they are not dirty on the underside so as to stain the tablecloths. Further, he is to be careful that no food is set before the convent at any time which is imperfectly cooked or putrid or stale, and further that no excessive noise or clattering takes place in the kitchen so long as the convent is in the frater.'

KNIGHTS HOSPITALLER

Knight Hospitaller

The order of St John of Jerusalem, an international and military order, whose work included provision and maintenance of hospitals. Their rule was based upon that of St Augustine and their habit was distinguished by a large black cloak with a 'Maltese Cross' in white over the left breast. Their English headquarters was at Clerkenwell which administered some 70 commanderies or cells (18 of which had been transferred from the Templars at their dissolution). These tended to be recruiting centres or farms for the maintenance of the order. All houses were characterised by hospitality to poor pilgrims and travellers and so were often called hospices. After London, Buckland, Somerset was their largest establishment whose brothers acted as chaplains and advisors to the sisters of the order (10 houses, remains at Aconbury). Elsewhere, their houses tended to be small, manned by three brothers (or less), with secular chaplains, clerks, officials and servants.

They normally supported a number of corrodians who were retired or incapacitated members of the order. Cells or 'camerae' were generally staffed by a bailiff, chaplain and servants. There are remains of a 'camera' at Llanwyddyn, a dependency of the commandery at Halston. The 'Angel' inn at Grantham belonged to the Hospitallers, passing to them from the Templars. Chibburn has the remains of a commandery, its buildings grouped round a court and consisting of chapel, hall and chambers for the staff of three members of the order, including preceptor and chaplain. Churches survive at Baddesley, Balsall, Dinmore, Garway, London (Temple and Clerkenwell), Maplestead, Ribstone, Rothley. New churches sometimes followed the Templar tradition in being provided with a round nave. Other remains at Barrow, Godsfield, Moor Hall, Poling, Quenington, Sandford, Slebech, Swingfield, Temple Bruer, Temple Combe, Yeaveley. There were three preceptories in Scotland (remains at Torphichen).

Internationally, the order was divided into 'Langues' and there is a splendid monument to the proctor of the Langue of Castile in the crypt of St John's Clerkenwell.

KNIGHTS TEMPLAR

An international and military order, arising out of the Crusades, which attempted to combine monastic and military virtues. It was famous for its valour, contempt for adverse odds and it adopted the Cistercian observance in 1128. Its chief house in England was the London Temple, most of its other houses (preceptories) were mainly recruiting centres or administrative bases for the farms which supported the order. There were hospitals for sick and infirm brethren at Denney and Eagle, Lincolnshire. Since every house practised the monastic virtue of hospitality (especially to pilgrims and other travellers), they are sometimes referred to as hospices.

Their houses were usually in charge of a preceptor who may have been assisted by one or two brethren. The chaplains were usually seculars and the clerks, bailiffs and other officials were usually paid employees. They had about 50 establishments in England, many commemorated in a place name containing the element 'Temple' and there are material remains of about a dozen. Besides their formal houses, the Templars possessed a number of dependencies called 'camerae' which were manors staffed by a chaplain, bailiff and other employees. The Templars amassed great wealth and became international bankers. At the beginning of C14 grave accusations were brought against the order, including sodomy, heresy and witchcraft. In 1308, Edward II ordered the imprisonment of all Templars in England (135 including six knights and eleven priests.) Judicial enquiry elicited nothing very derogatory but under torture some members admitted guilt in that they allowed lay members to give absolution. The master refused to admit to any crimes and was kept in Tower until his death. The whole order was suppressed by the pope in 1312 (mainly under pressure from the French king who had initiated their persecution) but members who were judged innocent were allowed either to transfer to another military order or to retire with a pension. In England most of the Templars' possessions were transferred to the Hospitallers and several of their houses were re-established under these auspices.

LADY CHAPEL

During C12, increasing devotion developed to the Mother of Christ because of emphasis on the centrality of the Incarnation. The movement was also related to courtly love but the exact relationship is unclear. St Bernard (q.v.) was a great protagonist of this cultus and all Cistercian abbeys were dedicated to Our Lady. Other abbeys added Lady Chapels i.e. chapels dedicated to the Blessed Virgin Mary, usually as an eastern addition behind the presbytery, though Durham is a notable exception with its Lady Chapel at the west end. Substantial monastic survivals in modified use at St Albans, Winchester though most did not survive mariaphobia of Reformation even when the main church substantially survived (e.g. Pershore,

Sherborne). Apart from the east extension a favourite site was parallel to the eastern arm of the church on the side away from the cloister (e.g. Ely, Lacock, Thetford). The so-called St Joseph's chapel at Glastonbury appears to be a Lady Chapel. With this devotion were associated a variety of liturgical practices: the Lady Mass, Anthems of Our Lady, Our Lady's Psalter, the Little Office (q.v.), etc.

LADY MASS

The morrow mass, sometimes known as the chapter mass. It was called the Lady Mass because it was celebrated in the Lady Chapel (q.v.) and often took the form of a votive mass of Our Lady.

'The brethren ought to meet at the mass of the Blessed Virgin which ought to be sung on every morning throughout the year, except Good Friday and Easter Eve, and there minister to the Blessed Virgin with all possible sweetness of voice and devotion of soul. All who can conveniently come should attend this mass that they may deserve to have her as an affectionate mediator with her Son, but especially ought the priest for the week and the juniors who have heartily performed their service to attend it daily; nor ought they to shrink it for the sake of reading or writing or singing private masses, unless they have obtained leave to do so. The novices also ought to attend it on principal feasts and on other days . . . if their master gives them leave.' (Barnwell Observances).

C14 Madonna and Child preserved at Ampleforth

LANDLORDS, MONASTIC

Since land was the principal form of endowment, the Benedictines and Cluniacs became great landlords and therefore involved in the feudal duties and responsibilities of this position. The Cistercians tried to avoid this problem by accepting waste i.e. land without indigent population and developing it through granges (q.v.). Not only was the function of landlord sometimes at variance with the monastic vocation but, particularly in later mediaeval period, involved them in conflict with tenants (see Insubordination). There seems to be some evidence that

Shepherd

monastic landlords were generally more considerate than secular ones but their position was invidious.

LAND UTILISATION

Up to mid C14, their lands were worked by the monks themselves for crops and animal husbandry. The Cistercians and Gilbertines specialised in sheep-farming but they were not alone in this form of land use. Monks also exploited the mineral wealth on their estates: coal, iron, lead (see Industry) as well as making full use of other resources such as fisheries and forest.

The Black Death produced a shortage of lay brethren and of labour in general, consequently there was an increasing practice of leasing out land, though a home-farm was always returned for the direct needs of the community. Other manors and estates were either leased to tenants or placed in the hands of lay stewards or bailiffs who acted as managers. Though there were disadvantages in this development it had the effect of freeing religious houses from the direct effects of bad harvests, droughts and floods, shortage of cattle-food, fluctuations in supply and demand of wool, pestilence among cattle and sheep (which had often produced financial emergencies and enormous debts).

LANE

An open space, often found in Cistercian houses, between the range of the conversi and the west walk of the cloister. Its purpose is uncertain: it may have provided a kind of lay equivalent to the monastic cloister or it may have been connected with some activity of the conversi which was necessarily noisy and therefore required 'damping' by the west walk of the cloister. It exists clearly at Citeaux and Clairvaux and there are traces of this provision at Beaulieu, Byland, Kirkstall, (substantial at Sibton). Lanes ran entire length of cloister (from which it was separated by a wall) and passed through frater range. Varied in width from mere passage (Byland) to a broad road (Kirkstall), usually with door to church at one end. There was a lane-like space separating church and cloister in some friaries.

Kirkstall Abbey (Lane)

Byland Abbey (Lane)

LANTERN

A name sometimes given to a great central tower with windows in upper storey which provide light at the crossing. More generally it was the source of artificial light. There was often a great lantern or candelabra in the vicinity of the great lectern and there were other lanterns or cressets to facilitate duties or to lessen chance of accidents (e.g. at corners of cloisters, by night-stairs, etc.). Night processions were led by a junior monk who carried a lantern. The circator (q.v.) carried a lantern at night as he went round the church and conventual buildings to see that no brother had been overcome by drowsiness. If he found anyone asleep when he should be at vigil, he placed the lantern before the weak brother's eyes and shook him, returning to his own place. The discovered brother then had to take the lantern and find another in like condition and repeat the process.

It was a minor office to trim the candles, see to the lanterns and fill the cressets.

Hand Lantern

LARDERER

Officer in charge of the larder, subordinate to the kitchener who had to keep him supplied with meat, fish and poultry. 'The larderer should be as perfect, just, faithful a servant as could be found. He had charge of the keys of the out-houses attached to the larder, the hay house, the stockfish house and the pudding-house.'

He was immediately subject to the kitchener and prepared raw materials for the cook for whom he got ready baked meats, venison, turbot and eels. All live animals passed through his hands and he saw to their killing, skinning and other necessary preliminaries.

Lantern Ely

LAUDS

A short office which was conjoined to Mattins and which was similar to Vespers. It began with an opening versicle followed by five groups of psalms sung antiphonally. The first three were followed by an O.T. canticle, the fifth always consisted of psalms 148-150 (the 'Laudes'). Then came a short reading, a hymn and versicle, the Benedictus (Lk.i,68ff), and closing prayers. In Benedictine houses, the reading or 'chapter' was a paragraph of the rule which was thus read through three times a year in the course of this office.

Cistercian Jug

LAUNDRY

Part of chamberlain's responsibility. He had to find laundress(es) of good reputation and character to wash monastic linen, both personal (sheets, shirts and drawers) and liturgical (albs, rochets, surplices). Altar linen was the care of the sacristan.

Personal linen was washed fortnightly in summer and every three weeks in winter. Detailed instructions occur in the Custumals concerning the keeping of tallies so that nothing was lost in the wash. Such losses, if they arose from the negligence of the laundresses, were to be made good by deductions from their wages.

LAVER   (Lavatorium)   see also *Ablutions*

Laver, Kirkham

Washing in the Middle Ages seems to have been invested with a formal and ritualistic quality as is evidenced by the lay romances as well as by ecclesiastical ceremonies. The holy-water stoup at a church entrance provided a symbolic cleansing as did the ceremony of the Asperges (q.v.) and the real washing which took place in the laver as in the maundy (q.v.) had more than overtones of symbol and sacrament.

The laver was located in the cloister near the frater doorway and was the place for washing hands before meals and for performing the morning toilet. There were two types: the long trough, usually recessed within an alcove with elaborate decorations and pinnacles. It was lined with lead, filled through brass inflows (sometimes in the form of lion's heads) and emptied through drain-pipes (possibly closed by stone or wooden bungs). The trough was usually partially let into the frater wall (e.g. Fountains, Rievaulx) but it could occupy other positions (west alley at Haughmond, Kirkham; beneath cloister windows opposite frater at Gloucester). There are remains also at Cleeve, Hexham, Norwich, Peterborough, Westminster, Worcester and the drain survives at Cambuskenneth. The other type, more frequent on the continent, consisted of an independent circular or polygonal building projecting into the cloister-garth. A circular basin surrounded a central pillar equipped with a number of individual taps. Such lavers existed at Canterbury, Durham, Exeter, Peterborough (where the laver was a marble bowl c.25ft in circumference), Wenlock. The laver from Sherborne survives in modified form in the so-called conduit erected in front of the abbey gate.

The water supply at Canterbury served a total of four lavers in the precincts. There are substantial remains of a water-tower there. Notices about plumbing and water-supply are frequent in the chronicles e.g. the new laver at Malmesbury (1284) and the provision of a new supply when the spring dried up at Waverley (1216).

Some great houses seem to have provided a special laver used on the way to the night office (e.g. Canterbury, Wenlock). Beaulieu has remains of laver serving frater of conversi and of another in ambulatory of church.

Towels were kept in a cupboard (free-standing or recessed into wall) near the laver (remains at Fountains, Gloucester, Westminster) and those at Durham seem to have had individual compartments. Towels were changed on Sundays and Thursdays.

Besides its use before meals and as a stimulus to wakefulness, the laver was also the scene of the weekly maundy (q.v.). It came within the fraterer's responsibility and he had to provide towels, keep the basin clean and see that no dirt or grit collected in it. He also provided a supply of sand and a whetstone so that the brethren could scour and sharpen their knives in the laver. Sometimes these duties devolved upon the chamberlain who was responsible for the supply of soap and hot water when required for bathing, shaving, foot-washing, etc.

LAXITY   see also *Corruption*

With the passage of time and the loss of original fervour most houses in later Middle Ages seem to have settled down to a kind of 'gentlemanly' existence which reached neither the decadent or flamboyantly unchristian behaviour asserted by polemical adversaries nor the ascetic ardour and zeal of their first centuries. Consequently, in the two centuries before the Henrician suppression, observance in the various orders tended to coalesce towards a lukewarm mean so that there was little difference in custom between them. The Carthusians are a notable and heroic exception to this generalisation (as were the Observant Franciscans), maintaining even unto death a stricter, more detached and ascetic rule than even the Cistercians in the days of their glory.

LAY ABBOT   see also *Commendators*

An abuse whereby a layman was appointed to the title and revenues of an abbacy by royal or papal commendation, producing almost inevitably not only economic but spiritual dissipation.

LAY ADMINISTRATOR   see *Adminstrator*

LAY BROTHER, SISTER   see also *Conversus*

A member of a religious order who is not bound to the recitation of the Divine Office and is mainly occupied in manual work. The institution arose in C11 when monks were increasingly priests and freed from manual labour. A similar development took place among nuns to free the 'choir' nuns for an elaborated office, mental prayer and intellectual pursuits. Lay brothers and sisters had to be daily present at mass and to recite a short office which often consisted of simple prayers conned by heart.

LAY OFFICIALS

In later Middle Ages, religious houses paid a number of officials to administer their estates. These included the receiver, the bailiff, and, most important, the steward who acted for the convent in all civil matters and exercised the authority of its superior in the manorial courts.

LAZAR-HOUSE

A hospital (q.v.) for lepers, deriving its name from St Lazarus, patron saint of lepers, and from the nursing order bearing his name which concerned itself with the care of sufferers from this disease.

LEAD

Lead was much used in complex monastic plumbing and in window glazing. It was also a very desirable covering for the vast areas of roof which were in constant danger from destructive fires. Consequently, as soon as the house's resources allowed, the church roof at least was covered with this very costly material.

At the Henrician suppression, lead together with brass and bell-metal was second only in the priorities of the plunderers to jewelry and gold and silver. To make it portable it was stripped from the church roof, melted into ingots using the stalls and other carved work as fuel. The resulting bars were stamped with Henry's mark of a tudor rose surmounted by a crown.

The lead stripped from the church roof at Rievaulx was stacked at the west end of the nave to await a suitable time for transport. Unfortunately the attack on the roof had been too impetuous and the entire upper fabric collapsed, burying the lead. It was thus lost until revealed by ministry excavation in 1920. It was presented to York Minster, whose arms also bear the Henrician crown, and was used to relead the Five Sisters window in the restoration of 1923-5.

LECTERN

In the middle of the quire stood a great lectern from

Lectern from Evesham

which the monks sang the lessons (lections, legends) from the scriptures, lives of the saints, or writings of the fathers. There was sometimes a second, and often doubled-sided, lectern for the use of the cantors. These lecterns were often elaborately carved and decorated. A somewhat mutilated stone lectern, allegedly from Evesham, survives in the parish church at Norton. Metal ones survive at Norwich and Peterborough and Newstead's, rescued from a lake, is now in Southwell Minster. Some lecterns were supported on a shaft socketed into the floor before the presbytery step and the stone which held it occasionally survives (e.g. Basingwerk, St Dogmael's, Titchfield). There was a special lectern for the reading at collation (q.v.) and at chapter (socket remains at Byland, Waverley).

Quire Lectern (Newstead)

LENTERN FARE

For 40 days before Easter (beginning on Ash Wednesday) a strict fast was prescribed. It was not to be broken before Vespers when a meatless meal was taken. This monotonous and frugal diet was sometimes alleviated in later Middle Ages by the addition of nuts and dried fruit (raisins and figs).

LEPROSY   see also *Hospital, Lazar-House*

A general name given to a variety of skin diseases which were gradually distinguished in Middle Ages. It was a scourge which waxed and waned and provoked different responses at different periods. It existed in Anglo-Saxon England, seems to have increased in C12-13, subsiding in later C14 but had not entirely disappeared in C15-16. The two earliest hospitals for its treatment ('Lazar-houses') were at Harbledown and Rochester, both founded before 1100, which were quickly followed by many others in first half of C12 under inspiration of monk-bishops (Gundulf, Lanfranc) and Queen Matilda. Foundations were also made by the abbot of Battle, Walter de Lacy, who 'especially compassionated the forlorn condition of those afflicted with leprosy and elephantiasis whom he was so far from shunning that he frequently waited upon them in person, washing their hands and feet, and with the utmost cordiality imprinting upon them the soothing kisses of love and piety' and by St Hugh the Carthusian in later C12.

Leper

LESSON   (Lection, Legend, Chapter)

The liturgical readings which were a central part of each office, especially Nocturns (q.v.), collation and chapter meeting. They were usually sung from a special lectern (q.v.), accompanied by a good deal of ceremony and preceded by careful rehearsal under the direction of the precentor. Readings also accompanied formal meals in the frater (q.v.).

LIBRARIAN   see *Armarius*

LIBRARY

All religious houses possessed libraries; their size was related to the importance and size of the monastery, though even small cells had their own collection e.g. the two monks who lived in the retreat of Farne had more than a dozen volumes available for their use, excluding the Bible and necessary service books.

Initially, the collections were small and probably adequately housed in the book-cupboards placed in cloister (often at north-east corner). At Durham these were ranged against the church wall, at Worcester there were two in east alley near entrance to chapter-house, while the original book store at Gloucester seems to have been in one of the carrels and two neighbouring cupboards in east alley.

The centralised Cistercians seem from the beginning to have planned book storage which usually included a recessed cupboard in east wall of cloister and a small room next to north transept of church entered from cloister (e.g. Cleeve, Fountains, Kirkstall). Cluniac Wenlock has a large vaulted chamber of three bays in this position (built in C13), as had Premonstratensian Titchfield. The Cistercians frequently provided book-cupboards in vestibule or west end of chapter-house (e.g. Calder, Fountains, Furness, Valle Crucis).

Monastic Library
(St Albans)

Increasing numbers of books eventually produced separate library rooms in later Middle Ages (e.g. Canterbury, Durham — the latter had a separate collection for the novices in the west alley of cloisters). In C14 Worcester a library room was provided over south aisle of church, at Bury, Norwich and at St Albans it was in a new upper floor of the cloister.

Books were collected by superiors, borrowed and copied in the scriptorium (q.v.), donated by benefactors and sometimes particular incomes of the house were ear-marked for book production and purchase (e.g. St Albans in late C11). No monastic library has survived as they were deliberately and wantonly destroyed at the suppression: their sheets were used as tinder to light the fires of carved

Wood Carving of Monk
studying

woodwork to melt the lead from the roofs or they were sold in job lots as wrapping paper for grocers and suchlike.

The friars emphasised learning and made special provision for studies and libraries (e.g. Gloucester, Clare) but catalogues have survived only from the Franciscans of Ipswich, the Austin friars of York and the Carmelites of Hulne. Three surviving lists indicate that hospitals also possessed libraries (Elsing, Ewelme, Gateshead).

Glastonbury had 400 volumes in 1247; Bury had over 2,000 before suppression; Canterbury Christchurch had over 600 before 1170, at least 1850 by 1300 and nearly 4,000 at suppression. The small abbey of Titchfield had, by 1400, an exceptionally fine library of nearly 1,000 different works collected in 224 volumes, exclusive of 102 service-books.

These books were the common property of the house, located in the library, church, chapter-house, frater and cloister but a particular volume could be assigned to a religious 'ad usum' and thus considered as belonging to that person for a fixed period. Such books had to be returned, checked and re-issued on the first Monday in Lent. In the later Middle Ages some books seem to have been available for external loan but the librarian was straitly charged about responsibility in this regard. Some books were chained and could only be read sitting or standing at desks near the shelves. Monasteries seem to have invented the library as we know it with procedures for the systematic care of books and catologuing and loan procedures. The

Study. Carrel. Cloister

Barnwell Observances declare that 'the press in which the books are kept ought to be lined inside the wood, that the damp of the walls may not moisten or stain the books. The press should be divided vertically as well as horizontally by sundry shelves on which the books may be ranged so as to be separated from one another; for fear they may be packed so close as to injure each other *or delay those who want them.'*

LIGHTING

The more utilitarian lighting was often provided by cressets, stone bowls filled with fat and provided with a wick. They were usually placed in the dorter, by the night stairs and in the church. Brecon has a fine one with 30 holes, together with fragments of smaller ones. It was the responsibility of the cook or larderer to see to their daily replenishing. There were sometimes lamps at the corners of the cloister (especially north-east) and brackets to support them occasionally survive (e.g. Lilleshall). Tallow candles were also used to light tables etc. in winter. Dark lanterns (to avoid unnecessary disturbance) were part of the equipment of the claustral prior and the circas (q.v.). The children and young monks were provided with lanterns whenever they went about the precincts after dark. There was usually one lantern between two but a single person had a lantern to himself.

Wax tapers were used in church, providing light on the altars but also being votive offerings, symbols and marks of honour. Provision of a candle of a specified weight before a particular shrine, image or altar could be the return for possession of a particular messuage or smallholding. Liturgical lights varied in number according to the solemnity of the occasion. Processional lights or tapers accompanied the great procession and also the book of Gospels, Blessed Sacrament, etc. The nave or chancel of great Benedictine houses was lit by a 'corona lucis', an elaborate metal wheel, much decorated and bearing a large number of candles. Canterbury had two, one in the nave and one in the choir, each bearing 24 wax lights. There is a modern example at Buckfast.

LITIGATION

Monastic records evidence a good deal of litigation concerning property; boundaries, rights and dues. This arises not so much from a fondness for litigation but rather from responsibility in maintaining what belonged to the house. The possessions of Durham e.g. were seen as the real patrimony of St Cuthbert and it was the superior's duty to maintain these possessions. Endowments had been given in return for spiritual services and privileges, particularly prayer for the benefactors and these required the material support of the intercessors. Thus litigation stemmed from many sources, varying from notions of sacrilege to those of contract. It was always expensive, particularly when it involved appeals (especially appeals to Rome sometimes requiring personal appearance there). During the later Middle Ages there was increasing tension, often involving law-suits, between growing towns and the monasteries under whose protection they originally developed.

LITERARY WORK

Monastic historians and chroniclers include such names as the Venerable Bede of Jarrow, Florence of Worcester, William of Malmesbury, Matthew Paris of St Albans, Jocelin Brakelond of Bury. There were also spiritual writers such as Richard Rolle of Hampole, St Ailred of Rievaulx and theologians such as Alexander of Hailes. Problems of times and seasons also led to some developments in

Mathew Paris of
St Albans

astronomy and mathematics as well as the technological development of clocks. R. W. Southern suggests that the increasing elaboration of monastic services in C10-11 developed historians, prose writers, poets and composers (not to mention scribes and illuminators).

LITTLE OFFICE

The Office of Our Lady, the Blessed Virgin Mary, which was added to the monastic breviary and formed a supplement to the great Hours during the Middle Ages. The Benedictine reformer, Benedict of Aniane, in late C8 added a short service in honour of Our Lady to the quire offices which developed with the Marian cult and in late C11 was ordered to be recited by all clerics for the success of the First Crusade.

This 'Little Office', somewhat elaborated, became popular with all clergy and spread to the devout laity and what had started as an appendix to monastic worship became the favoured prayer of the laity everywhere and became a separate entity as 'The Book of Hours' in C13.

'The fact that the Little Office was from the first concentrated on the Virgin Mary is of great significance. With no martyrdom or miracles associated with her in her lifetime, she became, through the mystery of the Incarnation, the central figure in an unprecedented devotion in which many of the deepest emotions of men and women were involved. The multiplicity of traces left in cathedral, chapel and shrine bear witness to this. Through their Books of Hours, with its personal prayers and private images lay folk were able to identify themselves with "Dei Genetrix", the Mother of God'. (J. Harthan).

God gave us Christ through Mary and, according to St Bernard, Christ desires us to have everything through Mary.

LOCUTORIUM   see *Parlour*

MAJESTAS

A representation of Christ in Majesty, a reminder of the Last Judgment (cf. Matt. xxiv, 29ff.) and therefore of purposes of religious life. It was one of the few images allowed in the strict Cistercian rule. The Majestas was usually placed in a dominating position: over the tympanum of the main entrance, sculptured or painted at the east end of the frater and elsewhere. A Majestas from York survives in the neighbouring museum its original position was probably at the east end of the chapter-house and a mutilated survival of a comparable figure exists in the former frater of Worcester (now school hall).

MALLARDY

A name for hospitals for the sick as distinct from other kinds of mediaeval hospice. Another contemporary designation of hospitals for sick was 'nurcery' (sic).

MALTHOUSE

A necessary facility for the production of the staple drink of beer and provided within the precincts, together with its associated kiln. It was usually located in the outer court but as such buildings were normally timber-framed, their existence is indicated only in records (e.g. Nunkeeling).

MANDATUM

The ceremony of foot-washing, derived from the antiphon 'Mandatum novum' (a new commandment) sung during the ceremony (see John xiii, 1-17, 34f.). Mandatum became modified to maundy. (q.v.)

MANUAL WORK   see also *Industry*

Early monasticism envisaged a three-fold division of waking time, more or less equally spent in prayer, study and manual work. The latter occupied a significant place in the primitive Benedictine rule but the increased demands of the choir office and other liturgical functions (under the influence of Cluny) reduced the time available and from C11 general manual work (apart from 'clerking' — book-copying, repairs, illumination, binding, etc.) was increasingly done first by lay brothers and then by lay servants. Remnants of manual work survived but it was

Manual Labour

largely notional and limited to repair of clothes, cleaning of
altar furniture, etc. Such work seems to have been done in
groups while a junior read to the workers from an edifying
book.

The Cistercians and Premonstratensians brought back
the centrality of manual work to the religious life and
consequently were able to reclaim worthless moorland,
drain swamps, convert barren land to pasture, plantation
and tillage. Their great abbeys became advanced farms,
cattle-breeding and wool-growing establishments which laid
the foundations of the country's agricultural prosperity (see

Maundy (Foot-washing)

Granges). But success brought some decline, accelerated by virtual disappearance of
conversi in C14 and by close of Middle Ages the number of lay servants considerably
exceeded the number of religious in almost every establishment.

MARBLE

As a rich and costly material suitable for adorning the house of God, marble was
frequently used in the more flamboyant monastic churches. It was used for altars,
colonettes, for flooring and for screens. Besides imported material, English marble
was used from Portland as well as local 'marble' (e.g. Fountains).

MARGARET, ST (1045-93)

Daughter of Edward the Atheling who, in spite of her leaning towards the
religious life, became the second wife of Malcolm III in 1069. Much influenced by
Lanfranc, she concerned herself with the reform of the Scottish Church and was a
great benefactor of the poor and of religious institutions. She founded the abbey of
Dunfermline which resulted in the introduction of Benedictinism into Scotland for
the first time. Her son David (q.v.), made Dunfermline the Westminster Abbey of
Scotland and founded many other religious houses.

MARTYROLOGY

An official register of Christian martyrs, giving the
name, place of death and sometimes a brief account under
the appropriate date in the calendar. The practice of
reading in quire at Prime the martyrology of the day was
practised in religious houses from C9.

Names of brethren, associates and benefactors who had
died a natural death and for whom the community owed
prayers were similarly calendared in the necrology (q.v.)
which was read at chapter and on other occasions.

The martyrology of Canterbury Christchurch is
preserved in Lambeth Palace library and contains, among

Decorative Roundel
(Resurrection) from Mazer

other documents, the martyrology of saints, the rule of St Benedict, calendar of
obits of archbishops, priors, monks and benefactors. These contents indicate that
this was the chapter-house volume.

MASS

A title of the Eucharist, dating from at least C4, and the commonest mediaeval
term for the central act of Christian worship. Mediaeval theology tended to
concentrate on the propitiatory and sacrificial aspects of this service which, among
other things, led to monks increasingly taking priests' orders and to the
multiplication of masses. This in turn affected church architecture, requiring
increasing provision of altars (q.v.) and the development of the institution of
chantries.

Besides the general, conventual, High Mass ('Missa Major') at which all the quire monks assisted a variety of other masses were offered in the course of each morning.

At about 8.30 am the 'Morrow' or Morning Mass ('Missa Matutinalis') was celebrated. It was variously called the Lady Mass, because it was usually celebrated at the Lady altar and, when the rubrics permitted it, was a votive mass in her honour, or the Chapter Mass ('Missa Capitularis') because, in other than Benedictine or Cistercian houses, it was followed by the chapter (q.v.). Later in the Middle Ages, half the community in priest's orders attended it while the others said their private masses (q.v.) at the altars scattered throughout the monastic church and elsewhere. The assistants at the Morrow Mass said their private mass during the conventual High Mass.

The term 'missa familiaris' could mean either a private mass or one sung for benefactors and friends (members of the extended 'familia'). Special psalms and prayers were also sung at the offices for the same intention ('Psalmi familiares'). This family concern is most obvious in the charitable prayers for the departed members of the household which included anniversaries of various length ('month's mind', 'year's mind', etc.) Such memorials were built into the corporate life (see Necrology) with appropriate prayers said not only in church but also in chapter and psalms were chanted in procession from quire to chapter when prayers were appointed for the dead 'at home or elsewhere' (see also Brief, Mortuary Roll).

Monk in Mass Vestments

Apart from the regular daily mass(es) for the convent, there were occasional masses for dead (Requiem) and special masses at visitations, election of superior, etc. Mass was also said daily in the farmery, at the chapel ante portas and for the lay brethren.

MASTER OF NOVICES   see *Novice Master*

MASTER OF SEMPRINGHAM
The 'prior of priors' or supreme governor of the whole order of Gilbertines (q.v.).

MATRICULARIUS   see *Sacrist*

MATTINS
The night office derived from the vigils of the early church and so called 'vigiliae' until C11. It was originally performed at midnight but Benedict's rule prescribed it for the eighth hour of the night i.e. about two a.m. It was long called 'Nocturns' from the units which composed it and made it equal in size and importance to all the rest of the (day) services put together.

After the silent recitation of the Lord's Prayer, Ave and Credo, the office opened with singing of versicles and responses, an invitatory and hymn varying according to feast and season followed, on Sundays and major feasts, by three Nocturns. Each Nocturn consisted of three psalms with their antiphons, versicle, paternoster and a short prayer called Absolutio to which are joined three lessons each preceded by a benediction. The lessons of the first nocturn are taken from scripture, those of the second are usually historical or hagiographical, and those of the third are usually from a patristic homily on the gospel of the day. Simple feasts and ferias have only one Nocturn, consisting of nine psalms and three lessons. Easter and Pentecost had one Nocturn consisting of three psalms and three lessons. The office concluded on feast days and Sundays (except those of Lent) with the singing of the Te Deum and Lauds (q.v.) followed immediately.

MATURIN   see *Trinitarian*

MAUNDY
    The ritual foot-washing as a reminder of the necessity for love of the brethren. There seems to have been a daily, weekly and annual maundy. The daily maundy was supervised by the almoner when one of the monks washed the feet of a fixed number of poor. (At Abingdon the daily number was three.) At the weekly maundy the brethren on duty in the frater and kitchen washed the feet of the superior and the rest of the convent in the south walk of the cloister, sometimes making use of the laver (as at Fountains). The Great Maundy took place on the Thursday of Easter week when it was the Benedictine custom to admit as many poor folk as there were members of the convent. After the singing of appropriate psalms and collects, each religious knelt before one of the poor, washed the feet, kissed mouth and eyes and then set the guest down to meat and ministered to him.
    The ceremonies of Maundy Thursday date, in one form or another, to C6 or earlier. The maundy benches survive at Canterbury and Westminster where the ritual took place in the cloister. Elsewhere it was performed in the laver or chapter-house.

MAZER
    An elaborate ceremonial drinking-cup passed round on great occasions. Its bowl was of wood (strictly speaking, bird's eye maple — hence the name) which, together with its stem, was often elaborately decorated. Such cups were often the gift of benefactors or confraters who were piously remembered on the occasions of their use and were often among the rich accoutrements of later fraters. Henry III gave one to Westminster and they sometimes survive in the treasuries of cathedrals as well as in museums

MEALS   see also *Breakfast, Dinner, Mixtum, Pittance*
    From Easter to Whitsun, dinner was eaten about noon and supper just before nightfall. From Whitsun to September 13 (eve of Exaltation of the Cross) dinner was about three p.m. on Wednesdays and Fridays and at this time daily from September 13 to beginning of Lent. During Lent supper disappeared and dinner was postponed until dusk.
    Strict dietary regulations prohibited the flesh of quadrupeds except as a concession to the weak and sick (see Farmery). Fish and poultry were counted as flesh meat and not allowed on fast days. Benedict's rule allowed for local relaxation in colder climes than Italy and some diminution became established e.g. mixtum and pittance. Though the strict rule about meat was relaxed it was never allowed in the frater (see Misericord).
    In the later Middle Ages, the basic porridge was supplemented by fish (fresh, dried or salted), meat which was generally beef or some form of pork (bacon or pickled 'sowce'). Mediaeval mutton was scraggy and rarely eaten. On festive occasions there could be fowls and some form of dessert. There was nearly always eggs, cheese and butter from the dairy and vegetables (though limited in choice) from the garden. There was a staple allowance of bread and beer made on the premises.

MEAT
    Benedict's rule forebade meat except to the weak and sick but with typical moderation it allowed superiors to make reasonable modification. C10 Abingdon allowed meat stew and meat puddings on certain feast days and meat became generally allowed except during fasting

Fish Cook (Misericord)

seasons. In C12 the ascetic Cistercians were only allowed two vegetable dishes, cooked without grease, but there was gradual relaxation against the entire prohibition of flesh meat. By the later C14 meat was generally allowed in religious houses 'for the reason that doctors and experience both teach that a total abstinence from meat is contrary to nature and hurtful to the system; so were monks to be confined to such diet, they would become weak and suffer, a thing the rule neither orders nor desires.'

MEDICINE   see also *Farmery*

A large religious community nearly always included a trained physician who may or may not have functioned as infirmarer. A good deal seems to have been known of the medical qualities of herbs (many of whose popular names indicate a monastic connection). Some monasteries had quite well developed pharmacies and most of the libraries contained standard works on medicine. At one time the monks gave great attention to medicine, partly out of natural interest and partly out of the desire to be self-sufficient (St Bernard did not like his 'sons' to consult physicians).

The physician of a monastery was sometimes a monk but in later Middle Ages more often not. At Bury in the time of Jocelyn he was a member of the community. The barber-surgeon, responsible for blood-letting (q.v.) was a kind of inferior physician — a Mr as distinct from a Dr.

MENDICANTS   see *Friars*

Religious who lived on alms, from 'mendicare' — to 'beg'.

Templars

MILITARY ORDERS

Their foundation was part of Christendom's response to capture of Jerusalem by Saracens (1076) and the ill-treatment of pilgrims to that place. They attempted to combine the life of a monk with that of a warrior and their institutions stretched across Europe from the Knights of St James in Spain to the Teutonic Knights in Eastern Germany. The most famous and widespread were the Templars and Hospitallers (qq.v.)

MILL

An important element in mediaeval economy whose possession was a privilege since it was a monopoly and its use involved a fee. They were powered either by wind or water and the latter are more common in association with religious houses since monastic sites were normally situated close to a river. It would seem that monastic mills were technically advanced, for in 1387, three mills in Southwark (two belonging to Henry Yevele the famous master-mason) were, according to the contract, to be modelled on the mills of Battle abbey. In these cases, at least, most of the structure was prefabricated.

Monastic mills sometimes survive (e.g. Abingdon, Fountains) and where they do not their former position can often be deduced from the mill leet or lade. Besides corn-mills, monasteries sometimes possessed other workshops operated by water power (e.g. fulling-mill at Durham, forge at Kirkstall).

MINISTER

A person officially charged to perform spiritual functions. The deacon and sub-deacon together with the celebrant at High Mass are known as the 'sacred ministers' and are provided with special seats in the sanctuary (see Sedilia).

MINOR RELIGIOUS ORDERS   see *Friars, Minor Orders; Fontrevault, Grandmontines, Savignac, Thiron*

MINORESSES
Female members of the order of Friars Minor, otherwise known as the Second Order of St Francis or Poor Clares after their foundress, St Clare (1219). They later divided into Urbanists and Collettines, (cf. Conventual and Observant Franciscans).

The Minories, London EC4 derives its name from a convent of Minoresses (1293-1539). There were other mediaeval foundations at Bruisyard, Suffolk; Denney, Cambridgeshire; Northampton; Waterbeach Cambridgeshire. Foundations were proposed at Clovelly, Hull and Newcastle but they did not materialise before Reformation. Few material remains: some may exist in Minories but only visible ones are at Denney. The order returned in C19 and now has some dozen houses in England, two in Wales and two in Scotland.

MINUTIO   see *Bleeding*

MISERICORD
From Latin 'misericordia' — mercy. The word is used of the projection of the tip-up choir stalls which provided some support during the long periods of standing during the office (especially Mattins). Some monastic examples survive e.g. Chester, Christchurch, Ely, Hampshire, Malvern, Minster, Sherborne, Winchester, Worcester.

Franciscan Prioress

The term is also sometimes used of a monastic dining-room set apart for religious whose health or age requires some relaxation of the strict rule, particularly in regard to meatless diet. It was often associated with the farmery. At Evesham it was beneath the dorter, not far from the bleeding-room and had a door into the farmery garden. It was under the frater at Kirkstall. Though 'misericord' was the usual term, others were used: 'loft' at Durham, 'deportum' at Canterbury, 'seyny' at Peterborough, 'oriel' at St Albans. This indulgence was originally only for sick monks or those recuperating after being bled but its use spread more generally in C13 and it had even entered Cistercian practice by late C14. With the increasing relaxation of discipline, there were some monasteries where the misericord became the normal eating place and the frater exceptional. In later Middle Ages new misericords were built at Forde, Furness, Jervaulx and Kirkstall.

MITRED ABBOT
The heads of some of the greater houses (including priors of cathedral priories) obtained this status by papal privilege. It allowed them the right to wear the mitre, carry the crozier and wear other episcopal insignia. Mitred abbots sometimes sat in the House of Lords but there was no connection between the two privileges. Except in the case of exempt houses, this papally granted dignity was confirmed

Mitred Abbot

by the metropolitan and diocesan bishops as it carried privileges affecting jurisdiction. By the end of the Middle Ages there were 29 abbots with this status, most of them Benedictine (Abingdon, Bardney, Battle, Bury, Colchester, Crowland,

Evesham, Glastonbury, Gloucester, Malmesbury, Peterborough, Ramsey, Reading, St Albans, St Augustine's Canterbury, Selby, Sherborne, Shrewsbury, Tavistock, Tewkesbury, Thorney, Westminster, York) but including the Cistercians at Beaulieu, Fountains and St Mary Graces London and the Augustinians at Cirencester, Thornton and Waltham.

MISSIONARY WORK

The conversion of the British Isles and the establishment of the Christian church there was due to monks at every stage: not only the Celtic monks whose names and activity are often only recorded in place names but others of whom more is known such as Gregory, Augustine, Paulinus, Aidan, Cuthbert, Wilfred, Theodore, Dunstan. After the church had been established much consolidation was done by saintly monk-bishops (e.g. Hugh of Lincoln) and the monasteries of England produced apostles for Germany, the Low Countries and Scandinavia. Remote establishments must have had considerable effect on 'home missions', perhaps particularly those of the regular canons.

MIXTUM

A meagre breakfast, consisting of bread soaked in wine, which was allowed to the old and infirm and to novices whose strength was not equal to the long morning fast which did not end until after midday. It was taken in the frater and signalled by three strokes on the bell at the church door. The time varied in different orders but it was before or immediately following Terce. One set of directions fixes the quota for mixtum at a quarter pound of bread and a third of a pint of wine or beer. It was preceded by a blessing and grace, consumed standing in silence, and followed by silent prayer for benefactors. The mixtum was not taken on fast days.

Canterbury and Winchester have some remains of the turn-table or 'rota' where the mixtum could be placed by the servitor and taken by the brethren without communication.

MODERN HOUSES

The religious life returned to these islands in a trickle in C17-18 and became a flood in C19. With the exception of the Gilbertines, all the major pre-Reformation orders are represented by the majority of the dozens of rules and hundreds of houses belong to post-Reformation orders and institutes. It is impractical and perhaps unnecessary to list these houses, varying from back to back dwellings in slums to architect designed abbeys in the country. But major abbeys have been mentioned as have houses in places where there is a mediaeval entry.

Fountains West Front
(restored with Nathex)

MODIFICATIONS

In the course of many centuries' occupation, monastic buildings had to be extended or modified to meet changing needs and the explorer will find traces of extensions, stairs and doors blocked up and buildings put to other uses. The Cistercians abandoned their distinctive style of frater (Cleeve, Croxden, Whalley) and extended the misericord (q.v.). The disappearance of the conversi after C14 produced further approximation of Cistercian and Benedictine plans and their former accommodation was taken over by the superior (Forde, Hailes, Sawley). Where the abbot already possessed adequate lodgings the buildings of the conversi were put to various uses. At Wykeham the first floor became a granary as at Rievaulx and at the latter

Castle Acre
(reconstruction)

the ground floor was divided into a number of small chambers with individual fireplaces. There was a general extension of private quarters: for obedientaries, scholars, corrodians, retired superiors (e.g. dorter undercroft at Byland and entire nunnery at Wilberfoss). Dorters were divided into individual cubicles by wainscot partitions and private wards were introduced into the aisles of farmery halls (Fountains, Tintern). the warming room (no longer the only domestic fire) became a common room (as at Durham) and was more drastically modified at Forde, Fountains and Rievaulx.

Normans introducing
Benedictine Reform

In small houses the domestic services were brought into the claustral ranges (Kirklees, Thicket, Yedingham, Wilberfoss, Handale) and even at the great Rievaulx the undercrofts of both dorter and frater became tanneries. It seems that in many smaller houses the superior's quarters became the centre of the communal life (e.g. Finchale). In other places (Lindisfarne, Muchelney) the frater became the great hall of the president.

In larger communities there was a tendency (for economic reasons) to divide the household into a number of separate units with their own kitchens (e.g. Bardney, Ely, Kirkham).

Norman Doorway: St
Albans (Benedictine)

The most drastic modification was the abandonment of the cloister itself (Forde, Lindisfarne, Valle Crucis).

MONASTERY

A community of men or women, devoted to the service of God and bound by a three-fold vow of poverty, chastity and obedience to a superior and to a rule.

MONASTICISM

A formal structure designed to permit a life of perfection in greater security than is normally possible in the secular world. Its chief aim is personal sanctification by fulfilling the Counsels of Perfection in poverty, chastity and obedience. The last is the most characteristic of the coenebitic life as the others may be practised in the world. The monk's activity is divided between prayer and work with the opus Dei or Divine Office being the centre and

Holy Contemplation:
reading in Dorter

source of both his private prayer and of his work. The latter, originally restricted to manual work, developed with monasticism itself to include copying manuscripts, teaching, art and scholarly research so that in the Middle Ages the monks were the chief teachers of Europe and an influential civilising power.

It originated in Egypt where St Anthony is usually regarded as its founder and was introduced to the west in C4 where the first monks usually followed eastern models, often marked by extreme austerity and a tendency to ascetic competitiveness. The rule of St Benedict (480-543) was the first detailed monastic legislation adapted to European needs and its genius brought the supercession of all other rules, including Celtic (q.v.) so that from C8-12, Benedictine monasticism was the only western form. It was brought to England by Augustine in 597, restored by the Anglo-Saxon reformers and encouraged by the Normans. This monopoly was overthrown by new developments, particularly the foundation of the Cistercians and Canons Regular (of which one form, the Gilbertines, was a home product).

Monasticism proper declined with the arrival of the mendicants (q.v.), but it

benefitted from the great spiritual revival of the Catholic
Reformation in C16. Monasticism was suppressed in
England by Henry VIII, briefly restored by Mary Tudor,
and returned in some fullness in C19.

MONASTIC HOSPITALS   see also *Hospitals*

Apart from the farmery and guest-house within
precinct, many religious houses supported an extern
hospital or hospice. A hospital under the direct control of a
major religious house tended to be even more monastic in
character than an ordinary hospital. Some are almost
indistinguishable from priories or cells, especially those of
the Gilbertines which were often infirmaries (e.g.
Clattercote and two in Lincoln).

Some hospitals became full priories, sometimes losing
their distinct eleemosynary character but providing the
usual monastic hospitality (e.g. Cockersand, Creake,
Tandridge). In other cases the change was only nominal
(e.g. Maiden Bradley). At St Bartholomew's Smithfield, the

Honest Toil

priory and hospital existed side by side in almost complete independence each with
their own revenue, staff and seal. Sometimes the titles of priory and hospital were
interchangeable — 'the priory at Wilton' was merely a hospital governed by a prior.

Augustinians were much concerned with hospitals, serving among others the five
largest London hospitals. Other Augustinian hospitals existed at Brackley,
Bridgwater, Dover, Newcastle St Mary, Newstead, Southampton. The Benedictine
rule was followed, not only by all hospitals under Benedictine monasteries but at
certain others (e.g. Bristol St Mark, Strood).

Franciscans in England, as distinct from their practice elsewhere, do not seem to
have been noticeably involved with lepers but there were relations between certain
hospitals and the friars.

MONASTIC LIFE   see also *Daily Round*

Walter Daniel described Ailred of Rievaulx as 'adorned with the three marks of
the monastic life: holy contemplation, sincere prayer and honest toil'. To the truly
called the life centred on adoration of God for what He is, intercession on behalf of
others arising from love of both God and neighbour and sanctified work according
to the Benedictine prescription and Pauline admonition. To the less sympathetic its
routine, monotony and utter weariness must have been almost inconceivable.

Even a comparatively sympathetic historian like Crossley says: 'They spent their
time in innumerable services and study, living a dull existence in silence, shut away
from the world and its excitement, for they lived on a low diet and suffered much
from indigestion, a prey to habits which cut across the precepts of good health, and
the constant and periodical bleedings were weakening. The average life of a monk
was 55 years. The picture of a monk's life during an English winter is not to be
envied, with no heating in the monastery, the dorter icily cold when he rose for the
long night service, going half asleep in the dark to a freezing church, perhaps filled
with a clinging fog, and being expected to sing and pray with fervour for an hour
and a half'. (English Abbey, p.28).

A contemporary wrote: 'I cannot endure the daily tasks. The sight of it all revolts
me. I am tormented and crushed down by the weight of the vigils and I often
succumb to the manual labour. The food cleaves to my mouth, more bitter than
wormwood. The rough clothing cuts through my skin and flesh down to the very
bones. More than this, my will is always hankering after other things, it longs for the
delights of the world and sighs unceasingly for its loves and affections and
pleasures'.

MONK

A word of uncertain origin (possibly meaning 'solitary' originally) applied to any member of a male religious community, living under the vows of poverty, chastity and obedience. Though it has no clear technical sense it contains the notion of a member of a secluded community and should not be applied to members of such later developments of the religious life as the Canons Regular, Clerks Regular and Mendicants.

Cloister: Centre of Monastery

Monks became divided into two classes — the quire monk and the lay brother (though this distinction is now disappearing again). In the Middle Ages the quire monks (with the requirements of literacy) were often of noble lineage or at least from the yeoman class. Many of the superiors came from the most distinguished families in the land. Nuns (apart from the Gilbertines) also generally came from the upper classes and Dartford e.g. received noblewomen both as postulants and as young girls for their education.

MORROW MASS

The mass (q.v.) between Terce and Chapter.

MORTUARY ROLL   see *Brief*

MURAL PAINTING

As in all mediaeval churches, monastic ones were decorated with murals, though the austere Cistercians severely limited their number. They were generally destroyed at the reformation but there are some survivals : substantial at St Albans, fragments at Durham. There was often a mural (representing the Crucifixion or Christ in Majesty) on the wall behind the dais in the frater (e.g. Lacock) and they also appear elsewhere e.g. chapter-house (Westminster).

Benedictine Black Monk

MUSIC   see also *Precentor, Succentor*

All monastic services, including grace at meals, were sung, originally to plainchant which the monks created and developed. Besides the practice, teaching and development

Monks descending Night Stairs

of plainchant, monasteries made other contributions. Some monks were instrumentalists (there is evidence of recitals in the farmery as part of the curative process), some were composers not only of masses, hymns and carols but also of 'secular' music. It is perhaps significant that 'Sumer is i-cumen in' occurs between the Latin lines of a manuscript from Reading abbey (and the Carmina Burana take their name from the Benedictine abbey of Beuron).

MUSTARDIUS

A minor kitchen official, appointed by the kitchener. He seems to have been the same person as the salter, responsible for seasonings and sauces including 'vert-sauce' with vinegar to go with lamb (and mackerel). In the later Middle Ages it was considered convenient if not necessary to take mustard with all salted food, meat or fish, and in winter, particularly, there was a good deal of salted food in the diet.

NARTHEX   see *Galilee*

NAVE

Except in the smallest churches, the church plan was cruciform with the nave forming the long vertical arm before the presbytery. It was often of great length in Benedictine and Cistercian houses: seven bays at Blyth, Buildwas; eight at Durham, Roche; nine at Binham, Rievaulx; ten at Furness, St Albans; Fountains and Peterborough had eleven; Byland, and Winchester twelve, while Norwich extended to fourteen.

In churches belonging to Benedictines and regular canons the nave was open to laity and often functioned as parish church (e.g. Brecon, Wymondham) and at Tynemouth the parish priest had a house attached to its north side. Such naves tended to survive the suppression (e.g. Binham, Bolton, Bridlington, Bristol St James, Chepstow, Cranborne, Davington, Deeping St James, Deerhurst, Dunster, Elstow, Freiston, Hatfield Broadoak, Hatfield Peveril, Hurley, Lapley, Malmesbury, Minster, Nun Monkton, St Bees, Shrewsbury, Thorney, Tutbury, York Holy Trinity, Bourne, Dunstable, Goring, Lanercost, Letheringham, Portchester, St Germans, Thurgarton, Waltham, Worksop.

At Crowland and Leominster one aisle alone served the parish, while at Sherborne the parish church adjoined the west end of the nave and at St Albans it lay outside the north aisle.

In Cistercian churches the nave was the church of the conversi and was cut off from the rest of the building by stone screens at its eastern termination and between the arches of the nave arcade (remains at Buildwas, Strata Florida, Tintern). The stalls of the brethren were placed parallel to the arcade screens and the aisles functioned as passage ways. Many small churches dispensed with nave aisle (Nun Monkton, Portchester) and even some large ones (Kirkham, Titchfield). Others only added an aisle on the opposite side from the cloister (to avoid expensive alterations) e.g. Bolton, Lanercost.

Friars' churches emphasised preaching and therefore they designed their naves as 'halls' with wide aisle and broad arcades.

When, in C14, conversi practically disappeared, the Cistercians tended to open up the nave and often placed additional altars against its piers. The nave then became a vast vestibule to the quire, an assembly place for processions, etc.

The main altar in the nave was the 'Jesus' altar, situated in front of the rood-screen which was normally at least one bay west of pulpitum (intervening space was called retro-quire e.g. St Albans). Occasionally sockets for rood-beams can be discerned and niches or recesses for statues in pillars.

The nave had two doorways into the cloisters, one at each end usually a great western doorway which was only used on ceremonial occasions. Occasionally there is a north doorway (e.g. Kirkstall) which was normally lay-folks' entrance where there were parochial rights.

NECESSARIUM   see *Rere-dorter*

NECROLOGY   see also *Martyrology*

The list of dead remembered by a particular house. Sometimes an order had a general necrology used in a number of their houses e.g. Cluniac. A French Cluniac necrology from late C12 has some 1500 names in it.

NIGHT OFFICE   see *Mattins, Nocturns*

NIGHT STAIR

A staircase giving direct access from the dorter to the church, usually via the south transept. Its head was often enclosed by a lobby at the north end of the dorter. Sometimes when space was at a premium it was reduced to a spiral stair or vice (e.g. Ewenny, Lindisfarne, St Radegund). Similar economy sometimes caused it to be contrived in the thickness of the west wall (e.g. Haverfordwest, Lacock).

Night stairs rarely survive but there is a perfect example at Hexham and a less perfect one at Bristol. Their position can often be recognised against the west wall of the transept (Neath has moulded stone handrail) e.g.Fountains, Kirkstall.

Cluniac houses (e.g. Castle Acre, Thetford) and the Augustinian Llanthony Prima did not provide for direct communication between dorter and church and presumably made use of day stairs at all times.

NOCTURNS

An older name for the office of Mattins (q.v.) derived from the units (Nocturn) which composed it and which varied in number according to the dignity of the feast.

NOMENCLATURE

Monasticism is complicated by the use of many synonyms: Regular Canons, Canons Regular, Friars, Mendicants, Austin Friars, Augustinian Friars, Black Monks, Benedictines, superior, president, prelate; monastery, house, convent.

Most parts of the monastery had three names: English (dormitory), Latin (dormitorium), Norman-French (dorter); refectory, refectorium, frater, etc. We have normally, following DE practice, used the last form.

Similarly officials can be called infirmarian or infirmarer, sub-cantor or succentor, etc.

NONE

The ninth hour of prayer i.e. about three p.m. A short office with similar structure to Terce and Sext. It consisted of a hymn followed by psalmody (part of Ps.cxix), a short reading with response and closing prayer.

NORMAN CONQUEST

Not only brought systemisation and reform to secular affairs but also to ecclesiastical ones. Under Cluniac inspiration the monasteries of Normandy had been reformed before William I's reorganisation of the English church on Norman lines extended this influence. Norman ideas and Norman personnel invaded the whole of English monastic life. Old monasteries were, with few exceptions, given Norman abbots and reorganised under the direction of archbishops of Canterbury, Lanfranc and St Anselm, both of whom had been monks of the reformed Bec. The king and his followers established new independent monasteries and dependencies of foundations in Normandy (see Alien Priories).

NORTH PANE

The northern cloister alley has no associated range since it is next to south side of church. This alley or 'pane' is usually wider than the others to accommodate the 'carrels' (q.v.).

NOVICE

When a postulant (q.v.) was admitted to a religious house, he or she became a novice, serving a probationary period before full acceptance into the community. Often there was special accommodation for novices, a building where they might 'meditate, eat and sleep', otherwise they were situated in a special part of a common building; cloister, frater, dorter. Besides the special responsibility of the novice-master (q.v.) the whole community was involved in the novice's formation so that 'anyone from a love of God and zeal for righteousness' might reprove, advise or warn him (with the master's permission). They had to leave chapter after the sermon, spend more time in church than the monks and make frequent confession.

Their instruction had academic and social elements as well as religious ones. If necessary they were educated in the monastic school until they could understand their service and their scriptures. If they had already reached this minimum requirement, they took more advanced lessons from the master or their tutor and, in the later Middle Ages 'if the master of the novices did see that any of them were apt to learning and did apply his books and had a pregnant wit withal' then he informed the superior who arranged for his transference to a house of studies in the university where he might study advanced divinity.

Novice taking Vows

Consideration for their youth and inexperience was shown in a variety of ways. They were under a slightly relaxed rule, particularly in matters of diet. They ate at a separate table in frater (sometimes partitioned off) and often had their own common room (often in the dorter undercroft e.g. Basingwerk), and at Peterborough and Westminster they had their own chapel nearby. They usually shared the recreation of the warming-house or 'common house' and often had special provision for their own recreation. At Durham and Tewkesbury they were provided with a garden and bowling green behind the warming-house where they might recreate themselves when not under instruction but their master stood by to see to their 'good order'. In addition they seem to have played a number of board-games such as 'nine holes' or 'fox and geese' and traces of these survive in the cloisters of Canterbury, Gloucester, Norwich, Westminster.

Receiving Tonsure

Their school seems normally to have been in the western alley of the cloisters and at Durham they had a special book-cupboard there. The period of the novitiate seems to have varied from six years to less than one but after mid C12 it was generally stabilised at one year.

'When a whole year had passed by in the cell where the tyros of Christ, are proven' and 'if the brethren approve of his behaviour and he of their way of life' (notice the double approval), the master instructed him to ask the prior and some senior religious to put the case for his permanent reception. This took place in chapter and if the suit was successful, the novice was sent for and reminded again of 'the hard and difficult things in our way of life'. If he reassured the chapter of his willingness to undergo all this, and more if need be, the brethren were finally asked if they wished to receive him into their number. If they agreed, their decision was confirmed by the superior and the novice left chapter to write out his profession or, if illiterate, to ask another to write it out for him, subscribing with a cross (the origin of 'making his mark'). He then read this out 'before the high altar in the church in the presence of all the community, as the law of blessed Benedict commands.'

After his formal profession, there followed an elaborate ritual which included the solemn blessing of the cowl and his investment by the superior with the words, 'May the Lord clothe thee with the new man who is created according to God in righteousness and the sanctity of truth'. Henceforth he was regarded as a full member of the monastic body but for three days he kept silent and received daily communion before joining in the full life.

There were usually about half a dozen novices at any time in the average house.

NOVICE-MASTER

Monastic school-master and spiritual director, who was responsible not only for the intellectual, social and spiritual formation of novices but also for their material needs, including food, drink and clothing which he drew from the cellarer and chamberlain. He supervised not only their study but also their recreation and slept near them in the dorter. His teaching could include reading, writing and psalmody as well as the rules and customs of the house and the nature of the monastic life.

He had obviously to be very perceptive, both for the sake of the novice and that of the community, as his continuous assessment was the weightiest evidence whether or not a novice should become a permanent member of the house. He had also to be very patient, as besides academic instruction, he had to instil the minutiae of monastic behaviour 'how to arrange his habit when he stands and when he sits, how to bow, how to keep custody of the eyes, how to dress and undress, even how to sit in the rere-dorter, how to behave at meals and services' including the complex rituals of the latter. Beyond all this was the heart of the matter: 'how he ought to please God . . . and whatever he does whether waking, praying, meditating or working, to do all for the sake of God.'

NUMBERS

The number of individual houses varied greatly from century to century but generally it grew to a peak in later C12, steadied in C13, declined in mid C14.

The Suppression Act of 1536 abolished about 370 smaller religious houses while the mendicants (nearly 2,000 friars) were suppressed after the Pilgrimage of Grace and all religious houses had disappeared by 1540. Some seven were restored by Queen Mary but these were abolished in 1559.

It is difficult to calculate the total number of religious houses which existed at the beginning of 1536 but it was probably about 1,000 with some 12,000 religious including c. 2,000 nuns.

Numbers in an individual foundation (quite apart from the servants, dependents, etc.) are difficult to calculate and, when an estimate is possible, they fluctuate considerably at different periods. The normal foundation number was 12 plus a superior and in C12 monasteries were full to overflowing, resulting in continual new foundations. By C13 large numbers were still being maintained but growth had largely stopped though there were still large numbers of conversi in Cistercian houses, usually double the number of quire monks (e.g. Louth had 150 to 66 quire monks). 1349 saw the Black Death's greatest impact, leading to the extinction of smaller houses which were often amalgamated with larger ones. Numbers never recovered from this havoc as there were not enough postulants to compensate for the sudden decrease though ground was slowly being regained in the early C16. In C15 few houses had the numbers that their resources could support: Norwich was reduced to 40-50, Walsingham to 17, while 25 was a large number for Premonstratensian priories. Conversi had practically vanished and the great monasteries of Furness and Bury had respectively 30 and 60 monks.

In normal times the number in a religious house depended on a variety of factors: the number of applicants, the 'entrance requirements' of a particular institution, the 'fashionability' of the order and, perhaps above all, the resources from which the community had to be supported.

For the intial numbers of some individual houses, see Foundation. The numbers at the suppression are collected conveniently in Knowles and Hadcock for England and Wales and in Cowan and Easson for Scotland.

NUNS   (Sanctimoniales, Monachae, Nonnae)

One of the surprises of the Middle Ages is the comparatively small number of female religious as compared with male (the reverse of the contemporary situation). In Middle Ages, nuns never seem to have exceeded 20 per cent of 'religious' population. Their houses increased in number from 12 in 1066 to a maximum of 152 just before the Black Death, falling to 136 just before the

Dominican Nun

Nunneries

suppression. The corresponding number of nuns was respectively 206, 3,247 and c.2,000. Their life was the same as that of the monks with a few necessary differences. The same means were used to the same end. The chief difference, is that men were often associated with convents, both as chaplains andservants or lay brothers (in case of Gilbertines e.g.) to do heavy work. Apart from the Gilbertines (and lay sisters), mediaeval nuns seem to have been almost exclusively recruited from the upper classes. Nunneries were also used as 'finishing schools' and many convents maintained schools for girls e.g. in 1336 Polesworth had 30-40 boarders — a large number for any mediaeval school.

Gilbertine Nun

There is not much evidence for nunneries being asylums for unrequited love but they were often refuges for widows and for relatives of male religious. Some nunneries had the reputation of being peopled not by young unmarried women but by mature women of noble rank including natural widows, relicts of soldiers (especially Crusaders), those rejected by their husbands (or daughters-in-law) and those co-operating with their husbands' desire to enter religion.

See also Augustinian Canonesses, Benedictine, Bridgetine, Cistercian, Hospitals, Nunnery, Poor Clares, Vowesses.

Nuns engaged in 'Opus Anglicanum'

As in the case of certain male religious, nuns were occasionally given permission (when judged worthy and apt) to attempt a life of greater seclusion as an anchoress. There was an anchoress cell attached to St Edmund's chapel near the bridge at Doncaster and there was a nun from Hampole in the chapel at East Layton. Some nunneries had their own anchorages within the precincts (e.g. Davington, Carrow, Polesworth). Barrow seems to have had a cell for a recluse and Julian of Norwich was one of the many anchoresses who came from Carrow. This movement seems to have been sufficiently popular in the later Middle Ages as to require books of direction, e.g. the Ancren Rywle.

Nuns in Procession

In Scotland there were never many nunneries and their houses were always comparatively small and poor, probably never numbering more than a score with about 250 professed religious.

NUNNERIES   see also *Repairs*

The spiritual and liturgical life in nunneries was almost indistinguishable from that of men in the same order. They could not, of course, provide priests from their own number and this necessity received a number of solutions. Wealthy houses sometimes provided a prebend for a chaplain, St Sepulchre Canterbury relied on a priest attached to a chantry founded in their church, others were supplied by a monk from the same order, others were double foundations.

There were related problems in the administration of lands and properties, since an abbess or prioress was often landlord and appropriator of churches and it was difficult to manage these affairs without breaking the rule of enclosure. Usually a layman was appointed as 'custos' or warden to see to the temporal administration. Such stewards were sometimes lodged within the precincts (e.g. at St Helens, Bishopgate).

All nunneries were subject to episcopal visitation and usually were small in size as well as being few in number. England had c.150 nunneries, Scotland very few but there were Benedictines at Lincluden (some remains) and of the nine Cistercian communities there are remains at Eccles and North Berwick. There were two priories of Austin Canonesses (including Iona) but scant remains and nothing of the Dominican nuns at Edinburgh or of the two houses of Poor Clares.

NUNNERY OBEDIENTIARIES
Parallel to those of monasteries but with some differences. The smallness of nunneries often led to one person holding more than one office. Nunnery obedientiaries nearly always included: prioress, sub-prioress, cellaress, sacristaness, treasuress, chantress, fratress, infirmaress, mistress of novices, chambress and guest-mistress.

NUN TOWNS
Just as there were towns which grew up under the shadow of a large abbey of men, so there were settlements which developed because of the previous existence of a nunnery e.g. Polesworth, Sheppey. These were usually little more than villages (whose name sometimes recalls their origin) but even in a large town such as Winchester a nunnery could be a significant employer of labour and contribute to the town's growth and economy.

'O's'
The 'O's were the great Advent antiphons: 'O Sapientia!' etc. each with its own complex chant. During the later Middle Ages each had acquired a secondary association with a particular obedientiary, e.g. 'O Clavis' with the cellarer, and the custom developed that when 'his' anthem was sung that obedientiary laid on a little party which helped to mitigate the rigours of the Advent fast.

OBEDIENCE
Of the three vows which are taken in every Christian monastic and quasi-monastic order, that of obedience is perhaps the most fundamental as chastity and poverty can be and are exercised outside the formal religious life. Mediaeval commentators associated this vow with the renunciation of Satan in the baptismal vow, the opportunity to exercise the virtue of humility to the destruction of pride which was seen as the chief of the Deadly Sins.

It lay at the heart of St Benedict's rule (chap.v.) and is related to his fundamental concept of a community under the absolute rule of a benevolent father (see Abbot).

Total Obedience was due to Abbot or other Superior

OBEDIENTIARIES   see also *s.v. Almoner etc., Officers*
The officers of a religious house who held 'obediences' i.e. departmental responsibilities to which they had been commissioned by the abbot or other superior who could also summarily dismiss them. As the function and departments of all religious houses were similar, they tended to have the same obedientiaries though in some places (especially in small houses) one person might combine two (or more) offices e.g. in C16 Durham the sub-prior was also fraterer and night-cursor.

Late in C13, those at Barnwell were prior (prelate), sub-prior, third prior, precentor, succentor, sacrist, sub-sacrist, cellarer, granger, receiver, sub-cellarer, fraterer, kitchener, chamberlain, hosteller, infirmarer, almoner. Unless some of these offices were held in plurality, the list implies that more than half and perhaps almost all members of the community held some office.

Oblate

Most obedientiaries had their own revenues and kept their own accounts which were presented for approval in chapter at least yearly and sometimes quarterly. Their term always ended with the appointment of a new superior and they had to surrender their keys to a new prelate on his appointment. He could, of course reappoint them if he saw fit.

Because of the demands of their offices, the rule was relaxed for obedientiaries: they were not compelled to attend all quire offices, they could travel out of the enclosure, they were sometimes allowed to sleep out of the dorter (often in the farmery or their own checker) and similarly they were allowed to eat in the farmery or their own checkers.

OBLATE   see also *Child*

'About St Benedict's time the Latin church innovated upon the discipline of former centuries and allowed parents, not only to dedicate their infants to the religious life but to do so without any power on the part of such infants, when they came to years of reason, to annul the dedication. This discipline continued for five or six centuries, beginning with the stern Spaniards, nor ending until shortly before the pontificate of Innocent III (1198-1215). Divines argued on behalf of it from the case of infant baptism in which the sleeping soul, without being asked, is committed to the most solemn of engagements', (J.H.Newman). Bede is one of the most famous of such oblates.

Benedictine Oblate: Bede

These 'pueri' and 'infantes' were given special care until the age of 15. They seem to have been excused the night office, they were taught reading and singing, had their own chapter and were given careful supervision and some indulgence. The child was offered (made an oblation) at the offertory in the mass, with the petition for entry and the boy's right hand wrapped together in the altar cloth. This petition was to embody the promises of stability, conversion of life and obedience.

'OBLEYS'

'Oblations' — a word used for the hosts or wafers of unleavened bread consecrated at mass. They were also called 'singing breads'. Their production was the responsibility of the sacrist or sub-sacrist (q.v. also Ovens).

OBSERVANCES

Monastic communities were governed by the rule of their particular order but whether this emanated from St Benedict or from St Augustine, it was a statement of general principles only and insufficient to meet the

Oblates at School

requirements of changing times and particular places. The details of daily life were governed by regulations originating in custom (hence their name, when collected, of 'customaries' or 'customals' which were often called the 'observances' of a particular house as in the case of the enlightening Barnwell collection).

OBSERVANTS

An austere reform of the Franciscans (q.v.)

130

OFFICE, DIVINE

The 'opus Dei', the main work of monks which occupied a substantial part of the day and night and which was their 'raison d'etre'. It consisted of the Day and Night Hours (q.v.) which were sung in quire (q.v.). It was, and is, the heart of monastic spirituality and a powerful element in religious formation: 'Those wholly unfamiliar with the monastic life are perhaps slow to allow for the moulding influence, upon minds and characters attuned to them, of the liturgical texts with their accompaniment of chant and ceremony, which brought to the thirteenth century, as they bring to those fortunate enough to know them at the present day, something of the purity, the austerity, the exquisite enjoyment of type, symbol and allusion, and the mingling of all that is best in the Hebrew and Roman genius, which was the supreme achievement of the age before the barbarians conquered Rome. Beauty of word and melody, beauty of architecture and ornament cannot create, and may even hinder, the purest spirituality, but pure spirituality is a rare treasure, and for men of more ordinary mould the liturgy in all its fullness may be a tonic nourishment as well as an ennobling discipline.'   (D.Knowles).

OFFICERS   see also *Obedientiaries*

Monastic officials tended to grow in number with the expansion of religious houses and tendency towards division of labour. The original rule of St Benedict (c.450 A.D.) mentions only the abbot, prior (praepositus, provost), priests (since most monks then were laymen), cellarer and porter. Other monks with special skills were appointed as artificers, while the rest followed a weekly roster which appointed them kitchen servers, frater readers, etc.

By C11 the chief officers were the abbot, major prior, deputy or claustral prior, circumitores (circae), cantor, sacrist, chamberlain, cellarer, guest-master, almoner, infirmarer. These tended to remain to the end of the mediaeval period with some additions and variations.

Besides the obedientiaries, officials of a religious house could include porters, butlers, yeomen of the cellar etc. on the one hand and, on the other, stewards, registrars, shrine keepers (at Durham this official was also third prior). In a great house all officials had assistants, deputies, clerks and servants.

OPUS DEI   see *Office, Divine; Horarium*

ORDER, RELIGIOUS

A group of dedicated men or women, vowed to poverty, chastity and obedience to a particular rule.

ORGAN

A musical instrument which reappeared in Europe in the Dark Ages. In C10 Winchester abbey had one possessed of 400 pipes and 26 bellows, presumably requiring at least 27 men to operate it.

Organs remained mechanically crude through the Middle Ages and often had large keys which were depressed with the fist rather than finger. A C14 document at Worcester records the payment of a musician 'to thump the organs, teach the quire boys and instruct any of the monks who wishes to learn the art of organ-thumping'.

Most monastic churches possessed at least one organ. Durham had one in early C13 and at Dissolution possessed three 'paires' in the quire. Besides these three quire organs, Durham possessed two others: one used for the Jesus Mass (most probably placed near the great rood) and another for the public services in the Galilee. A monastic organ was often located in a loft above the pulpitum.

ORIENTATION

Similar principles operated in the laying out of monastic churches and chapels as in others. They normally faced east and there are examples of 'weeping chancels' — most noteworthy at Bridlington. In some cases, exigencies of site made orientation impossible e.g. Rievaulx where alignment is more nearly north and south than east and west.

OUTBUILDINGS

Most monastic remains give little impression of the vast array of subsidiary buildings which clustered round the curia and the claustral buildings. The smallest house required at least a granary, bakery and brewery while the larger had various workshops, masons' lodge, mill, laundry, stables, etc. (see Offices). These subsidiary buildings were usually timber-framed and thatched and rarely survive. Even those constructed in stone rarely leave substantial remains though there are some at Canterbury, Fountains and elsewhere.

Among outbuildings might be included such structures as the great gatehouse, the chapel before the gate, almonry, pilgrims' chapels, hospitals, granges and court-rooms and a rare provision was the bath-house usually located some distance east of the cloister. More common were workshops, mills, factories, threshing floors, malt-kilns, stables, cowsheds, goatsheds, pigsties, sheepfolds, poultry-houses (sometimes with accommodation for their keeper) and stockfish ponds.

OUTER COURT see *Curia*

OVENS

Characteristic remains (usually of a beehive shape) of ovens survive in many monastic kitchens (e.g. Fountains).

Besides the general domestic ovens there was special provision for baking the eucharistic bread (obleys) with great care and ceremony under the direction of the sacrist. At Durham it still exists in the church but more usually it was located in the sacrist's checker where there are sometimes remains (e.g. Castle Acre, Thetford).

PANE

An alley or walk. The word is used e.g. of the cloister walk.

PANTRY

The bread ('pain') store. It was usually associated with the kitchen and sometimes had access to the frater via a service or dresser hatch. Sometimes, as in secular establishments, the pantry gave on to a screens passage or service lobby.

PARCLOSE SCREEN see also *Pulpitum, Screen*

A division, of wood or stone, separating off part of a church (e.g. chapel, chantry, shrine) from the rest.

PARISH CHURCH see also *Appropriation, Pastoral Work*

Monastic churches were essentially private chapels for the use of the community and members of the opposite sex were rarely admitted. There was provision for extern worship in the 'cappella ante portas' (chapel by the gate) e.g. Abingdon, Bury, Reading, York, and the Benedictines generally allowed the laity access to the nave which often became the parish church (Brecon, Binham, Bridlington,

Major Prior

Tynemouth, Wymondham). Sometimes another part served
the parish (an aisle at Crowland, Leominster; south
transept at Chester).

Any parochial use of the minster was likely to disturb
the silence and the monastic offices which were central to
the religious vocation and way of life, so often the monks
preferred to provide separate parish churches. At
Sherborne, it was joined to the west end of the nave and at
St Albans it was outside the north aisle. Chester built a new
church for the parish as did Bury and Coventry. Evesham
provided two churches within its precincts (which survive)

Music

and Wymondham provided a separate bell-tower as a result
of conflicts over bell-ringing. Rochester and Holy Trinity Aldgate London built
parish churches in their outer courts.

Nuns' churches too, were often shared with the local parish but sometimes the
utilisation was reversed: the nuns have the 'nave' and the parish the eastern arm (e.g.
Marrick, Nunkeeling).

This generosity or shared use explains the survival of many monastic churches
or parts of churches, which once belonged to Benedictines and Augustinians e.g.
Cartmel, Christchurch (see Nave). In some cases the parishioners exchanged their
rights in the nave for the use of the chancel and transepts (e.g. Boxgrove,
St Bartholomews Smithfield) while in others they bought the church or part of it
from the new owners (Great Malvern, Romsey, Pershore, Tewkesbury, St Albans,
Selby).

Parochial rights were rarely granted in naves (or any other parts) of
Cistercian, Cluniac or Premonstratensian churches, hence their almost universal
destruction.

PARLOUR   (Common House, Locutorium, Speke house)

A room where the rule of silence was relaxed to allow
necessary conversation ('parler'), including e.g. advance
discussion of chapter business.

There were often two parlours: a private or inner
parlour in the cloister, near church (often in or replacing
slype * q.v.) which was reserved for members of the

Nuns in Parlour

community (e.g. Kirkstall, Fountains) and another (often
in the west range * *) for meetings with outsiders
including artificers and merchants. It was in this position
at York and its outer gate known as the 'gate of Tobias'
(alluding to the stranger who revealed himself as an angel
in Tobias xii.15). Here strangers and travellers knocked
and three poor men were fed daily and other alms and
hospitality dispensed. At Durham by C15 the outer
parlour had become a place 'for marchaunts to utter their

waires'.

*   Inner parlour and slype were often side by side (e.g.

Monks in Parlour

Castle Acre, Fountains, Jervaulx, Rievaulx, Roche,
Thetford, Tintern).
**   Outer parlour was often in passage east of frater which gave external
access to cloister (Easby, Haughmond). Sometimes it was a large room
(Bridlington, Selby) projecting westwards and sometimes it was associated with
president's lodging (Castle Acre, Chester). At Rufford it occupies centre of great
cellar.

PASTORAL WORK   see also *Chapel*
Both the Celtic and early Benedictine monks were much involved in
evangelisation and pastoral care but this was, strictly speaking, no part of the
specifically monastic vocation. They continued to provide services in church and
extern services of charity and hospitality which often included provision of almonry,
schools, infirmaries and hospices. They often provided accommodation for the
worship of pilgrims and parishioners (see Parish Church) but rarely served as parish
clergy either in provided or appropriated churches and normally supplied a vicar. A
monastic church was not suitable for parish use for it had to be closed, like the rest
of the house, at night. This is exemplified in the case of Leominster which had long
served parochial needs when in 1283 Archbishop Peckham ordered 'that the said
monks shall build and complete within one year, outside their doors ('extra portas')
in a place suitable therefor, a decent chapel of reasonable size in honour of the
glorious martyr St Thomas (of Canterbury), to which there may be free access to
fugitives at all hours and in which the Body of Christ may be honourably kept for
sick parishioners'. This provision almost became the norm and a parochial church
can almost invariably be found in the near vicinity of the providing monastery (e.g.
St Margaret's, Westminster; St Olave's, York).
Since regular canons were, by definition, priests, they were more involved in
pastoral work. Premonstratensian Canons were generally allowed to serve the
churches belonging to their houses. Austin Canons were granted similar licence by
diocesan bishops, though with some demur. It may have been part of their original
purpose to supply parish clergy on their estates or provide a ministry to outlying
hamlets which lacked a parish church but such provision was checked in C13. The
great increase in appropriated churches seriously affected their own service in quire
and therefore they almost invariably supplied vicars. On the other hand, as late as
the abbacy of William of Clown (d. 1378) we hear that two monks from the abbey of
St Mary de Pré 'migrated to ecclesiastical benefices with cure of souls'.
Friars had a different ministry and vocation to that of monks; they were from
the beginning closely involved in city life, its problems and needs. Much of their
work was consequently pastoral, not only preaching, homilectics and spirtual
guidance but much practical care and charity. This led to their popularity and the
adverse comparison of monks with them. Unfortunately, their increasing
dependence on begging in the later Middle Ages tended to lose them their popularity
and eventually to make them the most disliked of religious orders in the period just
before the Reformation.

PARVISE   (Paradise)
The area between the west end of the church and the enclosure wall of the
precincts. It sometimes contained a bell-tower. The word is also applied to an
elaborate western porch and the chamber over it (e.g. at Peterborough).

PECULIUM
A personal allowance which developed from C14. From early times monks had
been allowed to receive small gifts in cash to distribute to the poor (including needy
relations). Later this allowance was increased to include medicines, spices and
holiday purposes. Parallel to this, the custom grew of giving a clothes allowance
instead of issuing clothing from a central single source. Sometimes clothing
allowance and pocket money were issued separately, sometimes they were combined
to produce a total annual allowance in C15 and C16 of about £1, which was
generally known as 'wages'. Reformers tried to abolish the custom but it persisted to
the suppression. 'Petty as were the sums in question and reasonable as were most of
the purchases and expenses, the custom of issuing money, and in particular clothes
money, had a demoralising effect; the dignified spiritual conception of common
property and common care was lost, and the monk, from being a son of the house,
became the petty pensioner with a small allowance.'   (Knowles)

PENAL CODE

The monastery was a society and had its regulations and sanctions. The purpose of the latter was to facilitate the keeping of the rule and to smooth internal regulations in a close and closed community. The internal discipline was supported by an external one.

The monastic penal code began in the desert and was particularly severe in its early forms. Later penalties could extend from reprimand, imposition of extra duties, mitigation of food or recreational periods, segregation, symbolic demotion (losing place as cantor, reader, lower place in processions, etc., kneeling where others stand, and so on) to corporal punishment in chapter and even

Discipline

confinement in prison. Penance could be private or public and was usually awarded by the abbot in private or the abbot in chapter. Prison was naturally for grave faults and could include solitary confinement and reduction of diet to bread and water. It appears that imprisoned monks were released for offices which they attended with their head covered. It was an important principle in the monastic code that faults should be willingly and spontaneously confessed and the punishment welcomed as just and positive.

PENANCE

Depends on the notion that sincere repentance for a fault is exemplified and aided by the performance of some unpleasant task. Its nature and extent was decided by the superior after public confession in chapter and by the confessor in private (auricular) confession. Penance could also be performed voluntarily and secretly in reparation not

Friar hearing Confession

only for one's own faults but for those of others. During the hour after Prime, those who desired to approach the sacrament of penance could be sure of finding a confessor in the chapter-house where alone the confessions of religious were heard.

PENSIONS

Increasingly in the later Middle Ages, religious houses supported a kind of pensioner called corrodian (q.v.). Almshouses or hospitals also supported poor throughout their history. Towards the close of the period there was a tendency for superiors to retire to special accommodation where they received allowances in kind and sometimes in cash.

At the suppression, superiors who co-operated were awarded grateful pensions, ranging from £60 to £100, derived from the former resources of the house until they could be replaced by stipends from bishoprics or other benefices in the newly constituted Henrician church. The rank and file in the same houses who were not only insignificant but could not co-operate so influentially with the king's purpose were given a mere £5. Those who resisted not only received no pension but were in danger of imprisonment or death.

PHARMACY   see also *Infirmary*

The mediaeval religious houses seem to have contained a pharmacy of greater or less extent within the infirmarer's chambers. Its contents were derived from herbs grown in the monastic herbarium (q.v.) or acquired from elsewhere. The infirmarer was expected to be skilled in their use and the monastic libraries usually contained herbals for reference. Sage was served to those who had been bled and the Barnwell Observances e.g. require the infirmarer to have always 'ginger, cinnamon, peony and the like, ready in his cupboard.'

Physician

PHYSICIAN   see also *Infirmarer*

It does not seem that there was generally a physician in the community though the life of St Ailred of Rievaulx may have been written by one. The infirmarer was expected to be able to dose with drugs, cordials and 'pick-me-ups' and the rule of St Augustine assumes the availability of a physician for consultation.

Physicians were among the rare seculars who had general leave to enter the farmery and could also be given permission to have their meals with the sick (Barnwell Observances). He naturally worked in close co-operation with the master of the farmery.

Physician and Patient showing 'Bleeding Points'?

PILGRIMS   see also *Shrine*

Religious houses often possessed a shrine, relic or remarkable image that attracted the devout and/or superstitious and they naturally made provision and provided assistance for pilgrims. The most popular shrine in England was that of St Thomas of Canterbury and the little bells carried by pilgrims were called Canterbury bells (hence the name of the flower). The other pilgrimage in England of European fame was that to the shrine of Our Lady of Walsingham. There are remains of chapels provided by religious houses for the benefit of pilgrims, e.g. Walsingham, on Glastonbury Tor, Red Mount, King's Lynn, St Catherine's above Abbotsbury, a chapel (now cottage) besides spring on way to Cleeve, and St Michael's chapel on approach to Fountains. Sometimes these chapels were simply served by a hermit or chaplain.

English houses also provided inns or hostels for the benefit of pilgrims and survivals include the George at Glastonbury and at Norton St Philip together with the Star and Cross Keys at Holywell. Holywell was a popular pilgrimage and was the subject of indulgences granted to Basingwerk and a house of Templars was said to be founded for protection of its pilgrims. Bardsey Island, Pembrokeshire, was sanctified by a settlement of Culdees (from before 516 AD) whose descendants seem to have been absorbed into the Augustinian foundation in C13. The route was marked by pilgrim's churches at Clynnog Fawr, Pistyll, Nevin, Llangwnnadl and Aberdaron. There is a marker cross carved on roadside near Pistyll and at Aberdaron, where the pilgrims embarked, the C13 hospice (now a farm) still stands and retains its popular name: Y Gegin Fawr ('The big kitchen').

Pilgrim

In Scotland the chief goals of pilgrims were St Andrews, Whitchurch, Whithorn.

Similarly, infirmaries were placed on pilgrim routes or provided by a convenient religious house e.g. the farmery at Castle Acre was used by sick and dying pilgrims who had been heading for Walsingham.

Other provision resulting from the influx of pilgrims includes churches for their devotions within the monastic precincts (e.g. St Lawrence, Evesham) and architectural developments to allow for easier access to shrine (wider ambulatories, one-way systems etc.) not to mention special buildings for board and lodging (e.g. Canterbury, Winchester).

PILGRIMAGE OF GRACE   (1536)

A popular religious rising in the counties north of the Trent in reaction against the suppression of the smaller religious houses and other aspects of Henrician policy. Under the banner of the Five Wounds of Christ some 40,000 men joined the protest of Robert Aske, a Yorkshire lawyer, and many religious returned to their recently dissolved houses: 'Work is done rapidly by willing hands' and within a week the 'king's tenants were universally expelled; the vacant dormitories were again peopled; the refectories filled with exultant faces. Though it was so late when they returned the monks sang mattins the same night.' Easby, Hexham, Lanercost, Newminster and Sawley were among the houses reoccupied and the men of the latter district took an oath to resist any further attempt to expel their community.

The government faced a serious crisis but the reasonable Aske voluntarily disbanded his forces on assurance that grievances would be redressed and a parliament convened at York. Immediately, the king acted with speed and utter ruthlessness. Aske was siezed and hanged in chains at York and German mercenaries hanged his followers in every town and village as a warning to other dissidents. Other leaders were barborously executed and the abbots of Sawley and Whalley were hanged at Lancaster. The pilgrimage was used by the crown to implicate some of the 'greater abbeys' in 'treason' so 'justifying' their forfeiture to the crown and spreading the extent of the Dissolution. The abbots of Rievaulx and Fountains were hanged, drawn and quartered at Tyburn.

PITTANCE

A very modest 'treat' or addition to the scant monastic fare, usually provided to celebrate a liturgical feast or some other event in the community's life, such as the anniversary of a benefactor. It usually consisted of an extra dish: eggs, fish or meat, or dessert. At Newminster the pittance consisted of bread, ale and salmon.

On Shrove Tuesday the pittance was often pancakes or fritters, called 'crisps' at Barking and 'flawnes' at Stamford St Michael. A pittance became customary on Maundy (or 'Shere') Thursday when e.g. the nuns of Barking had baked eels with rice and almonds and wine while those at St Mary de Pré had 'Maundy ale' and 'Maundy money' (see Peculium) and the convent of Stamford St Michael had beer with wafers and spices.

The system became so complex in some larger houses (e.g. Durham) that a special obedientiary called the pittancer was appointed to deal with this late institution* (At Worcester he had a special lodging.) Otherwise it came within the cellarer's purview.
* Sometimes the community voluntarily diverted the pittance to a worthy cause e.g. building repairs, beautification of church

PLACE NAMES

Street or place names may afford a clue to the former existence of a religious house though they may be misleading through being based on romanticism rather than history or tradition.

Street names in e.g. Bicknacre Essex yield Augustine's Way, Monks' Mead, Priory Lane. London has many: Canongate, Minories, St Sepulchregate, etc. Blackfriars, Whitefriars and Greyfriars are common in many places.

Names of individual buildings often indicate former use of themselves or of site e.g. Abbey, Bede, Bedern, Chantry, Grange, Hermitage, Priory.

Place names are often informative such as the elements 'llan' or 'clas' (glas) in Celtic sites or 'kirk', 'minster', 'stowe' elsewhere. Other elements are found e.g. Abbotsbury, Cerne Abbas, Canons Ashby, Nun Monkton, Priors Hardwick, Salford Priors, Swaffham Prior, Whitchurch Canonicorum, Whiteladies Ashton. It should be noted, however, that such places may indicate the possession of an estate rather than the existence of a community, as Tooting Bec reminds us that it once formed part of the considerable possessions of the great Norman house at Bec and had a Benedictine cell.

PLAINSONG   (Plainchant)

The traditional ritual melody of the western Christian church, inextricably associated with Benedictine (and other monastic) worship. It is synonymous with Gregorian (q.v.) and emphasises the unadorned (and unharmonised) musical accompaniment to words in the free rhythm of speech.

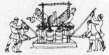

Organ to accompany
Plainsong

Plan

It came to England in 597, was largely lost at the Reformation though it affected Anglican chant and, in C19 and after, other liturgical music of the established church. It continues, though under some competition and attack, in religious houses.

PLAN

Planning was at first pragmatic but a type became established under the influence of the Cluniacs which became, from C11, the model in England. Its chief features were:

a. On the highest point of the site, a great church with aisled nave and presbytery to accommodate the quire offices and the great liturgical processions (q.v.).

b. The great cloister round its central garth with its north walk backing on to the church with doorways into it at the east and west ends, a south walk from angle of transept and nave providing access to east range (q.v.) whose length was determined by size of dorter which occupied upper floor with rere-dorter at south end (usually at right angle). From its north end issued the night stairs. Off the south cloister walk lay frater with its service kitchen outside the cloister range at south-west. The west range contained cellarage and checker with superior's accommodation later introduced above. At its north-west angle was an exit to curia and outer world. The cloister walk provided covered access to surrounding buildings as well as location for various subdued activities.

c. To south-east of eastern range, i.e. in most secluded part of precinct, lay farmery block, housing sick, temporarily disabled and aged who could not follow full round of monastic duties. It was consequently large and often resembled a small monastery in itself with its dorter, frater, chapel, infirmarer's quarters and herb-garden (sometimes within a lesser cloister). It also accommodated some obedientiaries and (later) cells for students and copyists.

d. To west of west range, where monastery made contact with world, lay the curia, entered by a gatehouse and containing a variety of busy and somewhat noisy offices. Sometimes there was an inner court between the curia and the cloister with its own gate.

There were modifications of the above basic plan due to peculiarities of the site, pre-existing buildings or natural features. Some orders had their own idiosyncracies. Such variations, and the reasons for them, often add additional interest to the examination of a site.

The Cistercians (q.v.) developed a uniform plan for all their houses. Austin Canons usually placed their frater on an undercroft, (part of which was the warming-house). The Premonstratensians were least architecturally ambitious or uniform in their planning while both Carthusians and Gilbertines developed a unique plan utterly unlike any others. In houses of friars the cloister was reduced to a corridor and the main entrance to their claustral buildings was usually through a north door in a transeptless church. In general the plans of nunneries resembled those of Benedictines or regular canons.

Illuminator

Besides differences between orders there were changes with time, resulting from the virtual disappearance of lay brethren, the growing desire for modest comfort and relative privacy and elements such as the elaboration of gatehouses, moats and fish-ponds.

POCKET MONEY   see *Peculium*

POOR CLARES   see *Minoresses*

POPULATION
It is difficult to estimate the population of mediaeval England but estimates give some 1,100,000 in 1086, rising to c. 3,700,000 in 1346. There had been a severe European famine c.1316 which caused many deaths. The figures dropped sharply in 1346-50 as a result of the Black Death and may have been reduced to something approaching the 1086 figures.

Porter?

PORCH   see *Galilee*

PORTER   (Janitor)
The gate-keeper or door-keeper. He was generally responsible for outer security and for the admission of wayfarers after nightfall.

In the later houses there was often more than one porter but the chief was custodian of the great gate (often living in gatehouse). Other porters were responsible for inner security, for locking the church, dorter etc. at night and for keeping the cloister uninterrupted and inviolate during the day. The chief porter handed on visitors, having enquired their business, to the superior or appropriate obedientiary, as prior, guest-master, novice-master, cellarer, etc. At Bury he was a lay employee of the abbey.

The was often a separate kitchen porter who dealt with a good deal of traffic from the outer-world. He prevented unauthorised access to the kitchen or disturbance to the cook; he checked the coming of seculars, begging clerks who lacked proper leave or proper business. He also received and distributed the daily alms of food to those waiting at the gate.

POST-REFORMATION ORDERS
With the exception of the Gilbertines, the orders existing at the suppression returned to these islands, mainly in C19 together with representatives of the large number of new orders and institutes which were founded after the Reformation, e.g. Jesuits and Sisters of Mercy.

POSTULANT
One seeking admission to a religious order. Initially he was lodged near the monastery gate for a few days after which he presented himself to the chapter (q.v.) on three consecutive days humbly petitioning to be accepted as a novice (q.v.).

POVERTY
One of the three monastic vows (q.v.) and specifically directed against the materialism of the world. 'They venerate poverty, not the penury of the idle and the negligent, but a poverty directed by a necessity of the will, sustained by the thoroughness of faith, and approved by divine love.' This state was an attempt to follow Christ: 'If thou wouldst be perfect; go, sell all thou hast and follow Me.'

It was a declaration of allegiance to God rather than mammon and a preference for the love and humility of community against the self-centredness of private property, Unfortunately, monks not only became corporately rich through work, benefactions and good management but also, in the later Middle Ages, private property (q.v.) crept in, in fact if not name, under the guise of 'peculium' (q.v.).

PRANDIUM
The main, and usually first, meal generally taken about noon.

PRAYER

A life of corporate prayer, continuing by day and night in the offices (q.v.) was the 'raison d'être' of the monastic life. Besides the daily masses and the Hours the community prayed for those who had made their vocation possible: the founders and benefactors of the house, living and dead. Thus, from one point of view the monastery could be considered, in a secondary function, as 'a great chantry foundation in which intercession for the dead never relaxed, coupled with prayers for the good estate of the living whose names were inscribed in the books of the church.' (A.H.Thompson).

Private prayer was secondary though the private mass and some spaces in the office might be regarded as such.

Private Prayer

Before each office there was a time for private prayer during which each religious said Pater, Ave, etc., and directed his own intentions silently before responding to the sung versicle 'O Lord open thou our lips . . . '

It should be remembered that a good deal of reading was meditative reading (in cloister, frater, chapter and collation) and could easily pass into private prayer.

PRECENTOR

One of the most important obedientiaries (q.v.). He was director of music and chief cantor. Besides the heavy responsibilities of organising the music of the services (all of which were sung), he conducted choir practices, rehearsed the readers for quire and frater, chose and taught the appropriate antiphons, corrected musical mistakes and was charged with ordering processions. He also made sure that the right music was available, that the quire-books were properly notated and kept in good repair. As a development of his responsibility for service books, he usually doubled as 'armarius' (q.v.) or librarian. As librarian, he was also usually the annalist, archivist and chronicler e.g. Eadmer of Canterbury, Symeon of Durham,

Precentor

William of Malmesbury. This work included preparing briefs (q.v.), mortuary rolls, etc.

As ruler of the quire, he picked those who were to sing the lessons and the responses and 'what he arranged to be sung had to be sung and what he decided to be read had to be read'. His position was on the right hand side of the quire, ('cantoris') and that of his assistant succentor (q.v.) on the left. He regulated the singing, particularly the time, and corrected mistakes. He drew up the duty list or tabula for services and readers and sometimes taught the cloister-boys to read but 'he was on no account to slap their heads or pull their hair' as this was reserved to the master of the boys' school.

'Let the precentor then — who may conveniently also be styled the chief of the singers, the leading singer, the foremost singer, the singer who sings remarkably or surpassingly or better than the rest — comport himself in his office which is a source of pleasure and delight to God, the angels and mankind, with such regularity, reverence and modesty; let him bend low with such reverence and respect, let him walk so humbly, let him sing with such sweetness and devotion that all his brethren, both old and young, may find in his behaviour and demeanour a pattern for the religious life and the observances required by the rule.'   (Barnwell Observances)

PRECEPTORY   see also *Commandery*
Strictly speaking, a house of the Knights Templar (q.v.) but name was often retained when these houses were transferred to the Hospitallers after the Templars were suppressed. The personnel of these establishments usually consisted of a small number of knights who wore a white cloak adorned with a red cross, together with chaplains, sergeant-commoners and servants who wore black. There were 23 preceptories connected with the London Temple, 18 of them were made over to the Hospitallers after 1312 and one, Ferriby, was refounded as an Augustinian priory. Most were small, functioning as estate management centres and sometimes as recruiting points.

PRECINCT
The area around and belonging to an abbey whose bounds were marked by ditch, bank or wall which was broken by one great gate, often a fine structure of which many examples remain. The precinct area was very extensive in order to provide space for all the monastery's physical needs and necessary services. At Glastonbury it covered 60 acres, at Fountains 90 and 100 at Jervaulx; at Furness there were 63, at Westminster 40, Canterbury St Augustine had 30, Tintern 27, Battle 20.
There are very substantial remains of the precinct wall at Battle, Bury, Fountains, Leicester but perhaps the most outstanding is that of York St Mary's.
One might see analogies between a castle and a great abbey with its outer curtain or ditch, one or more baileys or courts with their gatehouses, the conventual buildings proper representing the inner bailey dominated by the church as the keep of God. Like castle baileys, the monastic courts contained the ancillary buildings, often timber-framed.
The precinct of a great monastery, besides numberless stores, workshops, cattle-sheds, barns and the like, might contain chambers and checkers for obedientiaries, cemeteries and charnel-house, widely varying guest accommodation, orchards, gardens and vineyards.

PRELATE
One placed in charge ('prelatus') of a diocese or a religious community. At Barnwell the conventual superior (prior) seems always to have been called the prelate.

PREMONSTRATENSIANS
An order of Canons Regular (q.v.) f.1120 by St Norbert at Premontré, west of Laon. Its relation to Augustinian Canons is similar to that of Cistercians to Black Monks. The habit consisted of a long white cloak and hood over a white cassock with a white cap — hence their name of White Canons. It was founded as a reformed, singularly ascetic and rigourous community emphasising manual work for which special time was provided in their horarium.
Their similarity to the Cistercians included preference for remote sites, the dedication of their churches to Our Lady, the attachment of conversi to each house and the central organisation governed from the mother house at which chapters were held (annually). They came to England in 1143 with the foundation of Newham, Lincolnshire which in turn founded Alnwick (1147) and ten other abbeys before 1212. One of these, Welbeck (1153) produced seven more daughters between 1175 and 1218. they eventually had 31 abbeys in England usually consisting of 12 canons and abbot, together with

Premonstratensian

141

dependents of conversi and/or servants. Besides abbeys and non-conventual cells, Premonstratensians are found serving parish churches and acting as chaplains (to canonesses of their own order at Broadholme and to Cistercian nuns at Heynings, Legbourne, Stixwold, Swine).

Of Premonstratensian remains part of one church survives in modified use at Blanchland. Perhaps the most attractive ruins are at Dryburgh, followed by Easby and there are other remains at Bayham, Beeleigh, Coverham, Egglestone, Guyzance, Halesowen, Leiston, Shap, Titchfield, Torre. Soulseat may have been the earliest foundation in Scotland where there were eventually six houses with remains at Drybergh, Fearn and Whithorn.

The canons returned to England in 1872 with a mother house at Storrington and daughters at Crowle and Manchester.

PRESBYTERY

'The priest's place' i.e. the easterly section of the monastic church beyond the quire (q.v.) occupied by the High Altar and provided with its appurtenances and seats for the officiating clergy. C11 Benedictine presbyteries were apsed and aisled with subsidiary apsed chapels (St Augustine, Canterbury, Bury, Leominster, Muchelney, and with variant examples at Castle Acre, Durham, St Albans, Thetford, York). The apse did not last long in England and was usually quickly superceded by a square ended presbytery (Dover, Lewes, Romsey) which became general in C12.

These developments formed three main types:
(a) A square east end around which the aisles were returned with a projecting Lady Chapel roofed at a lower level (e.g. St Albans, Winchester) (b) Square-ended presbytery flanked by aisles (Alnwick, Castle Acre, Lanercost, Titchfield). Sometimes this modest plan was simplified even further by abolishing the aisles (e.g. Brinkburn, Easby, Lindisfarne, Monk Bretton). (c) The continental 'chevet' which was not popular in this country (Battle, Coventry, Tewkesbury, Westminster).

Aumbry, Piscina and Sedilia, Presbytery, Tynemouth

The austere orders expressed their ideals in simplicity of church design (Cistercians, Carthusians, Grandmontines and later the friars), restricting themselves to the minimum requirements of a narrow church with no architectural division between presbytery and nave (e.g. Brecon, (Dominican), Hulne (Carmelite), Lincoln (Franciscan), Mount Grace, Witham (Carthusian). The early London Charterhouse had a similar plan and the Grandmontine houses at Grosmont and Craswell kept the simplicity together with an apsidal east end inherited from the continent. Simplicity is maintained even in such cruciform churches as Haughmond (Augustinian), Torre (Premonstratensian), early Tintern, Waverley, Kirkstall and Valle Crucis (Cistercian). The modest presbytery of the Cistercians, often limited to two bays, was developed as a result of the need for more altars (e.g. Byland, Dore, Jervaulx, Netley, (late) Tintern). The final development was the great eastern arm exemplified in Thornton (six bays), Rievaulx, Whitby (seven), Carlisle, Kirkham (eight), York (nine). Fountains went even further and to its aisled presbytery of five bays added an eastern transept so spectacular that it was imitated at Durham.

Less ambitious developments simply extended the presbytery (e.g. Easby, Strata Florida,) while more flamboyant ones adopted the chevet idea (Beaulieu and more fully at Croxden, Hailes, Vale Royal).

The centre of the presbytery (or sanctuary) was the High Altar, often standing clear of the east wall and backed by a stone reredos (e.g. Durham, St Albans, Winchester). It was divided at its west end from the choir by a single (sanctuary) step called the 'gradus presbyterii'. This usually is discernible even in ruins and sometimes there are traces of the fixture for the lectern (e.g. St Dogmaels).

Sedilia (seats for the ministers at High Mass) are usually recessed into the south wall, together with a piscina (drain for washing sacred vessels) often associated with a credence (shelf for vessels containing wine, water and 'obleys'). There are usually traces of other fittings: the aumbries or lockers recessed in the wall which once protected relics, altar plate etc. and niches or bases for statues or support for screens. Many examples survive (Inchmahome, Fountains, Kirkstall, Tynemouth, etc.).

PRESIDENT see also *Abbot, Prior, Superior*
Also called prelate. The superior of a religious house.

PRIME
The first hour (q.v.) of the monastic day. It was said at daybreak and was sometimes followed by Prime of the Blessed Virgin Mary. In structure, it was similar to Compline and began with a hymn followed by a group of psalms and the Anthanasian Creed leading to a short lesson with its response. It concluded with the lesser litany, the Lord's prayer, apostles' creed, a series of suffrages including a form of general confession and absolution and an invariable collect.

PRIOR see also *Claustral Prior*
'The first among the brethren' second in command to the abbot and particularly charged with the maintenance of order in the cloister, both physical and spiritual. He was usually nominated by the abbot but occasionally he was elected from a short list of nominees. The prior of a daughter or dependent house was normally chosen from and by the senior members of the parent foundation. Sometimes this right was surrendered but the mother house retained the right of confirming the election (e.g. Westminster and Great Malvern in 1217).

Prior's Door, Ely

In cathedral priories and some non-Benedictine houses, the prior was the superior of the convent in which case he was assisted by a sub-prior who occupied the place of a prior under an abbot. In very large houses (e.g. Lewes, Peterborough) there could be a third and fourth prior as well as a sub-prior. These junior officers were originally known as circas (q.v.) or circatores since their chief function lay in making periodical 'rounds' of inspection in the convent.

PRIORY
i. A religious house governed by a prior or prioress. Among monasteries, a priory was usually a smaller establishment than an abbey except in the case of cathedral priories (q.v.). Daughter houses usually began as priories as did the dependencies of great abbeys. Most of the houses of Regular Canons (q.v.) were denominated priories as were all Carthusian establishments.
ii A small cell, (q.v.) accommodating agents on a distant manor or estate was often called a priory and similar dependencies of continental houses were called 'alien priories' (q.v.)

Bridlington Priory

Prioress

Apart from cathedral priories, the major remains in England include Bolton, Boxgrove, Cartmel, Castle Acre, Finchale, Guisbrough, Hexham, Kirkham,

Lanercost, Lindisfarne, Malvern, Mount Grace, Monk Bretton, Tynemouth, Watton, Witham.

Wales has Brecon, Ewenny, Haverfordwest, Llanthony and Pernmon. Small and dependent houses are rare in Scotland but among its priories one might instance: Archattan, Beauly, Coldingham. Inchmahome, Moneymusk, Restenneth, St Andrews, Whithorn.

PRISON

The monastery was a total community enshrined within a violent society and its own punishments were not always spiritual. It had to deal with a vast array of servants and dependents and when these layfolk were recalcitrant they were, if necessary, handed over to 'the temporal lawe' for punishment.

Great superiors had temporal jurisdiction as feudal lords with concomitant courtrooms and prisons. The latter were often located in the gate houses of abbeys (as they were in castles) e.g. Ely, St Albans.

But members of the community were sometimes imprisoned for serious indiscipline. Fountains had a series of cells in the basement of the abbot's house, each with its own garderobe and floor staple for the prisoners' shackles. Durham had a strong prison called the 'lying house' under the infirmarian's chamber 'which was ordained for all such as were great offenders'. The most severe punishment could extend to a year of solitary confinement with food let down by a rope. There was also a small prison next to the chapter-house (for punishment of sins confessed there?). It had a food hatch and its own latrine 'en suite'. Ely had a further prison in the farmery range called 'Hell'.

PRIVATE MASS

A mass said individually by a single priest with the assistance of a server or acolyte as distinct from the communal Morrow Mass or High Mass. The practice grew with increasing emphasis on the propitiatory element of the eucharistic sacrifice and the related notion that it was the duty of every priest to say mass at least daily. These masses were partly said at the priest's own discretion and for his private intentions but others were offered to fulfill obligations incurred by them in particular or the convent at large, especially masses for the dead.

This development necessitated the multiplication of altars (q.v.).

PRIVATE PROPERTY

In the original monastic rule the vow of poverty meant the abnegation of any kind of private property; of his own a monk, had 'absolutely not anything; neither a book, nor tablets, nor a pen — nothing at all'. Such things, including his clothes and bedding, were lent to him at need ('ad usum') but, by C12, private property on the smallest scale was beginning to creep in although it was strongly resisted by reforming superiors. The process continued, probably affected by the administrative development of allocating particular financial resources to specified obedientiaries (q.v.). So individual religious were given an allowance out of which to purchase their own clothes. One can appreciate the convenience of this system ('peculium' q.v.) but the introduction of merchants into the cloister and consequent bargaining cannot have been spiritually advantageous.

The development was encouraged by the institution of the 'pittance' (q.v.). At the same time there was a growing custom of individual gifts made by benefactors, friends and relations instead of to the community at large. All this was a gross breach of corporeity and of the idea of poverty and it had to be reformed.

PRIVY   see *Rere-dorter*

PROBATION   see also *Novice, Postulant*

The period (usually a year) between a postulant's request to join a community and his reception (novitiate). It was a time for careful consideration and deliberate decision based on experience of the religious life. 'Moreover, the year of probation is allowed as a favour both to the novice and to the convent for, should the novice be found amiable, sober, chaste, devoted to God, proper for a religious life, fit to take upon himself Holy Orders and well disposed to serve in them he will suit the convent. Further, if the novice be able and willing chiefly for the sake of God to endure with a good heart nocturnal vigils, a dull life in the cloister, continual services in the quire, prolonged silence, the strictness of the order and of the particular house, and the different characters of the brethren, it will suit the novice that leave should be given to him to profess at the end of the year.' (Barnwell Observances 1295/6)

PROCESSION

An important part of monastic liturgical practice. It emphasised their corporate disciplined endeavour to follow Christ (see Galilee) and it symbolised and reminded the participants of their ordered place in the church militant.

Procession (Cistercian)

The procession was so important that it affected church architecture (see Aisle, Ambulatory) and the stations taken up by certain participants in the procession were indicated by 'markers' on the church floor. At Fountains, limestone flags were let into the tiled floor and at Easby and Shap, where the name was flagged in stone, the places were marked by incised circles.

There was a procession of the whole convent every Sunday before High Mass led by cross, lights, thurifer, sacred ministers and novices. It first visited the altars in north transept where each was sprinkled with holy water to the accompaniment of anthems. Having made stations at each of the eastern chapels, the procession visited those in the transept next to the cloister which it entered through the eastern doorway in the nave. The chief claustral buildings were visited with stations at any altars contained in them and the procession returned from the cloister through the

Monks in Procession
(Benedictine)

west door into the church. Any altars at the west end were visited and the procession made its final halt in the middle of the nave before the great rood screen. After this, the community passed through the flanking doorways, reunited in the ante-chapel and re-entered the quire through the door in the middle of the pulpitum and the singing of High Mass began.

Solemn processions sometimes left the precincts of the convent e.g. at Durham on St Mark's Day the prior led the community to St Mary le Bow where there was High Mass and a sermon to the people of the parish. On Holy Thursday, Whitsunday and Trinity Sunday they had particularly grand processions.

The greatest processions were in honour of Corpus Christi when town convents were joined by the guilds and parishes, all with their own crosses, banners and relics swelling the procession behind the Body of Christ which was carried in a crystal monstrance accompanied by censors and thuribles. This procession concluded with a solemn Te Deum, accompanied on the organ, followed by a short service.

Rogation days were a general time of procession, during which litanies were sung and bounds beaten. Monasteries followed the custom, perambulating the enclosure or perhaps the area of sanctuary. The colourful Rogationtide procession at York had not only the usual cross, lights, incense and banners but also a dragon representing the devil. This was apparently kept in a recess of the tower of St Olave's by the gate where the procession issued from the monastic precincts.

PROFESSION   see also *Clothing, Novice, Postulant*
The solemn promise, including the three vows, involved in the entry to a religious order. It seems that, in the later Middle Ages, the minimum age for making this profession was 18 for quire monks and nuns, and 25 for lay brothers and sisters.

PROTECTIVE CLOTHING
Gloves and detachable sleeves were provided for the servitors in kitchen and frater and for manual work in the fields and elsewhere a kind of overall, called a 'scapular', was usually worn.

PSALTER   see also *Bible, Lessons*
Of all the books of the Bible the psalter dominated the prayer life to such an extent that the monastic hours were called 'psalmodia principalis' and the lesser hours or Hours of the B.V.M. 'psalmodia secundria'. The core of the worship consisted of the daily recitation of the psalter in the course of the seven offices (a division itself based on the psalmist's 'Seven times a day will I worship Thee'). The psalter was probably known by heart and it was even an advanced text book used in the first or elementary schools (e.g. at God's House, Exeter).

PUDDING HOUSE
An ancillary building not infrequently mentioned in monastic records. It was a dependency of the kitchen, probably always a timber-framed building, and seems usually to have been served by externs. It was used for making 'puddings' i.e. sausage, black-pudding etc. and had a heavy seasonable use at pig-killing time before winter as well as a lighter and more or less continuous function.

Pudding Cauldron

PULPIT
Originally a raised platform from which news was given, hence pulpitum (q.v.). Monastic sermons were usually given from the president's chair in chapter or quire or from a lectern, hence there are few, if any, monastic pulpits surviving. There were movable pulpits (e.g. in Durham Galilee) which were used for lay sermons. Sermons were also given from the steps of a 'preaching cross' (e.g. Blackfriars, Hereford). There was always a pulpit or reading desk in frater (q.v.) and that at Beaulieu is still in use.

PULPITUM
The great screen which closed the west end of the quire. It had a doorway in its centre, flanked by altars on either side of its western face. There was a loft above, reached by a stair, on which an organ was sometimes placed and from which on certain days the gospel and epistle were sung. It was adorned with statues or paintings intended to inspire beholders to imitation e.g. apostles, ascetics, pious kings, monastic saints, bishops and doctors of the church.

Norwich

The pulpitum was often double and occupied a whole bay of the name (e.g. Kirkstall, Norwich substantially survives). Elsewhere it was a single wall between the west piers of the crossing (e.g. Valle Crucis) or a wooden screen (e.g. Hexham).

Its position varied according to the demands of the quire. At Malmesbury it enclosed the first bay west of the crossing and its western wall now forms a reredos for the parish altar. At Canterbury and Durham the pulpitum connected the eastern piers of the crossing.

West Window, Valle Crucis

QUIRE

The place where the monk's fundamental work, the opus Dei, was carried out. This work was real and could be onerous, so that we have questions in visitations about 'the burdens of quire' and injunctions that nuns (particularly) should be physically and mentally 'able to bear the burdens of quire with the rest (of the work) that pertains to religious'. Nevertheless, this work was central and 'a place of prayer was built, because in it the brethren ought to praise God, to bless Him, to glorify Him and with the deepest devotion to sing psalms and hymns and spiritual songs.'

Monks in Quire

The quire occupied most of the eastern arm of the church, usually extended into the crossing and sometimes into several bays of the nave (e.g. Gloucester, Westminster). It was open to the presbytery (q.v.) on the east but separated from the aisles, transepts and nave by screens. The stalls (q.v.) of the monks were placed parallel to the screens dividing the quire from the aisles and transepts. To the west of the quire was the pulpitum (q.v.), the retro-quire (q.v.) and the rood-screen (q.v.).

Its furnishings, sometimes included an altar (e.g. Bury) and always a lectern in its midst, usually two or four-sided, to support the great music books (antiphonary, graduale, etc.) used by the cantors. It was ruled by the precentor (q.v.) who was instructed (at e.g. Barnwell) not to start a new and unfamiliar tune without the consent of the brethren. It was apparently the custom to ease the weight of the singing by alternating the decani and cantoris sides. Customaries not only lay down injunctions about singing e.g. 'At all singing of psalms brethren ought to be careful always to make a pause in the middle, and a verse should not be begun on one side before the verse on the other is ended' but give minute instructions about behaviour in quire. Punctuality is stressed, ritual behaviour (bows, genuflections, prostrations, turning east at certain points), the signs of reverence to superiors, brethren, altars, relics, the Gospel, the times of standing and sitting and the exact posture on these occasions. There are prohibitions in the Barnwell Observances against 'needless signs and conversation, cutting nails, writing, smiling, whittling, throwing one foot over the other, stretching legs, supporting body on elbows, sitting with legs apart.'

Instructions are also given about what to do if arriving late in quire, if office begins while saying a private mass, and such practicalities as 'Brethren should always be careful when they get up or sit down to raise or lower the seat gently and noiselessly with the left-hand.'

All this might appear rather tedious and pernickety but let Barnwell Observances have the last word : 'In these and all other observances according to the rule, brethren ought to be careful that, as the apostle directs, "all things be done decently and in order". For the place in which they stand to pray is holy. There is the sanctuary of God, there is the image of the Crucified One, there is the True Body of our Lord Jesus Christ which is received from the Blessed Virgin Mary and through which He redeemed us by His Blood. There are the divine mysteries consecrated, there is the frequent presence of the holy angels and there resound strains for the praise of God. Let servants of God therefore shake off indifference and carelessness, let them drive out of their heart idle and useless thoughts. Let them open the recesses of their hearts to the sovereign grace of God which is already ready to be bestowed upon those who pray for it with purity and sincerity. Let those who have the grace of song, sing willingly and energetically to improve the service of God. Let those who have not the grace of voice, vest those who sing and help the rest according to their capacity that they fall not under the reproof of that text which says "Cursed be he who doeth the work of God carelessly" but rather let them share the rewards of others who do their work well to whom the Lord will say: "Come ye blessed of my Father, etc." '

RASURA

Besides being tonsured, monks were also clean-shaven as, except in the case of mendicants and lay brethren (sometimes called 'barbati'), beards were regarded as a sign of pride. Thus the 'rasura' or shaving was not merely a renewal of the tonsure but also a general shaving session. It seems to have been on a monthly basis with additions before great festivals, etc.

It was an occasion of some solemnity, normally conducted in the cloister (probably in south walk near laver q.v.) and the customaries provide minute regulations e.g. at Canterbury the proceedings began with prayers for the dead and it appears that any canonical hour arising during the operation was said there, privately. Everyone was to wash his own head in preparation.

Rasura

Talking was allowed on the usual days when the psalms had been sung. Brothers were to go the office when summoned by the bell unless their shaving had already begun (Lancfranc: Constitutions). The material provision: hot water, towels, soap, etc. were the responsibility of the chamberlain (q.v.) and regulations usually required the seniors to be shaved first 'because in the beginning the razors are sharp and the towels dry'.

From about the middle of C13, the greater houses (e.g. Canterbury, St Augustine) at least hired a professional: a barber-surgeon who was a kind of inferior physician and may also have done the blood-letting. About the same time the frequency of shaving seems to have increased to fortnightly in winter and twice in three weeks in summer with four barbers in attendance at e.g. Canterbury.

St Augustine's Chair, Canterbury

READER IN FRATER   see also *Frater, Pulpit*

This office was considered so important that the reader was chosen and coached by the precentor and entered upon the 'tabula'. His duties were regarded as spiritual, silence was enjoined in frater so that his words could be heard and the brethren were enjoined 'nor let your mouths only take in food but let your ears also hunger after the word of God' (Barnwell Obervances). He was solemnly blessed in quire on Sunday, the day before he began his week's duty and he received a second blessing from whoever presided in frater before he mounted the pulpit. Dinner was not to begin until he had read the first sentence of the passage selected by the precentor who also provided the book. At Barnwell the readings were taken from the Bible and commentaries on it and the listing in the observances implies substantially reading through the whole Bible, book by book (but not in order) during the course of a year.

Frater Pulpit, Beaulieu

When the novices ate separately, they had their own reader: 'At which times of meals, the master (of the novices) observed this wholesome order for the continual instructing of their youth in virture and learning. That is, one of the novices, at the election and appointment of the master, did read some part of the old and new testament in Latin at dinner-time, having a convenient place at the south end of the high table within a fair glass window, environed with iron, and certain steps of stone with iron rails on one side to go up into it and to support an iron desk placed upon which lay the Holy Bible.' (Rites of Durham).

The frater reader operated at dinner and at supper (if there was any) but not at the readings in chapter and at collation which was normally the superior's privilege.

Sacred Reading

READING

Apart from the considerable reading involved in the recitation of the offices, the reading in chapter, frater and at collation, a good deal of the monk's time was allocated to private reading.

'At fixed times, the brothers ought to be occupied in manual labour: and again at fixed times in sacred reading . . . Moreover on Sunday all shall engage in reading excepting those who are deputed to various duties.' (St Benedict: rule chap.xlviii).

Reading included meditative reading, study and work on books: collating, copying, illuminating, etc. As the Middle Ages progressed reading began to oust manual work but was itself under pressure due to the encroachments of an increasingly complex liturgy which could occupy up to eight hours of the day. During the Dark Ages alternative occupations were found for the illiterate but they had largely disappeared from the ranks of the 'quire-monks' by C10. Inevitably, some abbeys (e.g. St Albans in later C12) contained more scholars than others but the increasing identification of literacy with the full monastic profession led the Benedictine General-Chapter at Canterbury in 1277 to order that 'in place of manual labour, the abbots shall appoint other occupations for their claustral monks according to their capacity: study, writing, correcting, illuminating and binding books.'

Thus, for 'work' in the horarium we can often substitute 'reading' i.e. in the very early morning, from chapter to Terce, from Sext to dinner, from None to Vespers, from supper to collation (some of these periods could be very short).

REBUILDING   see *Modification*

Was frequent for a variety of reasons: the expansion of initial community, the availability of resources to replace essentially temporary buildings, destruction or threatened collapse of existing buildings, the pride of a superior in his house, the glory of God, liturgical and doctrinal changes, the acquisition of a saint's shrine. e.g. there were three rebuildings at Meaux at end of C12 and beginning of C13. In 1091 the tower at Abingdon collapsed and that of Winchcombe was damaged by lightning.
About 1109 the fallen west end of Canterbury was rebuilt and four years later Worcester had to be repaired through damage from fire. The collapse of central tower at Ely in 1321 took 20 years to replace.

RECLUSE   see also *Anchorite, Hermit*

A person living a devout life in solitude. By no means necessarily a ragged figure inhabiting a cave. Some mediaeval recluses had guest rooms, servants and a private chaplain.

RECREATION   see also *Parlour, Warming-House*

Early monasticism makes little allowance for this but some indulgence was provided for children, novices and recuperating invalids. Later we hear of walks, of villagiatura, of strange pets and even of annual outings for the whole convent. There was also the relief of 'pittances' often accompanied by conversation in the common house.

Music was acknowledged as recreative, first for the sick and later for the whole. It is recorded of Sir William Corvehill, a monk of Wenlock who died shortly after the suppression of his house, that he 'was excellently and singularly experte in dyvers of the seven liberal sciences and especially in geometrie, not greatly by speculacon, but by experience; and few or non of hanye crafte but that he had a very gud insight in them, as the making of organs, of a clocke and chimes, as in kerving, in masonrie, and weving of silke, as in peynting, and noe instrumente of musike beying but that he coulde mende it.'

There is much evidence here of hobbies and creative recreations if Dom. Wm Corvehill was not unique. Games are not mentioned in the rule but some kinds would be forbidden on principle. On the other hand late mediaeval Durham had 'a garding and a bowlinge allie' for the novices and its cell at Finchale possessed a 'Player's Chamber'.

Monk at Recreation

There is some indication of skittle alleys, real tennis apparently originated in a cloister, and fives seems to have ecclesiastical connections. Restrained ball games were allowed in some houses, particularly at festivals and the Feast of Fools seems to have been kept at Christmas time in some places though it was frowned upon. There is also evidence of board games and a mysterious C14 reference to a 'sporting house' at Wylam.

There was a strong temptation to partake of the secular sports of the time, particularly hunting. Late in Middle Ages Cistercians had to be forbidden to keep, bears, cranes, peacocks, hunting dogs or hawks but Jervaulx was allowed to retain its mastiffs for the protection of its sheep from wolves. In C14 the monks of Canterbury St Augustine were prohibited from games of chess or dice, the use of bows or slings, running with poles, throwing stones of any size, being present at fights or duels, baiting or cock-fighting and

Nun at Recreation

from running in the woods with shouts and hounds in the profane sport of the chase.

In later Middle Ages there are records (e.g. Durham, Maxstoke, Thetford) of employment of paid entertainers (actors, fools, minstrels) as part of festal celebration, apparently in imitation of practice of lay lords.

The normal time allowed for recreation along with private work etc. was between None and Vespers.

RECRUITMENT

The monastic orders largely drew from the upper class, apart from their lay brothers and sisters. The mendicants were more socially mixed. Recruitment changed at different periods and each form of religious life had its high points when it was 'in fashion'. The recruitment of lay brothers substantially ceased after the Black Death, the creation of friars reduced entry into the older monastic orders and all religious orders seem to have lost impetus in C15 but later there was some evidence of revival, not only a modest general one but noticeably among the austerer communities such as the Carthusians and Observant Franciscans.

RECTOR

The ruler or head of a community, especially a college or parish. In the latter case he received the 'great tithes' as the most substantial part of his income. With appropriations, the rectorship was often vested elsewhere: religious house, college, etc., which provided a 'vicar' or substitute to serve the curé who was granted a stipend out of part of the rectorial revenues with the difference being retained to the profit of the appropriator.

RED FRIARS
A popular name given to Maturins or Trinitarians (q.v.)

REFECTORIAN   see *Fraterer*

REFECTORY   see *Frater*

REFORMATION
This is not the place to consider the complex elements of the Protestant Reformation which included sheer greed, envy and malice, economic and national factors as well as religious ones. The English Reformation had peculiar characteristics, not least of which was its direction by the head of state. The Protestant ethic despised or misunderstood the nature of the contemplative life and therefore was utterly hostile to the monastic ideal. The suppression of the monasteries was only supported by such motives, its prime motivation was plunder and its architect, Thomas Cromwell, had promised as a result to make his master Henry 'the richest Prince in Christendom'. The suppression of the monasteries (q.v.) can be seen as a major, and largely irrevocable step in the process of the English Reformation while their destruction in Scotland seems more peripheral.

REFRESHMENT   see also *Collation, Meals, Mixtum, Pittance*

REGISTRAR
An official not always found by name. He was the keeper of the monastic register, the records of all deeds of gift, conveyances, charters, etc., which gave legal authority for the house's possessions and rights. This function was sometimes carried out by the 'third prior' or even by the precentor.

REGULAR
One under a religious rule, sometimes called 'a religious'. Both words have implications of being bound. The regular was under rule, regulated by it to a sense of proportion and a measured mean. His whole life, the divisions of the day, the amount of food and sleep were all regulated, cf. Walter Daniel's panegyric of the early Cistercians: 'For them everything is fixed by weight, measure and number (Wisdom xi, 20): a pound of bread, a pint of drink, two dishes of cabbage and beans . . . no one takes a step towards anything of his own will. Everything they do is at the motion of the prelate's nod and they are turned aside by a like direction. At table, in procession, at Communion and in other liturgical observances, all of them — small and great, young and old, wise and ignorant — are subject to one law. Personal standing is merged in the equality of each and all, there is no inequitable mark of exemption, except the greater sanctity which is able to put one man above others.' This description was literally true: the community was strictly regulated and included children and old men, members of the nobility and of the lower orders.

Regular

REGULAR CANONS   see *Canons Regular*

Relics

RELICS   see also *Shrine*

The materialist, realist, incarnational nature of Christianity produced a natural devotion to relics and souvenirs from its earliest days. They were usually lodged for safe-keeping in religious houses (the very word chapel is derived from the room where St Martin's cloak was kept in the monastery at Tours). The abbot of Arbroath was the custodian of the relics of St Columba. Crypts originated as reliquaries and many great churches rose to house the relics of a saint (Durham, Bury, St Albans).

Shrine of St Thomas, Martyr (Canterbury Window)

St Cuthbert Shrine (reconstruction)

Relics attracted pilgrims and pilgrims brought money so that the possession of relics brought not only spiritual significance but income. Crowds of visitors not only made building necessary but provided the means for it. Pilgrims came to the Confessor at Westminster, to St Alban and St Andrew at their towns, to St Cuthbert (and Bede) at Durham, to St Thomas (and Alphege and Dunstan) at Canterbury, to St Swithun at Winchester, to the Holy Blood at Hailes, to a relic of the True Cross at Bromholm or Holy Rood, Edinburgh. At the beginning of C15 the church at Castle Acre was described as a repository 'in which are divers relics of saints and to which a great multitude of people resorts'. They also resorted to wonder-working images such as Our Lady of Thetford and the miraculous Rood of Bermondsey.

With the exception of Hailes and Rievaulx with its shrine of St William, Cistercian houses eschewed wonder-working shrines and relics lest pilgrims should invade the precinct and disturb their chosen solitude. (The Carthusians had a similar reaction).

Other houses had different reactions and welcomed pilgrims to such dubious saints, as Simon de Montfort (Evesham) and Edward II (Gloucester). It has been said that 'the acquisition of shrines and relics came to be an obsession with many Benedictine abbots' (G.H. Cook) and if we list only the foremost of their pilgrimage churches besides those already mentioned they would include Chester (St Werburgh), Crowland (St Guthlac), Ely (St Ethelreda), Malmesbury (St Adhelm), Rochester (St William of Perth), Worcester (St Oswald).

REMAINS   see also *Survivals*

There are not even vestiges of about a third of the houses which existed in the Middle Ages. There are minor remains of about another third while substantial remains of the remainder are often confined to the church.

Often the parochial part (usually the nave) of a monastic church was granted to the parish (often at a price) when the religious house was dissolved and the rest allowed to decay when the valuable lead had been removed from the roof and any valuable fittings looted (e.g. Bolton).

More rarely the whole church was retained though considerably denuded and modified (e.g. Christchurch, Selby, Westminster which was briefly used as a cathedral). The expelled monks of the cathedral priories were replaced by a reduced college of secular canons and six former abbeys and priories were made cathedrals of the new foundation.

Thus, with appropriate allowances and some imagination, the arrangements of a Benedictine monastery can be studied more or less satisfactorily at Canterbury, Chester, Durham, Ely, Gloucester, Norwich, Peterborough, Rochester, Westminster, Winchester, Worcester. Those of Austin Canons may be seen less well at Bristol, Carlisle, Cartmel, and Christchurch Oxford. The most complete series of ruined and abandoned houses are those of the Cistercians whose very remoteness has limited the amount of destruction and cannibalisation e.g. Fountains, Kirkstall, Netley, Rievaulx, Tintern. Benedictine, Cluniac and Augustinian houses have suffered more (Battle, Bury, York) but Wenlock represents a rare example of a Cluniac establishment while Bolton, Haughmond, Reading and Lilleshall do something to represent Augustinian foundations.

Only three Cistercian churches, in whole or part, remain in use for modified religious purposes: Dore, Holmcultram and Margam. The pre-eminent ruin is Fountains, followed perhaps by Rievaulx and Tintern. Less destroyed than most are the claustral buildings of Beaulieu, Buildwas, Cleeve, Croxden, Ford, Furness, Jervaulx, Kirkstall, Neath, Netley and Valle Crucis.

There are traces of most of the Premonstratensian houses (especially Easby and Bradsole) while part of the church at Blanchland is in Anglican use. Carthusian arrangements can be well studied at Mount Grace while those of the Gilbertines have been revealed by excavation at Watton.

Remains of nunneries are scanty but those of Benedictines at Jesus College, Cambridge and of Augustinians at Lacock deserve mention and the church at Romsey is substantially intact. Friaries are rarer but there are considerable Dominican fragments at Bristol and Norwich and Franciscan at Chichester. There is less at Augustinian Clare and Carmelite Hulne. The church of the Austin Friars in London survived in Lutheran use but has recently been substantially rebuilt while the Crutched Friars survive only in a street name. The quire of the Dominicans at Brecon is the chapel of a modern college and there are other fragments of friars' churches at Lynn and Richmond. Some sites at Cambridge are occupied by colleges: Sydney Sussex on a Franciscan one and Emmanuel, whose hall is substantially the former church, replaces the Dominicans.

Because of the more violent and radical nature of the Scottish Reformation, remains are scant — even in proportion (Scotland was a poor country and had fewer religious houses than England). The rare Premonstratensian ruins of Dryburgh fill a gap in the remains of Great Britain.

REPAIRS   see also *Rebuilding*

Religious houses were often extensive structures and repairs were a serious item in the balance sheet of every house. In spite of the continual expenditure shown by account rolls, visitation reports have much to say about crumbling walls and leaky roofs.

Perhaps nunneries had more troubles than male houses 'It was seldom that a . year passed without several visits from the plumbers, the slaters and the thatchers to the precincts of a nunnery; and once arrived, they were not easy to dislodge. If perchance the nunnery buildings stood firm then the houses of tenants would be falling about their ears; and once more the distracted treasuress must summon workmen. Usually the nuns purchased the materials used for repairs and hired the labour separately, and the workers were sometimes fed in the nunnery kitchen; for it was customary at this time to include board with the wages of many hired workmen'. (Eileen Power).

The causes were normal wear and tear, weather and bad workmanship, poverty which compelled poor materials, storm and tempest, and accident, especially fire. We must remember that there were always buildings of wood and thatch and even central buildings (such as cloisters) often remained in wood until late in the Middle Ages. The church of St Albans (c. 1235) was set on fire by lightning twice within three years and most of its nave collapsed in 1323.

RERE-DORTER (Domus necessaria, necessarium)

The main conventual latrine block which was always associated with the dorter. It was placed either at its further end or at right angles to that end, the position being determined by water supply. It consisted of a long gallery and usually contained a row of seats against one wall, each lighted by a window and divided from the next by a stone or wooden partition. At Furness the seats were ranged back to back against a central wall with a passage on either side of the cubicles. The partitions were carried by transverse arches over a flushed artificial drain or a diverted running stream and on the ground floor the drain was cut off from the vaulted undercroft of the rere-dorter by a solid wall. These rere-dorters were substantial buildings: that at Canterbury, nicknamed 'the third dorter' opened from the north-east corner of the great dorter, was some 150ft long, and contained 55 seats. The later necessarium at Lewes extended for 158ft, provided 66 seats and was separated from the dorter by a bridge and staircase.

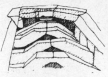

Part of Rere-dorter Drain
(Gloucester)

Rere-dorter
(reconstruction)

In spite of the accompanying lantern it was apparently very easy to fall asleep in the 'necce' (hence its nick-name at Canterbury) and the circa (q.v.) or third prior was specially instructed to look for sleepers there when he did his rounds 'with consideration and solicitude lest perchance some sleeping brother might still remain there. If he should in fact find one asleep, he is not to touch him in any way but modestly he should make the slightest noise which is sufficient to waken him.'

Besides the rere-dorter of the monks there was varied latrine provision elsewhere: guest-house, farmery, superior's lodgings, etc. There was normally latrines attached to prison cells. Separate rere-dorters were provided in the lay brothers' accommodation (e.g. Byland, Jervaulx, Roche, Rufford).

Considerable and interesting remains at e.g. Canterbury, Castle Acre, Easby, Fountains, Kirkstall, Lewes, Netley, Worcester.

REREDOS   see also *Screen*

The decorative 'backing' to the altar table, usually consisting of carving in high relief in stone or alabaster surrounding a central Crucifixion. There are rare survivals: St Albans, Christchurch Hampshire, but most went the way of that from Stafford priory which, together with a door and high altar, was knocked down at the suppression auction for seven shillings.

RETRO-QUIRE

The space between the pulpitum and rood-screen. It provided a gathering point for processions to unite before entering the single door of the quire after being separated by the two doors through the rood-screen. It also provided additional altar space, being furnished with two altars, one on either side of the pulpitum door. Its other uses were for monks arriving too late to enter the choir and for the accommodation of aged and infirm monks, attending quire offices. (For the more infirm there was a private chapel in the farmery (q.v.).)

The retro-quire seems to have been characteristic of Cistercian churches, but was found elsewhere and the mediaeval bench at Winchester may once have supported infirm monks in the retro-quire.

REVENUES   see also *Income*

Apart from the extensive estates (q.v.) which provided their main resource, the income of a religious house could come from a variety of things: mills, appropriated churches and, from town houses, especially markets and fairs with their profitable tolls. Bury had a fair, as had Dover. The latter also claimed passage dues, tolls on Saturday market, tithe of herring fishery and toll of sea and wreckage. Chester had a fair and a monopoly extending to a five mile circle. Besides the tolls from this it also rented out booths and stalls. At York there was conflict between town and abbey over the booths in Bootham. To help the building fund for the new Westminster quire, Henry III granted the convent a fortnight's fair during which all other shops in the vicinity had to be closed.

REVESTIARIUS

One of the sacristan's assistants in a great house. He was responsible for the care and mending of the vestments, curtains, veils etc., which adorned the ministers and the church. He had to issue them in the right numbers and colours on the appropriate occasions. His work-place was the vestry or revestry.

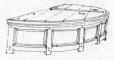

Revestarius Cope Chest
(Gloucester)

RISING

The monks slept in their habits, but without cloaks, girdle or footwear. At the summons of a bell before midnight, they rose, tidied their beds and completed their dressing by the light of the dorter cressets. When this was done and all were ready, they left the dorter for the cold church by the night stairs. Any spare time between rising, necessary functions and leaving the dorter was to be occupied in private prayer.

ROOD-SCREEN

A wooden or stone screen, usually one bay west of the pulpitum (q.v.) with an altar against its western face and with the great rood or crucifix with the attendant figures of Mary and John. Rood-screens remain amid the ruins of Crowland and Tynemouth and within the surviving church at St Albans and Dunstable. Their foundations or the holes to carry the rood-beam occur in many places. At Blyth, and possibly at Bolton, the rood-screen consisted of a wall taken to the full height of the nave with a painted crucifixion on its western face.

ROOFS

Often covered with thatch, tiles or wooden shingles. Whenever the resources allowed, the church roof at least was leaded and this valuable material was one of the chief objects of the royally commissioned looters at the Dissolution when bands of workmen under their supervision stripped off the lead and melted it down by fires fed with the woodwork of screens and stalls that had found no ready purchaser. The resulting ingots stamped with the royal badge were carted to royal store-houses unless the winter roads did not permit the passage of such heavy loads when it was stored or hidden locally. Some of the pigs from Rievaulx were lost until 1923 when they were used to relead the Five Sisters window in York.

Roof of Frater (Chester)

ROTA

A turn-table by which refreshment could be dispensed without communication or even sight. It was common in Carthusian houses, occured in Gilbertine establishments and there are remains of this contrivance at Canterbury between the cellarium and the north cloister alley.

Monk studying Rule

ROTULARIUS

A name sometimes given to the messenger (alternatively called the breviator (q.v.)), who carried the obit-roll from one religious house to another.

RUBRICATOR

A scribe specialising in capital letters especially those which marked the 'Red Letter Days' in the liturgical calender i.e. the major festivals which were so distinguished for advance warning and preparation.

RULE (Regula)

The constitution which laid down the principles and practice of the monastic or regular life. The basic code was that of St Benedict, modified and developed by e.g. the Cluniacs and Cistercians (especially in the Cartula Caritatis). The other seminal rule was that of St Augustine (q.v.) which underpinned the Canons Regular among others. These fundamental rules were also supplemented by subsidiary regulations in custumals or observances, some of which were general to a particular order but others included the idiosyncracies of an individual house.

C12 ms showing St Benedict giving Rule to Monks

All such codes and rules had a single aim — to provide a scaffold within which the Christian life might be lived in its fullest form. It was the genius of St Benedict which gave its particular direction to western monasticism and P. Johnson thus speaks of his rule:

'It is wholly lacking in eccentricity. It does not expect heroic virtue. It is full of provisions for exceptions, changes and relaxations in its rules; yet at the same time it insists that rules must be kept, once made. The monk must live to a time-table, and he must be doing something all the time, even if this only takes the form of eating and sleeping in order to enable him to labour afresh. "Idleness is the enemy of the soul": that is the keynote, echoing St Paul's advice to the earliest Christians as they awaited the "Parousia". And then the rule exuded the universality which had always been the object of Catholic Christianity, of Rome and, above all, of Gregory himself as a missionary pope who wanted to convert the world and society. The rule is classless and timeless: it is not grounded in any particular culture or geographical region, and it will fit into any society which will allow it to operate.'

SACCARIUM   see also *Checker, Treasury*

The counting-house or exchequer. Monastic finances were generally the care of the cellarer but other obedientiaries (q.v.) later had their own accounts.

SACRIST

A major obedientiary whose duties became so wide-ranging that, in the larger houses of the later Middle Ages, he had many assistants who could include not only the usual sub-sacrist but a master of works, treasurer, revestarius and assistant sacristan. His responsibilities could range from collecting salt from the kitchen for the consecration of holy water to the care of the cemetery.

Essentially the sacrist was responsible for the church, its furniture, fittings and supplies: 'Let the sacrist, then if he love the Lord, love the church. The more spiritual should he be, both day and night, to make the church useful and seemly in every way.' (Barnwell Observances). He was responsible for cleanliness, repair and security. This could include decoration, design and construction of fittings including altars and windows, wall-paintings and the

Sacristy in South Transept, Fountains

appropriate inscriptions for symbolic schemes. He had control of the clock, bell, ornaments and lights — not only the liturgical ones but the cressets, candles and lights needed for the community to see by.

He was responsible for all the church plate, shrines, reliquaries and their associated treasures. (The spoils of Canterbury at its suppression included nearly 5,000 ozs of gold and over 4,000 ozs of silver-gilt with over 5,000 ozs of plain silver) He had to provide watchmen and other security when appropriate and keep an inventory of all plate, vestments and altar furniture. He collected, secured and disposed of the income derived from mortuary dues, oblations, pilgrims' offerings and other altar dues (such as the town of Bury's obligation of £40 p.a 'to find lights for the church'). He could also, with the consent of the superior, take under his care extern deposits of gold, silver, deeds, bonds, chests and coffers. He exercised a general supervision over the entire fabric of the church (e.g. Durham, Ely, Worcester). However, when there was building or reconstruction on a large and long-continuing scale, the operation was placed under a special official or 'custos', sometimes known as the master of the works (so at Westminster for rebuilding nave in C14).

The sacristan usually had his own revenues apart from the offerings which came directly to the church. At Durham, the greater part of the regular income for this department came from estates in Sacristonheugh. The sacristan was one of the first obedientiaries to have his own office or 'checker' — see Sacristy.

Sacrist

SACRISTY

The office, store and administrative headquarters of the sacristan's department. It was sometimes a separate building annexed to the church or it could be provided, like some vestries, by partitioning off a section of the church. Occasionally the sacristan occupied more than one chamber and was thus able to divide store and workshop (sacristy) from administrative office (checker). Here he kept records, made up rota for use of altars, prepared accounts of income from the various sources under his charge and of expenditure on bread, wine, oil, wax, on lead, glass, timber, stone, on plate, silk, velvet, linen, cerecloth and on labour which could include masons and craftsmen, church-cleaners and bell-ringers. Here also he transacted business concerning the estates appropriated to his office, about crops, horses, cattle, poison for foxes, pitch for sheep-disease, carts and wagons, repairs to barns and other farm-buildings.

In Cistercian houses, the sacristy began as a small chamber leading from the south transept (Kirkstall, Fountains) and it is found in the same position in houses of other orders (Easby, Thetford). The latter possessed another sacristy in the north transept as did Castle Acre. Another popular position was against the north aisle of the presbytery (Durham, Whitby, York and a surviving two-storeyed building at Selby). In Worcester, high above north quire aisle, is the oriel window which once belonged to sacristan's checker and allowed him to see that all was well about the High Altar. At Ingham, he was accommodated above south porch.

SALTER

An assistant or kitchener, sometimes identical with the mustardarius (!), who is named because of the large amount of salt consumed in a large mediaeval establishment. With the lack of either advanced freezing or adequate winter fodder, animals were largely killed (apart from breeding stock) at the end of the summer and flesh, whether meat or fish, was salted down either by drysalting or brine curing. The decision was made on St Martin's Day (November 11th) when the great operation began in every stock-owning establishment. The purchase of the extra quantity of salt required occurs in the cellarer's accounts of Grace Dieu (1414-18).

Salt thus became practically significant as well as symbolically (where it indicated incorruption and wisdom). It was one of the ingredients used in the production of Holy Water and among the minor duties of the sacrist (q.v.) was the collection each Sunday of a platter of salt which was blessed for this purpose before High Mass. More was blessed than required for holy water and the remainder was taken to the frater where the sacrist himself placed a pinch of the blessed salt in every salt cellar there.

SALVE

The anthem 'Salve Regina', the earliest anthem or antiphon of the Blessed Virgin Mary commonly recited in the church. It was sung with special solemnity at the end of Compline and, in response to increased Marian devotion, it became highly developed musically with a dozen or more parts. It is the parent of all church anthems.

SANCTUARY

(a) That part of the eastern arm of a church between the quire and the screen behind the High Altar, otherwise known as the presbytery (q.v.).

(b) The privilege possessed by certain religious houses from Saxon times to the Reformation by which 'all manner of men who had committed any great offence such as killing a man in his own defence' escaped vengeance or the law by taking refuge within the sacred precincts.

Felon seeking Sanctuary at Shrine

William I systematised and defined the law of sanctuary and gave special privileges to his memorial abbey of Battle.

The 'frid'-stool or chair of peace still survives at Hexham and Durham still possesses the sanctuary knocker which brought the abbey's protection to any fugitive by rousing 'serten men that dyd lie alwaies in two chambers over the church dore . . . that when any such offenders dyd come and knocke, straight waie they were letten in at any our of the nyght.' Technically, sanctuary extended more broadly than this and the area of safety was often marked by crosses placed round the perimeter which often extended a mile or more from the church. Westminster was a famous and much abused sanctuary among the official and chartered refuges which numbered about a score, including Beaulieu whose 32 fugitives were summarily despatched by the king's commissioners when the abbey was dissolved.

SANITATION   see also *Laver, Rere-dorter, Water Supply*

Monasteries were pioneers in sanitation and the design of their buildings was far in advance of contemporary secular establishments. They were airy, well drained, plentifully supplied with water-points and facilities for evacuation and washing. Popular appreciation of this fact may be the origin of the proverb that 'cleanliness is next to godliness.'

SAVIGNAC   see also *Fontrevault, Tiron*

A religious reform originating in the abbey of Savigny (f.1112). The movement provoked considerable response but it lacked outstanding leaders and was so similar to the Cistercians that it was merged with them before the middle of C12. Furness (f.c.1127) was largely responsible for the spread of the Savignac rule in these islands where, by 1147, there were over a dozen houses of this obedience. After Furness, Buildwas was the most important foundation in England and others, for a time, included Byland and perhaps Jervaulx.

SCHOOLS

All religious houses gave instructions to interns: oblates and novices, but provision of schools for externs was no part of their vocation. Such education was the responsibility of diocesan bishops, usually acting through their chancellor, but C12 enthusiasm for monasteries tended to shift control of schools from him to the superior of the local monastery and the institution of cathedral priories (q.v.) further confused this responsibility. At this, time, several schools (e.g. Gloucester, Huntingdon, Reading) passed from the control of secular clergy to regulars and, in the remoter areas, monasteries occasionally provided a teacher for sons of their richer tenants.

It became fairly general for town monasteries to provide some education as a work of charity through the almonry (q.v.) and schools were sometimes built near the gate. In 1180's Abbot Samson of Bury provided a school-building and schoolmaster in School Hall Street. There was a large schoolroom in the dorter undercroft at York, known as the Schola Infantium in C14. This was probably for oblates but a large building attached to the almonry was built c.1318 as a school-house and its scholars provided a choir for the

Evesham (Chapter-House Arch)

daily Lady Mass. There were other almonry schools at Canterbury, Durham, Evesham, St Albans and Westminster at least. Some of these were grammar schools and some were 'song schools' providing a general education with emphasis on music. 'It is evident that, although there was some doubt about the canonical propriety of the application of alms in this direction, the education of poor children was a common part of the activity of monasteries.' (A.H. Thompson). Their 'canonical propriety' concerned whether such provision might lessen the available support for the indigent poor. These 'poor schools' disappeared with the almonries when the religious houses were suppressed.

Great monasteries provided another kind of education — that of a gentleman by the contemporary practice of 'apprenticing' him as a page in a great household. Glastonbury, among others, was a popular placement. Nunneries, in spite of adverse pressure, commonly provided a boarding school education for young gentlewomen.

SCOTLAND

In the Dark Ages, Celtic monasticism in the form of the Culdee communities had made a very considerable contribution to the evangelisation of Scotland, but by late C10 the missionary achievements and the golden age of Celtic Christianity lay in the distant past. Yet the Culdee life continued longer and in greater numbers than elsewhere in Britain and many mediaeval foundations were on sites hallowed by primitive monasticism and in some cases absorbed Culdee monks. The many Celtic saints were revered as holy individuals and as legendary rather than historical figures and the Culdees that remained had neither the strength nor the organisation to resist or influence the new developments in the country. These came in C12 under the influence of the sainted queen Margaret who first introduced the contemporary forms of the religious life at Dunfermline, a Benedictine abbey, and this development was continued and expanded on a vast scale by her son, David I (q.v.)

Melrose

Iona

The monastic families in Scotland continued to grow for half a century or so after the expansion had ceased in England, though their nunneries were always few and relatively small and poor. The friars reached Scotland a few years after their arrival in London and the country soon had its quota. C14 was a time of crisis in Scotland as elsewhere and was greatly aggravated by the wars with England since the chief and wealthiest monasteries lay unprotected and vulnerable in the basin of the Tweed. The monastic history of Scotland diverges from that of the rest of the British Isles markedly in C15 and early C16 where development and deterioration continue side by side in the former country. It accepted the new reform of the Franciscan Observants and also founded a Charterhouse at Perth. Foundations of all kinds were made with the greatest frequency in the years 1440-1540 and in one of these a lingering group of Culdees (of St Andrews) was transformed. Parallel to these positive developments was a general decline of observance in the monasteries hastened by their occupation by lay abbots, or commendators, in the last decades of C15. Simultaneously, the 'feuing' of monastic lands and the allotment of individual incomes to the religious was destroying both the property and the spirit of communities. Furthermore the houses on the border and near the Forth experienced the brutality of the Earl of Hertford in the so-called 'rough wooing' (1544). Nevertheless the end of religious houses came far more slowly in Scotland than in England and Wales. There was no total confiscation on the Henrician pattern but the urban houses, especially those of the friars, were sacked by the lawless element among the reformers. The abbeys continued, though with diminishing communities, until they were annexed to the crown in 1587 and even then, in many cases, did not legally come to an end until the turn of the century when one by one they were secularised by crown charters and acts of parliament. The dates for the dissolution of Scottish houses are difficult to establish because of the differences between the Scottish and English Reformations, the affect of lay commendators, the English support of Scottish Protestantism and their contribution to the destruction of abbeys during the 'rough wooing'. The C16 saw the establishment of a group of Scottish houses in Germany called 'the Schottenkloster' which survived until C19.

The earliest material monastic remains appear to be in Lothian and date from c.650 during the period of Northumbrian rule. Mediaeval Scotland was a poor and thinly populated country which affected both the size and the resources of monastic foundations. Religious houses were always sparse and there were hardly any north and west of a line Inverness-Perth-Glasgow. The total number of houses in the Middle Ages probably did not much exceed 130 but they represented all the major orders and some which were not found in England, such as the Valliscaulians. For other remains see under individual orders as Austin Canons, Benedictines, etc. There are records of more than 150 hospitals, of which about 30 seem to have been directly dependent on religious communities. There are remains of two or three (in Edinburgh, Soutra and possibly Thirlestane), but Alnwick was a Scottish foundation. There were two cathedral priories (St Andrews and Whithorn) though there were attempts to include Aberdeen, Inchaffray, Iona and Kirkwall among these institutions.

Religious life returned in C19 and there are modern abbeys at Fort Augustus and Pluscarden.

SCREENS

Monastic churches were divided into a number of compartments by screens of wood or stone. The main screens in church were the pulpitum (q.v.) and the rood-screen (q.v.). Their remains are scant, but at Lilleshall can be seen the bases of both, together with a wall further west screening nave from vaulted vestibule which may be ground-floor of an unfinished tower. An oaken screen rescued from the demolition of Easby survives in Wensley parish church.

Some idea of their former glory can be achieved by mentally putting together the shrine screen at Durham, the reredos at St Albans with survivals in parish churches (especially East Anglia where substantial decoration often survives). Monastic screens were decorated with painted or carved figures of appropriate saints: luminaries of the

St Albans Screen

order, apostles and/or famous ascetics. There might be monastic popes (especially St Gregory), pious kings including Jewish monarchs, Dark Age princes and English sovereigns, patriarchs and bishops who were monks, local saints, holy abbots and Doctors of the Church.

Besides the woodwork in the church, there were many screens and much wainscotting elsewhere: the carrels in south range of cloister, in the cubicles of the dorter, rere-dorter, farmery, frater and other domestic areas as well as subdivisions of cellars and undercrofts. It appears that some screens, e.g. those at the end of cloister alleys may have consisted of leather curtains. Often the frater was treated as a 'great hall' along with the guest-hall and abbot's hall and it would have the 'screens' which were found in all great mediaeval halls, together with the associated screen passage.

SCRIBE   see also *Illuminators*

'Clerk' and 'cleric' are cognate and the quire-monk was necessarily literate. It was natural that the use of his talents should centre round book production and reading and writing should become a dominant work. St Bernard had told his sons: 'Every word you write is a blow that smites the devil'. Writing was also suitable to the monastic vocation because of its silence, its communal value and the range of talents that could be used. Special accommodation was provided for this work in the scriptorium (q.v.).

Monastic Scribe

SCRIPTORIUM

There seems to have been a separate building used as a common scriptorium at the Celtic monastery of Tintagel. The early Benedictine practice was to provide individual studies or 'carrells' (q.v.) on the sunny side of the cloister. The south cloister walk was partitioned by richly-carved oak panelling into individual studies, each containing a desk and storage facilities for writing materials. The floor was covered with straw, hay or mats for quietness and warmth and each end of the walk that gave access to the scriptoria was screened to reduce draughts and increase privacy and silence.

At Chester, the cloister walk next to the church was built wider than the others to increase this accommodation but as it was still inadequate the carrells were continued along part of the west walk. At Wenlock it was probably in a large room over south aisle of church erected in C13. At Norwich it seems to have been extended to a second floor over the north walk (unusual in England) and similar provision was apparently made at Evesham c.1300. It is above sacristy at Selby.

It is to the monastic scriptoria that the modern world owes the preservation of many important books, both sacred and profane, from the ancient world. They were also the source of some of the most beautiful illuminations (q.v.) ever produced.

SEAL

In the Middle Ages the seal was the mark of authenticity in both state and church. The religious houses possessed a variety of seals: that of the house and those of individual obedientiaries as well as the superior's personal seal. The latter was destroyed at death and those of obedientiaries were recalled on the death of a superior. The great seal of a convent was placed in the joint charge of the three senior obedientiaries and was kept in a case which required three different keys to open it. Many seals have survived and they are useful sources of information.

Seal (Leominster)

SEATING   see *Stalls, Sedilia*

SECOND (and Third) ORDERS

Most mediaeval religious orders were initiated by and for men. Many of them developed a 'second order' for nuns following the same rule and inspired by the same ideas (e.g. Franciscans). Some had a 'third order' for men and women, living in the world, but associated in spirit and in work with a particular religious community (e.g. Dominicans).

SECRETARY   see *Sub-sacrist*

SECULAR CANONS

The group of clergy serving a cathedral or collegiate church. Though they were not monks, living according to one of the great rules, bishops increasingly insisted that they led a quasi-monastic life; celibate, eating and living in a common house and under some sort of regular discipline. Consequently, their accommodation tended to resemble that of monks so e.g. we are told that Giso, bishop of Wells (1061-1088) 'increased the number of canons in the church and made for them a cloister, dormitory and refectory'. Most mediaeval, secular cathedrals provided themselves with a cloister, chapter-house and buildings within an enclosure (close).

SECURITY

Maintained by a number of porters (q.v.) but keys seem to have been the responsibility of the second-in-command: the prior or sub-prior. He was responsible for the nightly locking up and kept the keys in his possession until morning when he opened up the common rooms and church and handed out keys to the minor official responsible for different stores and offices: porter, yeoman of the cellar, etc. The great obedientiaries maintained control of their own keys but all had to be handed in on the death of a superior, when they were maintained by the acting head until a new appointment was made. The new head distributed them to the officers of his own choosing.

SELF-SUFFICIENCY

It was Benedict's idea that the community should live off its own and all necessary facilities should be provided within the enclosure. This was an ideal rather than an actuality in the later period. Some rural monasteries, living austere lives, must have come very close but salt had to be imported if they had meat, iron was rarely found on monastic domains and there were other necessities which would have to be brought in from without such as tar to medicine sheep.

There was generally self-sufficiency in food and fuel, most structural materials (stone, timber, thatch), bedding (fern, heather or straw), floor covering (rushes and herbs) and in leather for footwear, harness, belts and wallets. The monastery produced its own fat for grease and for lighting, and its own wax for superior candles. Most clothing was derived from its own sheep and many processes in cloth-production took place within the precincts (though there seems no evidence of weaving).

The outer court or curia (q.v.) contained workshops for smiths and plumbers and sometimes even drawing offices and lodges for masons.

SERVANTS

Originally, religious houses had none, or as few as possible but, with the decline of lay brothers, changes in sources of revenues, increasing quire and extern duties, economic changes, etc., the number of servants steadily increased through the Middle Ages, especially in the great

Servant

Benedictine houses where they might reach as many as a hundred. 'Servants' is perhaps a misleading word and perhaps 'employees' (q.v.) would be better. They varied in function, status and remuneration and most of them did not reside on the premises. At the lowest level they might include fleeing serfs seeking sanctuary and protected from lordly claimants by the ceremony of placing a bell-rope round the neck of a fugitive. On the other hand they could include stewards of rank and great responsibility.

Some 'servants' were freemen, salaried employees of the house. Some were menials while some were formal assistants to the obedientiaries.

Servant

Other 'servants' could include altar-boys, bell-ringers, organists and medical practitioners, while the total staff of a large house in the later Middle Ages might, extend to artisans, smiths, carpenters, plumbers, tailors, tilers, shoemakers, those employed at the mill(s), bakehouse and brewery; workers within the grounds: gardeners, pig-keepers, poultry-keepers, etc.; those working in and about the stables, including drivers and messengers; indoor servants in gatehouse, frater, kitchens, cellarer's department, laundry, farmery and church, carters and bailiffs in the fields, labourers and shepherds on the farms.

Increasingly the superior had his own staff and attendants in imitation of the secular lord whose feudal equal he was: cooks and butler, chamberlain and chaplain, guards and attendants.

Even in a male house, some of these servants were women, laundresses and 'pudding wives' though the ordinances are strict about their choice; they had to be 'married, sober, of good repute and honest, that all danger of detraction from evil tongues be avoided.'

Generally a nunnery had proportionately more servants than a male community, for rough and heavy work and for protection.

SERVICE BOOKS
Included Antiphoner, Graduale, Rituale, Missal, Processionale etc. Their production, maintenance, up-dating and accuracy was the responsibility of the precentor (q.v.). He had to dust them, repair them and point them so that when they were used the brethren might not find any mistakes. They were not to be taken from the church or cloister since they were essential for the quire offices which were the monks' raison d'etre. All of them, especially the Gospel Book, were produced with great care, beautifully illuminated and among the most treasured possessions of the house.

SERVICE HATCH   see *Dresser Hatch*

SERVICES
For liturgical services in a religious house see hours, mass, processions. The external services or works of charity included the functions the almonry, school and hospital (q.v.) and the most obvious (and appreciated) was the 'ever-open door' of hospitality whether of doles or of meals and accommodation. Religious houses often served chaplaincies at nunneries, pilgrims' chapels and hospitals or paid vicars to fulfill these duties. (See also parochial responsibilities.)

SERVITORS
'Servitors' were members of the community, following a weekly rota, usually concerned with the service of meals (the word 'sizar' is cognate) in kitchen and frater and also in the work of the farmery e.g. 'Let the brethren serve one another and let no one be excused from the kitchen service, unless for sickness or because he is

occupied in some business of importance, for this service brings increase of reward and of charity.' (Rule xxv). Benedict characteristically legislated against overworking these 'willing drudges' and bringing sadness to their duty; 'Let everyone have help, according to the size of the community or the circumstances of the locality.' The weekly server had to ensure that all was shipshape for the next incumbent; towels washed, vessels scoured, etc. He and the incoming duty servitor conducted the weekly foot-washing.

They were given a 'biting on' an hour before the meal at which they were assisting (bread and a drink) and they took their full meal after the others had finished. Both incoming and outgoing servers were blessed and prayed for by the community according to Benedict's rule (xxxv).

SEXT
The day hour which took place about noon ('sixth hour'). It was similar to Terce and None, being short and simple, and consisted of a hymn, the singing of part of psalm cxix, a short chapter with its response and closing prayers which included the lesser litany, Lord's prayer and collect of the day. It usually followed, without interval, the High Mass.

SEYNIES   see *Bleeding*

SHAVING   see *Rasura*

SHEEP   see *Wool*

SHOES   see also *Boots*
Religious seem to have had two sets of footwear, the working boots worn during the day and the night shoes used for Mattins etc. These latter were felted and softer and were the equivalent of slippers which customaries allowed to be worn as an indulgence during periods of bleeding (q.v.) while their owners were in farmery etc.

New shoes were issued during Holy Week and the old pair were given to the poor by the almoner (q.v.). Originally they were made on the premises but tanneries are unpleasant neighbours and in later Middle Ages we find instances of shoes being supplied in place of rent e.g. Walter Cock supplied shoes to Meaux as part of his rent for a tannery, cobbler's shop and smallholding at North Grange.

SHRINES   see also *Pilgrimage*
'The saints' shrines of mediaeval Europe were not monuments to famous dead but gateways into the supernatural world.'

Many great abbeys (especially Benedictine ones) rose over the relics (q.v.) of a saint and the Austin Canons had St Birinus at Dorchester, St Frideswide at Oxford and St John at Bridlington. Certain images acquired thaumaturgic fame, especially that of Our Lady of Walsingham which led to the Milky Way being called the 'Walsingham Way'.

Relics were not only valued in themselves but they attracted other valuables producing the need for a shrine keeper (tumbarius) or master of the feretory, who assisted the sacrist and was responsible for the security of the relics and the associated treasury. He sometimes had his own checker or chamber, often associated with a special

Shrine,
St Werburga? (Chester)

watching-chamber (survival almost intact at St Albans). A falling candle in St Edmund's shrine in Bury in 1198 caused a fire which narrowly escaped destroying the church itself and regulations henceforth required two night-watchmen for the body and two others for the treasure and clock.

Nothing remains of the shrine of St William which was located in the Jesus chapel at Norwich and there is little more of the most famous shrine in England at Canterbury where a special chapel (the Corona) was built to house a fragment of St Thomas' skull. At the Dissolution, Henry, (who naturally had a special antipathy to this saint), required 26 carts to remove even the lesser treasures that had accumulated round his revered bones. The chapel of St Chad's Head survives at Lichfield with an exposition gallery above and there is a similar gallery at Norwich. There are fragmentary and denuded remains of the former shrines at Chester, Durham, Ely, Hereford, Oxford, Rievaulx, Shrewsbury, St Albans.

Shrine

SHRINE OFFERINGS

Perhaps not quite as an important source of ready cash as has sometimes been implied. Pilgrims undoubtedly gave of their treasure but in the case of major gifts it was almost as likely to be such a highly-prized curiosity as a unicorn's head, elephant's tooth or griffin's egg as an object of gold, silver or jewels. Since offerings belonged to the saint they were rarely converted into cash, even in times of crisis.

Shrine Offering

There were, of course, cash offerings, usually from the poorer pilgrims but these seemed to be falling away towards the close of the Middle Ages. In 1525 those at St Cuthbert's shrine amounted to £11-7-2 whereas a single emerald which survived until the Reformation pillage was valued at £3,000 in the money of the time. Cash offerings went to the sacrist's account and were spent on church building and furnishing.

All the shrines were destroyed and robbed 1537/8 on the useful and convenient grounds that the plunderers could attack superstition and gain great riches in a single act.

SICK, CARE OF   see also *Furmery, Illness, Hospital*

'The care of the sick shall come before and above all else, so that in every deed they may be served as Christ for He himself said: "I was sick and ye visited me" and "What you have done to one of these little ones, you have done unto Me." ' (St Benedict: Rule chap. xxxvi).

SIESTA   see also *Sleep*

Besides the broken night sleep, monastic constitutions allowed a return to the dorter in the afternoon from dinner until None except on Rogation Days. The time could be used for reading but, in the case of children, the time had to be occupied in actual sleep.

SIGNALS

Most of them were given by bells of which there was a wide variety and diverse manners of ringing them. Some kind of bell must have been punctuated the silence of the monastery almost every hour*. There were small hand-bells, even smaller table-bells and the great bells hung in church-turrets and towers.

Besides the signals of bell and gong (there seems to have often been a gong outside the frater), others were given by clapper or by beating a board and there were many silent signals given by hand gestures, including those in quire and the complex signs used in the frater, indicating requests for dishes, condiments, etc. Even these silent signals were to be limited for, as the Barnwell Observances say, 'needless and harmful signs are everywhere to be avoided.'

*   Bells were silent in Passiontide as a sign of mourning.

SILENCE

'Quiet, then, is the first step in our santification.'
(St Basil). The object, life and reward of monasticism was
'summa quies': the absence of all excitement, whether sensible
or intellectual, which might disturb the central contemplation
aimed at the achievement of the heavenly Sabbath.

The religious house was the home of silence, voices were
only to be raised in prayer and praise, silence (apart from
the measured words of scripture coming from the reader)
was maintained in frater, and silence brooded over the
whole house from Compline to the office of Mattins.

Silence

Outside the house, silence was supposed to be
maintained even between two religious accompanying each other (according to rule)
on a journey. Noisy activities were placed as far away from the cloister as possible
and even workmen in the extern shops and offices were to be silent during the
singing of the canonical Hours: 'While any Hour save Compline is being sung in
church, no brother shall talk to any officer of the monastery, nor within the bounds
of the great court, nor even in the farmery, save for the sick who are so straitened as
to be unable to keep silence for that space.' (Lanfranc : Constitutions).

This example must have been not without its effect on the external world as
'silent men were observed about the country, or discovered in the forest, digging,
clearing and building; and other silent men, not seen, were sitting in the cold
cloister, tiring their eyes and keeping their attention on the stretch, while they
painfully deciphered and copied and re-copied the manuscripts that they had saved
... by degrees the woody swamp became a hermitage, a religious house, a farm, an
abbey, a village, a seminary, a school of learning and a city . . . and what the
haughty Alaric or fierce Attila had broken in pieces, these patient meditative men
brought together and made to live again.' (J.H. Newman).

In spite of the rule, however, it became increasingly difficult to keep the hubbub
of the world from the silent cloister, especially if the monastery were on a pilgrim
route, the object of pilgrimage, or used by king and nobles for accommodation.
Even the house's own members, returning from a journey, might be irrepressible or
unable to resist demands for news from the great outside world. As such travellers
tended to return late, there was an almost continuous problem in the later mediaeval
period of preventing prolonged conversation (and potation) between returned
officials or other travellers and members of the community.

Originally speech was only allowed in the parlour (q.v.) but later restricted
conversation was allowed, with permission, in the cloister. Benedict was firm that
such permission should be rarely granted and almost all reforms of the Black Monks
included a return to strictness in this respect (e.g. Reformed Cistercians, Trappists).
Even this restricted conversation was to be on religious matters; 'Let no one dare to
ask about the gossip of the world, nor tell of it, nor speak of trifles or frivolous
subjects apt to cause laughter.' (Constitutions of St Augustine Canterbury).

'Let no one think himself a well-ordered, religious or God-
fearing canon, if he get into the habit of breaking silence
without urgent reason . . . for this want of control of the
tongue is an evident sign of a dissolute mind and a neglected
conscience . . . Therefore, let Canons Regular regard silence
as a precious treasure since through it a remedy against so
many dangers is applied.' (Barnwell Observances).

SINGING   see also *Music, Plainsong, Precentor*

All monastic services were sung, processions were
accompanied by singing, grace before meals and after meals
were sung, as were prayers for the dead in the cemetery.

Monks in Quire

The reading of the lessons was intoned (though perhaps not the reading in frater). The singing of the monks was sometimes supplemented by voices of boys from the almonry or song-school maintained by the monastery.

SISTERS   see *Lay-sisters, Canonesses, Nuns, Second Order, Vowess*

SISTERS OF THE ORDER OF ST JOHN OF JERUSALEM

About ten houses of this small nursing order are recorded in England (remains only at Aconbury).

SITE

The prime consideration in the choice of a site was the availability of a continuous adequate supply of water. The disposition of the conventual buildings was regulated by the relative positions of the water supply and the main site (though sometimes water channels were diverted, e.g. at Rievaulx). The ideal site was north of a stream flowing from west to east (e.g. Fountains where these are the natural conditions and Dryburgh where they were achieved artificially). The unusual siting of cloisters north of the church may be due to the awkward lie of the river in relation to the high point of the site where the church was built (e.g. Buildwas).

Other factors involved the current or potential use of the land which they had been offered. Available resources were another consideration: timber, stone, minerals. Monks often found and utilised neglected resources and developed waste by clearing, draining, liming and other back-breaking industry.

Except in the case of the later mendicants, solitude was a factor in the choice of a site but this has often been obscured by the subsequent growth of settlement under the protecting walls of a once remote house e.g. Bury, Durham, Ely, Norwich, Peterborough, St Albans. This development lay behind the renewed search for remote sites in the later Cistercian and Premonstratensian reforms. Inchmahome was built on an island in Loch Monteith; Ely, Crowland, Thorney and Glastonbury on firm land surrounded by marshes, Whitby and St Andrews on rocks jutting into the sea. Llanthony, Fountains, Rievaulx, Rosedale and Tintern were in remote valleys far from roads or tracks. Some houses were originally lost in a forest clearing: Kirkstall, Welbeck, Worksop. Even today the ruins of many are still in sites remote from the world: Blanchland, Buildwas, Beaulieu, Crowland, Llanthony, Strata Florida, Valle Crucis. Romantics, often comment on the aesthetic taste of monks in choosing 'such a beautiful site', forgetting that the beauty is almost invariably the result of hundreds of years of monastic industry which has transformed a most unaesthetic waste into what they see today.

Clearing Site

Some sites seem to have been related to a previously existing settlement of hermits and in some cases to a secular institution e.g. Austin Canons seem often to have served a castle chapel. Some sites were chosen on the basis of supernatural indications e.g. Durham, Crowland, and frequently they gathered round the tomb of an ancient saint: Bury, St Albans. Bristol was supposed to mark the place of meeting between St Augustine and Celtic missionaries, Battle consecrated the field which had given England to William while Glastonbury's site was a focus of many legendary associations.

Lindisfarne (Island Site)

Sleep

Once chosen, the highest point of the site was usually set aside for the church and the domestic buildings conveniently disposed about it to the south. Water supply and other site factors (e.g. Kirkham, Rievaulx, Tintern) could produce local variations and monasteries expanding within a constricted town site had sometimes to place their outer-court and farmery in unusual positions (e.g. Canterbury, Chester, Durham, Gloucester, Rochester, Thetford, Worcester).

Major site-work, besides clearance, could involve draining marsh (Byland), considerable earthworks (Bardney), excavating fishponds, constructing sea wall (Butley), canals (Dryburgh, Selby), diverting river (Rievaulx).

SLEEP

The hours of sleep were from sunset to midnight and from two or three a.m. to dawn, supplemented in summer by a siesta (q.v.)

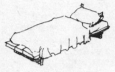

SLYPE

A through passage, usually at the north end of the east cloister alley giving access from the cloister walk to the monastic cemetery (e.g. Durham, Gloucester, Worcester). It was usually placed between the south transept of the church and the chapter-house and often is provided with seats, sometimes separated by elaborate arcading (e.g. St Albans). It sometimes functioned as a connecting link with the farmery and often served as a common-room or parlour (q.v.). It was closed by doors at both ends and the keys were kept by the sub-prior.

Sometimes it was placed at the southern end of the eastern cloister walk and its original position divided between sacristy and library (common Cistercian arrangement e.g. Kirkstall, Fountains, Valle Crucis) with access to the former from the church and to the latter from the cloister. At Thornton it was partly a parlour and partly a strong-room or treasury at Titchfield it was a library and at Thetford and Easby a sacristy.

Sometimes parlour and slype were placed side by side and the latter's position was affected by convenient access to the farmery (e.g. Castle Acre, Westminster). In Cistercian houses the slype was usually on the opposite side of the chapter-house from the church and it could be a structurally independent passage (e.g. Tintern) or simply a partitioned off part of the dorter undercroft (Fountains, Roche). It was often prolonged eastwards to form a gallery giving covered access to the farmery with a branch leading to the eastern arm of the church (e.g. Fountains).

SOLITARIES   see *Anchorite, Hermit, Recluse*

SONG SCHOOL

Song schools stood between the elementary and the grammar schools providing a technical education with good career prospects. Monasteries often used the members of their song schools to supplement the monastic singing or to provide it at particular services, particularly those to which the public were admitted. At Durham the song school was accommodated in two compartments of the dorter undercroft.

Song schools offered free tuition and sometimes board. Their numbers were small (six at Durham) but they offered quite a broad curriculum which included, besides a wide variety of musical skills, some mathematics, reading (probably writing) and Latin. The master of a song school often acted as assistant organist in the monastery (with a monk deputising for him at the night offices). At Durham, and possibly elsewhere, he was a secular clerk provided with a stipend, a house and board in the prior's hall. Song schools generally died with the abbeys but some survived or were revived as cathedral quire schools.

SOUTH (FRATER) RANGE

The cloister range opposite the church whose principal room was the frater which generally occupied most of it either on ground floor (e.g. Chester) or on undercroft (e.g. Durham and many houses of regular canons.) In Cistercian houses the frater was usually at right angles to south alley but in some cases it ran east and west (e.g. Sibton, Merevale). At Cleeve its axis was originally north and south but it was changed to east and west in C15.

Many houses had a passage through the range, east of the frater, which gave access to the dorter undercroft (e.g. Westminster) or outer court (e.g. Durham) or farmery (Gloucester, Peterborough, Westminster). When outer court lay south of cloister, this passage served as outer parlour (e.g. Easby, Haughmond, Westminster).

Laver (q.v.) was usually provided near entrance to frater and sometimes signs of its towel cupboard can be seen. The kitchen with its associated building usually lay beyond frater but in Cistercian houses it opened from western end of south walk.

SPAN   see *Bay*

SPITAL

Mediaeval form of the word 'hospital' and its occurence in place-names indicates the site of a hospital e.g. Romanby, Yorkshire, North Riding; Sherburn, Durham.

STABILITY

To the traditional three vows (q.v.) St Benedict added a fourth, of stability, by which a monk promised to remain until death in the house to which he was professed. Its effects have been judged critical in the development of European culture and civilisation. The basic meaning of 'stabilitas' in the rule seems to be 'perseverance' and the fixation of will and intention and love seems to have extended to the place where the vows were made. Some have seen 'stability' as a reaction to the unsettlement, the folk wanderings and physical disturbances of the time but it may be due more to the psychological insight that inward stability needs to be secured by outward stability, that we cannot bear fruit unless undisturbed roots penetrate deeply into the environment.

STABLES

In great monasteries stables were nearly as important an office as they were in castles. The guest-house provided stabling, the house required its own for transport and carriage. The more extensive and scattered the abbey lands, the more involved in state business its superior, the more horses were required.

Kirkstall had stables grouped round the courtyard of its guest-house, even little Nunkeeling had two stables; stables were often attached to the president's lodging and all houses had stables in the curia. As most of them were doubtless timber-framed, there are few signs of their existence remaining.

STALLS   see also *Quire*

The seats provided for those involved in quire services. The main community was seated in rows on either side of the quire and parallel to the aisles or quire wall with return stalls, facing east and backing on to the pulpitum, for the greater dignitaries.

As these were occupied for many hours in each monastic day, there was a slow diminution of their discomfort.

Movable Seat (Misericord)

Wooden screens were provided behind them and canopies above to minimise draughts, misericords (q.v.) were invented to give some support while standing during long offices, a ledge was provided in front of the stalls to support service books. (Also a warm quire habit was developed to provide some insulation in the unheated church).

Each monk had his own particular stall and his placement reflected his place in the community. The oldest monks sat towards the west of the quire, their juniors (in profession) towards the east. Novices were often given less elaborate provision in a second row of stalls in front of the others. In an abbey the abbot's stall faced east and backed on to the pulpitum on the south side of its doorway while the prior sat in the corresponding stall on the north. In a priory, these seats were occupied by the prior and sub-prior. At High Mass, the president had a second seat (usually a portable faldstool) in the sanctuary.

Occasionally the monastic seating survives in situ (e.g. Chester, Gloucester), in other cases only the foundations of the quire stalls survive (sometimes with resonators as at Fountains). Its development can be studied from early Winchester, C14 at Chester and Gloucester, C15 at Carlisle, Whalley, to C16 fragments at Bridlington, Jervaulx.

The quire stalls were usually used for firewood at the suppression but some were rescued e.g. Whalley's went to the parish church, some of those from Cockersand survive in Lancaster, and of Easby in Richmond.

STATIO

The place where the community asembled to take up their positions for a procession. At York it was in the west alley of the cloister before the parlour. The word was also used of the halting-places, for particular prayers in the course of a procession e.g. in the cloister, before the great rood, etc. 'Markers' sometimes survive, e.g. Shap.

Monastic Procession (Boss)

STATIONARIES

Old and partially retired members of the community for whom some of the rigours of the rule have been relaxed on account of their infirmity (called 'sempectae' among the Cistercians). They had 'quit themselves like men in the vineyard of the Lord for a great number (often 50) of years' and therefore ought to be treated with respect and consideration.

They were lodged in the farmery and excused from extra duties (such as those on the tabula) but they were expected to attend offices and mass, keep silence and persevere with their private devotions.

The indulgence could obviously be abused and the Barnwell Observances warn them not 'to repeat silly tales of old days with foolish hilarity or laughter, after the fashion of secular old men.' They are also to 'shun needless drinkings' and retire at the same time as the rest of the convent, if not before.

STEWARD   see *Lay Officials*

STONE

The source of its ashlar can often be seen in close proximity to a religious house (e.g. Fountains) though sometimes it was transported over considerable distances. Some religious houses had their own quarries, the canal which the monks of Selby built to transport stone from their estate at Monk Fryston (eight miles away) still survives. Others bought material (e.g. Kirkham acquired its stone through York Minster Fabric Department).

Wealthy abbeys imported stone (from Caen for St Albans) and Belgian marble was used for ornament until it was superceded by Purbeck. (The austere Cistercians e.g. at Fountains used a local 'marble'). The quality of building stone used in monastic building varies from almost intractable Cornish granite to the perishable chalk of Cherry Hinton and it can add additional interest to identify the particular material (and its source). Barnack stone was popular and occurs at e.g. Crowland, Ely, Peterborough, Ramsey, Thorney; Glastonbury drew much material from Doulting (near Shepton Mallet); Exeter used Portland; Bury, Ketton and the quarries of Quarr supplied the abbey there as well as Winchester. There is magnesian limestone at Roche and cretaceous (clunch) at Cambridge, Ely and Norwich, while Kirkstall used gritstone.

Besides Purbeck marble, alabaster (especially from Chellaston) was much used for internal sculpture, particularly altar-pieces.

STORE   see also *Cellar, Granary, Outbuildings*

STUDY

St Benedict expected study to occupy about a third of a monk's waking hours but monastic study was not conceived of as academic: it was linked to personal experience and regarded as a means not an end. It consisted of reading (usually aloud) from the scriptures, scriptural commentaries, and from the Fathers of the Church. It formed part of the pursuit of a better life and curiosity was not its purpose, since knowledge alone simply swells the mind.

Monk in Study

Study was really a form of meditation linked to prayer and religious experience and not (as in the universities) to disputation. It was an affective, not an academic activity. St Bernard, one of the finest representatives of monastic scholarship, said, 'My masters are not Plato and Aristotle but Christ and the apostles. They have taught me how to live and, believe me, that is no mean thing.'

Study was also meant to lead to a deeper understanding of the Divine Office, the significance of the mass, the events of Christ's life which gave shape to the liturgical year and the virtues of the saints who were celebrated in the ecclesiastical calendar. The insistence on silence (q.v.) was to allow the slow digestion of what had been read and marked in the periods of study.

Special provision was made for study in the carrells (q.v.) and elsewhere, including the farmery and the dorter (during the siesta).

SUB-CELLARER

Besides being the general assistant and deputy to the most important obedientiary in the community, the sub-cellarer had areas of special responsibility which centred round the provision of staple food and drink. His chief assistant was the granatorius.

In some houses, the sub-cellarer also had charge of the guest-house and the Barnwell Observances require him to be 'obliging, of cheerful countenance, temperate in his answers, courteous to strangers and of polished manners'.

Sub-Cellarer

SUB-PRIOR   see also *Third Prior*

The sub-prior was often a kind of Prefect of Discipline, responsible for order and the observance of the rule. He was sometimes called the warden of the order or the 'prior maius' and he and the prior shared a joint responsibility for the well-being of the religious house. It was his duty to see that all was in order in the dorter and farmery after Compline when he took all the keys of

171

the inner convent (e.g. the cloister and its surrounding buildings) into his charge until he redistributed them at the beginning of Prime.

In a cathedral priory, the sub-prior had the same duties as a prior in an abbey and was responsible for the day-to-day running of the community with a 'third prior' as his assistant. He could have his own accommodation (e.g. Canterbury Christchurch, Westminster, Worcester). His position was similar in a large priory (e.g. Barnwell) where the prior dealt with general and external matters and he was responsible for internal administration and oversight.

SUB-SACRIST

The sacrist's chief assistant and deputy, sometimes identified with Matricularius. 'It is his duty to assist the sacrist and act, in his absence, as deputy.' Apart from general duties he had specific tasks, chiefly acting as time-keeper for the house, responsible for the regulation of the clock and ringing the bells at the appropriate times. Sometimes he seems to have acted as a kind of porter, asking the business of those who knocked at the gates or doors of the church. Like the sacrist, he took his meals in church and also slept there in a special chamber or in a checker overlooking the church.

'In winter he ought to supply live coals in iron dishes to warm the hands of the celebrant'. He was responsible for seeing that the church was guarded at mealtimes, during processions and at other times when the general community was likely to be absent from it. He had to be skilled in bell-ringing of various kinds so that they gave clear signals (q.v.) — a complex matter which, the Barnwell Observances say, 'cannot be narrated in a few words'.

Sub-Sacrist

SUCCENTOR

The sub-cantor or chief assistant to the precentor (q.v.), particularly in quire where his place was on the 'decani' (i.e. north side) opposite the precentor's stall. The customals emphasise the importance of his possessing a strong voice and being skilful in all manner of singing. 'It is his business to set the tone for the psalms on one side, as the precentor does on the other; and on feast days to rule the quire with the precentor; to get ready the 'tabula' (q.v.) and to assist him in all other matters which belong to his office.' (Barnwell Observances).

SUPERIOR

The president or chief officer of a community who was given almost absolute power, was called abbot (or abbess) in major Benedictine, Cistercian and Premonstratensian houses.

In monasteries whose churches served as cathedrals, the head of the convent was a prior, though his position was almost identical with that of an abbot of a major monastery. The same is true of other large houses (especially those of Austin Canons e.g. Bolton) whose superior had the title of prior.

When the prior was superior of a dependency or cell (e.g. Finchale, Tynemouth) his powers were more limited as he was nominated by the head of the mother house and held office, not for life like a major superior but only at the nominator's will and pleasure. The priors of Dominican houses, the guardians of Franciscan ones and the superiors of 'alien' priories had less independence than an abbot (q.v.)

SUPERIOR'S LODGING

As the Middle Ages progressed, the superior's feudal status and responsibilities required a separate lodging: initially as appropriate accommodation for his guests: hall, bedrooms, chapel and parlour. For a time, the abbot or prior maintained his sleeping quarters in communication with the common dorter but eventually his chambers became quite separate, often with their own kitchen, and built round a minor court off the curia. This accommodation was often a development of the western range (except in Cistercian establishments where the western range was given over to the 'conversi'). At St Dogmael's, the abbot's hall was over the west range (with access to church via vice) with the guest-house behind.

Prior's Parlour, Castle Acre

Superior's Lodging, Castle Acre

This private opulence was not necessarily the superior's choice — sumptuous guest accommodation was practically forced on Bridlington Priory by the archbishop of York who required a comfortable base for his visitations of eastern Yorkshire.

In former cathedral priories, the prior's lodging was often appropriated by the dean after the Reformation and so survives in use at e.g. Carlisle, Durham, Ely. Other extensive remains may be found at e.g. Arbroath, Castle Acre, Kirkstall. Fountains has evidence of a gallery from the abbot's lodging giving on to a position overlooking the chapel of the Nine Altars.

SUPPER (CENA)

A light meal, served in frater, to supplement the major meal. It was not provided on fast days but when it was, it was accompanied by reading and similar ceremony to that which operated at dinner.

SUPPRESSION

There were a number of suppressions of religious houses in the Middle Ages due to an inadequacy of foundations, paucity of numbers or the inviability of a small order. More significant cases were the general suppression of the Templars and the slow abolition of alien priories. In both of these the resources and buildings were reassigned to very similar purposes to those of the original foundation.

In C16, Wolsey (with permission from Rome) suppressed a number of small and inefficient houses for the benefit of new collegiate foundations of an educational nature. These alleged precedents were used by Henry VIII to expropriate the great and 'unproductive' wealth of the religious houses. The smaller houses (those with an annual income of less than £200) were attacked on the grounds that their conventual life was slack and beyond reform and compared most unfavourably with that of 'the great and solemn monasteries wherein, thanks be to God, religion is right well kept and preserved,' to which the inmates of the suppressed houses were to be transferred.

There can be no doubt about Henry's real motives which had the two-fold aim of attacking institutions owing allegiance to the pope (with whom he had broken in 1532/3) and to reap the rich harvest revealed in the Valor Ecclesiasticus, the assessment of the church's wealth compiled in 1535. Royally commissioned preachers were sent through the land to prepare the general public for the siezure of monastic property and they were briefed to denounce religious as 'hypocrites, sorcerers and idle drones' and to declare that 'if the abbeys went down, the king would never want for any taxes again.' Simultaneously, commissioners were sent forth charged with collecting the evidence the king's propaganda needed from a visitation of religious houses. Under threats from the king in 1536 parliament passed

an Act of Suppression dissolving smaller monasteries and
its implementation led to the Pilgrimage of Grace (q.v.).

This resistance allowed the king to implicate some of the
greater houses which were also attacked piece-meal by a
variety of strategems including the intrusion of puppet
abbots who, by a legal fiction, could as 'owners' voluntarily
surrender their house to the king. Eventually by bribes,
threats, executions and fraud the majority of the greater
abbeys fell and the survivors were covered by an Act of
1539 which legalised past and future suppressions. The last

Bradford upon Avon,
Monastery

abbey to be dissolved was Waltham in March 1540 and
Cromwell had fulfilled his promise to make his master the
richest prince in Christendom. He had also implicated the
great landowners and crown servants in the maintenance of
the 'New Religion' since the return of the traditional one
might affect their pockets and possessions.

'Many private men's parlours were hung with altar-
cloths, their tables and beds covered with copes and many
made carousing cups out of sacred chalices. It was a sorry
house, not worth the naming, which had not somewhat of
this furniture in it; though it were only a fair-sized cushion
made of a cope or altar-cloth to make their chairs to have
somewhat in them of a chair of state.' (Heylin).

Byland (Cistercian)

But the king made the greatest haul: lead from the roofs, jewels and plate from the
churches, bell-metal for re-use in guns, farm-stock and land, contents of storehouses,
sale of buildings. The amount realised from church furniture and buildings alone came
to £26,502-1-0½ from April '36 to Sept. '47. Much stuck to intermediate hands, much
was paid out in bribes and presents, yet by 1547 the Court of Augmentations had
received £1,338,422 in contemporary money. It has been estimated that all this capital
had been wasted or squandered by the end of Henry's reign and the crown emptied the
dregs of the church's wealth in the reign of Edward VI.

The friaries went with the abbeys and, as for the hospitals, some fell with the
smaller priories (1536), others with the greater houses (1539), many, together with a
number of remaining schools, disappeared with the Edwardian Acts of 1545 and
1547.

SURVIVALS   see also *Remains*

The secular grantees who turned the religious house into
'a stately home' had little interest in or respect for the
church (e.g. Lacock). There is a contemporary description
of how Cromwell's demolition agent worked to destroy the
church in the priory of Lewes which his master had
acquired as part of his 'perks'. The new owner of
Stavordale actually converted the church into a residence
while the one at Repton had the church speedily demolished
lest the monks should one day regain it.

Leominster has Monastic
History of almost Nine
Centuries

Conversely, the great houses which were retained or
refounded as cathedrals tended to lose their conventual buildings though some
substantially survived. Churches which had parochial functions were often saved, at
least in part, but some of the greatest houses (Bury, Evesham, Hailes, York) were
entirely devastated, Jervaulx was blown up with gunpowder. Sites which were too
remote for their buildings to have alternative use often suffered severely though
sometimes the very solitude saved at least such buildings as the elements spared.
(Though Fountains Hall seems to have been entirely built from ashlar quarried from
the neighbouring abbey ruins).

Sometimes, the remains are of the most tenuous nature: a coat of arms (Boston), a tomb (Rosedale), displaced furniture. A ceiling from Shaftesbury survives at Marnhull, some quire-stalls from Lilleshall at Wolverhampton, the lectern from Newstead at Southwell. Sometimes a nave arcade or a timber roof has been re-used.

Elsewhere a building survives transmogrified out of all recognition: the hotel at Blanchland contains part of the abbot's house, a school at Battle incorporates some of the abbey, palaces (Dunfermline, Holyrood and some of the great houses of the 'Dukeries') hide within their secular magnificence fragments of a former religious house. Farms often occupy the remains of convents (e.g. Alberbury, Balmerino). There may be only a heap of stone, hummocks in the ground and individual churches or chapels quite frequently are reduced to barns. Sometimes all that is left is a place or street name.

TABULA

(a) the wooden board struck with a mallet as a monastic signal (q.v.),
(b) and more frequently the 'duty roster' read in chapter and published in the cloister which set out the Hebdomadarians (q.v.).

It was prepared by the precentor and read out in the chapter on Saturday since duties began after dinner on Saturday. The tablet was a thin rectangular board (in some cases measuring about 13×5 inches) which was coated with wax (apparently green in certain houses) on which the precentor or his assistant inscribed the names and duties with a stylus.

In the cloister at Fountains the recess in which the tabula was placed can still be seen.

Recess for Tabula
(Fountains)

TALK   see also *Silence*

Limited in both quantity and quality by rules and observances e.g. 'In multiplicity of conversation, sin cannot fail to be present and if the Truth says "of every idle word that men speak they shall give an account", there is no doubt that a just Judge will impose a far more severe sentence upon words that are false, scurrilous, censorious and treacherous. On this account, those who live according to a rule ought not only to restrain themselves from idle and wicked words but sometimes in certain places at certain hours, as the observances in accordance with the rule prescribe, to abstain even from conversation on sacred subjects, on account of the excellent result of silence.' (Barnwell Observances).

Silence was characteristic of monastic life and speech was intended to be directed only to the glory of God and the salvation of souls. There was little recreational conversation in a strict house though there might be some indulgence in the farmery where limited conversation was allowed inside the building and in the recuperative walks outside. Blood-letting (q.v.) seems to have been regarded as a time for sharing confidences and intimate conversation. Necessary conversation was catered for but it was confined to specific places e.g. 'Brethren who, during the time of silence find it necessary to talk must go into the parlour or some other retiring place outside the cloister where, without interrupting the general silence, they can talk together, providing always the senior brother first says "Benedicite" '. (Barnwell Observances).

There was sometimes a time when talk was allowed in cloister i.e. when an interval occurred between Chapter and Terce or between the latter office and High Mass when the brethren, once permission had been formally given, were allowed to talk sitting at their places in the cloister but there had to be no excessive laughter, noise or confusion. In the later Middle Ages the warming-house seems to have become a tolerated recreational centre and gradually developed into a common room where some relaxation and even celebration was allowed. The rules always required strict silence from Compline to Prime.

TANNING   see also *Shoes*

In spite of the unpleasant smells associated with the process, provision for
tanning seems to have been made within the precincts and, in the later Middle Ages,
Rievaulx used the undercrofts of both dorter and frater for tanning hides.

TAYLERY (Sartrina)

The tailoring department came under the chamberlain
who sometimes had an assistant responsible for this area. It
dealt with the making and repair of clothes and, in later
period, seems to have employed lay people who were
among the few allowed to enter the dorter (for fitting?). In
great houses the taylery was a considerable establishment
e.g. at Abingdon it included four lay officials and four servants.

At work in Taylery

The tailor's shop was usually placed in the great court or curia. It was beneath
the chamberlain's checker at Durham and in C14 York seems to have occupied the
upper floor of the guest-house.

TEMPERANCE

One of the four cardinal virtues, specifically the one which inclines us to keep
due measure and order (q.v.) in what we say or do. The architecture of the C12,
largely inspired by Cluny, was directed by principles of order and due measure, of
proportion, aptness and symbolism.

TEMPLARS

The 'Order of the Poor Fellow Soldiers of Jesus Christ
and of the Temple of Solomon' were given a rule by
St Bernard in 1128 some ten years after their foundation as
a small group of crusading knights to protect pilgrims to the
Holy Land. The rule was severe and ascetic, forebade all
luxury and display and enjoined constant devotional
exercises, fasting and mortification as well as the monastic
observance of the canonical hours. Templars took the usual
monastic vows to which they added knightly vows of fealty
and a promise only to engage the enemy at odds of three to
one. Their headquarters was in the mosque of Omar which
they believed to be Solomon's Temple and consequently
built their own churches with round naves in imitation of it.
(e.g. London Temple c. 1185). Hospitallers sometimes
followed the practice e.g. Little Maplestead.

The order recruited well and within 50 years became
numerous and powerful, wielding vast financial resources.

Templar

They became bankers and possessed of vast estates all round the Mediterranean as
well as an estimated 7,000 manors in Europe. Their wealth and secretiveness aroused
envy and suspicion and when Acre was retaken by the Saracens in 1291 they lost
their obvious purpose. Philip the Fair of France, envious of their wealth, used ill-
founded charges of heresy and immorality to suppress them with incredible
barbarity. He managed to gain the support of the pope, Clement V, who suppressed
the order in 1312. In England 18 of their 20 houses were transferred to the
Hospitallers (q.v.).

As recognised guardians of travellers, much of their local work was akin to that
provided by a hospital for wayfarers e.g. King Stephen gave them the manor of
Steynton, Yorkshire, on condition that they 'find a chaplain to celebrate divine
service daily and to receive and entertain poor guests and pilgrims there, and to
bring and blow the horn every night at dusk lest pilgrims and strangers should lose
their way'.

Similar services were doubtless provided at their other preceptories (23 in England and Wales) which also acted as recruiting centres and administrative offices for the manors in which they were situated. These preceptories are often alternatively called 'hospitals' e.g. Greenham, Berkshire, Sutton-at-Hone, Lincolnshire. St Thomas' Hospital, London began under the auspices of the Templars but it seems to have achieved quasi-independence by beginning of C14 and therefore was not involved in their suppression.

There are some remains of their houses at Balsall, Bisham, Denney, Dover, Garway, London, Ribstone, Rothley, Strood, Temple Bruer, Temple Combe, and Temple Hirst. Churches partially survive in Balsall, Garway, London, Ribstone, Rothley. The unique round chapel at Ludlow Castle may have Templar connections through Gilbert de Lacy.

Even slighter remains include the crosses with which they marked their possessions (e.g. in the Ainstey region of Leeds) and the tomb of Thomas Cantilupe in Hereford Cathedral. He was provincial Grand Master of the order in the late C13 and figures of 14 knights (as usual much defaced) decorate the base of his sepulchre.

There were three preceptories in Scotland of which Balantrodoch was the principal. There are no remains. There is a tradition that the Templars had a foundation near Basingwerk to protect pilgrims on their way to Holywell but Knowles denies its existence.

Other Templar sites, often only of manors in their possession, are indicated by surviving place names e.g. Temple Newsam, Leeds; the villages of Temple in Cornwall and Hampshire; and Temple Cowley, Temple Dinsley, Temple Ewell and Temple Guiting.

TEMPORARY ACCOMMODATION   see also *Rebuilding*

Early Cistercians and other monastic pioneers often found what initial shelter they could in the shadow of trees or rocks or in bivouacs made of tree branches (e.g. at Fountains). Other communities moved into temporary lodging in order to speed their occupation of a site e.g. at Meaux in 1150. Elsewhere this initial lodging seems to have been occupied by the conversi while they erected more substantial buildings for the monks to occupy when they had reached a suitable state of readiness.

Such temporary buildings were usually of wood and they were gradually built in stone (sometimes over centuries) when the resources became available e.g. St Dogmael's when cloister was rebuilt in stone only in C13.

TENTH CENTURY

After the disasters of the Danish raids and consequent decline and destruction, monasticism in England was revived in the second half of C10 where its continuous history really begins. Monasteries were reorganised and rebuilt and the strict rule of St Benedict was generally imposed. The chief architect was St Dunstan with the active support of St Ethelwold and Oswald. Their inspiration came from Fleury and they were enthusiastically supported by King Edgar who had declared that 'all the monasteries in my realm to the outward sight are nothing but worm-eaten and rotten timber and boards; and what is worse, they are almost empty and devoid of Divine service.' The houses restored or founded included Abingdon, Ely, Evesham, Peterborough, Pershore, Romsey, Westminster, Winchester and Worcester. This period, 958-975, has been described as the finest age of Anglo-Saxon monasticism.

TERCE

The short office sanctifying the third hour (i.e. about nine a.m.). It was similar in structure to Sext and None, consisting of a hymn, followed by the first part of Psalm. cxix, a chapter or reading with its response and usually concluded by the lesser litany, the Lord's prayer, versicles etc. and the collect of the day.

THIRD ORDER   see *Second Order*

THIRD PRIOR   see also *Registrar*
An office in cathedral priories which was equivalent to that of sub-prior (q.v.) in other abbeys. He was also called 'Deece' (Deice, Deace). He presided in the prior's hall in the latter's absence, generally acted as deputy and was also the prior's chaplain. He often had his own chamber next to the prior's (e.g Canterbury Christchurch, Westminster, Worcester).
Large abbeys also had a third and even a fourth prior who were disciplinary officers (see Circas), acting as a kind of domestic police. They were not allowed to rebuke the brethren directly but reported misdemeanours at the disciplinary part of chapter (q.v.).

THIRTEENTH CENTURY
Saw the rapid proliferation of regular canons come to a climax and early in this century they were joined by the two chief orders of friars: Franciscans and Dominicans who claimed to live off what they could beg (Mendicants).
The Dominicans, like the Austin Canons, were middle, sometimes upper-class and highly literate. Their main function was to provide efficient, orthodox preachers to combat heresy and explain the faith. The Franciscans were the only religious order recruited predominately from the lower classes and for a long time possessed a high proportion of lay brethren (and illiterates).
The friars had an urban vocation and did not seek solitude like the earlier orders. They were most numerous in Southern France, Spain and Italy but there were friars in most European towns.

TILES
Tiles were a domestic luxury in the Middle Ages but they were often used in monastic (and other) churches. Sometimes they were produced within the monastery, sometimes they were supplied from a nearby extern kiln. Because of their value, they tended to be looted from monastic sites after the suppression. Where tiles do not exist in situ, they are often preserved in neighbouring museum.
There are notable examples of monastic tiling at e.g. Byland, Malvern, Rievaulx, St Dogmael's and Strata Florida.

Fragment Westminster
Chapter-House

TIME   see also *Clocks*
The ordering of the Church's year, particularly by the establishment of the date of Easter, had required a high degree of technical skill and mathematical knowledge. This had been accomplished in the Dark Ages (where Bede had made a notable contribution to chronology) and the results were digested in the shape of 'perpetual calendars', a form of which still prefaces the Book of Common Prayer.
As the liturgy was an attempt to sanctify year and season, so the hours sanctified each day and night but the humble task of ensuring that services began at the proper hour was not easy before the monastic invention of clocks and when the natural day to which the monks conformed varied with the season. The problem was particularly acute in the early morning when the sequence of Mattins, Lauds,

Mosaic Tiling from
Rievaulx

Prime (and the early masses) was so rapid that any considerable miscalculation would throw the whole horarium (q.v.) into considerable disorder. Furthermore, the varying length of Mattins (q.v.) added a further complication.

The following C11 instructions for a nightwatchman at a monastery near Orleans show a typical solution before the introduction of mechanical clocks:

'On Christmas Day, when you see the (constellation of) Twins lying, as it were, on the dormitory, and Orion over the chapel of All Saints, prepare to ring the bell. On January 1 when the bright star in the knee of Artophilax (Arcturus in Boötes) is level with the space between the first and second window of the dormitory and lying, as it were, on the summit of the roof, then go and light the lamps.'

TIME-TABLE see also *Daily Round, Horarium*

Though adherence to a time-table is fundamental to western monasticism, it is difficult to translate the monastic horarium (q.v.) into modern clock hours (though the monasteries invented clocks, including alarm clocks, to improve the regulation of their time).

The monastic day (i.e. from sunrise to sunset) was divided into 12 equal parts, irrespective of the season, which were called hours. Thus winter hours could be 20 minutes shorter than summer hours and consequently there were different arrangements for winter and summer. The winter time-table operated from Holy Cross Day (September 14) until Easter (which itself could vary up to a month) and they were chiefly affected by the earlier bed-time.

Midnight was the half-way point of the hours of darkness and the time for the office of Mattins, followed by Lauds (see night office). When this lengthy service was over, the monks returned to bed before rising again for Prime (q.v.) which took place at day-break in winter and at sunrise in summer.

During the day there was a service every three 'hours' after Prime.

Besides the effects of seasons, there were other variations between the practice of different orders and changes within orders through the monastic centuries. Where manual labour was an important element in the rule (e.g. Cistercians, Premonstratensians) extra time was set aside for this.

The first meal (prandium) was taken about midday, shortly after Sext (q.v.). During it, the weekly reader (who had been allowed to dine earlier) occupied the frater pulpit (q.v.). Dinner was preceded and followed by an elaborate sung grace, taken in silence, and followed by the singing of 'Miserere' as the monks processed from the frater, through the cloister (sometimes with a deviation for prayers in the cemetery) to the church where further prayers were said.

In the afternoon the brethren usually retired to the dorter for a short siesta until None after which they returned to their particular work until Vespers. Vespers was followed by a procession to the frater (except on fast days) for grace, supper (cena) and further prayers. After supper, the community returned to the chapter-house or cloister for 'collation' (q.v.) and the day concluded with the appropriately named Compline ('Completorium'). All spare moments had to be filled with work or used for necessary personal needs, silence (q.v.) was rigorously maintained and necessary conversation confined to the parlour.

TIRON   see also *Savignac, Fontrevault*

A reformed Benedictine congregation in the diocese of Chartres, established in 1114 and whose members were called Tironians. The name was derived from the apprentices (tirones) who were united by its founder to pursue their trades and skills in the service of God (somewhat resembling the Cistercian 'conversi'). Over 100 foundations were made within a generation.

There were five priories in England of which St Dogmael's became autonomous while the others, apart from Caldey — a cell of the above, were cells of Tiron. There are considerable remains of St Dogmael's and rather less at Andwell, Caldey, Hamble and Pill.

In Scotland, this small order introduced by David I, exercised a disproportionate influence with eight houses, five of which were priories. There are remains at Arbroath, Kelso (abbey), Kilwinning and Lindores. Fontrevault, Tiron and Savigny all found their founders from a large group of C12 recluses dwelling in deserted heathland between Maine and Brittany.

TITHE BARN

From a very early date after the establishment of Christianity in England the notion had been established of God's 'tenth' — the custom (which became a due) of giving 10 per cent of income to the church. In an agricultural society much of the year's gain was in field produce and large barns were built to store it e.g. Abbotsbury (the longest surviving monastic barn), Doulton, Pilton, Torre. Many so-called tithe barns are not for this purpose but for storing the house's own produce (see Barn) but occasional examples survive in appropriated parishes e.g. Great Coxwell, Berkshire, (more than 50 miles from Beaulieu to which it belonged).

The strength, practicality and beauty of these utilitarian monastic buildings is worthy of comment.

TOMBS   see also *Burial, Cemetery*

Monks were usually buried in unmarked graves in the monastic cemetery but superiors were interred beneath the floor of the chapter-house (e.g. Rievaulx has the remains of the shrine of St William and the empty stone coffin of St Ailred). Less commonly they had a tomb or monument in the church. Tewkesbury has the tomb of abbot Alan and the Wakeman cenotaph; Pershore has the tomb of a C15 abbot with his mitre under his head, allegedly signifying that he resigned his office; Malvern has the tomb of its second prior Walcher, probably removed from destroyed chapter-house; Rosedale has a Cistercian prioress and there are other examples in former cathedral priories, e.g. St Dogmael's, Dundrennan.

Founders and confraters were often accorded the privilege of burial in the religious houses with which they were associated: Tewkesbury has a chantry chapel of its founder Robert Fitzsimmon; there is a brass of Ethelred in Wimborne; Dunfermline had a chapel-shrine of St Margaret. Royalty also sought this honour and apart from the Confessor's tomb-shrine at Westminster, other examples might include Queen Catherine at Peterborough; John at Worcester which also has the remains of Prince Arthur's fine chantry; Henry VII at Westminster. Wolsey has only a modern flag-stone set in the scant remains of Leicester; the tomb he designed for himself is in St Paul's and occupied by Nelson.

TONSURE   see also *Rasura*

The formal 'hair-cut' that marked the cleric i.e. the possession of major orders in the Christian ministry. It developed in early monasticism and was introduced into the west c. C7 as an indication of the clerical state. The differences between the

Celtic and Roman tonsure was one of the matters discussed at the Synod of Whitby (AD 664).

The western form involved shaving the crown of the head to leave a surrounding fringe which was taken to symbolise the crown and thorns and a reminder to the cleric of the difficulties in following Christ.

Roman Tonsure

The tonsure was normally renewed every three weeks with additional attention on the eves of the great festivals. The arrangements for this were the responsibility of the chamberlain (q.v.) who either appointed barbers from the community or, when the monastery was in a town, brought in professionals (the Winchester account rolls have an entry' 'for 36 shavings — 4s.6d'). The process normally took place in the cloister but the sick and others by permission could be shaved in the warming-house.

Celtic Tonsure

TOWER

In monastic churches its prime purpose was to house the necessary bells which marked the Hours and summoned brethren to service from the fields, but it could have other uses: look-out, defence-point, symbol. It was usually placed over the central crossing (e.g. Portchester, St Albans, Tewkesbury) but there were often western towers as well (Durham); Ely has a single western tower as had Bury. Sometimes a detached campanile was provided (c.g. Cambuskenneth, Evesham) or even a separate tower for parochial purposes (Wymondham).

Primitive Cistercian usage abjured the great tower as a symbol of pride and their early churches had only a low central tower (e.g. Buildwas) which initially contained only a single bell, small enough to be rung by one person. But in the later Middle Ages we hear of five bells at Hailes and Rievaulx and seven at Byland. Great towers were also raised towards the close of the period (Kirkstall over the crossing, Fountains adjoining north transept. Furness at west end, both Furness and Fountains attempted a great central tower) The erection of a great west tower at the Augustinian Bolton was in process when building was stopped by the suppression. A fine tower (St Rule's) survives from the same order's church at St Andrew's.

Detached Bell Tower,
Cambuskenneth Perthshire

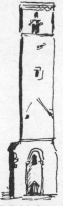

St Rule's Tower,
St Andrew's, Fife

Tower of Shap Abbey
(Premonstratensian
Canons)

181

TOWNS see also *Abbey Towns*

The growth of a town around an abbey resulted from the initial advantages to the settlers but the rights of the religious house to tolls and fairs, in fees and elections were increasingly resented by the growing dominance of the mercantile class. This resulted in physical violence in some places (e.g. Bury and Reading in C13-14).

Too much should not be made of the conflicts at Bury and Reading. We know that the relations at Burton always seem to have been good and the abbey provided the town with paved streets, market-hall, grammar school and water supply (though there were some complaints from neighbouring towns against the fairs at Burton and Abbots Bromley). Chester also seems to have maintained the good will of the town which grew up under its walls, as did Peterborough. The positive contributions of religious houses to towns included the maintenance of the defensive walls where they bounded their estates and also of manning them in times of crisis (so at Chester, Dover, Winchester, York).

Ely provided many roads and bridges in an area of bad communications (the tolls on its bridges went to the sacrist's account) and Chester repaired many bridges in its area. In C13 the houses at Crowland and Spalding constructed a number of bridges and in the same period Whitby bridged the Esk. Though road-making and bridge-building were regarded as religious works (with obvious symbolic significance), some superiors were accused of neglecting their alleged responsibility, perhaps because of not only the initial expense but of the power of precedent.

TRANSEPTS

The north and south arms of a cruciform church. Apart from their contribution to a symbol, they provided altar space and most had chapels opening from their eastern sides. At first these were apsidal (e.g. Romsey, Tewkesbury), but they soon yielded to the English preference of a rectangular termination formed by a simple eastern aisle with a chapel in each bay, separated by solid walls or, later by screens (e.g. Kirkstall).

The number of altars in a transept varied (e.g. one at Norwich, Gloucester, Tewkesbury; two at St Albans, York St Mary; three at Durham, Ely, Peterborough. There are substantial remains at Byland, Jervaulx, Strata Florida with tiles, fittings and most of altar).

South Transept, Fountains

Transept chapels could be aisleless but they often had eastern aisles, less frequently aisles on west or north and south. The Cistercian arrangement was normally to provide two or three chapels in eastern part of transept, separated by stone walls.

Besides altar provision the transept nearest the cloister (south) usually contained a night stair (q.v.) and also housed the monastic great clock. The south transept at Wenlock contained a laver in the west wall.

The north transept, especially among the Cistercians, often had a doorway leading to the monastic cemetery.

TRAPPIST

A name (derived from the house at La Trappe) given to the reformed Cistercians (O.Cist.Ref.) who have houses at Caldey, Coalville and Nunraw. Their rule is accessible in Appendix Two of 'Against All Reason', G. Moorhouse (London 1969).

Trappist

TREASURER

The officer responsible for the safe-keeping of the monastic treasures which could include cash, plate, rich vestments, valuable books and documents. Besides things belonging to the house he might also have been given charge of material from outside which had, with permission, been deposited in the house for security. Bury acted as a safe deposit for the town Jews.

The treasurer was sometimes a separate officer but often he doubled this responsibility as sacrist or assistant sacrist.

Sometimes the treasurer collected money rents but he could be assisted (or replaced) in this function by a receiver (receptor), bursar, or a garnerer or granger (granatorius).

TREASURY

The sacristy (q.v.) was a minor treasury but houses often provided an additional strong-room or safe-deposit for charters, evidences of rights and possessions, convent seal, rarer books, cash, plate or jewelry not only of the house but of patrons and others. The chapel of the Pyx at Westminster became the royal treasury during Edward I's campaign in Scotland. It was also regularly used for assaying the royal currency (hence name).

Recess in Treasury

The treasury was often located in an annexe to the dorter near the head of the night stairs and was vaulted in stone to protect its contents from fire. In this position it was under the immediate eye of the sacrist who usually had his bed in the vicinity. At Thornton it occupied the place of the slype and was provided with a complex entrance from the first floor level. At Durham it was in the dorter sub-vault between the parlour and the church. The treasury at Canterbury was placed between the farmery and one of the apsidal chapels of the church. At Gloucester it was over the parlour, between the chapter-house and transept. There are some remains of the treasury at Chester.

At Easby, as in many canons' houses, it was probably in the sacristy between chapter-house and church. The treasury was often annexed to the chapter-house because of the convenience of holding the seal, charters, etc., in proximity to the business meetings. It was sometimes placed over the east bay of the chapter house with the passage from the dorter to the night stair passing in front of it. Such a position gave strength, some concealment and automatic night-watch. The treasury / muniment room at Fountains, which substantially survives but currently is not open to the public, is in this position.

Subdivisions within the treasury, often including an inner room, were common in great houses. That at Durham still retains the strong outer door fitted with two locks and the lockable iron grille which separated the inner chamber from the outer. The treasury also contained separate chests and secure cupboards. The former were often furnished with three different locks which required the co-operation of three obedientiaries for access to their contents (Chests from Durham treasury survive in the modern library). Particular departments had their own coffers or a compartment within a larger one with its own slot so that money could be deposited without opening the box.

Trinitarian

TRINITARIANS

An order, f.1198, at Gerfroid in diocese of Meaux, also known as Maturins and Red Friars. They were not Mendicants but an austere order of priests based on the Augustinian rule. Their revenues were divided equally between their own support, charity to poor, especially travellers, and the redemption of prisoners in the hands of the infidel. The houses were usually small, consisting, of a superior (called minister or prior), three priest-brethren and three lay brothers. Sometimes the number was enlarged and the disappearing lay brothers seem to have been replaced by novices in 1267.

There were ten to a dozen foundations in England though only two (Ingham, Knaresborough) have left any trace. They were relatively strong in Scotland with eight houses (visible remains at Dunbar and Peebles).

TWELFTH CENTURY

Towards the end of C11, traditional monasticism was losing its attraction for generous souls.

In the face of this crisis arose many experiments which endeavoured to meet the problems of involvement with the world: some devout, some eccentric, some under rule, some individualistic. The resulting foundations sometimes provoked scandal and many were short-lived but from this effervescence came a renewal of the hermit tradition, internal reforms among the Benedictines and Cluniacs and the establishment of the Cistercians, Premonstratensians and Carthusians.

'It was on zeal and determination that the monastic church was founded, and in the twelfth century it was men of zeal who transformed it. Of the new and reformed orders that characterised the opening years of the century, the most influential was the Cistercian. Centrally controlled from the original Burgundian house at Citeaux, the Cistercians set a uniform standard of austerity very much in harmony with the best instincts of their troubled, but pious generation. They removed themselves, wherever possible, from the world they despaired of. And they sought at each of their many houses to establish a self-sufficient economy, to maintain the flesh but never to indulge it.' (Platt)

The influence was felt in England as well as everywhere else and, in spite of the anarchy of Stephen's reign, it was a time of many religious foundations and the impulse continued into that of Henry II when 113 new houses were founded. The revived monastic movement seems largely to have spent itself by the end of the century except among the Austin Canons who founded 80 priories after 1175.

TURNING WINDOW   see *Rota*

UNDERCROFT

The vault beneath a large building, usually the dorter (e.g. Gloucester, Westminster). It was usually, if not always, sub-divided to serve a variety of purposes, generally offices and stores. The undercroft of the dorter of the conversi at Fountains contained their frater as well as the cellarer's checker and store. At Evesham the undercroft of the monastic dorter accommodated two of the obedientiaries' offices as well as the misericord (q.v.).

Stocking Undercroft

The frater was sometimes raised on an undercroft (e.g. Rievaulx and the rebuilding at Cleeve) where the latter later functioned as a misericord e.g. Ford, Furness, Kirkstall.

The finest surviving undercroft is at Fountains but there is an excellent small example at Torre.

UNIVERSITIES

Developed without help from monks in spite of the ancient Benedictine tradition of learning. Indeed, Walter de Merton, the originator of the college system, excluded monks and in 1284 forebade his scholars to take religious vows. But the monks soon involved themselves and in 1283 Gloucester founded a house at Oxford for the use of its monks (there are traces of Gloucester Hall within Worcester College). Other great abbeys soon provided similar accommodation: Durham in

1290 on site now occupied by Trinity College; Ely founded a hostel in Cambridge in 1340 (afterwards incorporated in Trinity Hall); Crowland had its own hostel in 1428 (afterwards Buckingham College whose remains partly survive in Magdalene).

At first the Cistercians held themselves aloof from literary studies but the English houses in 1437 supported the foundation of St Bernard's College in Oxford on the site now occupied by St John's.

The regular canons (with the possible exception of the Gilbertines) did not possess a house of study but they owned the priories of St Frideswide in Oxford and Barnwell on the outskirts of Cambridge.

Friar Bacon's Study,
Oxford University

UNPOPULARITY

Monasteries declined in public favour and esteem from C13. The causes were many: their own loss of fervour, the rise of new forms of spirituality, the effects of the Black Death, the growth of new secular attitudes including the capitalist ethic. There was laxity and some real scandals, particularly in the smaller houses. They were the subject of incessant adverse propaganda, first of the friars, then of the seculars and finally of the Henrician (and subsequent) government.

To some extent they had lost their original function and were outliving their function (at least in their existing numbers). Much of their early pioneering work had been taken away by institutions which had developed subsequently and printing had deprived them of their characteristic occupation. New questions were being raised about the nature of piety and the essence of the Christian life and many monasteries were experienced as feudal powers rather than spiritual power-houses.

Above all there was their enormous accumulated wealth e.g. Westminster had possessions in 97 towns, 17 villages and owned 216 manors. Its total revenues in C16 were assessed at about £150,000 p.a. in contemporary money.

VACATION   see also *Villagiatura*

The original monastic ideal did not envisage any cessation in the work of the Lord until the achievement of the heavenly Sabbath hymned by Peter Abelard. Holidays were originally Holy Days centred round the joyful ceremonies of the day, spiritual in essence but sometimes marked with a little indulgence for the body in the way of food. (see Pittance). Later the increased relaxation associated with blood-letting made the occasion something of a relief from the toils of quire.

VALLISCAULIANS

A Benedictine reform, similar to that of the Cistercians, emanating from the abbey of Val des Choux in France. It reached Scotland in 1230 and eventually established three priories: Ardchattan, Beauly and Pluscarden (all of which have left some remains). The last became Benedictine in 1454 and the monks returned in the present century.

VEIL

The characteristic item in the habit of a female religious, hence 'taking the veil' became a synonym for making a religious profession or entering a nunnery. Quire nuns who made a more solemn and ceremonious profession were vested with a black veil, while lay sisters and other 'activists' wore a white one.

VESPERS

The evening service or Evensong which took place in the late afternoon between None and Compline. Its structure was similar to that of Lauds (q.v.) but the psalmody consisted of Psalms cx — clxvii and the Canticle was the Magnificat. In the later Middle Ages its music became much elaborated and, where convenient, it was attended by devout laity.

VESTIBULE

An outer-chamber or ante-room provided to give dignity or more privacy to certain monastic apartments. There was generally a vestibule to the chapter-house and some are of considerable architectural elaboration (e.g. Chester, Valle Crucis, Westminster). The head of the night stairs was often enclosed within a vestibule and access to the farmery was often through one.

Vestibule, Westminster
Chapter-House

VESTRY (Revestry)

Room where ministers equipped themselves in the appropriate vestments for quire or altar. These depended on the office being performed (celebrant, deacon, priest, acolyte, cantor etc), the nature of the service and the liturgical season. It contained aumbries and chests for the storage of albs, amices, copes, stoles, chasubles, surplices, etc. A cope-chest survives at Gloucester.

It was under the control of the sacrist or his assistant (large houses sometimes had an official called the 'vesterer' who was responsible for the care and maintenance of vestments, laying out the appropriate ones before service etc. but elsewhere this function was performed by bell-ringers.)

Valle Crucis West Door

The vestry (vestiarium) was sometimes combined with the sacristy (q.v.) but it often existed as a separate room and a large church might be provided with more than one. It was always placed in close proximity to the church to which it had direct access, either through the south transept or through the north or south wall of the eastern arm.

VICAR   see also *Appropriation*

A substitute or stand-in for the legal authority or rector (q.v.).

VICTORINES

An order of regular canons who founded their first English house at Wigmore, Hereford. Their greatest English foundation was St Augustine's Bristol, the church of which substantially survives. They were later subsumed under Austin Canons.

VIGIL

Night prayers either of a liturgical kind (Mattins (q.v.) was originally called vigils) or private and voluntary prayers in or through the night.

On great feasts, the night office became anticipated, i.e. said on the day before, or Eve, thus extending and giving greater dignity to the celebration e.g. Christmas Eve, Easter Eve, Pentecost Eve, All Hallows Eve.

Vigils were kept as devotion and for guidance before taking major steps such as making a religious profession or, in the secular field, before entering the estate of knighthood.

VILLAGIATURA

The modern name for a practice beginning in the later Middle Ages by which religious were given leave from their house for retreat to a small house in the country where the rule was relaxed to allow for spiritual, mental or even physical recuperation. Some houses maintained a manor, grange (q.v.) or small cell for this purpose (e.g. Durham's use of Finchale).

VINEYARD

For much of the Middle Ages, England was a vine-growing country and many monasteries established vineyards to produce their own wine. Sometimes the slopes can be seen (e.g. at Evesham) but sometimes only a name remains as at Abingdon, Ely). One of Bury's four gates provided access to the vineyard in its extensive precincts.

VISITATION

The formal inspection of a monastic (or other ecclesiastical institution) by the canonical visitor — usually bishop or religious superior.

Visitation (Ealing)

An official notice of impending visitation was sent to the house concerned, warning it to be prepared (e.g. by having necessary documents and records available and updated). When the visitor duly arrived, accompanied by his entourage which always included clerks, he was received formally and with outward marks of respect. The entire community met him and conducted him ceremoniously to the altar for the High Mass which opened the proceedings. Then the visitor and his clerks joined the entire community in the chapter-house where the visitor or one of his attendants preached.

After this, credentials were scrutinised before proceeding to the presentation to the visitor of the foundation charter of the house and the financial balance-sheet ('status domus') for the year.

When these preliminaries were completed, the main business began which was the individual and private examination of every member of the community with regard to the spiritual and physical well-being of the house. The chapter-house was cleared and every religious, beginning with the superior and ending with the youngest, was carefully questioned by the visitor. Each was encouraged to talk freely, while a clerk took notes ('detecta'), and make any criticisms or complaints. Sometimes the only result of this enquiry was a laconic 'omnia bene' in the record while on other occasions extensive 'detecta' had to be summarised and systematised into a report of 'comperta' (things demanding action).

When every individual had been interviewed, the whole community was recalled to the chapter-house and both 'detecta' and 'comperta' were read out, supplemented by verbal injunctions if the visitor thought them necessary. The visitation was then dissolved or, if urgent business was outstanding, it was prorogued to a later date.

After the visitor's departure, the community awaited the 'follow-up', for verbal injunctions were but an interim measure, always supplemented by a set of written injunctions delivered and expounded by the visitor's clerk.

Visitation and injunction provided the main machinery of external control and reform in religious houses but their effectiveness could be hindered by a variety of factors: haste through overwork on the part of the visitor or by external interference which prevented his arrival or otherwise interfered with his work (secular rulers were far from guiltless in this respect). Even a conscientious vistor could be deceived (and occasionally was) and reforming injunctions (particularly in the late Middle Ages) were not always obeyed.

VOW

The religious was bound (religere) by a triple vow, sometimes symbolised by three knots in the girdle, embracing poverty, chastity and obedience. They were seen as an intensification of the baptismal vows to which all Christians are committed.

Monk making Profession: taking Vows

Poverty was directed against the deceits of the world and ideally involved not only the renunciation of individual wealth, but the losing of self in community. All things were henceforth to be shared, held in common (Acts ii, 44): not only material objects but all the activities of life, eating, sleeping, working, worshipping, were done together and with little respect for idiosyncracies or personal likes and dislikes.

Chastity was the obverse of lusts of the flesh, rejecting not only extra-marital sex but marriage itself: the renunciation of a good for a greater good and the channelling of all creative energy into God's work (Matt.xix, 12).

Obedience was an antidote to the snares of the devil, particularly the sin of pride, held to be the chief and source of the Deadly Sins, It was the opposite of selfishness and self-will, being God-centred rather than egocentric, exemplified in Christ's incarnation and redeeming work (Phill. ii, 8).

The vows, once taken after long consideration (see Novitiate) were for life and irrevocable (apart from rare and complex dispensation). Once a monk, always a monk (see Apostacy) and the state could co-operate in returning a fugitive to his proper house.

VOWESS

A modified form of the religious life without solemn profession, resembling in some ways membership of a third order. In the Middle Ages it was often assumed by widows and included the vow of chastity and inhibited re-marriage. Such widows, sometimes called avowesses, had a distinctive habit (represented e.g. on the effigy of the Duchess of Sussex at Ewelme).

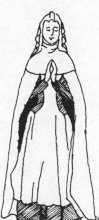

Vowess

WAFER, COMMUNION   see *Obley*

WALES   see also *Celtic Monasticism*

Early Christianity seems to have survived from Roman days or to have been subsequently renewed under monastic leadership. The names of church founders, traditionally canonised, survive in the dedications of churches on ancient sites. They are usually prefixed by 'Llan' ('the enclosure of . . .').

Scant architectural fragments rarely survive from the period C6-11 (e.g. Presteigne which came into the hands of Austin Canons in C13). But there are many carvings: Old Radnor, Newchurch, Trallong, Ystradfellte, Llanerfyl, Llandefaelog Fach, Llanfrynach, Llanhamlach, Neuadd Siarman.

Ancient sites, often enclosing graveyard, are indicated by their raised character and often circular shape.

By C10, Welsh monasticism had been reorganised round 'mother churches' ('Clas') with their dependent foundations. These 'closau', consisting of abbot, priests and hereditary canons were originally important centres of scholarship but they declined and had been absorbed into the Roman tradition of monasticism by c.1200. The ancient principality of Powys had séven such churches: Glasbury, Glascwm, Llanddew, Llandinam, Llangurig, Meifod, St Harmon. (The last retains its cruciform plan associated with 'clas' status.) Two churches, Patrishow, Pennant Melangell, possess specially planned graves constructed for their founder-saints.

From c.C12 Welsh monastic history is parallel to that of England: the same orders spread, similar foundations are made (though rarely as well-endowed) and they are suppressed under the same legislation. Even the building materials from Conway (Cistercian) and Bangor (Dominican) were robbed for Henry's fortifications.

There are some differences e.g. the Tironian foundation of St Dogmaels whose remains have no peer in England. Other major foundations at Bangor (Dominican),

Basingwerk (Cistercian), Brecon (Benedictine and Dominican), Cymmer (Cistercian), Ewenny (Benedictine), Haverfordwest (Augustinian), Llanthony (Augustinian), Margam (Cistercian), Neath (Cistercian), Penmon (Augustinian), Strata Florida (Cistercian), Talley (Premonstratensian), Tintern (Cistercian), Valle Crucis, Denbigh (Carmelite).

There was no Carthusian foundation in Wales and there are no remains of the Cistercian nunnery (f.c.1236) at Llanllugan. The Cluniacs had cells at Malpas and St Cleer and the Knights Hospitaller had a number of manors and one or two preceptories including the renowned Slebech. There was no Templar foundation in Wales though Kemeys Commander was a 'camera' belonging to the order.

WALKING PLACE

The passage, communicating with the domestic buildings, formed by two cross-walls between the nave and quire in friary churches. The tower was often built over this passage (e.g. Richmond).

WALL PAINTING   see *Fresco*

WARDEN

Title given to the superior of a collegiate or other quasi-monastic institution such as a hospital. Other titles included prior, custos, keeper, master, rector. The warden was usually a priest, often a religious, but he could be a layman.

The name 'warden' was also used within a monastic community with respect to oversight of a particular area (see *Warden of the Order*). A 'wardenship' or 'custody' was a name given to the regional division of the Franciscan (q.v.) order.

WARDEN OF THE ORDER

The officer (adjutant) of a religious house responsible for the maintenance of discipline, keeping rule, observances etc. Sometimes there was more than one (see Circas) but whether one or several they brought attention, in chapter, to any matter which required correction. Generally the warden of the order was identical with the second-in-command in a house; the prior in an abbey or the sub-prior in a priory.

WARMING-HOUSE (Calefactorium)

A room where a great fire was kept burning during the winter months in which the monks, particularly those occupied in sedentary work in the cloister, were permitted to briefly thaw out. In Cluniac houses it seems also to have been used for the operation of bleeding (q.v.).

It was usually located in the east range of the cloister but its position was to some extent influenced by that of the dorter (q.v.) since it served a secondary purpose of taking some of the chill off the sleeping quarters. When the dorter is moved from the east range, so is the warming-house e.g. Durham, Easby, Gloucester, Worcester. It is often at or near the junction of the south and east ranges (e.g. Basingwerk, Cleeve) but occasionally is in the undercroft of the dorter's extension beyond the cloister (e.g. Shap, Thetford) and it occurs in Cistercian houses as an independent building adjoining the frater in the south range.

Until the late Middle Ages it was the only room (apart from the kitchen and farmery) which possessed a fire but when this amenity was multiplied with the growth of private chambers or 'camerae' the single communal fire lost its significance. The warming-house ceased to be simply a place for warming chilled limbs and became metamorphasised into a common room for informal meetings, recreational conversation and minor celebrations in which, as at Durham, a cask of wine might ameliorate the occasion. This development brought change to the

Warming-House
(Fountains)

189

warming-room (e.g. at Fountains one of its great fireplaces was blocked up; at Forde it was abolished and at Rievaulx it was converted to domestic use). Elsewhere the warming-house was extended into or replaced by the 'common house' (that at Westminster had its own chapel) and a master of the common house or commoner appears. His duties were to maintain the fire (which might be a charcoal brazier) and to organise the little parties based on pittances (q.v.) including the 'Gaudys' (rejoicings at festivals) and the keeping of the O's 'where their banquet was of figs and raisins, ale and cakes and thereof no superfluity or excess but a scholastical and moderate congratulation among themselves.'

WASHING   see also *Laundry, Laver, Bath*

The observances required washing before Prime, before dinner and after None and additional facilities, besides the great laver associated with the frater, are mentioned in the conventual buildings towards the close of the Middle Ages.

Besides the provision in and about the cloister, facilities were provided in the chambers of the great obedientiaries, the superior's lodging, the guest-house and particularly in the farmery.

WATCHING LOFT

An observation post, overlooking sanctuary or shrine, for the purposes of security, to prevent theft or sacrilege. Its manning was the responsibility of the sacrist (q.v.). A rare example survives at St Albans and Worcester has an oriel above quire. At St Dogmael's such a chamber seems to have been built in C16 above the wall of chapel between presbytery and south-east corner of transept.

Watching Loft:
St Albans

WATER   see also *Conduit, Site*

'It circulates everywhere through a double system of pipes, one for fresh and the other for used water. The number of latrines and the care taken to provide them close to each dorter suggests the importance of cleanliness, and a similar care is evinced by the installation of baths for the community and by the way the infirmary is organised with a special room for washing the feet of sick brethren and for the laying out of the dead. Again a tub is provided for the disposal of soiled linen and the monks are directed to put clothes that need mending in a suitable place.'

The description is of the influential Cluny c.1050 but it is generally applicable to religious houses. At least two baths from mediaeval monasteries have survived in France and in England there may be remains at Shap and Kirkstall. Such facilities required complex supply and drainage systems. There were usually at least two supply sources: one

Detail Laver Basin
(Wenlock)

for washing, cooking, storing; another for power and flushing, and sometimes transport. The former came from walls or springs, the latter from streams. The stream (e.g. at Fountains) or the conduit (e.g. Beaulieu) was passed under the farmeries, rere-dorters and kitchens with branches to the superior's lodging and the guest-house. When the site was near the head of the stream, a lead for domestic use was sometimes drawn off above the house; more normally a supply of pure water was taken directly from a spring and brought by a conduit or pipe within the precincts. Fountains still has both a stream and a well, Netley preserves remains of impressive aqueduct, but the complex supply system of which an exemplary plan of

Canterbury survives have left few remains. A well-known Norman drawing of Christchurch depicts the system c.1165 which replaced the earlier provision from a number of wells. It was much more scientific and involved quite complex hydraulics, gathering water far outside the city's north wall under which it was piped after passing through five filtering tanks, designed for easy and effective cleaning. There were draw-off points along the route and a complex distribution system once it entered the monastic precincts. Water was often piped from distant sources: over a mile at Durham, from the present Hyde Park to Westminster, from Henwick Hill to Worcester. Although the walls of Waverley were washed by the Wey, it drew drinking water from a hillside spring and Stanley, Wiltshire, though surrounded by water-courses, piped spring water from a considerable distance. The monastic water-supply, sanitation and care of the sick in C12-13, were unsurpassed and probably reached a level which had never been equalled in Europe since the fall of the Roman Empire and were not equalled generally until modern times.

Mills required leets and sluices, stew ponds had to be constructed and fed and often sites (e.g. Byland) had to be drained before they were usable. Rievaulx made a canal c.1145, replaced with a second, improved version c.1160 and dug a third before the end of the century to provide transport from a new quarry.

WATER, HOLY   see *Holy Water*

WEEKLY OFFICERS   see *Hebdomarian, Precentor, Tabula*

WESTERN RANGE

Sometimes known as the cellarer's range from the 'cellarium' (great cellar or storehouse) which was its principal feature e.g. Canterbury, Chester, Norton, Peterborough. This consisted of a ground-floor room or basement usually vaulted from a central row of piers and originally was sub-divided by partitions. It was in the charge of the cellarer (q.v.) and divided from the church by a vaulted passage (sometimes functioning as an outer parlour) which provided the main access from the curia to the cloister. Elsewhere this parlour was more than a mere passage and a second and more or less private entry was provided opposite the west end of the south cloister alley.

Western Range

The floor above the cellarium was variously used: it sometimes provided accommodation for the superior and his guests e.g. Bradenstoke, Norton, where the first floor had a chapel, hall and chamber.

In Cistercian houses the western range was often called 'domus conversorum' since it contained the lay brothers' frater, dorter, rere-dorter and common room. The largest and finest surviving west range is at Fountains.

Conversus (West Range of Cistercian Houses)

There are three notable exceptions in regard to the provision of a western range: Worcester has none, due to proximity of river, and the cellarium was located under frater and dorter with parlour beneath was built at right angles to west cloister walk; Durham, which has a new range behind western walk built in C13; and at Easby, which is probably unique, the dorter occupies the west range.

WHITE CANONS   see *Premonstratensian*

WHITE FRIARS   see *Carmelites*

WHITE LADIES
Cistercian nuns or Augustinian Canonesses. The account book for 1414-1418 survives from the 'White Ladies' of Grace Dieu (Augustinian Canonesses). White Ladies Brewood (Boscobel) housed similar canonesses and White Ladies Aston was once a manor belonging to Cistercian nunnery at Whistones, now in northern suburbs of Worcester.

WHITE MONKS   see *Cistercians*

WINE
Besides the necessary provision for Holy Communion, wine occasionally appears as a beverage, either imported or produced from the house's own vineyard (q.v.). It is sometimes mentioned as part of mixtum (q.v.) or later collation (q.v.) but generally beer was the staple drink and wine was used medicinally in accordance with the apostolic precept (I Tim.v, 23).
The records of Westminster tell of a patient in a farmery who declared he could not drink beer to the infirmarer's incredulity. The prior was called in to judge the case and eventually ten shillings worth was bought for the sick brother's use.

WOOD
Monastic estates always included woodland and pioneer houses were constructed of wood. Some substantial buildings probably remained in timber until the end, leaving few remains after wilful destruction and long neglect. Late in monastic history wooden structures included not only barns, stables, workshops and the like but important buildings such as the cloister. The almonry at Bury was a wooden erection until abbot Samson rebuilt it in stone and the upper story at Evesham is timber-framed (as is the guest-house at York).
Apart from the large quantities used in furnishing and building (particularly roofs, floors and screens), wood was the general fuel for heating. With the development of corrodies (q.v.) the contract often specifies the wood allowance for firing.
Monastic employees sometimes include a woodward who was reponsible for the selection, collection, storage and use of wood as well as over-seeing its production. Woodsheds and wood-garths were usually provided near the warming-house (e.g. Fountains, Waverley) and kitchen.

WOOL
From second half of C12 an increasing proportion of national wool surplus came from monastic sheep (sharply increased by Cistercian enterprise). The mediaeval wealth of England largely depended on this major important (hence the Lord Chancellor's Woolsack).
Nearly all abbeys possessed flocks of sheep which were often their principal asset and whose wool was sometimes sold in advance to meet current financial difficulties (and often produced greater ones subsequently). Whalley had a middle-man in the port of Boston who received moneys for this commodity from foreign merchants. Dover in C15 received a royal export licence in conjunction with a London merchant to tranship a limited amount of wool to foreign parts beyond the straits of Gibraltar. Some of the

Weighing Wool on 'trone'

great Yorkshire abbeys (e.g. Kirkstall) developed tremendous debts due to miscalculation, disease and bad weather.
The Cistercians were pre-eminently sheep-farmers and wool-producers and in 1193 were compelled to surrender their entire year's product towards Richard I's ransom. In spite of this, they were similarly amerced the following year by the ransomed king.

WORK

'At fixed times, the brothers ought to be occupied in manual labour; and again, at fixed times, in reading.' (St Benedict: Rule chapl. xlviii). St Benedict laid great stress on the spiritual value of devoted manual work. His monks were expected to work in the monastic gardens and fields, (looking after their tools properly) and he arranged that any artificers within the community 'should work at their crafts in all humility'.

The pre-eminence of the 'opus Dei' as the central monastic work was emphasised by the Cluniac reform and eventually affected all Black Monks. The reduced time for work was given to intellectual activity which necessitated the introduction, first of lay brethren and then of servants to do the necessary 'chores'. (Established by General-Chapter of 1227).

The Cistercian and Premonstratensian reforms re-emphasised Benedict's stress and St Bernard consecrated the rule by his own example.

Monastic Workmen

The main work of mediaeval nuns, apart from the quire and administrative work, seems to have consisted in spinning and needlework, especially the fine embroidery which had a European reputation as 'opus anglicanum' and was much desired in rich church vestments. We know that the nuns of Grace Dieu received £10 for a cope they made for a neighbouring rector.

In the later Middle Ages, manual labour had lost any kind of central place in monastic life and most houses had at least as many servants (q.v.) as religious. Nevertheless set parts of the day remained devoted to work (now literary or theological studies, writing, reading, etc.) — usually from about noon to five p.m. in winter and from one to six in summer.

The Augustinian rule assumed that some artefacts were made for external sale to support the community and that all work would be done in meditative silence 'unless the need of the work constrain someone to speak'.

WORKSHOPS

A variety of workshops surrounded the curia (q.v.). There was always a brewhouse, bakehouse and stables. There was generally a smithy (Cluny had a goldsmith's workshop among its appurtenances), some of the greater houses had masons' lodges and drawing offices in the court. (e.g. Norwich). At Byland and Furness there were originally workshops in the dorter undercroft. Tynemouth had a special workshop for plumbers and foundations of general workshops are exposed in curia at Tintern.

FURTHER READING

Individual guides to particular sites, especially those published by the Department of the Environment. The notes on religious structures in the invaluable *Buildings of England* (Pevsner and others) and the initial volumes of the comparabl *Buildings of Scotland* and *Buildings of Wales.* The best short introduction is probably R. Gilyard-Beer's *Abbeys* (H.M.S.O.) and the most useful general books G.H. Cook's *English Monasteries in the Middle Ages* (1961) and F.H. Crossley's *The English Abbey* (1935).

The authority on English Monasticism is D. Knowles and the serious student is recommended to his extensive writings, particularly *The Monastic Order in Englan* (1966) and *The Religious Orders in England* (3 Vols. 1961). In association with J.K.S. St Joseph there is the illuminating *Monastic Sites from the Air* (1952) and with R.M. Hadcock the comprehensive listing of *Mediaeval Religious Houses, England and Wales* (1971). The survey for Great Britain has recently been complete by a companion volume — *Mediaeval Religious Houses, Scotland* by I.B. Cowan and D.E. Easson (1976). Mention should also be made of *Mediaeval Monasteries o Great Britain* (1979) by L. Butler and C. Given-Wilson.

Particular topics might be pursued e.g. for the idea of monasticism: *Against all Reason* — G. Moorhouse (1969); *Christian Monasticism* — D. Knowles (1969); founders of religious orders: *Warriors of God* — W. Nigg (1959); specific orders: *Benedictine Monachism* — C. Butler (1919); *The Cistercian Spirit* — ed. M.B. Pennington (1970); *Cluny under St Hugh* — N. Hunt (1967); *The Englis Austin Friars* — A. Gwynn (1940); *The White Canons in England* — H.M. Colvin (1951); *The Early English Friars Preachers* — A. Hinnebusch (1952); *St Gilbert of Sempringham* — R. Graham (1901); *Mediaeval English Nunneries* — E. Power (1922). For Celtic Church, see N.K. Chadwick: *The Age of the Saints in the early Celtic Church* (1961); Reformation: *England and Wales:* A.G. Dickens: Scotland: *Essays on Scottish Reformation* (1962),ed. D. McRoberts.

The purpose of the religious life: *Rule of St Benedict* — ed. J. McCann (1952), *Love of learning and desire for God* — J. Leclerq (1962), *Saints and Scholars* — D. Knowles (1963), the writings of T. Merton especially *The Sign of Jonas* (1953); mediaeval hospitals: *Mediaeval Hospitals of England* — R.M. Clay (1909). There are a number of other relevant volumes in the series of Antiquary's Books publishe in early C20 though some have been overtaken by later scholarship.

For the Monastic Grange, see C. Platt (1969), on the Dissolution: D. Knowles - *Bare ruin'd choirs* (1976). For church furniture and symbolism (including monastic see F. Bottomley: *Church Explorer's Guide* (1978).

Martyrdom of St Thomas
of Canterbury

GAZETTEER
of
Religious Houses
in
England, Scotland and Wales

I do love these ancient ruins:
We never tread upon them, but we set
Our foot upon some reverend history,
And, questionless, here in this open court,
Which now lies naked to the injuries
Of stormy weather, some men lie interred
Loved the Church so well and gave so largely to't
They thought it should have canopied their bones
Till doomsday. But all things have their end:
Churches and cities, which have diseases like to men,
Must have like death that we have.

(J. Webster: Duchess of Malfi, V.3) 1613.

GAZETTEER

County order: England, Scotland, Wales. Entries take the form: name of place, (old) county, OS map reference (omitting first two letters or numerical equivalent), dates of foundation or refoundation and dissolution. (This is followed by a brief description and account of remains, with a coding indicating access and classification. 'Working houses' are classified (A) irrespective of architectural quality. Figures in brackets following account of remains are page references to Glossary section (there may be more than one entry on page cited).

Every effort has been made to give correct information but the situation is a little fluid. The author will be pleased to receive corrections.

Abbreviations:

A	Abbey	dep.	Dependency of
ac	Alien Cell	DF	Dominican Friars
AC	Austin Canons	DM	Double Monastery
AF	Austin Friars	DN	Dominican Nuns
AN	Austin Canonesses	f.	founded, foundation
ap	Alien Priory	FFC	Franciscan Friars, Conventual
apc	Alien Priory Cell	FFO	Franciscan Friars, Observant
AS	Anglo-Saxon	FN	Franciscan Nuns
BM	Benedictine Monks	FS	Friars of Sack
BN	Benedictine Nuns	GC	Gilbertine Canons
BMF	Benedictine Monks (Fontrevault)	GD	Gilbertine Double House
BNF	Benedictine Nuns (Fontrevault)	GM	Grandmontines
BMC	Cluniac Monks	GN	Gilbertine Nuns
BO	Bonshommes	H, HH	Hospital, Hospitals
BR	Bridgettines	KH	Knights Hospitaller
C	Carthusians	KT	Knights Templar
c	Cell	OT	Order of Tiron
c.	Circa	P	Priory
Ce	Celtic	pc	Priory Cell (three religious or less)
CF	Carmelite Friars	PC	Premonstratensian Canons
CE	Carmelite Nuns	PN	Premonstratensian Canonesses
CM	Cistercian Monks	ref.	Refounded
CN	Cistercian Nuns	SH	Sisters of Order of St John
CP	Cathedral Priory (Abbey rank)	t.	Time
col.	Colonised from	TF	Trinitarians, Maturins, Red Friars
CrF	Crutched Friars	tr.	Transferred
d.	destroyed, dissolved, order changed	VM	Valliscaulian Monks

Access

+	(part of) church open to public
§	in private ownership, not usually accessible
DE	in care of Department of Environment
NT	owned by National Trust
AM	listed Ancient Monument (not necessarily implying free access).

Conventual parts of 'working orders' are not open to public, nor is even church in some enclosed orders.

Classification

A	First rate example, substantially complete
B	Considerable and interesting remains
C	Well worth a visit
D	Modest remains
E	Little surviving

Classification must be taken into relation with whole of foundation e.g. C might indicate only church of monastery and substantial remains of small hospital.

ENGLAND

ABBEY DORE, Herefordshire   3830   *1147-1536*
A (CM) f. from Morimond (Champagne). Little remains of conventual buildings, truncated
church in Anglican use. (8, 40, 142, 153)   + : C

ABBOTSBURY, Dorset   5785   *c.1044-1539*
A (BM). One of largest mediaeval barns in country, other sparse remains absorbed in later
buildings. (19, 136, 137, 180)   DE : E

ABINGDON, Berkshire   4997   *c.594-1538*
A (BM). AS f., d. Danes, ref. Dunstan. Dependencies included two town hospitals: St Helen's
(§), St John Baptist's (§). No remains of church, fragments of conventual buildings, gatehouse
with nearby hospital, extern chapel, barn (Christchurch). (2, 12, 19, 28, 32, 46, 84, 86, 117, 118,
119, 132)   AM : D +

ACONBURY, Herefordshire   4933   *c.1215; 1237+ -1539*
f. SH, became small P (AN). St John Baptist's church is substantially chapel of nunnery. (13,
105, 167)   + : C

ALBERBURY, Shropshire   1827   *c.1230-1414*
P (AC) changed to AP (GM). At d., endowments tr. to All Souls' College, Oxfordshire. Part of
nave and chancel, remains of St Stephen's chapel incorporated in farmhouse. (37, 85, 175)   § : E

ALDEBY, Norfolk   4593   *c.1120-1538*
P (BM), dep. Norwich CP. Church substantially survives, fragments of conventual buildings
incorporated in later secular structures.   + § : C-

ALKBOROUGH, Lincolnshire   8721   *1052-1220*
Small P (BM), dep. (for a time) Spalding which later appropriated and rebuilt AS church.   + : D

ALLERTON MAULEVERER, Yorkshire East Riding   4157   *1100+ -1414*
Cell (BM) dep. Holy Trinity, York became ap dep. Marmoutier in 1110. At d., endowments tr.
King's College, Cambridge. St Martin's church incorporates work from time of priory.   + : D

ALNWICK, Northumberland   1912   *1147-1539*
A (PC), col. Newsham. Dependent H, men's almshouse, in town, patron of nunnery at
Guyzance (q.v.). Substantial remains of C14 gatehouse, ground-plan of church. (37, 75, 141,
142). Fragmentary remains of H for poor — St Leonard's chapel.   AM : D +

ALVECOTE, Warwickshire   2404   *1159-1536*
Small P (BM) dep. Great Malvern. Sparse remains absorbed in (ruined) later house.   § : E

AMESBURY, Wiltshire   1541   *980-1157; 1177-1539*
AS A (BN), d. 1157, ref. ap (BNF). Later became large denizen P (BN). Anglican parish church
substantially priory minster. (20, 74)   + : C-

AMPLEFORTH, Yorkshire North Riding   5878   *1560, 1608, 1791, 1802-*
Large A (BM). When Westminster was d. for second time in 1560, survivors fled to continent, f.
abbey at Dieulouard, Lorraine in 1608. Returned to Acton Burnell (1791) and finally (1802) to
Ampleforth, largest religious house in England. (8)   + § : (A)

ANDWELL, Hampshire   6851   *t.Henry I - 1391*
Poor ap (OT), d. and endowments tr. to Winchester College. Sparse and incoherent remains:
flint walls, two doorways, garden on site of cloister-garth. (180)   § : E

ANGLESEY, Cambridgeshire   5262   *1212-1536*
Abbey occupies site of P(AC), developed from C12 H, remnants of conventual buildings
incorporated in mansion.   NT: E +

ANKERWYKE, Buckinghamshire   0273   *c.1160-1536*
Probably began as hermitage, becoming small P(BN) in later C12. Three sections of wall in
grounds of C19 house.   AM § : E

ARUNDEL, Sussex   *see Pynham*

ASTLEY, Worcestershire   7867   *c.1085-c.1414*
ac dep. St Taurin, Evreux (BM), d.endowments tr. college at Westbury-on-Trym. Church in
Anglican use.   + : C-

ATHERSTONE, Warwickshire 3097 *1375-1538*
AF in Lincoln 'limes'. General plan of friary church with chancel in Anglican use. (15) + : C-
St Scholastica's priory (DN), f. C19. + § : (A)

AXHOLME, Lincolnshire 7803 *1397-1538*
P (C). Scant remains AM : E

AXFORD, Wiltshire 2369 *?*
Priory farm incorporates remains of C14 chapel. § : E

AYLESFORD, Kent 7359 *1241-1538; 1949-*
Probably first CF f. in England. At d. church destroyed and two ranges of cloister perverted to house. ref. 1949, much restoration and new church. Mediaeval remains in gatehouse, south and west range of cloisters. (29) § : (A)

BADDESLEY, Hampshire 3920 *1167-1353; 1365-1540*
Originally ac of Godsfield (KH), relative positions reversed before 1355. Manor occupies site of preceptory which was KH Hampshire HQ after 1365. Anglican church preserves remains of chapel. (106) + : D

BALSALL *see Temple Balsall*

BAMBURGH, Northumberland 1834 *c.1121-c.1537*
i. Small P (AC) administering large estates of Nostell in this area. Ruins of chapel in east bailey of castle. (15) + : D-
ii. Small DF in York visitation. Scant remains lost in farm. § : E

BARDNEY, Lincolnshire 1169 *C7, C11-1538*
ap dep. Charroux (BM) on AS site. Became A in 1116, noted for hospitality; 'ever-open door' survives in Lincolnshire folk-saying. Of this famous and large house, nothing survives except ditch, masonry fragments and divers mounds and depressions. Extern church (in Anglican use) has abbot's monument and other gleanings. (23, 70, 87, 119, 121) AM : E +

BARKING, Essex 4584 *c.666-1539*
Original f. AS 'double monastery', d. Danes c. 870. Ref. 975 as large A (DN). Only outline of great 300ft minster, damaged east gate with chapel above, dependent (and provided ?) parish church. (1, 64, 137) § : E

BARLINCH, Somerset 9027 *c.1100-c.1537*
P (AC). Scanty ruins, almost lost in farm buildings, occupy picturesque setting. AM : E

BARLINGS, Lincolnshire 0774 *1154-1537*
A (PC), col. Newsham, moved to Oxeney from Barlin Grange. Remains of wall and scattered stones incorporated in adjoining cottages. AM : E

BARNWELL, Cambridgeshire 0485 *1112-1538*
P (AC) originally at St Giles from 1092. Nothing remains of great monastic house except fragment of cellarer's checker (Priory Rd) and extern chapel (Newmarket Rd) in Anglican use. (6, 14, 15, 23, 42, 51, 64, 78, 79, 90, 98, 102, 107, 112, 129, 136, 140, 145, 147, 156, 165, 166, 170, 171, 175, 185) § : D-

BARROW, Derbyshire 3528 *c.1240-1453; 1540*
Cell (KH), united to Yeaveley before 1453 as combined preceptory. Slight remains in later building (106, 128). § : D

BARROW GURNEY, Somerset 5267 *1212-1536*
Small P (BN). Conventual site occupied by Barrow court and chapel by C19 Anglican church. Some fragments of nun's church in churchyard wall. (20) § : E

BASWICK, Staffordshire 9422 *c.1174-1538*
P (AC) with one of earliest churches dedicated to St Thomas of Canterbury. Fragments of church and south range of cloister absorbed in farm. § : E +

BATH, Somerset 7464 *C7; C10-1539*
AS f., ref. A (BM) in C10, made CP in 1088. Dependencies in Cork, Dunster, Waterford and two local hospitals: St John Baptist :(§), St Mary Magdalene (+ §). No remains of AS church, little of Norman. A being rebuilt when d. stopped work, church substantially survives in Anglican use, no conventual buildings. (19, 20, 23, 31, 76) + : C +

BATTLE, Sussex 7416 *1067-1538*
A (BM) f. William I in thanksgiving for victory and to provide prayers for slain. High altar over spot where Harold fell. Dependencies at Brecon, Carmarthen, Exeter and local hospital. Nothing of C11 church, exposed remains of C14 crypt (within school buildings). Splendid gatehouse, hospice ('Pilgrim's Rest'), extern church (St Mary's) in Anglican use. (2, 8, 21, 46, 66, 67, 75, 83, 118, 119, 141, 142, 153, 158, 167, 175) AM/§ : D

BAWTRY, Nottinghamshire 6493 *1200-C16 ?*
In former hamlet of Martin, H almshouse of St Mary Magdalene. Some remains of chapel (rebuilt C19). + : E

BAYHAM, Sussex 6436 *1199-1208; -1525*
Col. from Premontre, settled at Otham, were moved to Bayham and joined by small community from Brockley to form rare A (PC). Most impressive monastic ruin in Sussex: much of church (with unusual polygonal apse) and conventual buildings (including gatehouse) recognisable. (142)
DE : B-

BEAUCHIEF, Derbyshire 3842 *c.1175-1537*
P (PC), col. Welbeck. Part of wall and other fragments attached to what is now Anglican parish church in Sheffield suburb. + : D

BEAULIEU, Hampshire 3801 *1204-1538*
Large A (CM), col. Citeaux after short stay at Faringdon. Became famous sanctuary. Little remains of largest Cistercian church in England, apart from plan. Some remnants of cloister, winepress, gatehouse with extern chapel(s) on first floor, conduit house ¾ mile north-east. Almost intact frater serves as Anglican church. (1, 16, 29, 35, 45, 50, 75, 79, 80, 83, 86, 108, 109, 120, 142, 146, 153, 158, 167, 180, 190) DE § : C

BEAUVALE, Nottinghamshire 4949 *1343-1539*
P (C) unique in county. Remains of one cell: monk's house with garden walls, now part of farm. (30) AM/§ : E

BEELEIGH, Essex 8406 *1172; 1180-1536*
P (PC), col. Newsham after brief sojourn at Great Parndon. Dependent H at Maldon. Fragments survive of west and south-west ranges, including chapter-house and dorter undercroft (warming room ?). Much incorporated in house built immediately after d. when church was utterly demolished. (37, 60, 142) § : D

BEESTON, Norfolk 1742 *c.1216-1539*
Small P (AC), apparently running a school and maintaining a scholar at Oxford. Substantial ruins of church, site neglected and unexcavated. AM : D-

BELMONT, Herefordshire 5141 *1858-*
A (BM) belonging to the English Congregation, associated school. + § : (A)

BERMONDSEY, London *1089-1538*
P (BMC), col. La Charité-sur-Loire, denizen in 1381 and elevated to abbey 1399. Possessor of miraculous crucifix 'Rood of Grace'. Only survives in street-names (Abbey Street, Crucifix Lane) and fragments of gatehouse in Grange Walk. (43, 64, 152) § : E

BICESTER, Oxfordshire 5822 *c.1183-1535*
Substantial P (AC). Church completely destroyed and conventual buildings converted to secular residence. 'Old Priory House' probably built from cannibalised material. § : E-

BICKNACRE, Essex 7802 *1175-1507*
Originally hermitage which became very small P (AC). The community died out in 1507 and its endowments were transferred to St Mary's Hospital outside Bishopsgate, London. All that remains is one tall, lonely arch. (137) AM : E

BILSINGTON, Kent 0434 *1253-1536*
Small P (AC). Only survival is much restored domestic block (farmery hall ?). § : E

BINDON, Dorset 8782 *1172-1539*
Small A (CM), col. Forde. Scant remains of church, chapter-house, dorter undercroft, fishponds. In C18 a retreat-house was established in grounds. (1, 37, 40) AM : D+

BINHAM, Norfolk 9740 *C11-1539*
P (BM), dep. St Albans. Interesting example of pc designed as miniature monastery (cf. Finchale). Considerable remains of church (some of it in Anglican use), less of conventual buildings and gatehouse. (20, 52, 124, 132) DE/ + : C+

BIRKENHEAD, Cheshire   3188   *c.1150-1536*
P (BM) with dependent H in Chester, much strained by travellers awaiting Mersey crossing.
Fragmentary remains apart from chapter-house (used as Anglican chapel), with room above of
unknown purpose. (37, 101)   § : E +

BISHAM, Berkshire   8585   *1337-1536; 1537-38*
f. as preceptory (KT), d. 1308-12. Site later occupied by large P (AC). d. was followed by brief
ref. A (BM) for dispossessed from Chertsey. Remains largely from KT period but remnants of
AC cloister, barns, dovecote. (177)   § : D

BLACKBOROUGH, Norfolk   0909   *c.1150; c.1170-1537*
P (BM) which became 'double monastery' (BMBNF ?) c.1170, finally P (BN) from c.1200. Scant
remains of some walls.   AM : E

BLACKMOOR, Dorset   7009   *1300-1424 +*
A community of hermits was formed here in C12 which seems to have adopted rule similar to AF.
Its end is unrecorded. Knowles indicates a church, Pevsner says nothing survives. (15)   + ? :?

BLACKMORE, Essex   6001   *c.1157-1525*
Small P (AC), d. Wolsey to endow educational foundations. Fine Norman church, slightly
modified when it became entirely parochial. (c.1526)   + : C

BLAKENEY, Norfolk   0243   *1296-1538*
CF, sparse remains incorporated in house called 'Friary'. (29)   § : E

BLANCHLAND, Northumberland   9650   *1165-1539*
P (PC), col. Croxton. d. 1536, ref. for few years. Modern village, including hotel (guest-house
?), substantially built from abbey remains which (apart from cannibalised materials) include
elements of church, prior's lodging, gatehouse, fragments of cloister. (142, 153, 167, 175)
       + /§ : C +

BLYTH, Nottinghamshire   6287   *1088-1536*
ap (BM), dep. St Trinité, Rouen. Independent P (BM) from c.1409. No conventual buildings
survive, church is 'sad, badly-treated fragment' (Pevsner). (5, 20, 124, 155)   + : C-

BODMIN, Cornwall   0767   *c.1124-1539*
Culdee settlement (Ce) associated with St Petroc, succeeded by AS monastery (BM) and then, in
C12, by P (AC) col. Merton with three dependent H. Fragmentary remains of priory church
only.   § . E
Town also possesses modern house (AF) serving scattered parishes.

BOLTON, Yorkshire West Riding   0753   *1194-1540*
P (AC), originally at Embsay, moving to Bolton c.1155, dep. Huntingdon until independent
c.1230. Scots caused abandonment of site in 1320. Substantial remains of church, (part in
Anglican use), gatehouse, (incorporated in hall), outline of cloistral buildings, rectory may be
reconstructed farmery. 'Very high place among monuments of Gothic genius' (D. Knowles). (4,
14, 16, 18, 37, 53, 68, 84, 101, 124, 143, 152, 153, 155, 172, 181)   + /§ : C +

BOSCOBEL, Shropshire   8308   *c.1200-1538?*
Small, poor P (AN). Ruins only of simple church. (15, 192)   DE : D

BOSTON, Lincolnshire   3244   *1288-1539*
Large DF in York visitation. Scant vestiges: odd stones from church (South Street), shell of
frater with undercroft (Spane Lane). (175)   AM : E

BOURNE, Lincolnshire   0920   *1138-1536*
A (AC). Much altered church of SS Peter and Paul is remnant of abbey, for the rest there are
some loose stones in church and blank arcading outside. (14, 124)   + : D +

BOXGROVE, Sussex   9007   *c.1110-1536*
ap (BM), dep. Lessay, became independent P in 1339. H (almshouse) attached. Apart from its
nave, priory church substantially survives. Few remnants of cloistral buildings but walls of
hospitium survive almost to full height. (5, 20, 133, 143)   AM/ + : C

BOXLEY, Kent   7759   *1143-1538*
Small A (CM) unique in Kent, col. Clairvaux. 'Pathetically sparse' remains.   § : E

BRACKLEY, Northamptonshire   5837   c.1150-1485
H (almshouse for poor travellers), ref. 1423, d. 1485 and annexed to Magdalen College, Oxford.
Chapel and remnants of hospital premises survive within College School. (122)   + /§ : D

BRADENSTOKE, Wiltshire 0079 *1142-1539*
Large P (AC), supported H at Wootton Bassett. On site only tower survives, marking lower
corner of north-west range and part of west range undercroft. Much removed by Hearst in 1930s
to St Donat's castle, including guest-house, prior's lodging and barn! (147) AM : D-

BRADFORD, Yorkshire West Riding *see Esholt*

BRADFORD ON AVON, Wiltshire 8620 *C8?; C13-1536?*
i. St Lawrence, rescued from profane use in 1856, may be rebuilding of monastic church of St
Aldhelm. No sign of domestic buildings. + : D-
ii. Tory chapel or hermitage, of unknown f., was at d. a 'hospitium with chapel in which
wayfarer could pray, a refectory in which he could eat and a room in which he could sleep.'
Chapel rebuilt C19. + : D-
iii. Barn belonging to grange of Shaftesbury. (16)

BRADSOLE *see St Radegund's*

BRADWELL, Buckinghamshire 8339 *1155-1525*
Small P (BM). Little survives except fragments of church incorporated in outbuilding of abbey
farm. AM/§ : E

BREEDON, Leicestershire 4022 *C7/8; 1122-c.1540*
AS monastic site c. 700, d. Danes. Ref. P (AC), dep. Nostell. No traces of monastic buildings but
church substantially survives with fascinating fragments of Saxon sculpture. (14) + : D +

BREWOOD *see Boscobel*

BRIDLINGTON, Yorkshire East Riding 1766 *1113-1537*
P (AC) with dependent HH in Bridlington and Saxton. One of largest houses of order. Of
conventual buildings only gatehouse survives. Church truncated and gutted c.1538 but worth visit.
NB reconstruction of section of cloister in north aisle. (4, 14, 83, 124, 132, 164, 170, 173) + /§ : C

BRIDPORT, Dorset 4692 *1240-1547*
H (almshouse), acquired by Society of Friends in 1697. § : E

BRINKBURN, Northumberland 1198 *c.1135-1536*
P (AC), dep. Pentney, independent -1188. Very little survives of conventual buildings, ruined
church sensitively restored 1858. (4, 14, 59, 142) + : D +

BRISTOL, Somerset 5872 *1142-1539*
i. Large and rich A (AC) f. Victorines with H (for poor) in town. Besides chancel (with many
original stalls) of fine church there are remains of conventual buildings: chapter-house, mutilated
claustral ranges, gatehouse. (14, 37, 54, 76, 81, 125, 152, 167, 186) + /§ : B
ii. P (BM), dep. Tewkesbury (1137-1540). Church (St James) survives in Anglican use, no
conventual remains. (20, 124) + : D
iii. Large P (DF), (1230-1538). Most of 'Quaker Friars' formed part of this house. (153)
AM/§ : E +
iv. Of 16 HH, there are traces of four: St Mark's, (for poor), in mayor's chapel + (95, 96, 122),
St Bartholomew's, (almshouse), f. 1207, fragment in Christmas Street, (15, 97), Three Kings
(almshouse), f. 1492 in Colston Street + §, Trinity, (almshouse), f.c. 1396 in Old Market Street.§

BROMFIELD, Shropshire 4876 *1115-1540*
Small P (BM), became dep. Gloucester 1155. At d., monastic buildings destroyed and church
converted to house. Remains restored to Christian worship 1658. Picturesque gatehouse.(4, 20)
+ / § :C

BROMHOLM, Norfolk 3324 *c.1195-1536*
f.P (BMC) dep. Castle Acre. Grew and became independent A and P of Cluny c. 1195, later
denizen. Acquired relic of Cross in early C13 and became very popular with pilgrims. Impressive
ruins include remains of church, part of conventual buildings, gatehouse. (4, 43, 152) AM : C

BROOKE, Rutland 8004 *1153-1535*
pc (AC), dep. Kenilworth. Only religious house in county. Some of masonry incorporated in
farmhouse. § : E

BUCKFAST, Devon   7367   *C10-1100?; 1137-1536; 1882-*
AS A (BM), ref. from Savigny in 1137. Remains include abbot's tower, St Anne's chapel in
undercroft, barn at Grange Farm. (19, 86)
Ref. in modern times by French BM who built own church by 1932 together with new domestic
buildings. (113)   + § : (A)

BUCKINGHAM, Buckinghamshire   6933   *1200-1279+*
H, (for poor), of St John Baptist. In late C13 seems to have been ref. as chantry with school.
Remains in Market Hill.   + : D +

BUCKLAND, Devon   4868   *1278-1538*
A (CM), col. Quarr. Domestic buildings destroyed by Richard Grenville who made his mansion
out of church. Tithe barn and other minor remains, gatehouse enclosed in later stables. (73)
                                                              AM /§ : E

BUILDWAS, Shropshire   6304   *1135-1536*
Modest A (CM) originating in col. Savigny. Never expanded due to Welsh depradation.
Substantial remains in simple, noble architecture with conventual buildings unusually on north
side of church. Some of library survived looting and is retained at Trinity College Cambridge and
Lambeth Palace. (40, 59, 124, 153, 158, 167, 181)   DE : B

BULLINGTON, Lincolnshire   4541   *c.1150-1538*
Large P (GD). All that survives are fragments built into stone pillar on Stainfield Road. (84)
                                                              AM : E

BUNGAY, Suffolk   3389   *1183-1536*
P (BN). Little remains except ruined choir of nuns' church and modified nave still serving a
parochial use. (20)   + /§ : C-

BURFORD, Oxfordshire   2512   *-1226-c.1538*
H, (for sick), under Augustinian rule, later almshouse for men. Large house built on site 1580 + .
In recent times returned to religious purpose, now occupied by Anglican nuns.   § : E +

BURNHAM, Buckinghamshire   9382   *1266-1539*
A (AN) of which more remains than any other Buckinghamshire religious house. Now part of
Anglican nunnery. (15, 64)   § : C-

BURNHAM NORTON, Norfolk   8243   *1241-1538*
Medium-sized house (CF) with substantial remains of gatehouse, fragments of walls, doorways
and further remnants incorporated in farmhouse. (29)   AM/§ : E +

BURSCOUGH, Lancashire   4310   *c.1190-1536*
Small P (AC), supporting H, (for lepers), in township. Fragments of church.   AM : E

BURTON, Staffordshire   2423   *1004-1539*
A (BM) with dependency at Blithbury. Centre of site under market hall, visible fragments of
farmery. (19, 64, 101, 103, 182)   § : E

BURY ST EDMUNDS, Suffolk   8564   *633; 1020-1539*
AS f., ref. A (BM) from St Benet's Hulme with later dependencies at Thetford and six HH in
town which grew under its protection. 'Wealthiest, if not greatest of English abbeys' but few
major f. have vanished so completely. Nothing of cathedral-like church, fragments of cloistral
buildings absorbed in subsequent erections. Two gatehouses and extern chapel survive, smaller
remnants in Moyse's Hall museum. (1, 2, 13, 19, 21, 28, 33, 41, 46, 49, 61, 64, 67, 71, 72, 75, 79, 83,
103, 112, 118, 119, 127, 132, 133, 139, 141, 142, 147, 152, 154, 157, 159, 164, 167, 171, 174, 181, 182,
187, 192)   DE : D +
    Material traces of three HH: St Saviour (c.1184-c.1539) for poor § (95); St Nicholas
(c.1215-1539) men's almshouse §; St Petronella (C12?-c.1539) for lepers, later for sick.   §

BUSHMEAD, Hertfordshire   1360   *c.1195-1536*
Small P (AC), remains of frater range attached to C18 house.   § : E

BUTLEY, Suffolk   3651   *1171-1538*
Large P (AC) with dependent school, bede-house and H for sick at West Somerton. Built sea-
wall, wharf and canal probably to assist landing of French building stone. Substantial and
interesting gatehouse survives, together with arch of church and parts of frater and rere-dorter
discernible in farm buildings. (168)   § : D

BYLAND, Yorkshire North Riding 5478 *1178-1539*
A (CM) col. Savigniacs from Furness after unsuccessful attempts at Calder, Hood, Old Byland, Stocking. After solving immense problems of draining site, great house established designed for 40 monks, 100 conversi. Impressive ruins of church, most conventual buildings distinguishable. Gatehouse fair distance to west. (1, 8, 17, 27, 28, 31, 33, 34, 36, 40, 53, 82, 101, 108, 111, 121, 124, 142, 154, 158, 178, 181, 182, 191, 193) DE : C +

CALDER, Cumberland 0506 *1143-1536*
A (CM) col. Savigniacs from Furness. First attempt d. by Scots and ended at Byland (q.v.). Second f. successful but always poor and never expanded due to continuing Scottish depradations. Ruins of church, east range. Private site not properly cleared. (36, 40, 112)
AM/§ : C-

CAMBRIDGE, Cambridgeshire 4658 *c.1135-1496*
i. P (BN) with ill-starred history of accident, financial ruin and moral decay, d. for f. Jesus College. Chapel and part of domestic buildings survive. (20, 64, 73, 153, 171) + § : C
ii. P (BM) dep. Ely established c. 1325 as house of studies, ref. 1428 with broader base as Buckingham College. After suppression became Magdalen College (1542). Scant monastic remains. (185) § : E
iii. P (DF), very large f. (1238 — 1538) as house of study for English Dominicans. d. and site occupied by Emmanuel College to spread Puritanism. Substantial masonry fragments on three sides of Second Court. (153).
iv. Town has modern f. (DF, FFC, AN)

CAMPSEA ASH, Suffolk 3356 *c.1195-1536*
Large P (AN) with attached small college for chaplains. A very little masonry survives in house and barn of 'Ash Abbey'. (15) § : E

CANONS ASHBY, Northamptonshire 5750 *c.1150-1536*
P (AC). At suppression, domestic buildings immediately converted into mansion. Fragment of church survives in Anglican use. (4, 137) + § : D

CANTERBURY, Kent 1557 *598; 997-1540*
i. AS f. by St Augustine, ref. as CP (Christchurch) which became one of richest abbeys (BM) in country with dependencies at Dover, Oxford and H at Thannington. Church, rebuilt in C12 from offerings at St Thomas' shrine, substantially intact apart from gutting. Considerable material remains (much altered) of domestic buildings once belonging to largest English monastery. Fine cloisters, chapter-house, dorter. (2, 7, 8, 15, 19, 20, 21, 25, 31, 34, 37,, 45, 46, 49, 60, 61, 63, 69, 70, 71, 75, 83, 84, 86, 87, 92, 95, 100, 103, 112, 115, 117, 119, 126, 132, 136,, 140, 146, 148, 149, 152, 154, 155, 156, 159, 165, 166, 172, 178, 183, 191) + /§ : A
ii. St Augustine's A (BM), the great extra-mural rival of Christchurch (C7 — 1538) with many dependencies including Minster in Thanet. C11 convent survived, largely unaltered, until 1538 when it was systematically demolished apart from two gatehouses and corner of church (incorporated in royal palace). Part of precinct now occupied by Anglican college. Fascinating archaeological site. (16, 19, 57, 64, 70, 86, 102, 104, 120, 141, 142, 148, 150, 154, 168, 191)
DE/§ : D +
iii. Large friary (AF) ›elonging to Oxford limes (1318-1538). Fragment. § : E
iv. Large friary (DF) in London visitation (1237-1538). Frater used as Anglican chapel, remains of guest-house? § : D
v. First Franciscan house in England (1224-1538) which became very large, d. 1498 (FFO) and produced many martyrs at Reformation. Altered warden's lodging survives. (77) § : E
Franciscans returned in C19, small house in Nunnery Road.
vi. There were at least six HH, remains of three: St John Baptist for poor f. c.1087 in Northgate (76, 95), §; St Mary (C) f. -1123 in Stour Street + §; St Thomas Martyr, travellers' almshouse f. c.1170 in St Peters Street. (95, 97) §

CARISBROOKE, Isle of Wight 4888 *c.1156-1414*
AP (BM), dep. Lyre, d. 1414 and endowments transferred to royal f. at Sheen (C). No conventual remains, most of church survives in Anglican use. + : C-
There is a modern P (DN) f. C19 of enclosed nuns. §

CARLISLE, Cumberland 3955 *C7-9; 1122-1540*
Early f. (Ce?) disappeared in Dark Ages, succeeded by large P (AC), made CP in 1133 with royal
support (Henry I) with dependent HH in town and at Caldbeck. Suffered greatly from Scots.
Chancel of church substantially survives in spite of Scottish aggression and English neglect. Some
original glass and stalls. Altered remains of some claustral buildings: frater, prior's lodging,
gatehouse. (8, 14, 31, 37, 75, 142, 152, 170, 173) +/§ : C
House (AF) f. C19 with dependent school. +/§ : (A)

CARTMEL, Lancashire 3778 *c.1190-1536*
P (AC), col. Bradenstoke, with important estates in Ireland. Temporarily reinstated as result of
Pilgrimage of Grace but sub-prior and several canons subsequently executed. Church survives in
Anglican use. No conventual buildings apart from gatehouse. (NT). (14, 59, 75, 133, 143, 152)
+/AM : B-

CASTLE ACRE, Norfolk 8115 *1087-1537*
P (BMC), dep. Lewes. Original f. in castle enclosure, moved c.1090. Became independent in later
C14 with own dependencies at Broomholm, Mendham, Norman's Burrow, Slevesholm. HH at
Racheness, Heacham (?). Possibly most impressive Cluniac remains: west front of church,
identifiable remains of claustral ranges, elaborate prior's house, gatehouse. Fragments of stalls
may survive in East Lexham church. (36, 43, 69, 104, 125, 132, 133, 136, 142, 143, 152, 154, 157,
168, 173) DE : B

CATESBY, Northamptonshire 5159 *c.1175-1536*
Uncertainty about rule of this f. which, for a time at least, was double monastery. Suggestions
include BM and BN, GD, CN with chaplains. Little, if anything, survives in later buildings on
site: doorway of church ? (64) § : E

CERNE, Dorset 6601 *987-1539*
A (BM) of ancient foundation but modest resources. Remains in garden of abbey farm and
neighbouring buildings: remnants of gatehouse, guest-house, porch of abbot's hall, barn,
scattered stones. (19, 137) AM/§ : E

CHACOMBE, Northamptonshire 4943 *t. Henry II - 1536*
P (AC). Scant remains incorporated in house called 'The Priory'. § : E

CHAPEL PLASTER, Wiltshire 8265 *-1400-?*
Pilgrims' hostel on way to Glastonbury H, almshouse for travellers. § : D

CHATHAM, Kent 7567 *-1108-?*
H for lepers and sick, dependent on Rochester. Part of much modified chapel survives. § + : D

CHERTSEY, Surrey 0466 *666; -964-1537*
AS f. (BM), d. Danes, ref. from Abingdon mid C10?, replaced by other BM in 964 when it
became A with dependency in Cardigan. One of most famous English abbeys which surrendered
to Henry VIII (who used materials for Hampton Court) on condition of ref. at Bisham (q.v.).
Sole remnants: stone arch in Colonel's Lane and possible remains of barn. (19, 46) § : E

CHESTER, Cheshire 4066 *1093-1539*
Preceded by AS f. (BN?) in C9, ref. Athelstan for secular canons, replaced by BM from Bec in
1093. Dependencies at Hilbre, Saighton. Moderately sized (for abbey) church substantially
survives, heavily modified; considerable remains of conventual buildings: cloisters, chapter-
house, warming room, frater, undercroft, abbot's chapel, gateway. Fine quire-stalls. (20, 26,, 29,
31, 30, 37, 53, 54, 60, 73, 78, 80, 86, 101, 104, 119, 133, 152, 154, 161, 165, 168, 169, 170, 182, 183, 186,
191) AM/ + : B
Grosvenor Street possesses a modern friary (Capuchin).

CHETWODE, Buckinghamshire 6429 *1245-1538*
Small P (AC), so impoverished in 1460 that it was reduced to pc of Notley. Twenty years later
priory church was granted to parishioners as their own was decayed and they added tower. (14)
+ : D

CHIBBURN, Northumberland 2798 *1313-1535 ?*
Small preceptory (KH). Overgrown, neglected but important (for its rarity). Remains of chapel,
living accommodation and small courtyard within moat. (106) AM : D +

CHICHESTER, Sussex   8605   *-1232; 1269-1538*
Quite large house (FFC) in London Custody, moved to site of ruined castle in 1269. Only remains
of church: noble fragment (choir) in Priory Park. (56, 77, 153)   AM/ + : D +
Remains of one of five HH: St Mary's f.1172, poor travellers, dep. cathedral. Some fine stalls
survive in chapel. (95, 96)   + § : C +

CHICKSANDS, Bedfordshire   1239   *c.1154-1538*
Larger P (GD). Some fragments incorporated in later house now occupied by USAF. (84)   § : E

CHIRBURY, Shropshire   2598   *c.1195-1536*
Small P (AC), originally f. Snead c.1190? About half of priory church survives in Anglican use;
of convent there is a solitary pier which may have supported chapter-house roof. Twelve badly
mutilated stalls in St Nicholas', Montgomery are said to be from this house.   + : D

CHRISTCHURCH, Hampshire   1593   *-1066-1539*
Former college of secular canons, ref. c.1150 as large P (AC), dependent H for sick at Rushton
St Leonard. No remains of conventual buildings, substantial fabric of church with some of quire
furnishings. (4, 14, 119, 133, 152, 154)   + : C

CHURCH GRESLEY, Derbyshire   2918   *t. Stephen ? - 1536*
Small P (AC). Part of church survives in Anglican use, even less of conventual buildings in
fragments to east.   + : C-

CHURCH PREEN, Shropshire   5398   *-1163-1539*
f. as ac dep. Much Wenlock, became denizen pc in 1384, same dep. Small Cistercian church
survives (much altered) in Anglican use; conventual remains probably beneath adjoining manor
house.   + : D

CIRENCESTER, Gloucestershire   0201   *-1066; C12-1539*
Ancient college (f. Egbert ?), replaced by P (AC) sponsored by Henry I, became rare A (AC) in
1131, one of largest houses of order with two dependent HH for sick in town. A survives only in
street names and part of enclosure wall, though some stalls may exist at Duntisbourne Rous. (14)
         § : E
Remains of H for poor: St John Evangelist f. -1135 in Dollar Street. (?)

CLARE, Suffolk   7645   *1248-1538*
House (AF), first to be established in England, later in limes of Cambridge. Detached fragments
of conventual buildings, nothing of church unless some stalls survive in St Paul's Belchamp,
Essex. (15, 81, 112)   AM : D
Friars have returned and have their English novitiate at Clare priory.

CLATTERCOTE, Oxfordshire   4549   *1148-1538?*
f. as H for lepers for members of Gilbertine order, apparently staffed by GN. Round mid C13
became P (GC). Scattered stones embedded in priory farm. (84, 122)   § : E

CLEEVE, Somerset   4566   *1198-1537*
Small A (CM), col. Revesby. Foundations of church survive with possible remains of collation
seat; rather more of claustral buildings, especially south range: frater, almonry. Gatehouse
inscribed 'Stay open gate and close to no honest person'. (1, 37, 40, 44, 53, 60, 79, 80, 83, 109, 112,
120, 136, 153, 169, 184, 189)   DE : B-

COALVILLE   *see Mount St Bernard*

COCKERSAND, Lancashire   4253   *-1184-1539*
A (PC), col. Croxton, incorporating and maintaining earlier H. After suppression, site much
robbed for sea wall. Chapter-house and fragments of wall survive and quire-stalls (Lancaster
parish church). (1, 37, 91, 122, 170)   AM : D

COCK HILL, Worcestershire   0558   *c.1180-1538/9*
Small P (CN). C18 house occupies part of site and incorporates remains of chapel.   § : E

COGGES, Oxfordshire   2547   *1103-1414*
Small ac (BM), dep. Fécamp, on d. endowments tr. Eton College. Benedictine church
substantially survives, no conventual remains.   + : D +

COGGESHALL, Essex   8522   *1140-1538*
A (CM), col. Savigny. Chapel by gate in Anglican use, fragments of claustral buildings including
earliest mediaeval brickwork in England, monastic barn at Grange Farm. (28)   § : E +

COLCHESTER, Essex　　　　　　　　0025　　　　　　　*c.1095-1536*
i. P (AC) first f. in England, replacing secular canons. Only ruined nave survives of great
Norman church, no conventual remains. (4, 14, 26)　　　　　　　　　　　　　DE : D
ii. A (BM), col. Rochester (1095-1539) with dependencies at Bedesman's Berg, Snaith, Wickham
Skeyth and town H for sick. Only restored gatehouse survives. (21, 58, 119)　　　DE : E +

COMBE, Warwickshire　　　　　　　4079　　　　　　　*1150-1539*
A (C) col. Waverley, became richest house in county. Replaced by C16 mansion incorporating
elements of conventual buildings.　　　　　　　　　　　　　　　　　　　　§ : E +

COMBERMERE, Cheshire　　　　　　5843　　　　　　　*1133-1539*
A (C), col. Savigny. Its own colonies included Poulton (1153), Whalley (1172), Hulton (1219).
Church utterly destroyed, fragment of frater in mansion which replaced A. (50, 54, 101, 103) § : E

COQUET ISLE, Northumberland　　2904　　　　　　　*c.684; 1125-1539*
Monastic site (Ce), became pc (BM) of Tynemouth, fortified C15. Cannibalised masonry in
lighthouse and cottages. (75)　　　　　　　　　　　　　　　　　　　　　　§ : E

CORNWORTHY, Devon　　　　　　　8255　　　　　　　*c.1220-1539*
P (AN). Only gatehouse and wall fragments survive. (15, 64)　　　　　　　　§ : E +

COVENTRY, Warwickshire　　　　　3379　　　　　　　*1043-1539*
i. AS A (BM), raised to CP in 1102, dependent H for sick in town. One of richest houses in
Midlands with cathedral-like church and appropriate conventual buildings. Only fragments
survive. (8, 19, 31, 133, 142)　　　　　　　　　　　　　　　　　　　　　§ : E
ii. Friary (FFC) in custody of Worcester (-1234-1538). No remains except church steeple
incorporated in C19 Christchurch (bombed). (77)　　　　　　　　　　　　　+ : D-
iii. Friary (CF) replacing C13 f. (1342 — 1538). Large house of which part of cloister is
incorporated in 'The Whitefriars'. Mutilated stalls survive (?) in Holy Trinity and Grammar
School. (29)　　　　　　　　　　　　　　　　　　　　　　　　　　　　§ : E
iv. P (CM) formed from pre-existing nucleus of hermits, dependent school (?). Scant remains.
　　　　　　　　　　　　　　　　　　　　　　　　　　　　　　　　　AM : DE
v. Of at least six HH, there are remains of Trinity (§) f. 1506, almshouse; Greyfriars (§) f.1529
almshouse; St John's (§) in Hales Street, dep. on CP, for sick, (95); Bond's f. 1506 (§) in Hill
Street, almshouse.

COVERHAM, Yorkshire North Riding　　0886　　　　　*c.1187; c.1200-1536*
Small A (PC), col. Durford ?, temporarily at Swainby, d. by Scots (1331) but recovered and
flourished to suppression. Of scant remains some are incorporated in neighbouring houses,
others removed to Bear Park. (5, 142)　　　　　　　　　　　　　　　　　AM : E +

COXFORD, Norfolk　　　　　　　　8429　　　　　　　*c.1140-1536*
P (AC), f. at East Rudham until c.1215, dependent H for sick at Boycodeswade. Fragments of
church, including one complete arch.　　　　　　　　　　　　　　　　　§ : E

CRANBORNE, Dorset　　　　　　　0513　　　　　　　*980-1540*
AS A (BM) with Tewkesbury as dependency, relations reversed in 1102 when latter became A and
former pc. No remains of conventual buildings but most of much altered church survives in
Anglican use. (20, 124)　　　　　　　　　　　　　　　　　　　　　　　+ : D +

CRASWALL, Herefordshire　　　　2836　　　　　　　*c.1125-1462*
ap (GM) dep. Grandmont, d. and added to endowments of Christ's College, Cambridge. Much
neglected site with nature completing work of Henry's commissioners. Nearby Holy Well. (37,
86, 142)　　　　　　　　　　　　　　　　　　　　　　　　　　　　AM/§ : C—

CREAKE, Norfolk　　　　　　　　8538　　　　　　　*-1189; 1206-1506*
Originally H for sick?, under Augustinian rule, became P (AC) in 1206 and A in 1231 with
dependent H at Gedney. Entire community perished in epidemic and endowments were passed to
Christ's College, Cambridge. Ruined remains of church and other fragments incorporated in
farm on site. (122)　　　　　　　　　　　　　　　　　　　　　　　　DE : C—

CROWMARSH, Oxfordshire　　　　6189　　　　　　　*-1142-C14?*
H for lepers, probably dissolved as need ceased, church became free chapel and ultimately parish
church. Norman church substantially survives.　　　　　　　　　　　　　+　D +

CROWLAND, Lincolnshire 2310 *C7; 714; 966+ - 1539*
Early hermit settlement (St Guthlac and companions). Monastery f. at his death d. Danes (870), ref. reign of Edred and became large, wealthy A (BM) with dependencies in Cambridge, Freiston, Peakirk. Survived earthquake and fire but not Henry VIII. Nothing remains of conventual buildings, ruined church with one aisle in Anglican use. (19, 20, 32, 46, 75, 87, 90, 103, 119, 124, 133, 152, 155, 167, 171, 182, 185) +/§ : D+

CROXDEN, Staffordshire 0639 *1178-1538*
A (CM), col. by Savigniacs from Aunay-sur-Odon. Impressive fragments of church (which had chevet) and recognisable claustral buildings on site cut by road. (28, 38, 40, 120, 142, 153) DE : B—

DALE, Derbyshire 4338 *+ 1180-c.1537*
Small P (AC) col. Calke c.1160 forced to withdraw some 30 years later. They were followed by col. Tupholme (PC) in 1180+ and Welbeck (PC) in 1194 but both had to be recalled. Finally a larger contingent from Newsham c.1200 was successful and P became independent A. Little remains on site but some glass is preserved in Risley church. AM : E

DARLEY, Derbyshire 1959 *c.1137-1538*
P (AC) inadequately endowed, ref. c.1146 with transference of majority of community from Derby whose old priory buildings were maintained as H for sick? Scant remains visible, mainly in part of house in Old Lane. AM : E

DARTFORD, Kent 5474 *1346-1539*
Very large P (DN) to which 'the best and noblest families of the country send their relatives both for education and for nuns'. The site survives in middle of iron-works with nothing much above ground except corner of occasional residence of Henry VIII which once occupied half of site. (59, 64, 123) § : E

DAVINGTON, Kent 2302 *1153-1535*
Largish P (BN) which steadily lost numbers from C14. When prioress died in 1535, the surviving nun left and priory became extinct. Nave of Benedictine church survives in Anglican use and west range of convent absorbed in C19 house. (20, 124, 128) +/§ : C—

DEEPING ST JAMES, Lincolnshire 1609 *1139-1539*
pc dep. Thorney (BM). Monastic church, with added C18 tower, survives in Anglican use; no remains of conventual buildings unless some exist under C19 house called 'The Priory'. (20, 124) +/§ : C—

DEERHURST, Gloucestershire 8729 *C9: c.1059-1540*
AS A f. early C9, ref. -970 d. Danes shortly afterwards, c.1059 became pc dep. St Denys, acquired denizen status P(BM) in 1443 but four years later tr. to endowments of Eton College. Restored to St Denys for accommodation of English Benedictines 1461 but decayed, becoming pc dep. Tewkesbury in 1467. East range of cloister partially survives in priory house; priory church is AS monument of first order. (19, 20, 124) AM/ + § : C +

DENNEY, Cambridgeshire 4968 *c.1159; c.1170-1312*
pc (BM) dep. Ely, tr. to KT c.1170 and from mid C13 became H for sick and aged knights. After d., unusually did not pass to KH but site occupied by FN (1342-1539) becoming one of only three houses with abbatial status and only nunnery of Poor Clares with any remains. Occupied by aristocratic and observant ladies who continued as a religious community at Coughton Court when ejected at suppression. Remains of church built into farmhouse, frater used as barn, precinct moats. (46, 77, 106, 177) DE : B—

DIEULACRES, Staffordshire 9857 *1214-1539*
A (CM), col. Combermere, after short stay at Poulton. Vestiges of church in situ and other fragments built into farmhouse. (102) § : E

DINMORE, Herefordshire 4848 *-1189-1535*
There was an early monastic settlement of unknown order whose property was granted to KH c.1180. The preceptory became very substantial with estates in Shropshire and Wales. It supported H for sick of St John in Hereford. Remains of chapel distinguishable and other remains partly belonging to manor. (106) § : C—

DORCHESTER, Oxfordshire 5794 *C7; c.1140-1536*
Originally AS missionary centre under St Birinus, later bishopric (tr. Lincoln C11) before tr. to P (AC). At d. their church bought by local philanthropist as parish church — survives in Anglican use. No other remains unless old school house contains remnant of guest-house. (5, 6, 14, 164) +§ : D+

DORE   *see Abbey Dore*

DOVER, Kent   3141   *C7; 1136-1535*
i. P (BM) dep. Canterbury, replacing AC (1131-36) who had replaced ancient collegiate f.
attached to castle and later tr. to St Martin's. Dover College preserves impressive frater, guest-
house and other remains. (74, 103, 142, 154, 182, 192)   § : D +
ii. Commandery (KT) occupied before tr. to Temple Ewell -1185. Foundations visible on Western
Heights. (177).   DE : E
iii. Four HH, of which largest was dependency of P. Remains of St Mary's (-1121-1544) another
large f. under Augustinian rule from 1239: Maison Dieu in Biggin Street, for sick travellers,
caring among others for Canterbury pilgrims. (95, 122)   AM/§ : D

DOWNSIDE, Somerset   6550   *1605, 1791, 1814-*
When religious orders were finally expelled by the Reformation, English exiles made new ff. on
continent. One of these was St Gregory's P (BM) at Douai which returned in 1791 to Acton
Burnell before settling at Downside, large A (BM) with associated school.   + § : (A)

DUDLEY, Worcestershire   9390   *1149-1539*
ap dep. Much Wenlock (BMC), became denizen pc same dep. in 1384 but remained small
community. Remains of varying extent include church, cloister and fragments of west and east
ranges.   AM : E +

DUNKESWELL, Devon   1407   *?1201-1539*
A (CM), col. Forde. Scant remains of church and conventual buildings, fragments in C19
church, ruined gatehouse.   AM/§ : E +

DUNSTABLE, Bedfordshire   0221   *1132-1540*
P (AC) with dependent HH at Dunstable and Hockliffe. Remains of gatehouse and guest-house
(enclosed in house called 'The Priory'), part of nave of church preserved in Anglican use. (14,
103, 124, 155)   + AM : C

DUNSTER, Somerset   9943   *1090+ - 1539*
Small and poor P (BM), dep. Bath. Church substantially survives in Anglican use, scattered
fragments of conventual buildings: prior's house, barn, dovecote, well-house. (20, 124)   + /§ : C

DUNWICH, Suffolk   4770   *-1277-1538*
i. House (FFC) in Cambridge custody. Ruins of part of south range and gatehouse survive.   § : E
ii. There were two HH: part of chapel survives of St James (-1199-1754 +) originally for lepers,
later for sick.   § : D—

DURHAM, Durham   2742   *1083-1539*
i. f. of secular priests from 995, replaced by large A (BM) in 1083, greatly increased by C12.
Became wealthy CP with dependencies at Coldingham, Farne, Finchale, Jarrow, Lindisfarne,
Lytham, Monkwearmouth, Stamford, Warkworth; HH in town and Witton Gilbert, for poor
and sick; attached school. 'Probably most famous religious house in England'. Magnificent
remains of great church in Anglican use, gutted and unsympathetically restored; most of
conventual buildings survive in modified form. (2, 6, 8, 9, 18, 21, 26, 29, 31, 32, 33, 34, 36, 37, 42,
45, 49, 52, 60, 63, 64, 69, 71, 72, 79, 83, 85, 88, 89, 99, 100, 101, 104, 106, 109, 112, 113, 118, 119, 121,
124, 126, 129, 131, 133, 137, 140, 142, 145, 146, 148, 150, 152, 157, 158, 159, 160, 165, 167, 168, 173,
176, 181, 182, 183, 184, 189, 191)   + § : A
ii. Of five HH, remains of two: St Giles, Kepier (1112-1546), large staff following Augustinian
rule, joined by sisters in C14, for poor, (75, 95) §; St Mary Magdalene (c.1240-1540 +), dep. CP,
almshouse.   §

EALING, London   1781   *1897-*
Modern A (BM) with associated school, English Congregation. P (AC) with associated school.
                                                                                 + : (A)

EARL'S COLNE, Essex   8528   *1111-1536*
P (BM), dep. Abingdon. C18 house on site, little above ground. De Vere monuments from priory
church moved to Bures, Suffolk.   § : E

EASBY, Yorkshire North Riding   1800   *1151-1135/7*
A (PC); col. Newsham, enlarged 1392, canons ordered to be hanged for resisting suppression.
Attached and dependent H, almshouse. Substantial remains of abbey: ruined church (some
quire-stalls survive in St Mary's Richmond), cloister (especially south range), farmery, abbot's
lodging. Extern chapel with mediaeval murals survives in Anglican use. Sloping site produced
skilful rearrangement of conventual buildings. (33, 48, 56, 61, 70, 79, 83, 104, 133, 137, 142, 145,
153, 154, 157, 160, 168, 170, 183, 189, 191)   DE : C +

EASTBOURNE, Sussex 8922 *-1248-1536*
P (AN). Domestic buildings largely incorporated in house occupying site. Nuns shared parish church, later 'neglected and catastrophically restored.' (15) + § : D

ECCLESFIELD, Yorkshire West Riding 3393 *t. Henry I - 1386*
Large ap (BM), dep. St Wandrille. In 1337 community withdrew, leaving skeleton staff to maintain house as hospice. In 1386 tr. to endowments of Coventry (C). Some survivals, including chapel, in house called 'The Priory'. Carthusians have left token of their passing in (Anglican) parish church — see westernmost north window. (5) + /§ : C

EDINGTON, Wiltshire 9252 *1351; 1352-1539*
Secular college, converted to BO, at desire of Black Prince. Rare remains of this order in magnificent church. Some domestic buildings may be incorporated in house called 'Priory' with monk's well near west entrance. (23) + /§ : C

EGGLESTONE, Yorkshire North Riding 1615 *-1198-1540*
A (PC), col. Easby, small and never rich in spite of status. Ruined and scattered by Scots, 1323; fully restored by C15 with much pastoral responsibility. Comprehensible ruins of church, fragments of claustral buildings, especially north-east of precinct. Many irregularities of plan. (1, 142) DE : B-

ELLERTON, Yorkshire North Riding 2597 *-1227-1537/8*
Small P (CN), certainly very poor in C16. Fragment of ruined church. AM : D

ELSTOW, Bedfordshire 0547 *c.1075-1539*
A (BN), large. Part of church in Anglican use with unusual detached belfry, brass to abbess, outer parlour ?; fragments of west range and other masonry incorporated in Hillersdon Hall. (20, 64, 124) + § : C

ELY, Cambridgeshire 5380 *673; C9; C10; 1109-1539*
A first f. (DM), destroyed by Danes; A (BM) f. c.966, became CP in 1109 with dependencies at Denney, Mullicourt, St Neots, Spinney and H in town. Substantial remains of priory church with unique octagon, savagely mutilated Lady Chapel. Little preserved of cloister but notable prior's door, chapel and guest-hall (now headmaster's house), gatehouse, fragments of farmery absorbed in later buildings, remains of abbot's house, sacristy, almonry, goldsmith's tower. (13, 19, 20, 21, 31, 34, 49, 56, 60, 66, 69, 70, 72, 76, 82, 83, 104, 107, 119, 121, 144, 149, 152, 157, 165, 167, 171, 173, 177, 181, 182, 185, 187) + /§ : A-
There were originally two HH (for poor and lepers), combined mid C13, remains of buildings of St John Baptist. (§)

ESHOLT, Yorkshire West Riding 4144 *C12-1539*
Small P (CN). Laundry at rear of former hall contains monument to last prioress and a part of domestic buildings. Site now enclosed in Bradford sewage works. (64) § : D

EVESHAM, Worcestershire 0344 *701 + ; 989-1539*
A (BM), early history confused, changing from monastic to collegiate twice but continuous existence as A (BM) from 989 though in C11 its community of 173 included a few BN. Wealthy house with dependencies in Alcester, Penwortham and Denmark; almonry school. Scant remains of its large provision of buildings include almonry, gateway, fragment of church and chapter-house, detached belfry and two provided churches (one for pilgrims). (6, 18, 19, 21, 22, 28, 46, 64, 66,, 67, 71, 83, 98, 102, 111, 119, 133, 136, 152, 159, 161, 174, 177, 181, 184, 187, 192)
AM : D +

EWELME, Oxfordshire 6491 *1437-?*
H called 'God's House' almshouse, living under rule and early example of organisation of accommodation round quad; school (remains) f. at same time. Fine church, connected to H by covered passage, with monument to founder and brasses of two masters. (95, 112, 188) + § : C +

EXETER, Devon 9292 *1087-1536*
i. P (BM), dep. Battle. Remains of one range of cloisters, fragments of another. (7, 19, 41, 104, 109, 171) § : E +
ii. P (AN), site occupied by Deanery: remains of chapel, undercroft and solar according to Pevsner, not in Knowles. + § : C
iii. There were 11 HH: remains of almshouses are: St Katherine's f. 1457; God's House f. 1436; St Anne f. -1418; Liverydole f. early C15.
iv. Largely destroyed abbot's lodge (townhouse of abbots of Buckfast). See also Polsoe.

EYE, Suffolk   1473   *c.1080-1537*
i. ap, dep. Bernay; denizen and expanded in 1385, P (BM). Fragments of church and other
masonry in farm.   § : D-
ii. H (for lepers, later sick), C12-c.1547, St Mary Magdalene.   §

FAREWELL, Staffordshire   0811   *c.1140-1527*
Small A (BN), declined to P in mid C13, d. Wolsey and tr. Lichfield cathedral. Remains of nuns'
chancel (with some stalls) in Anglican parish church. (20, 64)   + : D

FARNBOROUGH, Hampshire   8753   *1947-*
A (BM), col. Prinknash, Subiaco congregation.   + § : (A)

FARNE, Northumberland   2337   *c.651; c.1255-c.1538*
Long used as hermitage, but only became PC (BM) dep. Durham c.1255. St Cuthbert's church
probably occupies site of saint's cell (hermitage). Prior Castell's tower, with inner and outer
courts, and fragments of two chapels remain of PC. (31, 32, 75, 90, 111)   AM/ + : C

FAVERSHAM, Kent   0161   *1148-1538*
i. Small A (BMC), col. Bermondsey. Nothing of church unless stalls in Anglican church came
thence. Some masonry may survive in farm on site.   § : E
ii. Modern P (CF) with press, hostel and parochial responsibilities.   + § : (A)

FINCHALE, Durham   2947   *c.1196-1538*
Former hermitage of St Godric, became PC (BM) dep. Durham, ruled by distinguished monks
from mother house and used as kind of 'convalescent home'. Most important ruined monastic
remains in county. Priory enclosed hermitage chapel. Misericords in St Cuthbert's Darlington
may be related. (21, 31, 36, 52, 90, 101, 121, 143, 150, 170, 186)   DE : B-

FLANESFORD, Herefordshire   5897   *1346-1536*
P (AC), intended large f. blighted by Black Death. Remains only of ruined frater, unusually
situated on first floor.   AM : E

FLAXLEY, Gloucestershire   6915   *1151?-1537*
A (CM), col. Bordesley, Worcestershire. Poorly endowed, never expanded. Ground floor of west
range substantially survives in later mansion, other remains (including church) under garden.
(4, 73)   § : E +

FLITCHAM, Norfolk   7226   *c.1217-1538*
P (AC), dep. Walsingham. 'Some featureless masonry remains in house called "Flitcham
Abbey"' (Pevsner).   § : E

FLIXTON, Suffolk   5195   *1258-1537*
P (AN). Wall with arch attached to succeeding house. (15)   § : E

FOLKESTONE, Kent   2336   1095-1535
ap of Lonlay (BM), serving castle. Moved outside in 1137, became independent P (BM) c.1400.
Half-ruined church almost entirely rebuilt C19 but some remains include presumed relics of St
Eanswythe (AS abbess), benefactor's tomb with monk 'weepers', fine C13 sanctuary and tower.
           + : D

FORDE, Dorset   3505   *1141-1539*
A (CM), dep. Waverley, moved from Brightley after stay of five years. Flourished and colonised
Bindon and Dunkeswell. Church entirely destroyed; some domestic quarters survive in C17
mansion including chapter-house, frater, dorter, kitchen. (34, 60, 120, 121, 153, 184, 190)   § : E +

FORDINGBRIDGE, Hampshire   1413   *-1271-1546+*
H of St John Baptist (for poor, later poor travellers), became dep. St Cross Winchester 1445.
           § : E

FOUNTAINS, Yorkshire West Riding   2768   *1132-1539*
A (CM) f. BM from St Mary's York seeking more austere rule, regarded as col. of Clairvaux.
Perhaps greatest Cistercian house in Britain. Seven colonies (1138 — 1150), involving departure
of nearly 100 monks. Community (up to Black Death) normally consisted of 30-40 monks and
200 conversi. Dependent extern hospital (f. Richard I for poor travellers). The best preserved of
all abbey ruins in England. 'There is no other place in the country in which the mind can so
readily evoke the picture of C13 monastic life, and the eye a picture of the vast extent and yet the
crispness and freshness of Cistercian architecture in the wild North Country forests' (Pevsner).
(1, 6, 8, 16, 18, 25, 26, 28, 31, 32, 34, 36, 40, 47, 52, 53, 56, 60, 61, 63, 67, 69, 70, 73, 75, 79, 80, 82, 83,
86, 87, 92, 98, 104, 109, 112, 115, 117, 118, 120, 121, 124, 125, 132, 133, 136, 137, 141, 143, 144, 145,
153, 154, 157, 167, 168, 170, 173, 175, 177, 181, 183, 184, 190, 191, 192)   DE : A

FREISTON, Lincolnshire   3743   *1114 + - 1539*
P (BM), dep. Crowland. No domestic remains but good deal of priory church in restored
Anglican building. (20, 124)   + : D +

FRIARSIDE, Durham   1754   -1312-C15?
Possible H for poor travellers. Roofless ruin of C14 chapel survives.   § : E +

FRITHELSTOCK, Devon   4619   *c.1220-1536*
P (AC). Extensive ruins of church. Church farm incorporates prior's house.   AM : C-

FURNESS, Lancashire   2271   *1127-1537*
A (CM), col. Savignac, after brief stay in Tulketh. Became one of largest Cistercian houses with
nine daughters, dependencies included school for children of tenants and H, almshouse. Large
precinct of 70 acres contain 'ruins remarkable for extent, beauty of architecture and
idiosyncracies of plan' including remains of church, largest dorter in England, well-preserved
extern chapel, gatehouse incorporated in hotel. (1, 28, 31, 36, 37, 40, 50, 59, 70, 75, 83, 85, 103, 112,
119, 124, 127, 141, 153, 154, 158, 181, 184, 193)   AM/DE : B

GARENDON, Leicestershire   4919   *1133-1536*
A (CM), col. Waverley? Poor and did not develop. Only remains seem to be a few stones in a
wall.   § : E

GARWAY, Herefordshire   4522   *c.1186-1308 +*
Commandery (KT), most important house on Welsh border. After d. tr. to KH and continued as
H and preceptory. No conventual remains (apart from dovecote ?) but interesting remnants of
church, partly in Anglican use. (106, 177)   + : C-

GLASTONBURY, Somerset   4938   *C6?; 943-1539*
i. Early Ce f., ref. c.705 and again in 943 as A (BM) with dependencies at Bassaleg, Lamanna and
in Ireland. HH in town and Curry Rivel. Perhaps most famous abbey in Britain occupying
legend-filled site of immemorial antiquity. Its associations and traditions made it one of the most
revered and richest monasteries in England. Remains of transept of abbey church, plan in grass;
ruins of Lady Chapel; little left of very large cloister but fine kitchen, fragment of almonry, more
of gatehouse, tower of pilgrims' chapel, courthouse (Tribunal) and hospice ('George'). (1, 16, 19,
21, 33, 35, 49, 53, 58, 66, 73, 98, 103, 104, 107, 112, 120, 136, 141, 159, 167, 171)   AM : B—
ii. Of its two HH, St John Baptist for poor sick seems to have been nearly as old as abbey, rebuilt
1246 and ref. C16 as almshouse for women.   +/§ : C

GLOUCESTER, Gloucestershire   8318   *c.681; -1017-1540*
i. First f. DM, ref. 82⁸ for secular canons and again 1017 as A (BM), ref. 1058 after fire and
became large and prosperous with dependencies at Cardigan, Ewenny, Ewyas Harold, Hereford,
Kilpeck, Leonard Stanley, Llanbadarn Fawr, with school and three HH. Gutted but magnificent
church largely survives as Anglican cathedral; remains of cloister and some surrounding
buildings: vestry, library, chapter-house, undercroft, misericord. Bishop's palace preserves some
of abbot's lodging, deanery some of prior's. Also remains of outer parlour, gates, almonry, site
of cemetery. Completeness of monastic remains inferior only to Durham and Ely. (7, 19, 20, 21,
26, 28, 29, 33, 36, 37, 42, 49, 60, 70, 83, 84, 86, 98, 104, 109, 112, 120, 126, 147, 152, 158, 168, 169, 170,
182, 183, 184, 186, 189)   +/§ : A—
ii. One of three HH survives in part: St Margaret f. c.1150, for lepers later almshouse.   §
iii. AS f. of secular canons became P (AC) in 1153, ruins of aisle.   AM : C—
iv. P (DF) in Oxford visitation, some conventual buildings converted into factory (-1241-1538).
     AM : E +
v. Large house (FFC) in Bristol custody (-1230-1538). Remains of nave and aisles. (77)   AM : E
vi. Remains of Llanthony II (q.v.), gatehouse and ruined barn (AC).   § : E

GODSFIELD, Hampshire   6337   *-1171-1355*
Early preceptory (KH) which moved to Baddesley before 1355, reducing Godsfield to 'camera'.
Chapel with attached presbytery near Old Alresford. (106)   AM : C—

GODSTOW, Oxfordshire   4810   *1133-1539*
A (BN), with associated community of men until late C13. Fragmentary remains only of precinct
wall, chapel of abbess' lodging. Approach bridges near Wolvercote. (64)   AM : E

GORING, Oxfordshire   6080   *c.1120-1536*
f. as small P (AN) which expanded greatly at end of C13. Much of nuns' church survives in Anglican use. (14, 15, 124)   + : D

GRACE DIEU, Leicestershire   4122   *c.1239-1538*
Large P (AN) with attached H for poor. Account-book survives, see Gasquet, *English Monastic Life* (1904), pp. 158-176. Confused ruins requiring excavation and preservation. (15, 64, 157, 192, 193)   AM : E +

GREAT BRICETT, Suffolk   0350   *c.1115-1444?*
ap, dep. Nobilia, Limoges (AC), d. and endowments tr. to King's College, Cambridge.
Fragments of domestic quarters in farmhouse adjoining church which is nave of canons' church.
AM/ + : C—

GREAT MALVERN, Worcestershire   7845   *c.1085-1540*
P (BM), became dep. of Westminster after 1090, maintained large associated H for poor, other dependencies at Alvecote, Barton, Colwall, Llandovery. Only gatehouse survives of monastic buildings; church saved by purchase for town and retains some mediaeval furnishings.
(20, 23, 48, 60, 84, 102, 119, 133, 143, 144, 178, 180)   + /§ : C

GUISBOROUGH, Yorkshire North Riding   6115   *1119-1540*
Large P (AC) whose dependencies included Lowcross H, for lepers, then sick. Fragment of church, dovecote and gatehouse. Parish church preserves Brus cenotaph from priory.
(49, 86, 144)   DE : D

GUYZANCE, Northumberland   2103   *c.1147-1500*
Small P (PN), apparently under control of abbot of Alnwick. Never wealthy and became extinct before C16. Ruins of nuns' chapel. (141)   AM : D—

HACKNESS, Yorkshire East Riding   9690   *-680; -970; c.1095-1539*
AS nunnery, perhaps later DM, d. Danes c.870. Ref. c of Whitby (BM) after Norman Conquest.
AS features in church and memorial cross to abbess; stalls from later Benedictine use. (32)
+ : C =

HADLEIGH, Suffolk   0242   *1497-*
11, almshouse, rebuilt C15 and chapel survives in Pykenham almshouses.   + : D—

HAILES, Gloucestershire   0530   *1246-1539*
A (CM), col. Beaulieu. Popular pilgrimage centre and home of philosopher Alexander of Hailes.
Fragments in situ and museum witness to departed glory. Outline of unusual Cistercian church, unfortunately prettified with ornamental trees, site of shrine of Precious Blood. Distinguishable remains of cloister ranges. (27, 34, 40, 59, 113, 142, 152, 174, 181)   NT : C—

HALESOWEN, Worcestershire   9683   *1215; 1218-1538*
Small P (PC) col. Welbeck, became A in 1218 with dependency at Dodford. Fragments mixed up with manor farm include remains of church, cloister, frater, abbot's lodging or guest-house (with monuments). Some stalls may survive in St Matthew's, Walsall. (142)   AM : E

HAMBLE, Hampshire   4806   *-1228-1391*
ap, dep. Tiron, at suppression endowments tr. Winchester College. Priory church substantially survives in Anglican use. (180)   + : D +

HARBLEDOWN, Kent   1358   *c.1084-c.1550?*
Probably first H for lepers in England. At end of C14, with decline of leprosy became H for poor. Very large house in C16. Most of chapel survives with some original decoration and furnishing (including four mazers). (76, 94, 96, 111)   + : D +

HARDHAM, Sussex   0317   *1248-1534*
Small and poor P (AC). Remains of frater (murals survived into C20), fine chapter-house, one misericord in St Botolph's. Unexcavated.   AM : E +

HARTLAND, Devon   2624   *-1066; c.1165-1539*
Pre-conquest f. secular canons, became A (AC) mid C12. Little above ground except masonry of abbot's lodging converted to C16 mansion.   § : E—

HATFIELD BROADOAK, Essex 5516 *c.1135-1536*
ap, dep. St Melaine, Rennes; became independent denizen P (BM) in 1254. Nave of Benedictine
church survives in Anglican use. (20, 124) + : D

HATFIELD PEVEREL, Essex 7911 *1100+ - 1536*
College of secular priests (f. William II) converted into P (BM), dep. St Albans t. Henry I. Part
of nave of priory church survives in Anglican use. (20, 52, 124) + : D

HAUGHMOND, Shropshire 5517 *c.1130-1539*
P (AC) almost immediately became A, large house with dependencies at Ranton, HH at
Oswestry, Whitchurch. Very unusual plan with fragments including foundations of church,
chapter-house, frater, dorter, kitchens, farmery, abbot's lodging. (4, 5, 14, 37, 70, 109, 133, 142,
153, 169) DE : C—

HEALAUGH PARK Yorkshire West Riding 4947 *-1180; 1218-1535*
Original f. was group hermitage which may have become formally associated. Ref. 1218 as P
(AC) with dependent hospital in Yarm. Fragmentary remains of domestic buildings scattered
among three farms. § : E

HELSTON, Cornwall 6527 *C13?-1537?*
The Blue Anchor Inn is claimed to originate in monastic hospice. § : D

HEREFORD, Herefordshire 5040 *-1246-1538*
i. Large house (DF) in Oxford visitation. Remains of west range and uniquely surviving
preaching cross. (146) AM : E
ii. Site of house (FFO) of Greyfriars above Bridge Street. AM : E
iii. Of nine mediaeval hospitals, remains of two: St Giles, for lepers and poor, f. 1150+
administered by Hospitallers of Dinmore (St Owen Street). § : E
St John's (f. 1221 +) From 1340+ also served by KH, for poor men, ref. C17 as Coningsby's.
Interesting museum related to KH. § : E +

HEXHAM, Northumberland 9364 *1113?-1537*
AS f. of cathedral with secular canons, ref. as large P (AC), survived frequent destruction by
Scots and fierce resistance to Henrician suppression seems to have kindled Pilgrimage of Grace
after which many canons were executed. Dependency at Ovingham and H in town. Crypt of AS
church survives and a good deal of Austin priory: magnificent night stairs, remains of rood-
screen, stalls, lectern (probably from frater), some painting, chantries of two priors. Fragmented
conventual buildings: laver in police station, undercroft, slype, chapter-house, frater undercroft,
warming-house, gatehouse. (14, 75, 76, 109, 125, 137, 143, 146, 158) + /AM : B-

HEYNINGS, Lincolnshire 8184 *+ 1135-1539*
P (CN) with, until mid C14, PC as chaplains, and conversi (CM). There may be remains of
domestic quarters incorporated in Knaith Hall, nave of nuns' church (with fragment of
monument) survives in Anglican use. (40, 64, 142) + § : C-

HICKLING, Norfolk 4124 *1185-1536*
P (AC) f. with guidance from St Osyths. Fragments of cloister survive at priory farm. § : E

HIGHAM, Kent 7174 *1148-1522*
ap (BN), dep. St Sulpice, Rennes. Became denizen P after 1227 but remained poor and very
small. Suppressed by Wolsey and endowments tr. St John's College, Cambridge. Abbey farm
occupies site. Much modified parish church in Anglican use may have been extern provision. (20)
  + ?/§:E

HURLEY, Berkshire 8283 *-1087-1536*
P (BM), dep. Westminster. Nave of church survives in Anglican use; fragment of frater in house,
together with dovecote and barn. (20, 124) AM + /§ : C-

ILFORD, Essex 4586 *c.1140-*
H, for lepers later almshouse. Remains of chapel survive in modern H. + : D

INGHAM, Norfolk 3825 *1360-1536*
P (TF) for whose accommodation existing church was enlarged. This arrangement constitutes a
rare survival. Sacrist's checker above south porch, traces only of other domestic buildings.
(157, 184) + /§ : C

IVYCHURCH, Wiltshire 0227 *t. Henry II - 1536*
P (AC) which flourished until devastated by Black Death. Fragments only: some in situ, some in
farmhouse and its garden. § : E

IPSWICH, Suffolk 1744 *1263-1538*
i. Large P (DF) in Cambridge visitation. Only part of wall survives (School Street). AM : E-
ii. P (AC) f. c.1177-1538. Site occupied by Christchurch Mansion,.now museum which preserves
fragments. § : E +
iii. Friary (FFC) f. -1236-1536?. Short piece of wall in garden of 8 Friars Road. (112) § : E
iv. Gateway in College Street is remaining fragment of Wolsey's College of St Mary to endow
which he obtained permission to d. number of small religious houses. § : E

ISLEHAM, Cambridgeshire 6474 *C11-1254*
ac, dep. St Jacut-de-la-Mer, abandoned and tr. to sister ac at Linton in 1254. Endowments of
both tr. Pembroke College, Cambridge 1414 or earlier. Small conventual chapel survives near
parish church. DE + : D-

IVYCHURCH, Wiltshire 0227 *t. Henry II - 1536*
P (AC) which flourished until devastated by Black Death. Fragments only: some in situ, some in
farmhouse and its garden. § : E

JARROW, Durham 3265 *681; 1074-1536*
Originally AS f. A (BM) from Monkwearmouth. Became dependent P of Durham in 1083.
Remains of most venerable monastery in kingdom, now surrounded by docks: chancel of church,
tower with abbot Ceolfrid's inscription, badge of prior Castell, 'Bede's chair', two walls of C11
monastery. (19,21,66,101,113) AM/ + : C

JERVAULX, Yorkshire North Riding 1785 *1156-1537*
A (CM), col. Byland after having been at Fors for about five years. Last abbot hanged and
buildings demolished by gunpowder. Little remains of church (described by contemporary as
'one of fairest churches') but good deal of cloister and surrounding buildings: misericord,
abbot's lodging with chapel, farmery of unusual design. A little neglected. (8, 33, 35, 38, 40, 53,
69, 70, 102, 104, 119, 133, 141, 142, 150, 153, 154, 158, 170, 174, 182) AM/§ : C-

KENILWORTH, Warwickshire 2872 *c.1125-1539*
P (AC), became one of larger houses and elevated to A after 1438. Dependencies at Brooke,
Calwich, Stone. Anglican parish church, probably built by canons c. 1280 to relieve parochial use
of priory church, contains fragments including tiles. Site somewhat neglected, extensive but not
very informative ruins probably included detached octagonal campanile, remains of gatehouse,
guest-house. One stall from canons' church may survive in St Mary's, Halford. AM : C-

KERSEY, Suffolk 0044 *c.1218-1443*
Original f. was H, for sick, but soon became P (AC) with continuing associated H ? Greatly
impoverished in 1347 and incapable of supporting establishment, d 1443 and endowments tr. to
King's College, Cambridge. Major fragment of church survives, other remains incorporated in
succeeding secular buildings. AM § : D-

KEYNSHAM, Somerset 6568 *c.1170-1539*
A (AC), large, well-endowed house Scant remains: part of pier of church in situ, fragments in
archway of Keynsham House. § : E-

KINGS LANGLEY, Hertfordshire 0702 *-1308-1538*
Very large P (DF), Incorporating school for friars going on to university. Dependent nunnery
(DN) at Dartford. One room of priory incorporated in private school. Tomb of Edmund Langley
tr. to (Anglican) parish church. § : E

KINGS LYNN, Norfolk 6220 *1100-1539*
i. P (BM), dep. Norwich, used as convalescent home for invalid monks and helped support H,
for sick, in town. Church (St Margaret's) survives in Anglican use, meagre conventual remains in
Priory Lane. (20,31) +/§ : C
ii. Friary (FFC) in Cambridge custody. Scant remains at Greyfriars in St James Street. (5, 77, 153)
AM : D
iii. P (CF). Only remains: Gateway in Bridge Street. (29) AM : E
iv. Friary (AF). Site occupied by St Augustine's (private house) in Chapel Street, an original
archway in garden wall. § : E-
v. Of seven mediaeval HH, remains only of St Mary Magdalene, for lepers then sick travellers,
f. 1145. § : D
vi. Redmount chapel (f. 1485) provided mass and shelter for Walsingham pilgrims. (35,97,136)
+ : C

215

KINGSWOOD, Gloucestershire   7491   *1139; 1150-1538*
A (CM) with complex early history but ultimately col. Tintern. Only C16 gatehouse survives (one of last monastic erections before Reformation), together with fragments of enclosure wall.
(16, 35, 40, 83)
         § : E +

KINGTON ST MICHAEL, Wiltshire   9077   *-1155-1536*
Small P (BN). Church completely destroyed. Fragments of cloister and guest-house in priory farm.
         § : E

KIRKBY BELLARS, Leicestershire   7117   *1315; 1359-1536*
Original f. of college of secular priests changed into P (AC). No remains of domestic buildings, church substantially survives in Anglican use. (76)
         + : D

KIRKHAM, Yorkshire East Riding   7365   *c.1122-1539*
P (AC), one of larger houses of order. Emerged from financial difficulties of C14 into new flourishing state. Dependencies at Carham, Bolton. H for sick. Fragments of church, cloister with chapter-house, dorter, frater (with impressive laver), kitchen, superior's lodging and guest-house. Magnificent gatehouse. (4, 8, 48, 61, 75, 76, 83, 109, 121, 124, 142, 143, 168, 170)   DE : C-

KIRKLEES, Yorkshire West Riding   2022   *C12-1539*
Always small and poor P (CN). Remains largely obliterated by grandiose hall and its ancillary buildings. (121)
         § : E

KIRKSTALL, Yorkshire West Riding   2635   *1152-1540*
A (CM), col. Fountains after five years intermediate sojourn at Barnoldswick. Joined by some hermits already on site. Highest remaining buildings of pre-Reformation Cistercian house, including church, cloister with parlour and chapter-house. Rather less of farmery, frater, abbot's lodging, large guest-house and other ancillary buildings. Gatehouse incorporated in neighbouring museum. (1, 14, 17, 33, 37, 40, 50, 60, 79, 87, 91, 98, 101, 104, 108, 112, 118, 119, 124, 125, 133, 142, 146, 153, 154, 157, 167, 168, 169, 171, 181, 182, 184, 190, 192)   AM : B-

KIRKSTEAD, Lincolnshire   1762   *1187-1537*
A (CM), col. Fountains, f. 1139 moved to present better site in 1187. Last abbot and several monks executed. Former chapel by gate in Anglican use. Only scattered fragments of monastic church and conventual buildings. Abbey Lodge Inn may incorporate monastic outbuilding.
(28, 85, 101)
         AM : D +

KNARESBOROUGH, Yorkshire West Riding   3557   *c.1252-1538*
A house (TF) was f. near famous hermitage of St Robert but nothing survives except street-name and chapel of Our Lady of the Crag with more than life-size effigy of St Robert. (91, 184)   § : E

LACOCK, Wiltshire   9168   *1232-1538*
A (AN), wealthy and aristocratic house, virtuously observant up to their ejection when abbey was immediately converted into palatial mansion occupying twice residential space of convent. Unrequired portions, including church, totally destroyed but a good deal of claustral buildings incorporated, leaving more remains of domestic buildings of nunnery than elsewhere in England.
(14, 15, 37, 53, 76, 104)
         NT/ AM/§ : C

LANCASTER, Lancashire   4761   *-1428-C15*
ap (BM), suppressed C15 and endowments tr. Syon A. Substantial remains of church in Anglican use, nothing of conventual buildings. Some stalls may be survivors of priory; alternatively, they may have come from Cockersand in 1537. (19)
         + : E +

LANERCOST, Cumberland   5563   *c.1165-1537*
P (AC), suffering much from Scottish depradations. Involved in Pilgrimage of Grace and Henry instructed his creature Norfolk 'without pitie or circumstance to cause all the canons that be in anywise faultie to be hanged without further delaye.' Substantial remains of church in Anglican use, west range of cloister converted to house, prior's lodging (pele tower), fragment of gatehouse, beautiful bridge. (5, 14, 75, 124, 137, 142, 144)
         + /DE : C +

LANGLEY, Norfolk   3500   *1195-1536*
A (PC), col. Alnwick with extensive parochial responsibilities. Neglected and unexcavated site with substantial remains of west range (now barn), little of chapter-house, less of church, farmery and stables?
         AM : E

LANIVET, Cornwall   0364   *1411-1535 +*
H, for lepers later sick, lost in re-used building. Anglican parish church has a capital which may have come from Bodmin priory.
         § : E

LAPLEY, Staffordshire   8713   *1061-1414*
ap (BM), dep. St Remi, Rheims. In 1414 endowments tr. Tong College. Substantial remains of priory church in Anglican use. No trace of domestic buildings unless there is cannibalised masonry in Park House. (20, 124)   + : D +

LATHOM, Lancashire   4508   *1500-*
H, almshouse. Restored chapel and almshouse survive.   + : D-

LASTINGHAM, Yorkshire North Riding   7290   *660; 1078-1086-*
AS A (BM), associated with St Chad etc. Seems to have been revived for short time in later C11 when a group of monks fled from Whitby before moving to York. Energetic building produced unforgettable crypt (with fragments of earlier work) and, above ground, apsidal chapel. No domestic remains. (50)   + : D +

LATTON, Essex   4709   *-1200-1534*
Small P (AC), abandoned in 1534 when, for a long time, it had only contained a single canon. Part of church survives in barn.   AM : E

LAUNCESTON, Cornwall   3384   *1127-1538*
P (AC) replacing college of secular priests in castle. One of larger English houses of order. Scattered and scanty remains: behind St Thomas' church and re-used doorway in White Hart hotel.   § : E

LAUNDE, Leicestershire   7904   *1119-1538*
Large P (AC), devastated by Black Death but recovered. Chancel of priory church survives in use as part of Thomas Cromwell's mansion.   + /§ : C-

LEDBURY, Herefordshire   7037   *1232-c.1547*
H of St Katherine, f. as almshouse but became more general almshouse for poor travellers. Old range and master's house incorporated in C19 rebuild.   + § : C-

LEEDS, Kent   8253   *-1119-1540*
Large P (AC). Revealing site but hardly anything above ground. (15)   § : E

LEIGHS, Essex   7317   *-1200-1536*
P (AC). Largely destroyed for Lord Rich's mansion but fragments of church and excavations.
        § : E

LEICESTER, Leicestershire   3904   *1143-1538*
i. Large and wealthy A (AC), one of greatest of order in England, scene of Wolsey's death. Rather pitiful remnants: enclosure wall, fragments, unreliable lay-out on lawn, small items in museum. (6, 9, 141, 180)   § : E
ii. Of some half dozen HH there are remains (chapel, hall) of St Mary's f. 1330 for poor and sick which, 25 years later was turned into a great college (Newark), with almshouse with a very large attached hospital for sick. (96)   + § : C
iii. Modern P (DF) in New Walk. (1777; 1825-)   + § : (A)

LEISTON, Suffolk   4464   *1183-1537*
A (PC), col. Welbeck. So successful that it colonised Langdon in 1189. Continual increasing numbers and resources led to building new convent (1363) on site one mile west and old abbey became pc (with anchorage). Part of church incorporated in succeeding house, recognisable remains of cloister. Remains will become more comprehensible following DE acquisition. (142)
        AM/DE : E +

LEOMINSTER, Herefordshire   4959   *c.666; 1123 + - 1539*
Ce f. (DM), d. Danes and replaced by collegiate church, later tr. to nunnery (BN), d. 1046. After 1123 became pc (BM), dep. Reading. Substantial remains of priory church in Anglican use (preserves mediaeval tiles, mural, altar plate). Fragments of conventual buildings apart from 'Priory House' (rere-dorter ?). (20, 114, 133, 134, 142)   + /§ : C

LEONARD STANLEY, Gloucestershire   8003   *c.1125; 1146-1538*
f. P (AC), tr. to pc (BM), dep. Gloucester in 1146. Priory church substantially survives in Anglican use; remains of conventual buildings include (extern) chapel used as farm building, barn with dovecote, fishpond.   AM/ + : C

LESNES, Kent   4977   *1128-1525*
A (AC), neither wealthy nor unusually large in spite of status. Dissolved by Wolsey and endowments tr. to his Oxford College. Exposed foundations show plan (apart from farmery).
        AM : E +

LETHERINGHAM, Suffolk 2757 *-1200-1537*
Small P (AC), dep. Ipswich. Fragment of nave of priory church incorporated in Anglican parish church. Scattered masonry in churchyard wall, gatehouse. Site of domestic buildings recently excavated. (14, 124) DE + /§ : C

LEWES, Sussex 4110 *c.1080-1537*
i. ap (BMC), first in Britain, col. Cluny. Quickly flourished, became denizen in 1351. Dependencies: Castle Acre, Clifford, Heacham, Monks Horton, Monkton Farleigh, Prittlewell, Stansgate. Two HH in Lewes, almshouse and for the poor. Not much remains of priory and its 450ft long church: fragment of tower, undercrofts and other remnants of claustral buildings, scattered bits of masonry (including some in museum and chimney-pieces in Southover Grange), ruined gatehouse. Anglican church of St John Baptist may have been earlier guest-house. (43, 86, 142, 154, 174) AM : E +
ii. Large friary (FFC) has left street name and archway. § : E

LICHFIELD, Staffordshire 4553 *c.1237-1538*
i. Smaller friary (FFC) in custody of Worcester. Parts of precinct wall along St John's Street, fragment of domestic buildings in 'The Friary', nothing of church. (77) §AM : E
ii. Of several HH, remains of St John Baptist almshouse f. -1208: some original walls, part of chapel and C15 ref. § : C-

LILLESHALL, Shropshire 7315 *c.1143; c.1148-1538*
Small house (AC, originally Arrousian) with A status, col. Dorchester, after short stay at the Lizard and then at Donnington Wood (c.1144). Became prosperous f. with dependencies at Alderbury and Bridgnorth H for poor. Impressive ruins of church and conventual buildings, in spite of Reformation and Civil War. Some stalls may survive in Wolverhampton parish church (Anglican). (1, 5, 101, 113, 153, 160, 175) DE : B-

LIMEBROOK, Herefordshire 3770 *c.1189-1539*
Small P (AN). Only remains are ruins of single (C13?) building. AM : E

LINCOLN, Lincolnshire 9771 *-1150-1539*
i. PC (BM), dep. St Mary's York, looking after estates in vicinity. Ruins (in Monks Road) of church and other buildings. AM : C-
ii. Large house (FFC) in York custody, remains in museum (undercroft of church?). (142) 1230-1539. AM : E +
iii. Of some half dozen HH: remains of St Giles, f. c.1275, for poor, tr. c.1280 for sick priests. In Lamb Gardens, some fragments incorporated in church. § : E

LINDISFARNE, Northumberland 1343 *635; 1082-1537*
Name of Holy Island derived from its use as missionary base by Ce monks. Became P (BM), dep. Durham, later fortified, C14 against Scots. Housed visitors (convalescents ?) from Durham as well as small permanent community. Impressive ruins of church, fragments of claustral buildings, brewhouse, bakehouse, curia with gatehouse and barbican. (9, 20, 66, 89, 121, 124, 142, 144) DE : C

LITTLE COGGESHALL *see Coggeshall*

LITTLE DUNMOW, Essex 6521 *1106-1536*
P (AC). Lady Chapel of priory church survives in Anglican use. 'Flitch Chair' is a botch of part of C13 stall. Note Fitzwalter monument (benefactor). (14) + : D

LITTLE MALVERN, Worcestershire 7741 *1171-c.1537*
P (BM), dep. Worcester. Truncated remains of priory church survive in Anglican use. Prior's hall incorporated in 'court' together with cannibalised masonry from priory. (20) + : C-

LITTLE WYMONDLEY, Hertfordshire 2126 *-1218-1537*
Original f. H for sick which seems to have become P (AC) with attached H. A few arches inside farmhouse and barn. Some of quire-stalls said to be in Stevenage (Anglican) parish church. AM : E

LITTLE MAPLESTEAD, Essex 8223 *-1186-1540*
Preceptory (KH). Rare example of round nave survives heavy C19 restoration. No other remains. (106) + : D +

LODERS, Dorset 4994 *c.1106-1414*
Larger ap, dep. Montebourg (BM), tr. to endowments of Syon. Church substantially survives in Anglican use, walls of Loders Court may reproduce walls of priory buildings. + : D

LONDON   *see also Bermondsey, Ealing, Southwark, Westminster*
i. Charterhouse (Finsbury), 1371-1539. Intended (1348) as secular college but f. as P (C). Grown
to large Carthusian community by C16 of whom one third were martyred for their resistance to
Henry VIII. Survivors returned to Sheen at Marian Restoration. Expelled by Elizabeth, they f. a
house in Belgium d. French Revolution. Great Cloister still recognisable in Medical College. (31)
                                                                                          § : E
ii. Minories. Large A (FN) of which nothing survives above ground except name (cf. Minching
Lane — 'Mynechene' = (Benedictine) nuns). (77, 119)   § : E-
iii. St Bartholomews (Smithfield), f. 1123-1539. Large and wealthy P (AC) with dependent H for
sick which became independent community under Augustinian rule in C13. Chancel survives in
Anglican use, nave entrance (gateway), restored cloister. (14, 23, 122, 133)   + /§ : C-
iv. St John's (Clerkenwell), f. c.1144-1540. Large house (KH) and English HQ of order. No
remains except gatehouse and crypt of church with magnificent monument to high official of
KH. (104)   AM + : D
v. St Helen's (Bishopsgate) f. -1216-1538. Large P (BN). Church substantially survives in
Anglican use. (20, 64, 128)   + : D
vi. Temple. f. c.1128; 1308-1540. Large house (KT) and English HQ. 'Old Temple' was in
Chancery Lane, moving to 'New Temple' in 1184. After d., ref. by KH in 1324. Remains of
original porch, nave and chancel have survived new use and heavy restoration. (104, 176) + : D +
vii. Of more than 20 mediaeval hospitals, there are remains of one: Elsing Spital for sick
(St Mary without Cripplegate) f. 1331 on site of decayed nunnery with accommodation for 100
patient i. In 1340 it was placed under AC and suppressed as lesser monastery in 1536. Tower-
porch of chapel survives opposite St Alphege's Garden (Barbican). (15)   § : D-
viii. A number of modern houses (including Anglican religious) comprehend P (AF) in Fulham
Palace Road; P (BM of Olivetan Congregation, Bramley Road, N14), friaries: DF in
Southampton Road, NW5; FF in E7 and SE15; CF in Kensington Church Street; CN in
St C arles Square.

LOUTH PARK, Lincolnshire   3287   *1139-1536*
A (CM) col. Fountains, after two years in earlier site at Haverholme. Fragments of walls
belonging to chapels 'picturesque in a certain light'. (47, 127)   AM : E

LUDLOW, Shropshire   5175   *1486-*
Of four mediaeval HH, remains of St John Evangelist (large almshouse), maintained by a college
of the Palmers Guild. College was west of St Lawrence church which contained their chapel. (96)
                                                                                      + § : E +

LYME REGIS, Dorset   3492   *-1336-?*
H (first for lepers, later sick), Scant remains incorporated in house.   § : E

LYMINSTER, Sussex   0204   *c.1082-c.1414*
P (BN), dep. Almenèches, reduced by French wars and suppressed as ap. Revenues tr. Eton
College. Church, with substantial Saxon masonry, survives in Anglican use. (20)   + : D +

LYNN   *see Kings Lynn*

MAIDSTONE, Kent   7656   *1244-1547*
H almshouse, incorporated in later college but continued (1395 +). Chapel unsatisfactorily
incorporated into (Anglican) St Peter's.   + : D

MALDON, Essex   8506   *c.1164-1536*
H (first for lepers, later sick), dependency of Bicknacre P, later (1481 +) on Beeleigh A. Ruins of
large chapel (part of chancel and transepts).   AM : D-

MALLING, Kent   6857   *c.1090-1538: 1916-*
Large A (BN), much reduced by Black Death. Remains much modified by intruded C18 house.
Anglican nuns occupied site in 1916 and built new church and cloisters. Ewell Monastery houses
another Anglican community of enclosed nuns.   AM/§ : (C)

MALMESBURY, Wiltshire   8787   *C7; c.965-1539*
i. At beginning of C7 allegedly a nunnery (Ce), replaced by monks (Ce?) which became secular
college c.950, tr. A (BM) c.965, strengthened and codified in C11. Dependency at Pilton.
Fragments of cloister, gatehouse; other remains incorporated in abbey house (rere-dorter) and
Bell Hotel (guest-house). Substantial gutted fragment of abbey church (about half original
minster), preserved in Anglican use, retains some original architectural magnificence, especially
south porch. (1, 19, 20, 56, 60, 109, 113, 120, 124, 140, 146, 152)   AM/ + : C
ii. Of three mediaeval HH, remains of St John Baptist for poor?   § : E

MALTON, Yorkshire North Riding   7871   *c.1150-1539*
i. P (GC) f. as 'retreat house' for canons. Supported HH in town, Broughton, Norton. Little remains of domestic buildings: undercroft beneath abbey house. Gutted, decayed and reduced church (with mediaeval quire-stalls, inscription to prior) survives in Anglican use. (84)
AM/ + : C-
ii. Dependent H for poor travellers of St Mary Magdalene. Undercroft beneath Cross Keys. § : E

MALVERN   *see Great Malvern*

MAPLESTEAD   *see Little Maplestead*

MARHAM, Norfolk   7110   *-1249-1536*
Rare A (CN), poor and, in spite of status, remained small. Remnants: south wall of nave, substantial fragment of west range with outer parlour. (40)
AM : B-

MARRICK, Yorkshire North Riding   0798   *c.1155-1540*
Large P (CN, possibly BN) with dependent H at Rerecross. Some remains cannibalised by C19 church, ruins of chapel in situ, incorporated in new secular building. (64, 133)   AM : E

MARTON, Yorkshire North Riding   5867   *t. Stephen - 1536*
f. c.1154 (DM — canons and nuns). Nuns tr. to separate f. at Moxby -1167 and Marton became P (AC). Survived d. Scots in 1322. Some fragments built into farmhouse ('Marton Abbey'), others in Anglican parish church.   AM : E

MATTERSEY, Nottinghamshire   6899   *c.1185-1538*
Small P (GC) which did not recover from disastrous fire of 1279. Rare remains of Gilbertine house include fragments of original church, masonry of later one (and two fine alabasters) in Anglican church; ruins of part of cloister including frater. (27, 62, 84)   DE : C-

MAXSTOKE, Warwickshire   2368   *1331; 1337-1536*
f. as college of secular priests, became P (AC) in 1337. Remains include: ruined crossing tower of church, wall of farmery, two gatehouses, precinct wall. Modified extern chapel may survive in Anglican parish church. (150)   AM : C-

MEARE, Somerset   4541   *C15?-*
Almost complete remains of 'fish house' belonging to nearby Glastonbury which was almost an island in Middle Ages. It seems to have been equivalent of 'grange', used by abbey's fishermen. (73)   AM : D

MEAUX, Yorkshire East Riding   0939   *1151-1539*
A (CM), col. Fountains. Sparse remains of great house collected into converted cottage once one of ancillary buildings. (1, 28, 59, 67, 70, 73, 84, 102, 149, 164, 177)   AM : E

MENDHAM, Suffolk   2783   *-1155-1537*
ap. dep. Castle Acre, enlarged and became denizen P (BMC) in later C14. Knowles indicates 'remains of importance', but I am unable to locate any unless they survive in 'Mendham Hall'. (43)   § : E ?

MEREVALE, Warwickshire   2897   *1148-1538*
A (CM) col. Bordesley. No remains of abbey church, fragments of domestic buildings in and around farm. Extern chapel (probably with some glass from abbey) may survive used as Anglican church. (28, 79, 169)   § : E +

MICHELHAM, Sussex   5609   *1229-1536*
P (AC), devastated by Black Death. Church utterly destroyed at Reformation, some claustral buildings distorted into secular dwelling, gatehouse survives together with barn, wide moat and approach bridge.   § : E +

MILTON ABBAS, Dorset   8001   *c.933; 964-1539*
Originally collegiate f., replaced by BM who formed large A, considerably reduced in C14. Church, truncated and clipped, in Anglican use contains interesting fragments (rare tabernacle, some quire-stalls). Ornate abbot's hall largely survives in school. (19, 20)   + /§ : C

MILTON, Kent   1255   *c.1155-1524*
H, for lepers, later almshouse, under Augustinian rule. Remains of chapel and hall incorporated in The Terrace.   AM : E

MINSTER, Cornwall   1090   *c.1088-1407*
ac, dep. St Serge, Angers. tr. to rectory early C15. No remains of claustral buildings but priory church (modified) may survive in Anglican use.   + : D

MINSTER IN SHEPPEY, Kent   9573   *-1087-1396; 1536?*
Early AS nunnery f. c.670, ruined by Danes and deserted before Conquest. Ruins seem to have
been occupied by BN in later reign of William I. Apparently ref. 1130 as P (AN), returning to
Benedictine rule by 1186 and back to Augustinian in 1396 until Henrician suppression. Some
remains of AS church and later convent church. Much altered after Reformation but fascinating
fragments survive including C12 Madonna. Only gatehouse remains of domestic buildings.
(15, 20, 124, 129)   + § : C

MINSTER IN THANET, Kent   3164   *C7+ C11; 1207-1536*
Large AS nunnery, twice d. Danes, twice ref. Deserted after 1011 and site occupied by a few
seculars. After 1207 became dep. St Augustine's Canterbury which established large grange with
chapel (Minster Court §). (86, 119, 124)
Ref. 1930s A (BN) who occupy site, including some Norman buildings.   + § : (A)

MISSENDEN, Buckinghamshire   8901   *1133-1538*
A (AC). Church utterly d.; some parts of cloister absorbed in C18 mansion.   § : E

MONK BRETTON, Yorkshire West Riding   3706   *1153+; 1280-1539*
ap (BMC), dep. Pontefract. Became P (BM) c.1280. Most of remains date from BM period.
Survived disastrous fire in 1386, remained observant house and, when expelled, took books and
continued monastic life at Worsborough in house belonging to one of community for at least 20
years. General arrangement of site discernible amid rather sparse remains. (27, 36, 61, 62, 142,
144)   DE : B-

MONKLAND, Herefordshire   4557   *t. William II - c.1414*
ac (BM) of Conches, tr. to endowments of Coventry Charterhouse in 1399 but then seems to
have returned dep. Conches until 1414 when it was granted to Windsor College. No remains of
domestic buildings; some fragments of abbey church survive Reformation and C19 rebuilding.
                                                                               + : D-

MONK SHERBORNE, Hampshire   6056   *c.1125-1414*
Large ap, dep. Cerisy-le-Foret (BM), endowments tr. first to St Julian's H for poor and
travellers, Southampton, thence to Queen's College, Oxford. Part of church survives in Anglican
use; scant other remains.   + § : C-

MONKS HORTON, Kent   1140   *1142-1536*
ap, dep. Lewes (BMC). Became independent P c.1160. Fragments of church and west range
absorbed in C20 house.   § : E

MONKS KIRBY, Warwickshire   4683   *1077-1536*
ap dep. Angers (BM) tr. to Epworth (C) in 1397. No remains of priory except church in Anglican
use which still shows conventual origin in architectural arrangements.   + : D

MONKTON FARLEIGH, Wiltshire   8065   *1125-1537*
Large ap dep. Lewes (BMC) which became independent P c.1360. Fragments of masonry (some
in shed) in and about 'manor'. On hill above are almost complete remains of 'Monks Conduit',
covering a spring from which water was piped to priory in valley below. (45)   § : E

MONKWEARMOUTH, Durham   4057   *674; 1075; 1083-1536*
AS f. (BM) revived by Normans. In 1083 its members, together with those from Jarrow, were
transferred to Durham CP and status of Jarrow was reduced from A to pc. Some remains of AS
church f. Benedict Biscop and of mediaeval alterations and additions. Fragments of sculpture
include part of abbot's throne. (19, 21, 66)   + : D+

MONTACUTE, Somerset   4916   *c.1102-1539*
Large ap dep. Cluny which became independent denizen P (BM) in 1407. Dependencies at
Holme, Kerswell, Malpas, St Carrock. No remains except gatehouse range. (43)   § : E+

MOOR HALL, Middlesex   0588   *C12-?*
Preceptory (KH) reduced to 'camera' by 1338. Scant remains incorporated in hall. (106)   AM : E

MOTTISFONT, Hampshire   3226   *1201-1536*
P (AC). Due to economic difficulties nearly dissolved in 1494 but managed to survive until
Reformation. Site, including church, converted to secular dwelling house.   NT § : B/E

MOUNT GRACE, Yorkshire North Riding   4598   *1398-1539*
P (C) f. which expanded c.1416. Best preserved Carthusian ruins in British Isles. Part of guest-
house incorporated into secular residence. (5, 8, 30, 142, 144, 153)   AM/DE : B

MOUNT ST BERNARD, Leicestershire   4519   *1835-*
A, (CM of Reform — Trappists) f. in rough moorland of Charnwood Forest which has since
blossomed under their labours. (182)   + § : (A)

MUCHELNEY, Somerset 4224 *C8; c.950-1538*
AS monastery, becoming A (BM) c.950 after d. Danes in C9. Plan discernible and some substantial remains (abbot's lodging) and extern church in Anglican use. Interesting survival of mediaeval parsonage belonging to latter. (19, 27, 62, 121, 142) DE : B-

MUCH WENLOCK, Shropshire 6200 *C7; 1080-1540*
C7 AS A (BN) d. Danes. Restored early C11 but again decayed. Ref. as ap, dep. La Charité (BMC) in 1080. Became independent denizen P in 1395. Dependencies at Church Preen, Dudley, St Helens. Considerable remains: unique upper chamber in ruined nave, chapter-house, laver, sacristy, farmery, prior's lodging, gatehouse. (37, 43, 63, 70, 101, 109, 112, 150, 153, 161, 182)
AM / DE : B

NASHDOM, Buckinghamshire 9083 *1914-*
A (Anglican BM), formerly at Caldey, in house built 1910 for Princess Dolgorouki. + § : (A)

NETLEY, Hampshire 4508 *1239-1536*
A (CM), col. Beaulieu. Seriously embarrassed financially in C14 as a result of hospitality to sailors and their depredations. Remains: ruins of church, recognisable cloister ranges (including beautiful sacristy/library) and abbot's lodging. (1, 40, 70, 142, 153, 154, 190) DE : B-

NEWARK, Surrey 9612 *t. Henry II - 1538*
P (AC). Much robbed ruin with remains of church, little else. AM : D-

NEWBURGH, Yorkshire North Riding 5774 *1145; c.1150-1539*
P (AC), col. Bridlington, first settling at Hood for about five years. Became large community with Hood as dependency. Scant remains incorporated in C17-18 mansion. § : E

NEWBURY, Berkshire 4666 *-1215-?*
Of three mediaeval HH, remains of St Bartholomew's (for poor and aged), under Augustinian rule. 'Litten chapel', truncated and misused, in Argyle Street. § : D
There is an English community of enclosed Franciscan nuns f. Brussels, 1621 tr. Taunton, before settling in Newbury. § : (A)

NEWCASTLE, Northumberland 2464 *-1239-1539*
i. Large P (DF) in York visitation. A certain amount can be pieced together in Low Friar Street including general shape of cloister. No remains of church. § : E
ii. Remains of church tower of P (AF) behind Holy Jesus Hospital, City Road. (122) § : E
iii. Scant masonry of P (CF) at 18 Forth Street. § : E
There is a modern P (DF) serving central parish. + § : (A)

NEWMINSTER, Northumberland 1985 *1138-1537*
A (CM), one of 'three daughters of a single birth' from Fountains when latter was only seven years old. Became one of largest houses in north, colonising Pipewell, Roche, Sawley and supporting HH at Allerburn, Mitford. First abbot was a former monk of Whitby who had joined exodus from York — St Robert of Newminster. Considerable fragments remain of 'strangely neglected ruins of one of most notable monastic houses in Northumberland'. (75, 85, 137)
AM / § : D?

NEWSTEAD, Lincolnshire 0005 *-1164-1538*
Small P (GC). Part of frater survives as room in Priory Farm 'with precious and beautiful reading pulpit'. (84) § : E

NEWSTEAD, Nottinghamshire 5252 *c.1163-1539*
P (AC). Substantial remains of church and monastic buildings absorbed into Byron palace. (5, 111, 122, 175) § : C-

NEWTON LONGVILLE, Buckinghamshire 8431 *c.1080-1414*
apc, dep. Longueville (BMC), never more than residence for monastic agents. Denuded remains of chapel in Anglican use. + : D

NORTHAMPTON, Northamptonshire 7561 *c.1145-1538*
i. Large A (BNC), originally at Fotheringay (c.1141). Some masonry and general shape preserved in County Record Office, formerly mansion. (21, 43) § : E
ii. 'Abington abbey', now museum, has pre-Reformation work in south range, but it was never an abbey.
iii. Of four HH, there are material remains of St John's, for poor, under Augustinian rule. Part incorporated in Catholic church (Bridge Street). + : C=
There is a post-Reformation community of nuns in Abington Street.

NORTH CREAKE, Norfolk 8538 *-1189; 1206-1506*
Original f. H for sick, becoming P (AC) in 1206. Dependent H almshouse at Gedney. Became A
in 1231. Entire community perished in epidemic of 1506 and endowments tr. Christ's College,
Cambridge. Remains of ruined church and other fragments in farm. DE : C-

NORTON, Cheshire 5581 *c.1115; 1134-1537*
P (AC), originally at Runcorn, moving to Norton in 1134 and becoming one of largest houses of
order, raised to A c.1422. Remains of west range and other fragments in house which replaced it
immediately on suppression. (31, 60, 191) AM § : E +

NORWICH, Norfolk 2308 *1094-1538*
i. CP as centre of see tr. from Thetford. Monastic buildings ready for occupation by 1101. For
previous seven years community occupied St Leonard's P which afterwards became dependency,
along with Aldeby, Hoxne, King's Lynn, Yarmouth. CP supported two large HH in Norwich
and school attached to monastery. Magnificent church, now used as Anglican cathedral, with
superb stalls, mediaeval retable, interesting reliquary arch, perhaps best cloisters in country with
fine bosses. Some remains of domestic buildings: prior's lodging converted to deanery,
gatehouse, granary. (2, 20, 31, 70, 83, 109, 111, 112, 124, 126, 127, 146, 152, 161, 165, 171, 182, 193)
 +/§ : A
ii. Priory (BN) of St Mary of Carrow (1146 — 1536). Prioress' lodging substantially survives,
together with fragments of nunnery, on neglected and private site. (64) AM : E +
iii. Large priory (DF) in Cambridge visitation (1226 — 1538), moved to site of Friars of Sack in
1307. Church transmogrified into St Andrew's Hall, a rare survival in any form.
(5, 59, 81, 152) AM/§ : C +
iv. Priory (CF) f. 1256, only remains arch in Cowgate. (7) AM : E
v. House (AF), f. c.1272 only remains arch in King Street. AM : E
vi. Mediaeval city had some sixteen HH. Remains of St Mary Magdalene's, for lepers then poor,
f. 1119 in Sprowston Road. (§:E +); St Mary in the Fields (almshouse later college), f. 1250 —
small fragments in west wing of assembly rooms; great H of St Giles f. 1246 — much remains,
including chapel (now Anglican church of St Helen), though vastly altered. (97) C +

NOSTELL, Yorkshire West Riding 3815 *c.1114-1540*
Formerly hermit settlement, formed P (AC) c.1122. One of larger houses of order with
dependencies at Bamburgh, Breedon, Hirst, Skewkirk, Woodkirk and two HH, almshouses, in
Pontefract. Only name remains apart from discrete stones in outbuildings of succeeding
mansion. (15) § : E

NOTLEY, Buckinghamshire 4427 *-1164-1539*
Large f. (AC) made A from f. Dependencies included Chetwode, Sheringham. Nothing survives
except enormous dovecote (4-5,000 boxes) and abbot's house transmogrified into secular
mansion. § : E

NUNEATON, Warwickshire 3592 *1155-1539*
Original f. belonged to order of Fontrevault P (DM) until 1424 when it became denizen P (BN).
'Mangled fragments' of church in Anglican use, scant remains of claustral buildings, brewhouse.
(20, 25, 74) + § : C-

NUN MONKTON, Yorkshire West Riding 5057 *-1147-1536*
P (BN), probably not large. Truncated church in Anglican use. (5, 20, 64, 124, 137) + : D

OAKHAM, Rutland 8509 *1398-C18*
H, almshouse, of St John Evangelist and St Anne. Former chapel in William Dalby Street. + : D

OLD BUCKENHAM, Norfolk 0691 *c.1146-1536*
P (AC) given site of old castle when it moved to (New) Buckenham with permission to build
house from castle materials. Nothing remains except lump of stone south of Tudor manor house.
 AM : E

OLD MALTON *see Malton*

OSNEY, Oxfordshire 5205 *1129-1539*
P (AC), elevated A c.1154, becoming one of most important houses of order in Britain.
Dependencies included Crowmarsh H. Of great P with 332ft long church, nothing remains except
minor conventual building and recast bell. (18) AM : E

OSPRINGE, Kent   9960   *-1234-1516*
H, for poor and travellers, conducted by order of Holy Cross to 1470, afterwards by seculars.
Remains in two mediaeval houses, one with C13 undercroft (Maison Dieu) in Water Lane.
           DE : E +

OTTERHAM, Sussex   7954   *c.1184-1210*
A (PC), probably from Durford, moving to Bayham early in C13, leaving Otterham as
dependent grange. Otterham Court incorporates some remains, including early C14 chapel. § : C-

OVINGHAM, Northumberland   0863   *1378-1537*
pc (AC), dep. Hexham. Church, which preceded priory, in Anglican use; vicarage incorporates
part of domestic quarters.   + § : C-

OWSTON, Leicestershire   7708   *-1177-1536*
A (AC) though not particularly large or well-endowed. Chancel of abbey church survives in
Anglican use with fragments of domestic buildings incorporated in vicarage.   + § : C-

OXFORD, Oxfordshire   5106   *1002; 1122-1542*
i. St Frideswide's was originally served by secular canons, replaced by P (AC) in 1122. Priory d.
Wolsey in order to f. university college on site. Truncated priory church survives to double as
college chapel and Anglican cathedral. Watching loft, fine quire, part of cloister largely remains,
scanty remnant of modified dorter, more of frater, impressive chapter-house. (14, 152, 163, 185)
           + /§ : C +
ii. St Bernard's (1437-1542) was a C House of Studies under a 'provisor'. After Henrician
suppression it was reorganised as St John's College by Mary I (some remains incorporated in
latter). (185)   + /§ : C
iii. Other monastic houses of study included Gloucester College P (BM), tr. Worcester College
(+ §); Durham College P (BM), tr. Trinity College (§); Canterbury Hall, later College; St Albans
Hall later combined with Gloucester; London College (all BM).
iv. Remains of friars' houses of study: (DF) from 1221, gateway at south end of Littlemore
Street, (FFC) from 1224, remains of church under Sainsbury's and fragments of wall elsewhere.
(77)
v. Frewen Hall in New Inn Hall Street was originally St Mary's Hall (AC) f. 1435 for canons
studying at university (part of gatehouse and cellar survives).
vi. There were some half dozen HH. Remains of (a) St Bartholomew's (f. -1129), for lepers, then
sick. Became dependency of Oriel College to which sick members of college could retire.
Remnants in Cowley Road chapel and nearby farmhouse.   + § : C-
(b) St John Baptist (c.1180-1457), (originally for travellers, then sick including poor scholars),
under Augustinian rule. tr. Magdalen whose front range incorporates some remains.
vi. Modern houses include P (DF) in St Giles Street, House of Franciscan Capuchins in Iffley
Road, a retreat house belonging to Carmelites in Boars Hill, St Benet's Hall (BM) in St Giles
Street.

PARKMINSTER, Sussex   1136   *1876-*
Large Charterhouse (C), of French origin, designed to accommodate 34 Carthusians. Two cells
d. by bombs 1940. Guest-house.   § : (A)

PATRIXBOURNE, Kent   1855   *c.1200-1409*
apc (AC), dep. Beaulieu, Normandy. Church later appropriated to Merton P (AC), Surrey. In
1409 cell sold to Merton. Splendid Norman priory church substantially survives in Anglican use.
No remains of domestic buildings.   + : D +

PEAKIRK, Northamptonshire   1606   *C8; 1000-1048*
AS monastic f. later pc dep. Crowland (BM) and a hermitage after 1066. No conventual remains;
chapel which succeeded St Pega's cell (interesting remains in Anglican church including murals).
St Pega was sister to St Guthlac, f. of Crowland. (19)   § : D +

PENTNEY, Norfolk   7213   *-1135-1537*
Large P (AC), much reduced by Black Death, dependency at Brinkburn. Imposing gatehouse
only remains above ground.   AM : E +

PERSHORE, Worcestershire   9446   *c.689; c.972-1535 +*
Original AS f. for secular canons, replaced by monks for a period, then canons returned. Ref. A
(BM) c.972. Substantial part of abbey church (originally same length as Tewkesbury) survives in
Anglican use. Nothing of conventual buildings, extern parish church of St Andrew. (19, 20, 66,
86, 106, 133, 177, 180)   + : D +

PETERBOROUGH, Northamptonshire   6037   *c.655; c.966-1539*
AS monastery, d. Danes (870) ref. C10 as A (BM), becoming rich and powerful with
dependencies at Oxney and a number of HH: two in city: St Leonard, f. -1125 for lepers, later
men's almshouse; St Thomas Martyr, f. c.1180, sick, later women's almshouse §; four in
Stamford, others at Cotes and Southorpe. Magnificent remains of abbey church, now serving as
Anglican cathedral: retro-quire, fragments of shrine, many abbots' monuments, lectern.
Remains of other buildings include: gates, prisons, abbot's lodging (now much-altered episcopal
palace), prior's lodging (now private house), much of cloister, guest-house (largely lost in
deanery), impressive remains of farmery, outbuildings, fragments of precinct wall. (2, 19, 20, 23,
26, 27, 46, 61, 66, 70, 72, 76, 83,, 102, 109, 111, 119, 124, 126, 143, 152, 167, 169, 171, 177, 180, 182,
191)   + /§ : B +

PILTON, Devon   5534   *C12-1539*
Small P (BM), dep. Malmesbury. Much altered church in Anglican use. Merest traces of site of
conventual buildings, some of whose masonry may be incorporated in neighbouring houses.
(180)   + : C

PINLEY, Warwickshire   3181   *early C12-1536*
A (CN), one of earliest and perhaps one of smallest. Ruined nave wall of church. Neighbouring
half-timbered house may have been abbess' lodging or guest-house.   § : E

PIPEWELL, Northamptonshire   8385   *1143-1538*
A (CM), col. Newminster. Nothing visible on site. Dubious report that four stalls survive in
Great Oakley parish church.   : E-

PLYMPTON, Devon   5356   *-1066; 1121-1539*
AS secular college, ref. 1121 as P (AC) and became one of largest houses of order in Britain with
dependencies at Marsh Barton, St Anthony-in-Roseland H for lepers, later sick, in town.
Neglected and unexcavated site: fragments above ground include gatehouse with re-used
masonry from undercroft. Extern chapel (St Mary's) in Anglican use.   § : E

POLESWORTH, Warwickshire   2602   *-839?-1539*
AS nunnery whose inhabitants were apparently expelled soon after 1066. They retired to Oldbury
to form a P (BN) but were brought back to Polesworth c.1130 as A (BN) with Oldbury as pc.
Part of nunnery church (with effigy of abbess) preserved in Anglican use. Little of conventual
buildings: gatehouse, part of claustral buildings incorporated in vicarage?, and ancillary
structures in cottages. (20, 64, 128, 129)   + § : C

POLING, Sussex   0405   *?-1540*
Preceptory (KH). Such remains as there are incorporated in Fairplace Farm. (106)   § : E

POLSLOE, Devon   9292   *-1160-1539*
Largish P (BN). All that remains (guest-house?) of aristocratic nunnery is incorporated in
farmhouse which lies west of cloister.   § : E

PORTBURY, Somerset   4975   *?-1536*
pc (AC), dep. Bristol. No visible remains but eight quire? stalls were rescued and placed (without
exactly fitting) in (Anglican) parish church at Weston-in-Gordano.

PORTCHESTER, Hampshire   6105   *1133-c.1150*
P (AC) tr.Southwick between 1145 and 1153. Site was in south-east of outer bailey of castle.
Church substantially survives in Anglican use; nothing above ground of conventual buildings
except garderobe exits in south fortress-wall and mark where cloister abutted nave of church.
(14, 124, 181)   + § : C-

PORTSMOUTH, Hampshire   6501   *-1214-1540*
Of two HH, there are remains of God's House for poor men under Augustinian rule and f. in
association with Southwick P (AC) as was chapel of St Thomas which became parochial in 1320
and Anglican cathedral in 1927. Modified H church survives in Garrison Church, nave (ruined by
Germans) represents H hall. (14)   AM + : C-

POUGHLEY, Berkshire   3474   *c.1160-1525*
f. as hermitage which became small P (AC), d. and endowments tr. to Wolsey's new Oxford
college and buildings were used as temporary accommodation for scholars awaiting completion
of their rooms. Church entirely demolished at Reformation, part of west range incorporated in
farmhouse now owned by RAF.   § : E

PRINKNASH, Gloucestershire   8713   *1928-*
A mediaeval grange, dep. Gloucester, laicised at Reformation and modified C19. Benedictines
(from Caldey) returned in 1928 and their A (BM) incorporates this house with modern
extensions, including church. Colonies at Farnborough, Pluscarden. Famous pottery.   + § : (A)

PRITTLEWELL, Essex 8787 *-1121-1536*
ap (BMC) dep. Lewes, became denizen between 1351 and 1374. Prominent remains of frater,
prior's lodging, much of west range. Church indicated by part of ruined walls. (43) AM § : C-

PYNHAM, Sussex 0107 *-1151-1525*
pc (AC), serving chapel (St Bartholomew), undertaking repair of causeway and bridge,
maintaining small H for poor and travellers d.Wolsey for endowments of his great Oxford
college. Remains of priory in fragmented tower incorporated in farmhouse; of H, 'Maison Dieu',
near bridge. § : E +

QUARR, Isle of Wight 5692 *1132-1536; 1908-*
i. A (CM), col. Savigny. Church utterly demolished at Reformation, fragments of masonry
scattered in later buildings around site, much of precinct wall survives. § : E
ii. A (BM of Solesmes Congregation), next to ruins and centred in Victorian house with
modifications and extensions of some architectural merit. (171) + § : (A)

QUENINGTON, Gloucestershire 1404 *c.1193-1540*
Preceptory (KH). Site occupied by lay mansion after suppression. Interesting dovecote and
gatehouse survive but, as often, nothing of church or other religious buildings. (106) § : E +

RAMSEY, Huntingdonshire 2885 *c.969-1539*
i. Large, well-endowed A (BM) with dependencies at Modney, St Ives. Much quarried after
suppression for Cambridge colleges and towers but remains of Lady Chapel and gatehouse.
Some of stalls are said to survive in Anglican parish church of Over, Cambridgeshire.
(19, 46, 66, 69, 120, 171) § : E +
ii. Abbey maintained H (poor travellers and orphans?) outside gate to which church of
St Thomas, in Anglican use, belonged. + § : D +

RANTON, Staffordshire 8324 *1149-1539*
P (AC), dep. Haughmond. Unexcavated site with visible tower and fragment of church wall.
(102) § : D-

RAVENDALE *see West Ravendale*

RAVENSTONEDALE, Westmorland 7203 *-1300-1536?*
P or pc given to Gilbertines of Watton in late C12. Not very informative ruins and foundations
immediately north of church. (84) § : E

READING, Berkshire 7272 *1121-1539*
i. AS f. nuns, replaced by A (BM) in 1121. Cluniac affinities to end of C12. Dependencies at
Leominster, Cholsey and in Scotland. Two HH, for poor travellers and lepers, in town. Last
abbot of Henry I's favourite monastery executed by Henry VIII. Bits of church, cloistral
buildings, restored inner gatehouse, fragments in museums. Extern church (St Lawrence) in
Anglican use. (2, 23, 36, 37, 58, 120, 123, 132, 158, 182) AM : B-
ii. Franciscan friary in Oxford custody. Church reconstructed C19. No domestic remains. (77)
  + : D
iii. Remains of H (St John Baptist) f.1190 for poor travellers with chapel in north aisle of
St Lawrence's church. Seems to have become redundant in 1479 and abbot, with royal
permission, tr. it to Grammar School. Part of hospitium survives north of church. + § : E +

REDLINGTON, Suffolk 1871 *1120-1537*
P (BN). Church in Anglican use may contain remains of nuns' church and barn to south
probably belonged to conventual buildings. (20, 64) + § : C-

REIGATE, Surrey 2550 *C13?-1536*
Small P (AC) supporting attached H for sick. Church completely destroyed and domestic
buildings converted into mansion immediately on suppression. AM/§ : E

REPTON, Derbyshire 3026 *c.660; c.1155-1538*
Ce monastery, d.Danes 875, at which St Guthlac was once a monk. Replacement church is one of
glories of AS architecture. Site occupied in C12 by P (AC), became large house with dependency
at Calke. Fragments: church, cloister, prior's lodging incorporated in school buildings.
(90, 102, 174) § : C-

REWLEY, Oxfordshire 5305 *1281-1536*
A (CM), col. Thame. For a time was college for student monks but ceased to serve this purpose
before end C14. C15 doorway and fragment of precinct wall (north of Blackwells) alone survive.
  AM : E

RIALTON, Cornwall   8362   *C15?-1539*
'The Priory' seems to have been a grange of Bodmin (AC) occasionally used for prior's
villagiutura. Apart from chapel, a good deal survives, including study and bedchamber of prior
Vivian. Well.   § : E +

RIBSTONE, Yorkshire West Riding   2963   *c.1217-1308; 1312-1540*
Preceptory (with Wetherby) of KT which, on their d., was tr. to KH. Dependent 'camera' at
Mount St John in C15. Modified chapel survives, attached to C17 house occupying site.
(106, 177)   + : D

RICHMOND, Yorkshire North Riding   1701   *-1146-1539*
i. P (BM), dep. York with its own dependent H for York monks for lepers and sick. Scanty
remains in Frenchgate.   AM : E
ii. Large house (FFO) in Newcastle custody. Main survival is crossing-tower characteristic of
friary church. (5, 77, 81, 153, 189)   AM : E +
In late C12, there was P (BN). No trace.

RIEVAULX, Yorkshire North Riding   5784   *1132-1538*
A (CM), counted as daughter of Clairvaux and most celebrated monastery in England within few
years of f. Many col. of which Melrose was most famous (1136). St Ailred was abbot (1147-1165)
ruling 140 monks and 500 conversi. Later suffered severely from Black Death and changing
economic conditions. Magnificent and extensive remains, second only to Fountains. Unique
chapter-house, interesting waterworks, extern chapel incorporated in (Anglican) parish church.
Intelligent and industrious re-modelling of inconvenient site. (1, 8, 9, 17, 28, 33, 34, 37, 39, 40, 47,
48, 52, 53, 61, 70, 76, 79, 80, 82, 86, 103, 109, 110, 113, 120, 122, 124, 132, 133, 136, 137, 142, 153, 165,
167, 176, 78, 181, 184, 190)   DE : B +

RIPON, Yorkshire West Riding   3171   *C7-?*
i. AS monastery (BM) f.St Wilfred. Remains include remarkable crypt, cathedral, chalice.
(19, 50, 88)   (+) : D +
ii. Remains of three HH: St Mary Magdalene, f. -1139 (for lepers, travellers and blind) in
Stonebridge Gate (96), AM : D + ; St John Baptist, f.c.1110 (almhouse for poor clerks) § ;
St Anne's, f. -1438 (almhouse for travellers) AM.

ROBERTSBRIDGE, Sussex   7323   *C13?-1538*
A (CM), col. Boxley, changing site from Salehurst in C13, dep.H (men's almshouse) in Seaford.
Fragments of masonry much involved in farm occupying site.   AM : E +

ROCHE, Yorkshire West Riding   5489   *1147 1538*
A (CM), col. Newminster. Important monument for development of Gothic style. Ruins of
church, especially east end; recognisable fragments of cloistral buildings, farmery, abbot's
lodging, gatehouse. Four quire-stalls may survive in Anglican church at Loversall.
(1, 40, 69, 104, 124, 133, 154, 168, 171)   DE : B

ROCHESTER, Kent   7467   *604; 1080-1540*
AS f., ref. CP (BM) with dependencies at Felixstowe, Darenth, HH at Chatham for lepers and
sick, and for a time, Strood for poor travellers. Magnificent remains of priory church, used as
Anglican cathedral. Good deal of rest: gateways, cloister, frater entrance, fine chapter-house,
ruined dorter undercroft. (9, 20, 21, 31, 37, 63, 76, 133, 153, 168)   + § : B

ROMSEY, Hampshire   3521   *c.907; -1539*
AS f. probably DM. After 1301, A (BN). Became very large house (90 in 1333) and though much
reduced later remained considerable. Dependent H for poor where parents and relatives were
received as sisters (consorores). Town grew in shelter and as dependency of aristocratic
community. Modified church in Anglican use, nothing visible of unexcavated convent. (7, 20, 46,
59, 64, 72, 95, 133, 142, 153, 182)   + : C +

ROSEDALE, Yorkshire North Riding   7296   *-1158-1536*
Small P (CN) whose chapel served parish. Temporarily scattered in 1322 by ravaging Scots.
Anglican church occupies site of chapel and preserves tomb. Scant remains: corner buttress of
tower, inserted window. (64, 167, 175, 180)   (+) : D-

ROTHLEY, Leicestershire   5812   *c.1220-1308; +1312-1535*
House (KT) tr. KH united to Dalby -1535, having been 'camera' before 1338. Secular house on
site may preserve some masonry of conventual buildings and certainly preserves substance of rare
chapel of military order. (106, 177)   (+) § : C

ROYSTON, Hertfordshire   3541   *+ 1163-1537*
f. as small secular college, became P (AC). Part of church survives in Anglican use. No remains
of conventual buildings.   + : D

227

RUFFORD, Nottinghamshire 6464 *1146-1536*
A (CM), col. Rievaulx. Church utterly destroyed by expropriators. Within ostentatious mansion
(now in decline), one room of conventual buildings survives. (31, 40, 133, 154) § : E

RUMBURGH, Suffolk 3581 *1047-64; 1140-1528*
pc of St Benets Hulme (BM), later ap of St Melaine, Rennès. In 1140 became pc of St Mary's
York. Church substantially survives in Anglican use: interesting watching window (originally
from dorter). Farmhouse on site of frater. + : D +

RYE, Sussex 9220 *-1350-1538*
P (AF) in 'limes' of Oxford, f. on East Cliff but, from fear of French, moved within town walls
in 1378. Remains of chapel on Conduit Hill. (15) AM : D-
Another house (FS) c.1263-1307. Knowles lists 'remains' but cannot trace anything other than
'Old Hospital' in Mermaid Street (C15). (81) § : ?

ST ALBANS, Hertfordshire 1507 *c. 793; c.969-1539*
Original f. seems DM (BMN). Became decadent but revived c.969 and remained DM until 1140
when nuns moved to Sopwell. Became A (BM), powerful and very wealthy with large numbers of
monks and dependencies at Bedlow, Belvoir, Binham, Hatfield Peveril, Hertford, Millbrook,
Pembroke, Redbourn, Tynemouth, Wallingford, Wymondham, St Albans Hall Oxford.
St Mary de Pré (BN) with H, for lepers, Sopwell (BN), two HH, for male lepers and sick, in town
and school were also dependent on house whose ruler claimed to be premier abbot of England.
Magnificent remains of abbey church used as Anglican cathedral containing fragments of
shrines, watching loft, murals, monuments of abbots. Less of conventual buildings: slype, trace
of cloister, gatehouse. Some of ejected quire-stalls, damaged through weathering, were saved for
Leighton Buzzard (Anglican) church. (2, 6, 8, 13, 15, 19, 21, 23, 26, 31, 34, 41, 46, 52, 60, 64, 67, 71,
72, 76, 80, 83, 88, 90, 98, 102, 106, 112, 113, 119, 124, 133, 142, 144, 149, 152, 154, 155, 159, 160, 164,
167, 168, 170, 181, 182, 190) AM / + : C +

ST ANTHONY IN ROSELAND, Cornwall 8532 *-1288-1538*
pc (AC) dep. Plympton. Modified remains of church in Anglican use. C19 mansion ('Place')
occupies some of site. + / § : D

ST AUGUSTINE CANTERBURY *See Canterbury*

ST BEES, Cumberland 9611 *1120-1538*
AS nunnery f.650, d. Danes. Ref. P (BM) dep. York St Mary and produced colony of its own at
Neddrum, Ireland. Substantially complete church in Anglican use. No remains of conventual
buildings unless some are incorporated in C16 buildings of school. (20, 101, 124) + : D +

ST BENET HULME, Norfolk 2417 *c.800; 1019-1539*
AS monastery (BM) d. Danes in 870. Site reoccupied by hermits in C10. A (BM) f.1019 and
helped to staff Bury in 1020. Dependencies at Rumburgh and two HH: Horning for poor
travellers, Gt.Hautbois for poor. Never legally suppressed and Anglican bishop of Norwich thus
legally abbot. Site enclosed by river and great dyke. Gatehouse only recognisable remains.
Fragments of four stalls preserved at Ranworth. (5, 19) AM : E +

ST CONSTANTINE'S CELLS, Cumberland 4654 *?*
Three man-made caves, used as hermitage (in C14 at least) and later provided refuge for monks
of Wetheral against moss troopers. (91) AM : D-

ST FRIDESWIDE'S *see Oxford*

ST GERMANS, Cornwall 3557 *c.1175-1539*
AS collegiate f., cathedral for about century after 936, united to Crediton in 1042. Secular
canons replaced by P (AC) about a century later. Priory church substantially survives in Anglican
use. Conventual buildings largely obliterated by house ('Port Eliot') which incorporates
undercroft and frater. (14, 124) + : C-

ST MICHAELS MOUNT, Cornwall 5130 *-1050; c.1090-1414*
Important Ce monastery (C8-11), became ac of Norman namesake (BM) before 1050, elevated to
ap c.1090. Granted to Syon in 1414 which established small college of secular priests on site.
Substantial remains of chapel, gatehouse, frater modified into salon, early crosses and
alabasters. + / § : C

ST OLAVES, Suffolk 4797 *c.1216-1537*
Small P (AC). Rather confused remains, divided by lane and affected by post-Reformation
conversion into house. Discernible outline and considerable fragments of north range including
frater undercroft. DE : D

ST OSYTH, Essex   1215   *1121-1539*
Large and wealthy P (AC), elevated to A c.1160. Dependency at Blythburgh. Transformed by
Lord Darcy into mansion and church totally demolished. Unexcelled gatehouse substantially
survives with parts of precinct wall. Parish church served by canons and reconditioned by Abbot
Vyntner. (15, 23, 83)   AM : D

ST PIRAN, Cornwall   7752   *C6-C11?*
Ce monastery, possibly f. St Kieran of Saiger. Later secular college until shortly after Norman
Conquest. (33)   AM : E +

ST RADEGUNDS, Kent   2742   *1193-1536*
Small A (PC), dependency at Blakwose. In 1590 remains converted into secular residence,
centred on frater of which a good deal survives. Church tower made into gatehouse, fragments of
cloister and guest-house. Mutilated ruins constitute, apart from two cathedrals, most extensive
monastic remains in county. (53, 124)   AM : D +

SALISBURY, Wiltshire   1429   *-1214-*
Of some five HH, remains of St Nicholas, almshouse for travellers, probably under Augustinian
rule.   § : E +
Rebuilt Trinity H, for sick, f.-1379 preserves some mediaeval glass. (96)

SALMSTONE, Kent   *C11?-1538*
Early grange of Canterbury St Augustine with chapel and residential buildings for occupying
monks. (BM)   + § : C

SANDFORD, Oxfordshire   5108   *+ 1312-1540 ?*
House, originally KT, tr.preceptory KH. Remains of church used as barn, some conventual
buildings incorporated in farm. (106)   § : E

SANDWICH, Kent   3358   *1217-*
Of at least four HH, remains of St Bartholomew's almshouse probably under Augustinian rule.
Denuded chapel with effigy (founder?).   + § : C-
Entrance porch of gateway of St Thomas', f.1392.

SAWLEY, Yorkshire West Riding   7746   *1148-1536*
A (CM), col. Newminster. Always small and poor but developed scholarly tradition. Dependent
H, for lepers, later sick, at Tadcaster. Remains include much of outer wall of church, discernible
cloister with surrounding buildings, abbot's house partly incorporated in cottage, C19 arch
constructed of mediaeval materials which are also scattered elsewhere. (1, 34, 40, 120, 137) DE . C-

SEATON, Cumberland   0130   *c.1190-1537*
Very small P (BN), for a time pc dep.Nunburnholme. Independent after 1313 but never large.
Fragment of church and re-used material in neighbouring house.   § : E

SELBY, Yorkshire West Riding   6132   *c.1070-1539*
A (BM), dependencies at Snaith and H, almshouse, in Brigg, Lincolnshire. Earliest great
Benedictine house in north. Church preserved in Anglican use (sacristy and scriptorium), no
discernible trace of rest of buildings. (1, 8, 20, 21, 66, 72, 84, 120, 133, 52, 157, 161, 168)   + : D +

SHAFTESBURY, Dorset   8622   *c.888-1539*
AS f. which became largest nunnery in England A (BN) with over 120 nuns in 1326, considerably
reduced by Black Death but still c.60 at suppression. Supported two hospitals in town, for poor,
and men's almshouse, and another at Bradford for lepers. Substantial remains of reduced church
in Anglican use (crypt, tiles), little of convent above grounds, some of fragments in museum.
(1, 16, 24, 86, 175)   + AM : D

SHAP, Westmorland   5615   *c.1200-1540*
A (PC), col.Cockersand located at Preston Patrick for about ten years before moving to Shap
c.1200. Large community until Black Death with HH at Brough (for travellers) and Appleby, for
lepers then poor. Imposing ruin of church tower, recognisable remains of most domestic
buildings. (5, 17, 142, 145, 170, 190)   DE : C

SHERBORNE, Dorset   6316   *c.993; 1075-1539*
Original AS f.-672, became see 705. Reconstituted CP (BM) c.993. See tr. Old Sarum (1075-8)
but bishop remained titular abbot until 1122 when Sherborne was made A (BM). Dependencies
at Horton, Kidwelly, and H, for poor, in town. Most of minster survives in Anglican use (some
quire-stalls), some conventual remains incorporated in school. (19, 20, 31, 88, 107, 109, 120, 124,
133)   + ./ § : C+
Some remains of H in Trendle Street which passed from Augustinian to Benedictine rule c.1404,
ref. some 30 years later with added almshouse. (96)   + / § : C

229

SHERBURN, Dorset   3142   *c.1181-?*
Great H of SS Lazarus, Martha and Mary, begun as leper house to which monks and nuns were
sent. It accommodated 65 patients and entire community lived under strict (Augustinian ?) rule.
Reconstituted 1434 as college with provision for surviving lepers and added men's almshouse. In
1501 it seems to have lost its almshouse function. Gatehouse and fragment of chapel survive.
(95, 96, 169)   § : C-

SHOBDON, Herefordshire   3961   *+1131-1170*
Short-lived P (AC), tr. to Wigmore. No remains of conventual buildings, fragment of church
converted to C18 'eye-catcher'.   § : D-

SHREWSBURY, Shropshire   4912   *c.1095-1540*
i. A (BM), col. Seez. Dependency at Morville. Substantial remains of abbey church in Anglican
use. No conventual remains apart from frater pulpit. (20, 36, 80, 101, 120, 124, 169)   + : C
ii. House (FFO) in Worcester custody. Masonry fragments. Some glass preserved in St Mary's.
(77)   § : E
iii. Of five HH, remains of St Giles f.-1136, for lepers and sick, dependency of abbey. Remains
of chapel incorporated in Anglican church of St Giles.   + : C-
St Mary's not only contains some glass from Greyfriars but also from German Cistercian houses.
(81)

SHULBREDE, Sussex   8729   *-1207-1536*
Small P (AC). Church completely destroyed, some conventual buildings (part of west range)
converted to secular dwelling-house, moated site, fish-ponds.   § : E +

SIBTON, Suffolk   3770   *1150-1536*
A (CM), col. Warden. Dependent H, for poor travellers, f.-1264. Only Cistercian house in
county. Neglected and sparse remains of cloister, frater, kitchen. Some masonry from destroyed
church may have been used to restore Anglican parish church in C19. (79, 85, 108, 169)   § : E +

SNAITH, Yorkshire West Riding   6422   *c.1310-1539*
Church granted to Selby (BM) c.1110 which provided two monks to serve it. In 1310 it was
constituted pc. Nothing visible of conventual buildings but substantial remains of reduced priory
church in Anglican use.   + : D

SOUTHAMPTON, Hampshire   4212   *c.1197-?*
St Julian's or God House was H, for poor travellers, under Augustinian rule, tr. to Queen's
College, Oxford 1343 but continued function into C16. (96, 122)   § : ?

SOUTH KYME, Lincolnshire   1452   *-1169-1539*
P (AC) which flourished to suppression. Anglican parish church (much restored C19)
incorporates fragments of great priory church. No domestic remains.   + : D-

SOUTHWARK, Surrey   3278   *1106-1539*
P (AC) probably replacing earlier community of secular canons. Dependent H, for poor, in
township. Nothing remains of conventual buildings but a large part of the priory church of
St Mary Overie (much altered in C19) survives in Anglican cathedral. (14)   + : D
There are a number of modern houses of nuns, including Anglican one.

SOUTHWELL, Nottinghamshire   7053   *-1208-1534-*
H (for lepers then sick) of St Mary Magdalene.   § : ?
Magnificent collegiate church, used as Anglican cathedral, contains lectern and candlesticks
from Newstead where they were thrown into pond at suppression.

SOUTHWICK, Hampshire   6308   *c.1150-1538*
P (AC), tr. from Portchester, f. Domus Dei, for poor travellers, and St Thomas' church (now
Anglican cathedral) at Portsmouth. Priory church utterly destroyed at suppression, part of
cloister converted to mansion. Apart from fragments incorporated in Anglican parish church,
only scant remains of undercroft are visible in much altered and unexcavated site in naval
occupation.   § : E

SOUTH WRAXALL, Wiltshire   8364   *C14-C16?*
H, for travellers. Hall and attached chapel incorporated in manor farmhouse.   § : C-

SPALDING, Lincolnshire   2422   *1311-1539*
Outside town is Wykeham chapel, once part of summer house of prior of Spalding (BM). (23
182)   + : D-

SPORLE, Norfolk   8411   *-1123-c.1414*
ac, dep. St Florent-sur-Saumer (BM), tr. to resources of Eton College. No remains of conventual
buildings, Benedictine church in Anglican use.   + : D-

STAMFORD, Lincolnshire   0207   *658; c.1082-1538*
i. AS monastery f. St Wilfrid, d.Danes C9. Site reoccupied late C11 by P (BM), dep. Durham.
Only remains of ruined church   AM : D-
ii. Large P (CF), in St George's Square -1268-1538. (29)   AM : E +
iii. P (AF) in 'limes' of Lincoln, 1343-1538. Remains incorporated in George Hotel. (15)
        AM : E +
iv. H almshouse, All Saints' in Broad Street, f.1485. (96)   + § : A-
Peterborough (BM) maintained three other HH; remains of St John Baptist, for poor travellers
f.c. 1174 incorporated in Burghley H. Chapel preserves some misericords (from Fotheringhay?).
(96)   (+) § : D-

STANBROOK, Worcestershire   8555   *1625; 1838-*
A (BN) f. by 'English Ladies' at Cambrai, fled French Revolution to Abbot's Salford (1807-38)
after which they moved to Stanbrook Hall to which they added piecemeal as numbers increased.
        + § : (A)

STANSGATE, Essex   9305   *-1121-1525*
apc (BMC), dep. Lewes, became pc between 1351 and 1374. Neglected site: one visible wall,
cannibalised material in Anglican church (rebuilt C19)? (43)   § : E

STAVORDALE, Somerset   7532   *-1243-1539*
Small P (AC), seems to have become dep. Taunton in last six years. Nothing of conventual
buildings; church perverted into private house. (174)   § : D

STEVENTON, Berkshire   4691   *1100 + - 1363 +*
Large ap, dep. Bec. Sold after 1363, endowments tr. Westminster before 1400. 'The Priory' (NT)
may represent guest-house. Benedictine priory church in Anglican use.   + § : C-

STIDD, Lancashire   6536   *1216-?*
H for sick, taken over by KH in 1265. Preceptory chapel largely survives in Anglican use. (98)
        + : D

STOGURSEY, Somerset   2042   *c.1105-c.1442*
ap. dep. Lonlay (BM), tr. endowments of Eton College. Site unexcavated. Of conventual
appurtenances, only dovecote shows above ground. Priory church largely survives in Anglican
use.   + : C-

STONE, Staffordshire   9034   *c.1135-1536*
P (AC), dep. Kenilworth, becoming independent in 1260. Austin priory probably succeeded AS
f. (DM). Some walling in Abbey Street, and undercroft in house called 'The Priory'.   § : E
In Margaret Street is a modern convent: mother house of English Congregation of Dominican
sisters. At nearby Oulton, modern A. (BN)   § : (A)

STONELEIGH, Warwickshire   3272   *1156-9 - 1536*
A (CM), col. Bordesley. At Red Moor (1141-56) before settling. Church completely destroyed.
Monastic remains (cloister, slype, chapter-house, warming room?, hospitium, gatehouse) much
involved in Leigh mansion. (85)   § : C-

STORRINGTON, Sussex   0814   *1872-*
Mother house of returned PC in England. Other houses near Doncaster and at Scunthorpe,
Spalding, Holbeach, Manchester. (142)   + § : (A)

STOURBRIDGE, Cambridgeshire   0485   *-1169-c.1279*
H for lepers, but with decline of leprosy became free chapel of St Mary Magdalene. Disused and
gutted chapel survives.   + : D-

STOW, Lincolnshire   8781   *1005 +; 1091-5*
f. secular canons, later temporary A (BM) from Eynsham. Monumental collegiate church rebuilt
as abbey church survives in Anglican use. No conventual remains (probably never built in stone).
        + : D +

STRATFORD, Warwickshire   2055   *1269-1547*
H for sick priests and poor, supported by guild, under Augustinian rule. In C15, almshouses
were attached and shortly afterwards H tr. to collegiate church for maintenance. Same guild,
until its suppression in 1547, supported town Grammar School. Survivals: modified chapel and
almshouse, guildhall.   + § : C

STROOD, Kent   7369   *?-1308*
Possibly preceptory (KT) but more likely 'camera' which ceased to belong to Templars before
their dissolution. Chapel destroyed but manor substantially intact in 'Temple Manor'.
(96, 122, 177)   DE : C-

STUDLEY, Oxfordshire 5912 *-1176-1539*
Large P (BN). Church utterly destroyed. House on site contains masonry fragments from
domestic buildings. § : E-

STUDLEY, Warwickshire 0763 *+1135-1536*
P (AC), f. at Witton, t.Stephen, moving to Studley c.1155. Dependent H for sick. Fragments in
and about Priory Farm. In (provided?) Anglican church is C13 memorial to anonymous prior:
'flower of virtues, ornament of Augustinian order and specially of its priors. . .' § : E

SUDBURY. Suffolk 8741 *c.1115-c.1538*
pc (BM), dep. Westminster. Fragments of ruined remains of chapel in grounds of Brundon Hall.
§ : E +

SUTTON COURTENAY, Bedfordshire 5093 *C14-1538?*
'The Abbey' mainly incorporates C14 grange of Abingdon. (BM) § : D

SWAFFHAM BULBECK, Cambridgeshire 5562 *c.1155-1536*
P (BN). Church utterly demolished. Undercroft survives in 'Abbey House' which also has some
indistinct walling in grounds. (64) § : E

SWAINBY, Yorkshire North Riding 4701 *c.1187-c.1200*
A (PC), probably col. Durford; tr. Coverham about turn of century. Scant ruins of church,
nothing else. AM : D-

SWAVESEY, Cambridgeshire 3669 *-1086-c.1401*
ap, dep. St Serge, Angers (BM), seems to have lost conventual status in late C13, tr. to
endowments of Coventry (C). Sole remnants of conventual buildings are slight traces in rough
grass north of church which may have belonged to priory (fine mediaeval benches.) (19) AM : C-

SWINE, Yorkshire East Riding 1335 *-1153-1539*
Most important of later DM, consisting of CN, PC and conversi with similar arrangements of
Gilbertine houses. Became P (CN) mid C14. No domestic remains but parochial portion of nuns'
church survives in Anglican use (mediaeval stalls). (40, 64, 142) + : D

SWINGFIELD, Kent 2343 *-1180-1540*
Preceptory (KH), and house of sisters of order before transferred to Buckland. C13 chapel of
St John and associated hall survive (modified) in lay occupation. (106) § : B-

SYNINGTHWAITE, Yorkshire West Riding 4243 *c.1160-1536*
P (CN). Sparse fragments: arch and cloister arcading. Re-used material in house occupying site.
§ : E

SYON, Middlesex 1675 *1431-1539*
Rich A (BR) f. Henry V, begun 1415 at Twickenham. After Henry VIII community continued at
Dermond, Flanders before returning to Syon, ref. Mary in 1557. On Elizabeth's accession, fled
again to continent but have returned in modern times (Devon). General plan and undercroft
survive in palace of Somerset and Northumberland. (17, 48, 73, 82, 86) § : E

TADDIPORT, Devon 4816 *1334-*
H for lepers later almshouse. Some remains of original chapel. + § : D-

TAMWORTH, Staffordshire. 2004 *-1150-1535+*
H (for poor becoming men's almshouse in late C13). Much altered spital chapel in Wiggington
Road. § + : D

TARRANT CRAWFORD, Dorset 9203 *-1199-1539*
f. by three ladies with their servants who eventually adopted Cistercian rule (-1228) when
flourishing community was adopted as A (CN) and became one of richest nunneries in England.
Remains: perhaps church in Anglican use, part of barn, re-used masonry in Tarrant Abbey
House. (9, 40) AM : C/D +

TATTERSHALL, Lincolnshire 2157 *1438-*
H almshouse, attached to former college. Remains behind houses on north side of Market Place.
(7) AM : E

TAUNTON, Somerset 2324 *c.1120-1539*
i. Large P (AC) with H, for lepers later almshouse in town and dependent P in Stavordale.
Church utterly destroyed, fragments used to patch village churches in vicinity. Remains of
domestic buildings etc.: fragments of walling in Canon Street, priory barn incorporates
conventual building (Priory Avenue). (16) § : E
ii. H (above) remains in Hamilton Road (much altered C17 and later.) § : E

TAVISTOCK, Devon   4774   *c.980-1538*
AS monastery, d.Danes 997, ref. a few years later (BM) with dependencies at Cowick, Modbury, Scilly, Denbury. Only scattered fragments of religious house which created town: bits of church wall, some of farmery (incorporated in Unitarian chapel), gates, precinct wall, tower. (19,120)
     AM : D

TEMPLE BALSALL, Warwickshire   2376   *1140-1308; 1322-1496; 1540*
Preceptory (KT), ref. after dissolution (KH). Hospitallers moved to Temple Grafton in 1496 and Balsall became dependency. Remains of much restored church in Anglican use; possible remains of conventual buildings in cottages to west. (106,177)   § + : C-

TEMPLE BRUER, Lincolnshire   0053   *-1185-1308; 1312-1540/1*
One of richest houses of KT, passing to KH after dissolution. In mid C14 its dependencies included Eagle and Beverley, cameras in Rowston and Kirkby. Substantial remains of chapel (mysterious C14 tower attached to church; masonry fragments in farmhouse.) (106,177) AM : C-

TEMPLE COMBE, Somerset.   7022   *c.1108; 1308-1540*
House (KT) passing immediately to KH on dissolution. During demolition of outhouse in 1951, panel-painting discovered portraying head of Christ possibly derived from Holy Shroud which may have been in Templars' possession. One of charges made against them was their devotion to a mysterious male head. Painting now in (Anglican) parish church. Scanty remains of preceptory in and about manor farm. (106,177)   § : C-

TEMPLE CRESSING, Essex   7920   *1136-1310*
First English settlement of KT. No remains of house but two ancient and splendid barns dating from KT occupation. It was tr. KH after 1312 and leased out privately from 1515. (16)   § : E +

TEMPLE HIRST, Yorkshire West Riding   6025   *1152-1308*
House (KT) which does not seem to have continued in religious use after their dissolution. Uninvestigated remains embedded in buildings of Temple Farm. (177)   § : E

TEWKESBURY Gloucestershire   8933   *c.715; c.980-1540*
AS f. seems to have decayed by C10, ref.c.980 as P (BM), dep. Cranborne. Positions reversed 1102 when Tewkesbury became A. Other dependencies at Bristol, Cardiff, Deerhurst, Goldcliff, Llantwit Major. H almshouse in town. Half magnificent church survives in Anglican use (misericords); rather less of conventual buildings: gatehouse, guest-house, abbot's lodging (now vicarage), mills, barn. Bell Hotel may incorporate some domestic buildings and claims bowling green. Abbey cottages belonged to abbey and were built (as shops?) in Middle Ages. (1, 8, 20, 21, 34, 46, 50, 102, 120, 126, 133, 142, 180, 182)   + § :C +

THAME, Oxfordshire   7006   *1140-1539*
A (CM) col. Waverley, earlier (1137) for a time at Otley. Site largely obliterated by 'Thame Park' which incorporates abbot's lodging and some of cloister range. Church utterly destroyed.   § : E

THATCHAM, Berkshire   5167   *-1446-*
H (for poor travellers and wounded soldiers on way home) with St Thomas' as chapel. AM + : D

THETFORD, Norfolk   8783   *c.1139-1536*
i. Small and poor P (AC). 'The Canons' in Brandon Road, preserves what little is left: fragment of ruined church. (53)   AM : D
ii; P (DF) in Cambridge visitation. Remains built into Grammar School.   § : E +
iii. P (BN) moving from Ling to deserted Benedictine house (c.1160). Remains of large nunnery off road to Euston: church perverted to barn, domestic remnants in and about farmhouse. (7,64)   § : E +
iv. P (BMC), col. Lewes, first installed in old cathedral before moving to permanent site in 1114. Achieved indpendent denizen status 1376 with dependencies at Horkesley, Wangford. Impressive but eroded remains of church, monastic buildings, gatehouse d.1540. (24,,43,70,83,104,107, 125, 132, 133, 142, 152, 157, 168, 189)   DE : B-

THORNEY, Cambridgeshire   2804   *C7; c.972-1539*
Original hermit settlement d. Danes c.870. Ref. A (BM) c.972 and became island of Christian civilisation in fens and as late as C15 monks were being licenced as parish priests in locality. Dependencies: Deeping St James, Trokenholt, attached H for poor. Fragment of church survives in Anglican use, vicarage may incorporate some masonry from east range of cloister. (19, 20, 23, 83, 120, 124, 167, 171)   + : C-

233

THORNTON, Lincolnshire 1119 *1139-1539*
P (AC), col. Kirkham, flourished and made A in 1148. Dependencies: Thwaite, H for poor, attached large school. Site robbed almost to foundations but clear and comprehensible plan discernible. Most substantial survival perhaps finest monastic gatehouse in country, probably included abbot's lodging. Impressive fragment of chapter-house. (1, 8, 37, 73, 75, 83, 120, 142, 168, 183)   DE : C

THURGARTON, Nottinghamshire 6949 *c.1125-1538*
Large P (AC). All that remains of church, similar to Southwell, is 'terribly mangled fragment' and of conventual buildings: whatever lies under gardens and within house called 'Thurgarton Priory'. Four quire-stalls survive in church. (5, 14, 15, 124)   + / § : D-

TILTY, Essex 6026 *1153-1536*
A (CM), col. Warden. Fragment of cloister. Extern chapel in Anglican use. (28)   AM : E

TINTAGEL, Cornwall 9588 *C9-?*
Small Ce monastery on unforgettable site. Dependency of Bodmin long before Norman Conquest. (32)   DE : D +

TISBURY, Wiltshire 9429 *-710-983; 1539*
AS f. (BN). declined towards end of C10 and became grange of Shaftesbury. Remains in Place Farm House: largest barn in England, outbuildings, two gatehouses. (83, 86)   § : D +

TITCHFIELD, Hampshire 5305 *1232-1537*
A (PC), col. Halesowen, serving at least two parish churches. After suppression quickly converted to pretentious mansion, using church as basis of gatehouse. Other remnants: fragments of chapter-house, barn. (73, 111, 112, 124, 142, 168)   DE : C-

TIVERTON, Devon 9512 *1517-*
H, almshouse. Much restored chapel and reconstructed almshouse in Fore Street.   + § : C-

TONG, Shropshire 7907 *c.1410-*
H, almshouse attached to college. Present almshouses seem C18 rebuild.   § : E?

TORRE, Devon 9164 *1196-1538*
A (PC), col. Welbeck, became one of largest and wealthiest houses of order. Barely recognisable plan of destroyed church; discernible remains of some conventual buildings in usurping residence: gatehouse, abbot's lodging, barn. A misericord may survive in St George's, Cockington. (5, 83, 142, 180, 184)   AM / § : B-

TORTINGTON, Sussex 0005 *c.1180-1536*
Small P (AC). Fragment of church abused as barn.   AM : D-

TOTNES, Devon 8060 *c.1088-1536*
f. ap, dep. St Serge, Angers (BM), became denizen P in early C15 with priors nominated from Canterbury CP. Remains incorporated in Guildhall and private house called 'The Priory'. Chancel of parish church was responsibility of priory, separated by one of most perfect stone screens in country.   § : E

TUPHOLME, Lincolnshire 1580 *c.1160-1536*
A (PC), col. Newsham. Outer wall of frater with fine pulpit, masonry fragments in farmhouse.   AM § : E +

TUTBURY, Staffordshire 2129 *1080+ - 1538*
ap, dep.S.Pierre-s-Dives, became independent denizen P (BM) early C15. No remains of conventual buildings, about a third of Benedictine church in Anglican use. (20, 124)   + : D

TYNEMOUTH, Northumberland 3769 *C8?; 1089-1539*
Early AS f., d.Danes 875. Ref. as P (BM), dep. Durham in late C11 but tr. St Albans before 1089. Own dependencies: Coquet Isle, large H, almshouse for sick in town. Largest monastery in Britain built within castle. Substantial ruins of once magnificent church (fine chantry), plan of cloisters, signs of some ancillary buildings. Much of defence works (maintained after suppression). (14, 31, 24, 52, 75, 101, 124, 133, 143, 144, 153, 172, 193)   DE + : C

ULVERSCROFT, Leicestershire 5012 *t.Henry II - 1539*
Originally group hermits, living under own rule. Reconstituted 1134 + as P (AC). Site walled and moated because of location in wild wood (Charnwood). Recognisable church and tower, some parts of cloister, much involved in farm. (5, 14)   AM § : C-

UPHOLLAND, Lancashire 5105 *1310; 1319-1536*
Originally college of secular priests; ref.1319 as P (BM). Chancel of Benedictines used as nave of Anglican church; fragments of domestic masonry among houses east of church. (20)   + : C-
Modern house (CN) at Stony Brow.

WALSINGHAM, Norfolk   9336   *c.1169-1538*
i. P (AC) serving England's most famous shrine of B.V.M. Dependency at Flitcham. Remains: gatehouse, frater, east wall of church, other fragments. Extern chapel in Anglican use; pilgrims' chapel at Houghton St Giles restored to Catholics. (15, 127, 164)   AM : C-
ii. House (FFC) in custody of Cambridge, maintaining large H for poor travellers. 'The only house of the English province where mendicant plan can be seen in its totality.' (among farms and kitchen gardens!). Substantial remains of guest-house, fragment of great church. (77, 81, 136)   § : D

WALTHAM, Essex   3800   *-1060; 1177-1540*
Pre-Conquest collegiate f., ref. large P (AC), raised to A in 1184, becoming most important Austin monastery. Last religious house suppressed by Henry VIII. Dependency: Wormley and attached H for poor. Sparse remains of conventual buildings include gatehouse. About third of abbey church survives in Anglican use. (14, 83, 120, 124, 174)   + / DE : C

WALTHAMSTOW, Essex   3788   *c.1515-*
H, almshouse to which Grammar School was attached in 1527. Rebuilt C18.   § : E

WANGFORD, Suffolk   4679   *-1159-1540*
ap, dep. Thetford (BMC), became denizen P in 1376. No sign of conventual buildings; priory church substantially survives in Anglican use.   + : D +

WARBLETON, Sussex   6018   *1413-1536*
P (AC), tr. from Hastings where site was endangered by erosion. Never large and most of canons may have returned to Hastings. Fragments incorporated in farmhouse and outbuildings.   § : E

WARE, Hertfordshire   3614   *-1351-1538*
Small house (FFC) in custody of Cambridge. Part of cloister and guest-house (?) incorporated in council offices. (77)   § : E +
Modern enclosed community (CN) at Ware Park.

WARWICK BRIDGE, Cumberland   4756   *C19?-*
At Holme Eden is a modern A (BN) of English Congregation.   § : (A)

WATTON, Yorkshire East Riding   0791   *c.1150-1539*
Probably largest P (GD), ground plan almost completely recovered by excavation, once accommodating 220 religious. Prior's lodging and barn. (5, 84, 144, 153)   AM § : E + +

WAVERLEY, Surrey   8645   *1128-1536*
A (CM), col. L'Aumône. One of largest in order, but never rich. First Cistercian f. in Britain, with five daughters. Extern infirmary for layfolk attached. Not very important in spite of spurious fame of Scott's novel. Sole remnants are sadly neglected fragments. (33, 36, 40, 47, 104, 109, 111, 142, 191, 192)   AM : E

WELBECK, Nottinghamshire   5674   *1153-1538*
A (PC), col. Newsham. Large community with responsibility for many local parishes and so successful that it colonised Durford, Hagneby, Beauchief, Léiston, West Dereham, Torre, Halesowen. Traces of west range in basement of grandiose secular mansion on site. (141, 167)   § : E

WELLS, Somerset   5445   *c.1207-1539*
i. H for poor, ref. 1350 as almshouse. Fragments survive in 'The Priory'.   § : E
ii. H, almshouse, f. 1424, surviving as 'Bubwith' almshouses, Chamberlain Street.   + § : C +

WENDLING, Norfolk   9213   *c.1267-c.1536*
Small A (PC), survived Wolsey's planned tr. to be suppressed by Henry VIII. 'Low heaps of rubble' close to abbey farm.   § : E

WENLOCK   *see Much Wenlock*

WEST ACRE, Norfolk   7715   *t. Henry I - 1538*
Large P (AC). Dependencies at Great Massingham, Weybourne and supported advanced students at Cambridge. On same scale as Castle Acre but remains only of gatehouse, fragment of chapter-house, tower.   AM : C—

WEST DEREHAM, Norfolk   6602   *1188-1539*
Large abbey (PC), col. Welbeck. Site south Abbey farm, masonry in ruined later house.   § : E

WEST MALLING   *see Malling*

WEST MERSEA, Essex   0112   *-1066-1400*
Large ap, dep. St Ouen, Rouen (BM), endowments tr. to Higham Ferrers college early C15. No visible remains of conventual buildings; priory church substantially survives in Anglican use.
        + : D

WESTMINSTER, London   2979   *958-1540*
Early AS monastery (C7), d. Danes, ref. St Dunstan as P (BM) soon perhaps richest A in Britain, due to royal patronage. Dependencies at Great Malvern, Hurley, Sudbury and HH at Westminster for lepers, Knightsbridge, for lepers, later poor. Substantial remains of church, now 'royal peculiar' in Anglican use as repository of memorials and stage for state religious occasions (fine misericords in Henry VII chapel). Good deal of modified claustral buildings: cloister, chapter-house, dorter undercroft, frater chapel, abbot's lodging, cellarer's range, guest-house, part of precinct wall. Abbey was temporarily restored in 1556 and suppressed again in 1560 — see Ampleforth. (1, 7, 8, 19, 20, 28, 34, 36, 37, 42, 48, 49, 53, 60, 63, 64, 66, 67, 71, 72, 75, 76, 80, 89, 90, 101, 104, 109, 117, 120, 123, 126, 134, 141, 142, 147, 152, 154, 157, 158, 159, 168, 172, 178, 180, 183, 184, 186, 190, 191)   DE + /§ : B +

WEST RAVENDALE, Lincolnshire   2891   *c.1202-c.1414*
apc, dep. Beauport, Brittany (PC), tr. to Southwell in C15. Neglected ruin of extern chapel alone remains.
        (+) : E

WETHERAL, Cumberland   4654   *c.1110-1538*
Small P (BM), dep. York St Mary. Gatehouse substantially survives and some wall from east range of cloister.
        AM : E

WEYBOURNE, Norfolk   1143   *early C12?-1536*
P (AC), dep. West Acre. Became independent 1314 but remained small and poor, using pre-existing building of which ruined tower remains. Part of priory church and parochial aisle in Anglican use. Confused and fragmentary remains of conventual buildings invaded by later private house.
        + AM : C

WHALLEY, Lancashire   7335   *1296-1537*
A (CM) originally at Stanlaw, 1172, col. Combermere. Foundation only of church but considerable (modified) conventual remains, some in Anglican, others in Catholic use. Much altered stalls may survive in Whalley and Blackburn (Anglican) parish churches.
(1, 40, 83, 137, 170, 192)   AM § : C—

WHITBY, Yorkshire   9011   *C7; -1077-1539*
AS f. c.657 (DM), location of famous Synod and home of St Hilda and Caedmon, d. Danes 867. P (BM) f. mid C11 by mission from Evesham, elevated to A before 1109. Dependencies at Hackness, Middlesborough, York (Físhergate), H, for lepers, later poor, in town. Monumental remains of ruined church, hardly anything of domestic buildings except remains (kitchen?) absorbed in 'Abbey House'. Cross. (1, 8, 10, 19, 21, 31, 66, 85, 142, 157, 167, 182)   DE : C—
At nearby Sneaton Castle is Anglican community of nuns, based on Benedictines.

WHITE LADIES   *see Boscobel*

WHITTLESFORD, Cambridgeshire   4748   *C13-1357*
H, almshouse, under Augustinian rule, tr. to chantry by 1357. Chapel belonging to H, near station.
        + : D +

WIDMERE, Buckinghamshire   8191   *-1248-1338*
Probably small commandery (KH), but farmed out by 1338. Chapel with undercroft incorporated in farmhouse.
        § : E

WIGMORE, Herefordshire   4169   *1179-1538*
f. as small P (AC) in Shobdon c.1140, after four moves settled at final site where they flourished and achieved status of A. Dependency at Ratingcope. Fragments of church, converted abbot's lodging with detached building of unknown purpose. Some quire-stalls said to be preserved at Leintwardine (Anglican) church. (186)   AM : C—

WILMINGTON, Sussex   5404   *-1100-1414*
ac, dep. Grestain (BM), became ap before 1243. At suppression endowments tr. Chichester cathedral. Always poor house from which survive unrelated fragments of conventual buildings and church in Anglican use.
        + AM : C

WILTON, Wiltshire   0931   *830; 890-1539*
i. P (BN), ref. by Alfred, became A in C10 and developed into great house. Remains only of outlying building called 'The Almonry'. (1)   § : E +
ii. Of three HH, remains of St John Baptist, for poor, f. 1187. Chancel of chapel and possibly other derelict remains in St John's Square.   § : C—

WIMBORNE, Dorset   0199   *1216-1547*
H, for lepers, later women's almshouse, dep. Wimborne College. (76)   + § : C—

WINCHCOMBE, Gloucestershire   0228   *c.798; c.972-1539*
AS ff. first of great nunnery c.787 and then very large monastery c.798 which became
secularised, replaced by BM c.972. Dependent H (leprous monks) at Charlton Abbots. Of mitred
abbey described at end of C15 as 'equal to a little university' nothing survived desolation of
Seymour. One house on site is said to incorporate malt-house and former Abbey Hotel
incorporates mediaeval material. Chancel of (Anglican) church of St Peter built and maintained
by abbey until suppression (tiles from site with initials of Abbot Kidderminster).
(11, 16, 19, 65, 66, 68, 149)   § : E

WINCHELSEA, Sussex   9017   *1243; 1269-1538*
i. Friary (FFC) in London custody, moved to vacant site of castle in 1269. Ruins of chancel in
garden of 'Greyfriars', reset doorway in Back Lane, gable of one range in Hastings Road.(77)
               AM : D
ii. Of four HH remains of St John's, almshouse 1292-1557.   § : E

WINCHESTER, Hampshire   4829   *c.604; 964-1539*
i. Many traditional ff., earliest allegedly in 169. AS monastery in early C7 and CP (BM) from
964. Dependencies included Piddletrenthide, Sisters H women's almshouse. Largest unruined
Benedictine church in world preserved in Anglican use. Fragments only of conventual buildings
apart from prior's lodging (deanery), pilgrims' hospice, gatehouse. (19, 20, 26, 31, 34, 46, 64, 74,
106, 119, 120, 142, 170, 171, 177, 181, 182)   + § : B
ii. A (BN) f. 965 when it was called New Minster. Moved to Hyde, outside city in 1010 until
d.1538. Only gateway survives (end of King Alfred Place). (1, 19, 20, 64, 70, 72, 124, 129, 131, 136,
152, 154)   AM : E
iii. Of half a dozen HH, remains of (a) St Cross (f.1132) f.KH as almshouse which, inter alia,
served 100-200 men with daily dinner. Left control of KH in 1185 and decayed from mid C13,
recovered, ref. Beaufort mid C15 but his full plans as college, large almshouse etc. never entirely
achieved. Still functions as almshouse and issues daily dole of bread and beer. (7, 96, 98)   + § : A-
(b) St John Baptist f. 1289 (almshouse for travellers, sick and lame soliders). Chapel survives in
spite of bus station.   + § : D +

WINDSOR, Berkshire   9676   *1348; 1483-*
Of five HH, remains of (a) St George's f.1348 (almshouse for poor and infirm knights), (b)
chantry with bede-house and almshouse f.1483. Both attached to college with castle. Remains
absorbed in much altered chapel and college buildings in lower ward.   § : E

WITHAM, Somerset   7440   *1178-1539*
First Carthusian priory in England, col. direct from Grande Chartreuse. After difficult
beginnings established by third prior, St Hugh of Avalon, later bishop of Lincoln. Only dovecote
survives of ancillary buildings. Present Anglican church (with C19 additions) absorbs fragment
of church where St Hugh worshipped and retired for contemplation even when a bishop.
(30, 142, 144)   + :D

WITTON GILBERT, Durham   2345   *c.1157-1532 +*
H for lepers later almshouse of St Mary Magdalene, dependency of Durham CP. Some masonry
incorporated in Witton Hall.   § : E

WIX, Essex   1628   *1122-1525*
Small P (BN), suppressed for Wolsey's college at Oxford and nuns, as usual, transferred to larger
house. Nothing visible of conventual buildings (foundations in grounds of 'Wix Abbey') but
something of nuns' church may remain in Anglican parish church. (20)   + : D-

WOLSTON, Warwickshire   4175   *c.1090-1394*
ac, dep. St Pierre-sur-Dives (BM), sold to Coventry Carthusians in 1394. Always small f., any
material remains probably in house called 'Priory'.   § : E

WOODKIRK, Yorkshire West Riding   2625   *t.Henry I - 1540*
pc (AC), dep. Nostell. Only tower survives in substantially C19 Anglican church.   (+) : D-

WOODSPRING, Somerset   3268   *c.1210-1536*
Large P (AC), originally at Dodlinch. Considerable ruins include part of church, frater (?), tithe
barn, absorbed in farmhouse and appurtenances. Five rescued stalls in Worle church, served
from P.   § : C-

WOOLHAMPTON, Berkshire   5766   *C19?-*
Douai is A (BM) of English Congregation with associated school.   + § : (A)

WORCESTER, Worcestershire 8555 *c. 743; c. 975-1540*
i. AS cathedral c.680 served by clerks and monks. St Mary's was f. c.743 (DM) and later became cathedral church. Ref. for BM and increased in importance as CP shortly after Norman Conquest. Dependencies: Little Malvern, Westbury-on-Trym, HH in Worcester, for male lepers, then poor, Droitwich, men's almshouse. Monastic church survives in Anglican use. Other remains: cloister with slype, fine chapter-house, dorter (unusually sited), traces of guest-house (its C14 roof is in Buildings Museum at Stoke Prior), frater undercroft, substantial ruins of farmery, gateway. (7, 10, 20, 27, 28, 31, 33, 34, 46, 48, 61, 65, 66, 70, 79, 87, 109, 112, 113, 119, 131, 137, 149, 152, 157, 168, 172, 178, 180, 189, 191) + § : B
ii. 'Greyfriars' is former guest-house of friary (FFC) f. c.1227. 'One of finest timber-framed houses in county.' (Pevsner) NT : D
iii. Of HH there are remains of St Wulstan's (c.1085-1540) under Augustinian rule, almshouse for poor, and sick monks. (96, 98) + § : C+

WORKSOP, Nottinghamshire 5879 *1103-1538*
Large P (AC) with dependency at Felley. Impressive church in Anglican use. Only gatehouse survives of conventual buildings. (4, 14, 83, 124, 167) + § : C

WORTH, Sussex 3134 *1933-*
Modern A (BM) of English Congregation with associated school. + § : (A)

WROXALL, Warwickshire 2271 *-1135-1536*
Small P (BN). Part of church survives with surprising amount of mediaeval glass. Fragments of convent (chapter-house and frater?). (20) + § : C

WYKEHAM, Yorkshire North Riding 9685 *c.1153-1539/40*
Small P (CN). Solitary remnant is north wall of church in grounds of 'Wykeham Abbey'. (34, 120) AM : E

WYMONDHAM, Norfolk 1101 *-1107-c.1538*
f. as dependent P (BM) of St Albans. Became independent 1449. Remains only of modified church in Anglican use (abbatial monument, corporal case) whose twin towers recall parochial dispute. (20, 124, 133, 181) + AM : D

WYMONDLEY *see Little Wymondley*

YARMOUTH, Norfolk 3589 *-1101-1539*
i. Small P (BM) dep. Norwich, acting as 'rest house' and accommodating secular priests serving parish. Remains (frater?) absorbed in 'Priory School'. § : E
ii. Friary (FFC) in Cambridge custody. Scant ruins of west range off South Quay. (77) DE : E+

YEAVERLEY, Derbyshire 1840 *+ 1188-1540*
Preceptory (KH). Site occupied by Stydd Hall, incorporating one wall of chapel. (106) AM : E

YEDINGHAM, Yorkshire East Riding 8979 *-1163-1539?*
Small P (BN or CN) which expanded in C13. (25, 121) § : E

YORK, Yorkshire 6052 *-1055; -1086; -1539*
i. ASP (BM), f. from Lastingham which seems to have declined. Before 1086 St Olave's church was given for A (BM), ref. 1088 as St Mary's on larger site nearby. Dependencies: Lincoln, Richmond, Rumburgh, St Bees, Sandtoft, Wetheral, Neddrum (Ireland). Monks from St Mary's f. Fountains. Spectacular ruins of church. Remains of conventual buildings in basement of museum which preserves countless interesting fragments, gatehouse, hospitium with attached remains of water-gate, part of abbot's house incorporated in King's Manor, unique precinct wall, extern chapel. (8, 9, 21, 36, 37, 45, 52, 53, 56, 73, 79, 82, , 83, 86, 88, 90, 114, 132, 134, 141, 142, 145, 153, 155, 159, 174, 176, 182, 192) AM § : C+ +
ii. Holy Trinity, originally ap dep. Marmoutier, f. 1089. Became denizen P (BM) in 1426. Dependencies: Allerton Mauleverer, Hedley, Tickford, HH in York, almshouse; Scarborough, almshouse for poor. Part of much altered priory church in Anglican use, no visible signs of conventual buildings. (20, 124) + : D
iii. Of some two dozen HH, remains of St Leonard's 1135-1540, succeeding St Peter's f. 936? One of greatest English H, conducted by brothers and sisters under Augustinian rule, caring for over 200 resident sick with special provision for babies and delicate children. Remains in Museum Street of passage, undercroft and chapel. (76) AM : C—

SCOTLAND

ABERCORN, West Lothian 0878 *C7-?*
AS monastery and episcopal see, d. Picts 685 but apparently restored temporarily. Traces revealed by excavation (1963) but only obvious survivals are fragments of crosses preserved in room of church adapted for Presbyterian use. § : E

ABERDEEN, Aberdeenshire 9305 *1469-1559*
Friary (FFO). Marischal college occupies site and re-uses some material. § : E

ABERLADY, East Lothian 4679 *C13-C16*
Friary (CF). 'Pitiful remnant' of church, with founder's tomb, used as outbuilding to Luffness House. (29) AM § : D—

ARBROATH, Angus 6340 *1178-1606*
A (OT), col. Kelso, f. William the Lion, buried there. Dependencies: Fyvie, attached H, almshouse. One of greatest and wealthiest abbeys much involved in country's development. 'Fragments of magnificence' include: ruined cloister, abbot's lodging, much robbed church. (2, 94, 102, 152, 173, 180) DE : B—

ARDCHATTAN, Argyllshire 9734 *1230-1602*
P (VM) with obscure history. Scant and fairly uninformative remains include transmogrified prior's house, ruined church with tombs and sculptures. DE : C—

BALANTRODOCH, Midlothian 3158 *c.1140-c.1309*
Principal seat of Scottish KT, f. David I. After dissolution tr. KH and in early C15 church seems to have become parochial. (177) AM(+) : D—

BALMERINO, Fife 3524 *c.1227-1603*
A (CM), col. Melrose. Ruins of part of church, scant remains of cloister, barn. All much involved in farmyard. Well at Overmoln. Two cells (?) accessible only from roof. (2, 39, 40, 175) DE : E +

BEAULY, Inverness 5426 *c.1230-1634*
P (VM). Poor house which, after papal dissolution of order in 1510, seems to have become P (CM) dep. Kinloss. (144, 185) DE : D +

BIRSAY, Orkney 2328 *?*
'Remains of mediaeval monastery', possibly TF but no record. § : D

BRECHIN, Angus 5960 *-1267-C17?*
'Rare traces of mediaeval H', for poor, fragment of chapel in town centre. § : E

CAMBUSKENNETH, Stirlingshire 8094 *c.1146-1604*
P (Arrousian, became AC and A). Distinguished place in Scottish church history. Burial place of James III. Little above ground save detached belfry. Very small cloister. Little of robbed site excavated. (2, 14, 18, 27, 52, 94, 109, 181) DE § : D +

COLDINGHAM, Berwickshire 9065 *-1139-1606*
P (BM), dep. Durham. Much involved in military and political clashes. Some remains of church in Presbyterian use. (21, 144) AM + : D

COUPAR ANGUS, Perthshire 2139 *-1164-1606*
A (CM), col. Melrose, possibly on earlier Culdee site. Richest f. in country, popular with kings. Thoroughly quarried site. (39, 40) § : E

CROSSRAGUEL, Ayrshire 2708 *-1216-1617?*
Small P (BMC), col. Paisley, became A -1270. Country's best preserved mediaeval religious house with substantial remains of church, claustral buildings, two courts, corrodians' houses, commendator's tower house and gatehouse. (2, 43) DE : B—

CULROSS, Fife 9885 *1217-1589*
A (CM), col. Kinloss, occupying earlier (eremitical?) site associated with St Serf and St Mungo. Scant remains of part of cloisters, central tower and choir of church restored for Presbyterian use. (2, 39, 40) DE + : C—

DEER, Aberdeenshire 8846 *C6; 1219-1587*
Important Ce settlement, associated with St Drostan and St Columba, produced first known Gaelic ms. (Book of Deer) in C9. May have disappeared long before f. on site of A (CM). Substantial remains of latter. DE : C

DRYBURGH, Berwickshire 5931 *1150-1606*
A (PC), col. Alnwick. Produced saintly Adam of Dryburgh who became C at Witham. Suffered greatly from English marauders, finally burnt out in 1544 after two raids in same year. Hallowed site associated with St Modan (Ce abbot). Substantial claustral remains (east range and gatehouse), less of church. Ingenious solutions to problems of site level. 'One of country's loveliest ruins'. (2, 14, 52, 94, 142, 167) DE : B—

DUNBAR, East Lothian 6878 *c.1245-C16*
P (TF). Rare Trinitarian fragment — tower (converted into dovecote) which once typically straddled passage between quire and nave. (81, 184) § : E +

DUNDRENNAN, Kirkcudbrightshire 7447 *1142-1606*
Wealthy A (CM), one of many col. Rievaulx where its first abbot succeeded St Ailred. Important contribution to development of Scottish architecture. Substantial ruins of church (with many abbatial monuments), fragments of claustral buildings (much quarried e.g. Kirkcudbright Tolbooth). (2, 39, 40, 52, 94, 180) DE : B—

DUNFERMLINE, Fife 0987 *c.1070-1593*
A (BM) on site of earlier Ce monastery. Religious centre of Fife and much involved in Scottish culture. Substantial remains of church nave, some claustral ruins, especially frater, foundations of chapel-shrine of St Margaret to which Queen's Ferry conveyed pilgrims. Scriptorium, guest-house absorbed into palace and abbot's house into later building. Pretentious tower is C19. (2, 19, 21, 27, 94, 115, 175, 180) + DE : C

ECCLES, Berwickshire 7641 *1156-1609*
P (CN), suffering severely from English invaders in C16, culminating in its being 'brent, rased and cast downe' in 1545. Finally extinguished by commendators and Scottish Reformation. Scant remains. (129) § : E

EDINBURGH, Midlothian 2674 *see also Holyrood -1537-*
Out of some ten HH, only remains of St Mary Magdalene, men's almshouse, in Cowgate. § : E + There are modern houses of friars (DF in George Square; FFC in Lothian Street and Criagmillar.)

ELGIN, Moray 2162 *-1494-c.1559*
Friary C13 (FFC) replaced by FFO in C15. After Reformation, convent converted to Court of Justice and church to Presbyterian use. + § : D

EYNSHALLOW, Orkney 3529 *c.1100?-C15 ?*
P (BM) of obscure origin. Uninformative remains on island site. § : D—

FEARN, Ross and Cromarty 7782 *1221?-1609*
A (PC), col. Whithorn, related to shrine of St Duthus, much visited by James IV, though some accounts connect it with translation of St Ninian's relics from Galloway. Site tr. c.1238 to New Fearn, abbey rebuilt mid C14 but ruined by commendators a century later. (142) + § : D +

FORT AUGUSTUS, Invernesshire 3709 *1876-*
A (BM) f. Simon, Lord Lovat. Attached school. § : (A)

GLENLUCE, Wigtownshire 1858 *1192-1602*
A (CM), col. Melrose. Much given to hospitality for pilgrims to St Ninian. Scant ruins (mainly east range including chapter-house) of architectural interest. (2, 39, 40) DE : D +

HOLYROOD, Midlothian 2674 *1128-1606*
Rich P (AC), providing royal lodgings and eventually elevated to A and sort of palace-chapel. Substantial remains of what was one of most splendid churches in county. (2, 14, 52, 94, 152, 175) DE : C—

INCHAFFRAY, Perthshire 8621 *1200-1609/69*
P (AC), replacing earlier hermit community, A in 1220, proposed as see in 1237. Relic of St Fillan carried at Bannockburn. 'Isle of Masses' said to possess ruins of abbey but these unrecorded in Cowan-Easson. § : ?

INCHCOLM, Fife 1882 *c.1153-1609*
P (AC), replacing hermitage, A 1235. 'The Iona of East Scotland'. Extensive and well-preserved remains (rere-dorter flushed by sea) described as 'most interesting monastic ruin in country'. (2, 14) DE : B—

INCHMAHOME, Perthshire 6004 *+ 1238-1604*
P (AC) On island site, apparently with parochial responsibilities. Comprehensible remains. (143, 144, 167) DE : C

INVERKEITHING, Fife   1383   *1268?-1559*
Small house (FFC) whose hospitium survives incorporated in private dwelling. (77)   § : E

IONA, Argyllshire   2723   *563; -1203-1587/8?*
f. St Columba as monastic (Ce) and missionary HQ. Royal burial place. d. Norsemen 802, 808,
828. BM and AN established c.1203, became CP. Restoration in C20 by Iona Community
(Presbyterian). Remains of St Oran's chapel, royal cemetery and few Ce crosses out of hundreds
destroyed by Reformers. (2, 21, 27, 32, 129)   AM/§ (+) : C—

JEDBURGH, Roxburghshire   6520   *1138-1696*
P (AC), f. David I on Ce site, col. Beauvais. Made A 1152 seven years after moving site, now cut
by modern road. Substantial ruins of magnificent church and rather more than foundations of
claustral range. (2, 14, 52, 94)   DE : B—

KELSO, Roxburghshire   7333   *c.1113; 1128-1607*
A (OT), originally at Selkirk. Wynton's Chronicle said to have been produced in scriptorium.
Dependencies at Fogo, Lesmahagow. Much damaged by English, especially Dacre in 1528. Little
remains of great church except tower and even less of conventual buildings. (2, 52, 94, 102, 180)
        DE : C—

KENMORE, Perthshire   7745   *1122-?*
Island in Loch Tay said to contain ruins of P (AC) allegedly f. Alexander I and burial place of his
queen, Sybilla.   § : ?

KILWINNING, Ayrshire   3043   *c.1175-1592*
A (OT), col. Kelso on Ce site (St Finnan's ?). Remains not very informative, remains of church
in Presbyterian use. (2, 180)   AM + : C—

KINLOSS, Moray   0661   *1150-1601*
Wealthy A (CM), col. Melrose, f. David I. Colonised Culross, Deer. Fragmentary remains, much
quarried and not very communicative. (2, 39, 40, 94)   AM : E +

KIRKCUDBRIGHT, Kirkcudbrightshire   6851   *c.1450-1569*
Friary (FFC), f. James II. Church in Presbyterian use, scant remains of friary buildings. (77)
        + § : E

LINCLUDEN, Kirkcudbrightshire   9678   *1174-1389; 1389-1560*
P (BN), suppressed in 1389, replaced by large collegiate f, with dependent H, men's almshouse.
Scant remains of nunnery, rather more of college (tomb of provost in church). (129)   DE ; C—

LINDORES, Fife   2612   *1191-1600*
A (OT), col. Kelso f. David, brother of William the Lion. Dependent school in Dundee
Considerable remains, somewhat neglected. (2, 180)   AM § : C—

LUFFNESS   *see Aberlady*

MELROSE, Roxburghshire   5433   *c.650; 1136-1609*
Early Ce f. associated with St Cuthbert and St Aidan, disappeared. Replaced centuries later by A
(CM) col. Rievaulx. Generosity of David I and learned sanctity of St Waldef made it prime abbey
in Scotland. Most spectacular ruins in country. Substantial remains of magnificent church and
much else: claustral range, lay brothers' accommodation, interesting water-works. Scanty
remains of abbot's lodging, more of commendator's (now museum). (2, 39, 40)   DE : B

MONEYMUSK, Aberdeenshire   6815   *-1245-1617*
Small, poor P (AC), dep. St Andrews. Absorbed earlier Ce settlement. Remains cannibalised to
build Moneymusk House apart from church in Presbyterian use. (14, 144)   + : D

NEWBATTLE, Midlothian   3365   *1140-1587*
Large A (CM), f. David I. Benefitted from quarry and earliest coal-mine. Incorporated into
mansion of Kerr 'who did so metamorphose the building that it cannot be known that ever it did
belong to the church'. Now educational establishment with remains in cellars (dorter
undercroft), precinct wall. (39, 40, 76)   § : E

NORTH BERWICK, East Lothian   5485   *c.1150-1587/6*
Wealthy A (CN). Ferry terminal for pilgrims to St Andrews via Earlsferry and hospitality much
abused. Scant remains in grounds of old people's home, seemingly part of north range.
(76, 94, 129)   AM § : E +

NUNRAW, East Lothian   5670   *1946-*
The village of 'Nuns Row' originally belonged to Haddington P (CN). Now outside it is A (CM),
col. Mount St Bernard, a modern Trappist monastery part of whose church is usually open to
public. (182)   + § : (A)

PAISLEY, Renfrewshire   4864   *1163-1587*
P (BMC) originally f. at King's Inch. Shortly after move raised to A and colonised Crossraguel.
Many links with Scottish history. Famous school. Burnt by English 1306, by accident 1498,
rebuilt in time to be destroyed by Reformers. Conventual buildings converted into mansion.
Church rebuilt for Presbyterian use. (2, 43, 84)   (+)/§ : C—

PEEBLES, Peebles   2540   *-1296-1560/1*
Obscure f. (TF), col. Val de Choux. Declined mid C15 to pc (BM) dep. Dunfermline. Remains of
west limb of church, west range of cloister, other fragments of conventual buildings. Restored to
religious use in 1948: P (BM), col. Prinknash. (21, 185)   + /§ : C— (A)

PLUSDARDEN, Moray   1457   *1239-1454; 1454-1587*
A VM), col. Val de Choux. Declined mid C15 to pc (BM) dep. Dunfermline. Remains of west
limb of church, west range of cloister, other fragmants of conventual buildings. Reatored to
religious use n 1948: P (BM), col. Prinknash. (21, 185) + /§ : C— (A)

QUEENSFERRY (SOUTH), West Lothian   1278   *1440-1565*
Friary (CF). Rare survival. Much of church in Episcopalian use (Heavily restored C19). No trace
of conventual buildings. (29)   + : D

RESTENNETH, Angus   4550   *1153-1606*
P (AC), col. Jedburgh. Probably f. David I to succeed earlier Ce settlement. Burnt by Edward I
of England who seems to have contributed to rebuilding. Substantial remains of church,
including tower, little else. (14, 144)   DE : C—

RUTHWELL, Dumfriesshire   1067   *C7-?*
Magnificent cross, 'earliest and most graceful of Runic monuments' preserved in Presbyterian
church. Sole souvenir of Ce monastic f.   § : E + +

SADDELL, Argyllshire   8635   *c.1150-1508*
A (CM), col. Mellifont, so reduced by C16 that James IV received papal permission to tr.
revenues to bishopric of Argyll. Much robbed, fragments in houses and farmsteads. (39)   § : E

ST ANDREWS, Fife   5116   *c.4?; C8; 1154-1592*
i. Apart from legendary f., there seems to have been a religious house (Ce) in C8. Priory (AC),
col. Scone, f. 1154 on site still occupied by Culdees (ruins of their church), became CP in 1157
and extremely wealthy corporation with dependencies at Loch Leven, Pittenween and
Moneymusk. New church 1318, mitred priory 1418, archiepiscopal see 1472. Much robbed site
but outlines of most buildings discernible, interesting details include C10 sarcophagus, precinct
wall with towers, gateway. (14, 26, 44, 52, 136, 144, 152, 159, 160, 167, 181)   DE : C—
ii. Small priory (DF), established in C15, grew in C15 and provided student hostel at university.
(59, 94)   DE : D—

ST MONANS, Fife   5201   *1471-c.1557*
Small collegiate establishment, ref. James III as small priory (DF) but it declined through
inadequate endowment. Remains of church in Presbyterian use. (59)   + : D

SOUTRA, Midlothian   4361   *1164-C16*
Soutra Aisle on Soutra Hill represents fragment of church and H (for travellers, later almshouse)
under Augustinian rule. (94)   § : E

SWEETHEART, Dumfriesshire   9666   *1273-1624*
A (CM), col. Dundrennan. Named from embalmed heart of John Baliol, buried there by his
widow Devorgilla, founder and benefactor of this and many other religious houses. Maintained
famous school. Substantial remains of church, precinct wall, rather less of conventual buildings.
Mutilated statue of f. (2, 39)   DE : B—

TEMPLE, Midlothian   3158   *C12-1312*
Scottish HQ of KT until suppression. No visible traces of conventual buildings and some think
mediaeval church postdates KT.   + : D—

THIRLESTANE, Berwickshire   5647   *-1541?-?*
Ruined building to east of farmhouse has been identified as H, for poor, but the matter is
uncertain.
                    § : E

TORPHICHEN, West Lothian   9672   *1168-C16*
Only KH house with remains: conventual buildings outlined on grass, fragment of church with
monument to preceptor, traces of decorative painting and rare working drawing. (106)
                    DE + : D—

TYNINGHAME, East Lothian   6179   *C8-941*
A well-endowed monastery (Ce) grew round hermitage of St Baldred (died 756/7), d. Danes.
Ruined C12 church in grounds of Tyningham House on site.   § : E

WHITEKIRK, East Lothian   5981   *c.1300-1537·*
Parish church, dep. Holyrood, whose nearby well gained reputation for healing C14. Vast
crowds of pilgrims provided with HH, for poor travellers, demolished by Sinclair who added
tower to surviving abbey tithe barn. (136)   + § : D +

WHITHORN, Wigtownshire   4440   *c.1175-1612*
Wealthy P (PC), of obscure origin but probably col. Soulseat, with some responsibility for
pilgrimage church of St Ninian. (His cave is four miles away on coast with crosses cut in rock by
mediaeval pilgrims.) Apart from remains on site, some in museum which has fine collection of
early Christian inscribed stones including oldest Christian memorial in country.
(136, 142, 144, 160)   DE : C +

WALES

ABBEY CWMHIR, Radnorshire   0571   *1176-1536*
A (CM), col. Whitland, possibly rcf. of unsuccessful Ty Faenor (1143). Damaged by English
1231, practically destroyed by Welsh 1401. Church a third longer than Brecon (cathedral). Only
slight remains on extensively robbed site: columns at Llandiloes church, screen to Newton
Montgomerys, masonry to Llanbister church. Earthwork and fishponds. (2, 27)   § : C +

ABERCONWY   *see Conway*

ABERGAVENNY, Monmouthshire   2914   *c.1090-1536*
ap (BM), dep. St Vincent, Le Mans. Denizen in 1415. Little remains of conventual buildings
(wall fragment adjoining church which is substantially preserved in Anglican use — stalls,
fragment of Jesse window). Nearby Holy Mountain (Skirrid Fawr) has masonry remains of
possible hermitage attached to priory. (14)   + : C—

ABERGELE, Denbighshire   9477   *C8*
Mother-church of Ce monastery. Site occupied by C15 church containing lid of 'abbot's coffin'.
    + : E—

ANGLESEY, Carnarvonshire   *see also Penmon, Holy Island*
Many monuments of Ce Christianity: Cemaes, Llaneilian, Lligwy, Saint's Cave (near point of
Eilean Bay)

BANGOR, Carnarvonshire   5872   *525-C11*
I. Ce monastery, f. St Deiniol, church acquired cathedral status. Daughterhouse at Bangor
Iscoed, Flintshire. tr. to collegiate church during Norman reconstruction. Remains of this and
later mediaeval church now part of Anglican cathedral.   + : C—
ii. Small priory (DF) in York visitation (-1251-1538). Some remains may be incorporated in
'Friars School'. (188)   § : E +

BARDSEY, Carnarvonshire   3643   *C13-c.1537*
Large monastic settlement of hermits (Ce?) which became A (AC) in C13. Slight remains of
church and conventual buildings. (2, 14, 33, 136)   AM : C—

BASINGWERK, Flintshire   1976   *1131?-1535*
A (CM), col. Savigny. Because of its situation it was fortified. (HQ of Edward I during building
of Flint castle). H for lepers, then sick, at Coventry from C13. Scant ruins of church, rather more
of claustral buildings (especially east and south ranges). Later frater in unusual position. Jesse
window in Dyserth church said to be from here. (2, 40, 102, 111, 136, 177, 189)   DE : C—

BEACHLEY, Monmouthshire   5991   *?*
Hermitage at St Thecla's chapel, with well. Possibly associated with Severn ferry.   + : D

BEDDGELERT, Carnarvonshire   5848   *C6; c.1200-1536*
Ancient Ce which CM of Conway tried to absorb in C12. Community seems to have become P
(AC) to maintain its independence. At dissolution granted to new A (BM) at Bisham which lasted
only months. No apparent conventual remains but part of church survives in Anglican use.   + :D

BRECON, Brecknock.   0428   *-1269-1538*
i. Small priory (DF) in Oxford visitation. Buildings occupied by college of Abergwili, using part
of church as school chapel. Six stalls may survive from priory. (5, 142, 153, 189)   + : C-
ii. Priory (BM), dep. Battle, c.1110-1538, replacing earlier Ce foundation. A great deal of priory
church survives in Anglican cathedral, together with fragments of conventual buildings (some re-
used), parts of claustral range, former prior's lodging, tithe barn, almonry. (113, 124, 132, 144,
189)   + /§ : B—

CALDEY, Pembrokeshire   2285   *C6; 1113 + - 1536; 1928-*
'Island of Saints'. Ce f. associated with SS David, Dyfrig, Gildas, Illtyd, Maglorius, Paul,
Samson. C12 ref. P (OT), small and poor becoming dep. St Dogmaels. Remains of monastic
buildings, priory church (Ogham stone). (180)   + § : C—
In C19 saw beginnings of Anglican experiment in Benedictinism. Community split in C20,
minority continuing at Nashdom, majority becoming Catholics and f. Prinknash. Caldey site
became A (CM), col. Chinay, Belgium. (182)   + § : (A)

CARDIFF, Glamorganshire   1877   *-1242-1538*
i. Small P (DF) in Oxford visitation.   AM : E +
ii. Small friary (FFC) in Bristol custody. (1284-1538)   AM : E +
Fragmentary remains of both. (77)

CARMARTHEN, Carmarthenshire   4120   *-1284-1538*
Friary (FFC). Site in Friars' Park. Utterly d. except for ap Rhys, tomb which was salvaged and
tr. St Peter's Church (Tudor supporter).   § : E

CHEPSTOW, Monmouthshire   5393   *-1071-1536*
ap (BM), dep. Corneilles, became independent c.1442. Originally castle chaplaincy, later part of
church served town growing under walls — substantially survives in Anglican use. No domestic
remains. (20, 124)   + : D

CONWAY, Carnarvonshire   7777   *1190-1283*
A (CM), col. Strata Florida. First f. Rhedynog-felen, then moving to Conway and finally to
Maenan until c.1538. Abbey church substantially survives in Anglican use, otherwise only
fragments (processional cross in museum). See also Rhos. (2, 188)   + : C—

CWMHIR   *see Abbey Cwmhir*

CYMMER, Merionethshire   7219   *1199-1536*
A (CM), col. Abbey Cwmhir. Small and poor house on periphery of Cistercian movement.
Hence never remodelled and interesting for that reason. Some ruins of church, outline of
cloister, other remains obliterated by or incorporated in farm on site. (2, 5, 40, 104, 189)   DE : D

DENBIGH, Denbighshire   0566   *-1289-1538*
House (CF) with rare ruins. (29, 189)   DE : C—

EWENNY, Glamorganshire   9078   *1141-1540*
P (BM), dep. Gloucester. 'Remarkable example of semi-fortified monastery'. Nave of priory
church survives in Anglican use; of conventual buildings: frater (incorporated in modern
dwelling-house), part of prior's lodging, great defensive wall with gates and towers.
(75, 124, 144, 189)   + /DE : D—

GARWAY, Monmouthshire   4522   *1185/8-c.1310*
House (KT), tr. KH (1312 + - 1489), merged with Dinmore 1489 + . Much of C13 church
survives, dovecote, conventual buildings incorporated in farm?   + § : C—

GOGARTH, Carnarvonshire   7277   *?*
On west side of Great Orme in grounds of 'Old Abbey Memorial Home' are scanty ruins of
'Gogarth Abbey', said to be occasional residence of bishop of Bangor. No confirming evidence
and not noticed in Knowles and Hadcock.   § : E +

HAVERFORDWEST, Pembrokeshire   9515   *-1200-1536*
P (AC). Scant and uninformative ruins in meadow. In town, church of St Thomas has tomb of
palmer, pilgrim to Rome; while fine St Mary's has one of pilgrim to Santiago. (124, 144, 189)
                    AM : E +

HAY-ON-WYE, Brecknock   2342   *1250-1550?*
Effigy of monk under gallery stairs in (Anglican) parish church. Related to former H for poor
travellers, of St John?   (+) : E +

HOLY ISLAND, Anglesey   2381   *C6; -1536*
Early Ce monastic settlement, associated with St Cybi, later apparently pc dep. Penmon (AC).
On top of Holyhead mountain are ruins of Ce cell, one of about half a dozen which formed early
'clas', protected by walls of deserted Roman fort.   (+)§ : C—

HOLYWELL, Flintshire   1875   *C7-*
Pilgrimage centre associated with well of St Frideswide, abbess of Gwytherin. Well enclosed in
C15 chapel, served by modern convent and H for travellers. (136, 177)   + § : (A)

KIDWELLY, Carmarthenshire   4106   *-1115-1539*
pc (BM), dep. Sherborne. No conventual remains. Priory church largely survives in Anglican
use.   + : D +

LLANBADARN FAWR, Cardiganshire   6081   *C6-?; 1116-1136*
Early Ce f. of St Padarn, became pc (BM) dep. Gloucester for short time in C12, then collegiate
until tr. to Vale Royal A (CM) in C13. Church in Anglican use occupies Ce site and may have
been used by BM.   + : D

LLANDAFF, Glamorganshire   1578   *C6-c.1108*
Ce monastery, associated with St Teilo, with famous school. Became seat of bishop and some
for a of Ce monasticism may have continued until 1108 when it was apparently tr. to secular
canons.   (+) : D

LLANDEGAI, Carnarvonshire   5970   *C5?-?*
Apparently site of monastic settlement of St Tegai but not noticed in Knowles and Hadcock.
Much restored C14 church, in Anglican use, contains 'curious monument' said to be from
Llanfaes (FFC).   (+) : E

LLANDEGLAY, Radnorshire   1363   *?*
Probable site of H for sick, using mineral springs. Surviving church in Anglican use (dedicated to
St Tegla, patron of falling sickness) provided for pilgrims.   + : D—

LLANDUDNO, Carnarvonshire   7782   *C6-?*
i. Restored church of St Tudno in Anglican use probably occupies site of cell of eponymous Ce
saint. Open air pulpit and reading desk on south side.
ii. 'Hiding Cave' under Great Orme Head may have been monastic hermitage associated with
Gogarth. 'Ty-yn-y-graig' under Little Orme provided refuge for Catholic priests after
Reformation.   +§ : C—

LLANDYSILIO, Anglesey   5572   *C5-?*
Ce monastic settlement from which parts of church are said to survive.   + : D-

LLANFAES, Anglesey   6078   *1245-1538*
Friary (FFC) f.Llewellyn the Great. Some of contents (misericords and monuments) preserved in
Beaumaris and Llandegai churches.   § : E-

LLANGENNITH, Glamorganshire   4291   *-1119-c 1414*
ac, dep. St Taurin, Evreux (BM), tr. to endowments of All Souls, Oxford in C15. Largest church
in Gower is substantially priory church. Only fragments of conventual buildings survive
incorporated in later structures.   + § : C-

LLANGURIG, Montgomeryshire   9070   *C6-C16*
Site of Ce 'clas', f. St Curig (died 550). Became dependency of Strata Florida (CM) from c.1180.
Much altered church (but retaining C12, C15 elements) survives in Anglican use on site with
characteristic circular raised graveyard.   (+) : D

LLANLLUGAN, Montgomeryshire   0402   *-1236-1536*
Small P (CN). Only remnant is part of church in Anglican use. (40)   + : D

LLANTARNAM, Montgomeryshire   4313   *1179-1536*
A (CM), sometimes called Caerleon, col. Strata Florida. Barely discernible remains, apart from
barn, incorporated in later buildings.   § : E

LLANTHONY, Monmouthshire/Gloucestershire   2827   *c.1103-1539*
i. P (AC), developing from earlier hermit settlement. Grew into very large house of more than 40
canons, most of whom moved in 1136 to new settlement — Llanthony Secunda — near
Gloucester. Nucleus remained in Monmouthshire which became pc of Llanthony II in 1481
(reversing previous relationship). Dependent H for sick in Gloucester. (15, 125, 144, 167, 189)
a. Considerable ruins of church sacristy. Fragments of cloisters, chapter-house. Prior's lodging
incorporated in Abbey Hotel. Other portions, including gatehouse, absorbed in neighbouring farm.
Extern chapel in Anglican use.   DE : B-
b. Abused site in industrial suburb of Gloucester. Not very informative fragmentary ruins:
gateway, precinct wall, remains of barns, guest-house (?) incorporated in private house. Library,
saved by last prior, now in Lambeth Palace.   § : E +
ii. 'Monastery', four miles up valley from Llanthony I is monument to eccentric (1870) attempt at
Benedictine revival in Church of England. Somewhat derelict remains except for portion
occupied as private residence.   § : C-

LLANTWIT MAJOR, Glamorganshire 9768 *C6-1100-1547?*
Ce monastery, associated with St Illtyd, possessing famous school. About beginning C12 apparently became pc or grange of Tewkesbury (BM). Very interesting church of notable monastic character in Anglican use. (2, 33, 86) AM / + : D +

LLANWHADEN, Pembrokeshire 0717 *1287-C16*
H (for poor travellers and orphans) which became dependency of St David's cathedral in 1501.
§ : E

LLOWES, Brecknock 1941 *C7-?*
Site of Ce f. associated with St Meilig. Church in Anglican use occupying site preserves ancient font and C7 cross. (+) : E +

MAENAN, Denbighshire 7963 *1283-c.1538*
A (CM) tr. from Conway due to castle-building. Only remains seems to be rood loft preserved in (Anglican) parish church at Llanwrwst. § (+) : E-

MALPAS, Monmouthshire 3090 *-1122-1539*
ac (BMC), dep. Montecute. Became denizen 1407 but remained very small. No conventual remains, church in Anglican use. (189) + : D

MARGAM, Glamorganshire 8086 *1147-1536*
A (CM), col. Clairvaux, became one of largest C houses in Wales. Fragment of church incorporated in modern building, some remains of cloister, chapter-house (unique Cistercian example). Collection of Ce stone crosses housed in churchyard building. (2, 37, 40, 153, 189)
NT AM / + : C-

MONMOUTH. Monmouthshire 5113 *1086-1540*
ap (BM), dep. St Florent, Saumur, became independent P (BM) in 1415. Some fragments of priory church survive in much restored Anglican church. Fraction of conventual buildings (part used as school room) + : D-
Catholic church has processional cross which may have come from Evesham.

NEATH, Glamorganshire 7597 *1130-1539*
A (CM). col. Savigny. Rebuilt 1224 after burning by Welsh. Described by Leland as 'fairest abbey in all Wales'. Remains include plan of church and ruins of west front, gatehouse, domestic buildings (much modified to requirements of secular expropriators.) (2, 40, 53, 82, 125, 153, 189)
DE : B-

NEVERN, Pembrokeshire 0840 *C6-?*
Site of Ce f., associated with St Brynach. Ogham stones in (Anglican) church and nearby pilgrim's cross (remains of wayside shrine for pilgrims to St Davids from Strata Florida.) AM : E

PEMBROKE, Pembrokeshire 9901 *c.1098-1539*
ap, dep. St Martin Sée (BM), became denizen P after 1441 and subsequently dependency of St Albans. Only remains of conventual buildings are ruined fragments among farm buildings. Priory church substantially survives serving as Anglican parish church for Monkton. + § : C-

PENMON, Anglesey 6381 *C6;1221; 1414?-1536*
Ce monastery, maintaining hermit tradition into C13. Possibly ref. as P (AC) in 1221 but hermit tradition may have persisted. First sure evidence of regular P in 1414. Dependency (for hermits ?): Puffin Island. Prior's house, now secular dwelling, much of cloister south range remains of conventual buildings. Priory church, with best preserved Romanesque detail in North Wales, substantially survives in Anglican use. 80 metres north is holy well and remains of anchorite's cell. (33, 61, 144, 189) + § : C +

PILL, Pembrokeshire 5275 *1113+ -1536*
P (OT), dep. St Dogmaels. Fragments only survive. (180) AM : E

PORTHCAWL, Glamorganshire 8176 *?*
There seems to have been a grange or pc (CM), dep. Margam. After d. transmogrified into Nottage Court. Masonry fragments of chapel embodied into walls of village. § : E

PUFFIN ISLE, Anglesey 6481 *-1066-1536*
Early Ce hermit settlement, probably becoming pc (AC), dep. Penmon when latter became P (AC). Earliest community, associated with St Seiriol, d.Danes 853. Tower survives from AC cell.
AM : E

RHOS-ON-SEA, Denbighshire 8480 *C13-1538?*
pc (CM) of Conway which had tithes of fish caught at weir. Chapel of St Teilo, now in Anglican use, may represent cell chapel. + : D-

RHUDDLAN, Flintshire   0277   *-1258-1538*
P (DF) in Oxford visitation. Partial remains incorporated in farm buildings (Plas Newydd).
Some inscribed slabs preserved in (Anglican) parish church.   § : E

RUTHIN, Denbighshire   1257   *1310-1535*
Rare example (BO). Substantial remains of their church in Anglican use with some part of
conventual buildings incorporated in vicarage. (23)   + § : C

ST ASAPH, Flintshire   0374   *c.560-1066*
Ce settlement f. St Kentigern, succeeded by Asa or Asaph. As often, became episcopal see but
this died out before Norman Conquest. Cathedral occupies part of site. (ref. 1143)   § : E

ST CLEAR'S, Carmarthen.   2716   *c.1160-c.1414*
ac (BMC), dep. St Martin-des-Champs, Paris. Endowments tr. All Souls, Oxford on dissolution
of apc (188) Church in Anglican use.   + : C

ST DAVIDS, Pembrokeshire   7525   *C6-1115*
i. Ancient Ce monastic.site, established by St David, becoming episcopal see and pilgrimage
centre. Oldest parts of church (Anglican cathedral) date from Norman period when it was,
unusually, reconstituted from monastic to secular canons. Presbytery dominated by Tudor tomb
salvaged from Greyfriars, Carmarthen. Portable altar stone attributed to St David whose shrine
and reliquary also survive   (+) : C?
ii. H (for infirm monks and general almsgiving) f.c.1280. annexed to St Mary's College (ruins)
c.1377. Possibly under Augustinian rule.   § : E

ST DOGMAELS, Pembrokeshire   1646   *c.1115-1536*
Ancient Ce site, occupied by P (OT), elevated to A before 1120. Dependencies at Caldey, Pill.
Fragments of church and (adapted) conventual buildings. Parish church (with Ogham stone) may
be former extern chapel. (2, 50, 70, 73, 11, 142, 173, 178, 180, 188, 190)   DE : C—

ST GOVANS HEAD. Pembrokeshire   9792   *C7?, C13?-*
St Govan's chapel once belonged to a hermitage (C13?) with an associated Holy Well much
favoured by pilgrim cripples from all over Wales who left their crutches as votive (apparently into
early C19). The well has been filled in.   + : D

SLEBECH, Pembrokeshire   0315   *later C12-1540*
Largest house of KH in west of Britain, far-famed for its hospitality. Slebech Hall (1780) may
incorporate some masonry. Church 'a picturesque ruin.' (106, 189)   § : D

STRATA FLORIDA, Cardiganshire   7465   *1164-1539*
A (CM), col. Whitland, first f. at Yn Hen Fynachlog, two miles south-west before moving to
final site in 1200. In spite of great damage in Welsh wars became one of main centres of national
literature and culture. Cloistral remains largely obliterated by farm. Scant ruins of church,
cloister (with rare survival of collation lectern), chapter-house, fragments of west range.
(2, 33, 40, 44, 60, 124, 142, 167, 178, 182, 189)   DE : D

STRATA MARCELLA, Montgomeryshire   2611   *1170-1536*
Seems to have been f. on different site as P (CM), dep. Whitland. At beginning of reign of
Edward III, Welsh monks tr. English houses, replaced by English and dependency to Buildwas.
Own dependencies at Pen-y-Llwyn, Cwmhir, Montgomery. Largely unexcavated site with rare
masonry fragments visible. 'Tragic victim of Glyndwr iconoclasm and Dissolution.'   § : E

TALLEY, Carmarthen   6332   *-1197-1536*
Site probably occupied by Ce before Rhys ap Gruffydd f. A (PC), col. Amiens. Because of
distance, Halesowen later made mother house. Limited resources and nearness of Cistercians at
Whitland led to contraction. Recognisable site but part still under farm. (2, 189)   DE : B-

TENBY, Carmarthern   1300   *C14; C19*
i. Catholic church of Holy Rood and St Teilo is part of failed scheme to restore GD. Vestry
preserves pre-Reformation crucifix from Brecon priory.
ii. St Mary's church in Anglican use has monument of nuns or vowess.
iii. West of this church are two arches attributed, apparently without authority, to CF said to be
f. here in 1399. Some C15 stalls were rescued from mason's yard in C19 and tr. to Anglican
church at Colton, Staffordshire.

TINTERN, Monmouthshire   5300   *1131-1539*
A (CM), col. L'Aumone. First Cistercian house in Wales and one of earliest in Britain. Rather
undistinguished house with uneventful history. Main fabric of church almost complete.
Distinguishable claustral buildings, sometimes standing to fair height. Infirmary cloister.
Abbot's lodging (converted to dwelling-house.) (2, 34, 40, 41, 44, 70, 82, 121, 124, 133, 141, 153,
167, 168, 189, 193)   DE : B

TOWYN, Merionethshire 5800 *C6-1291+*
Ce f. by St Cadfan. Had become principal 'clas' under an abbot by 1147. Church survives in Anglican use. (33)
+ § : D

USK, Monmouthshire 3701 *-1236-1536*
P (BN). No conventual buildings survive but part of convent church in Anglican use. (20)
AM + : D

VALLE CRUCIS, Denbighshire 2044 *1201-1538*
A (CM), čol. Strata Marcella. Badly damaged by fire in C13. Named from Eliseg's Pillar, Ce cross, four or five centuries older than abbey. Small and poor house but considerable remains, especially of church and east range. (2, 33, 36, 40, 53, 60, 104, 112, 121, 142, 146, 153, 167, 168, 186, 189)
DE : B

WHITLAND, Carmarthenshire 1916 *c.1151-1539?*
CM from Clairvaux reached Wales 1140 and settled for a time at Trefgarn, whence they colonised Cwmhir. Moved to Whitland A c.1151 which became mother house of Cistercian mission to Wales, colonising Strata Florida (1164), Strata Marcella (1170). Slight remains of church and conventual buildings.
AM : C-